ULTIMATE WORDPRESS

Disclaimer:

This book is three books combined into one.

WordPress Domination

WordPres Plugins and Themes Review Guide

WordPress Security

155

WordPress Security: Protection from Hackers

BOOK ONE

WordPress Domination: Beginner to Ninja in 7 Days

Introduction

Hello everyone, this is Lambert Klein and this time I'm bringing you the definitive WordPress guide that will turn you into a WordPress ninja in just 7 days. This guide is designed to take you by the hand and familiarize you with how to get set up on WordPress, how to enhance the basic WordPress setup, and how to monetize your site for maximum revenue. While this guide is perfect for beginners, it was also created to meet the needs of intermediate and advanced users.

One of the best things about using the WordPress platform is that it's incredibly easy to get started. An experienced user can have a site up and running in less than an hour. However, WordPress doesn't exactly come with an instruction manual, and many new users can end up feeling lost, or worse, spending hours and hours looking up YouTube tutorials on how to do the most basic of tasks. At the same time, intermediate and advanced users may have WordPress down to a science but might also have trouble effectively monetizing the site, beating Google's Panda update, and driving targeted traffic.

The good news is that regardless of your skill level this guide will be your WordPress instruction book and make sure that nothing is left to chance when it comes to fully optimizing your WordPress website. Whether you're an Internet marketer looking to make a full-time income online or just a person looking to start a blog for the fun of it, this guide will help you make it happen!

One thing that should also be mentioned is that this book is best read when sitting in front of your computer. A lot of the material goes into extensive detail about how WordPress works, how to configure domains/web hosting, and more. It really helps to actually be doing this at your computer as you read this guide so that you don't get lost.

Also worth mentioning is that while much of the content in this guide is very specific, some is more general. This is because factors such as what web hosting you're using, what theme you have installed, and what plugins you're using make it impossible to give step-by-step instructions for certain things. In cases such as these, I seek to give you a general understanding of the topic to get you started. However, you may need to look up resources using Google or tutorials on YouTube for your specific situation.

Once you're done reading the main part of this book, don't forget to check the Resources chapter at the end. There is some good stuff in there, including links to tutorial videos that help you with some of the more complicated tasks.

Now that you understand how this WordPress instruction manual works, let's jump right in and get started. Stick with this guide and in 7 days you will have a fully functional, completely optimized WordPress website that you can be proud of!

Day 1 – Getting a Domain Name

The first day of building your WordPress website is going to be one of the easiest. In fact, you won't be using WordPress at all today. What you're going to be doing is first learning the difference between WordPress.com and WordPress.org, two similar yet different platforms.

I'm also going to be showing you how to purchase a domain as well as the factors that go into determining the perfect domain name for your website. Choosing the right domain name is the first major SEO task that you will complete, and it is very important for making sure that your site ranks well in Google and other search engines.

Chapter 1: WordPress.com vs. WordPress.org

The reason the WordPress platform is so popular is that it allows you to create websites without having to learn complicated HTML and CSS code. Before WordPress you would have to spend months learning this complicated programming language if you wanted to build a site. Now, thanks to WordPress, you can have a site up and running with a few clicks of a mouse.

The very first thing you need to understand, if you are new to the WordPress platform, is that there are two different types of WordPress: WordPress.com and WordPress.org. While these two platforms are very similar in function, there are some **major** differences as far as what you're allowed to do on each of them. Let's take a look at each platform so you can figure out which one is best for you.

WordPress.com

WordPress.com is a website that allows you to create a blog using the WordPress platform. When you sign up you have several URL options, such as [your blog name].wordpress.com which is free and other domains such as .com, .me and more that you have to pay for. The free option is generally the most popular.

The blog will also be hosted on WordPress's servers for you, and there are paid and free options. With the free option you only get the blog, but with the paid option you get the following:

- Domain name and mapping (allows you to register a domain name of your choice)
- 10GB space upgrade (adds more storage space)
- No ads (your free blog will have ads on it so WordPress can make money)
- Custom design (allows you to customize your font and theme CSS)
- Video press (allows you to upload and play HD videos)

All of these paid options cost $99 per year total, although there are discounts available at times. Even with the domain name and mapping, your site will still be hosted on the servers at WordPress.com and you will still be subject to their terms of service. In other words, WordPress owns your website.

With the free variant you get many different themes to choose from, but you will be unable to upload your own themes. You will also not be able to edit the themes you choose from the gallery either. However, you will be able to add your own custom header.

In addition, WordPress will also have the right to display ads on your site. The good news is that the ads are very infrequent, and logged-in users won't see them. For a $29.99 annual fee you can have ads removed entirely, if you didn't choose the paid version that removes them automatically.

Another major downside to WordPress.com (if you're looking to make money on your site) is the fact that you are not allowed to have any third-party advertisements on it. While you can sell your own products (which is great if you're a Kindle author or something of that nature), WordPress.com simply isn't ideal for a strong marketing effort.

One odd notable exception to this rule, as stated in the WordPress.com terms of service (TOS), is that you can write your own movie and video game reviews and link people to Amazon.com.

In addition to affiliate blogs, other types of blogs that Wordpress does not allow are autoblogs, SEO blogs, and scraper blogs.

You also can't add plugins to your WordPress.com site. Plugins are special programs that you can add to WordPress.org that enhance your site in various ways. Some browser-based WordPress plugins, such as Zemanta, do work with WordPress.com because they don't have to be uploaded onto the site itself.

Here is a quick recap of the pros and cons of WordPress.com:

Pros

- Very easy to set up
- Don't have to learn HTML or CSS
- Great for blogging
- Basic variant is free
- Don't have to worry about buying hosting or a domain name

Cons

- ⮤ Can't upload custom themes
- ⮤ Advanced features and ad removal come with a yearly fee
- ⮤ Can't sell affiliate products, advertising space, or post AdSense ads
- ⮤ Can't use plugins
- ⮤ No control over your hosting
- ⮤ Can't sell the site

In the end WordPress.com is really only useful if you plan on blogging for the fun of it or if you run a service-based business online and just need a website as quickly as possible and for free. WordPress.com is **not** recommended for anyone who is serious about online business, with one of the top reasons being that SEO (search engine optimization) is discouraged on WordPress.com, and this will limit your traffic. Also, third- party advertising is not allowed, which limits your business model to selling only your own products. For those who are serious about making money online, WordPress.org is going to be your best choice.

WordPress.org

WordPress.org is, quite simply, the easiest way to create a website that is designed to make money. While it does take a bit more effort to set up, and there is a bit more of a learning curve involved, its advantages over WordPress.com are many.

One of the best things about WordPress.org is the level of customization available to you. You can choose from **many** pre-made themes that can be found across the Internet for free, such as Flexibility, or you can choose from one of the Wordpress-provided themes. You can even hire someone to create a custom theme for you or make one yourself if you have the talent for that. You can also go into the CSS and edit your themes.

Another huge benefit of using WordPress.org is the fact that you can use plugins. As previously mentioned, plugins are programs that you add onto your site that perform different functions. Some plugins filter spam, some make your site load faster, while others give you extra fonts. There are thousands of plugins available, and we'll get into which ones are the best for your site a bit later.

WordPress.org is also the preferred platform for website flipping. If you want to build a site, rank it high in the search engines, drive traffic, and produce a revenue stream so that you can sell it, WordPress.org is perfect for you. WordPress sites tend to sell very well because most people are familiar with them and how they work, as opposed to HTML sites.

There are many other ways to monetize a WordPress.org site. You can participate in affiliate programs, create autoblogs, create websites with curated content, post AdSense ads, sell ad space, and much more. Because you own the site and are hosting it on your own hosting service, you can do whatever you want when it comes to monetization.

Also, because your site isn't hosted on the WordPress.com servers, you're free to do as much SEO as you want. Not only that, SEO is very easy to do using WordPress, especially if you have the right plugins for it. Doing SEO will help to drive plenty of traffic to your site, which can help explode your revenue.

Here is a quick rundown of the pros and cons of WordPress.org:

Pros

- Very easy to use once you learn how
- Don't have to learn HTML or CSS
- Have complete control over the site
- Can sell the site
- Can use SEO
- Can use custom themes
- Can edit themes
- Access to thousands of plugins
- Have control over hosting
- Can monetize your site any way you want

Cons

- Takes a bit longer to set up
- More of a learning curve

⚼ Responsible for obtaining your own domain name and hosting

As you can tell, the pros drastically outweigh the cons. WordPress.org is functionally superior to WordPress.com in almost every way, making it the clear winner here unless you just want to be a casual blogger. Because of this, the remainder of this guide will focus on WordPress.org, how to set it up, optimize it, and monetize it. However, due to the similarities between WordPress.com and WordPress.org, much of the information in this guide about how to set up your site will be applicable to the WordPress.com platform as well.

Now that you understand the difference between the two WordPress platforms we can move on and get you set up. As mentioned before, you do have to purchase your own domain name for WordPress.org, and that will be your task for Day 1.

Chapter 2: Purchasing a Domain Name

The first step for getting started with WordPress is purchasing a domain name. This is incredibly easy and can be done in less than 5 minutes. However, there are some things to keep in mind before you rush out and buy a domain name. This is especially true if you plan to monetize your website.

Branding

The first thing you want to think about is branding. This is important whether you plan on monetizing your site or not. You want to pick a domain name that perfectly describes your website or blog and encapsulates what you're all about. Your domain name should also be something memorable and easy to spell.

An example of good branding would be a site that sells cat litter boxes and has the domain name "buycatlitterboxes.com." Just from hearing the URL you can tell exactly what the site is about.

An example of poor branding for this business would be "cat-tastic.com." Even if the product itself is named "cat-tastic" no one is going to have a clue what the site is about just by hearing the name. Another problem is that it is hard to remember how to spell, thanks to the hyphen. As a rule you should avoid hyphens and numbers (8, 3, 12, etc.) in domain names at all costs.

Also remember that domain names with two words are great, if you can find them. They tend to be worth much more than domain names with more words. The thing is, two-word domain names are incredibly rare these days, so you may not be able to find one suitable for your website. Don't worry about this too much; just get a three-word name. Generally speaking, the more words in your domain name, the less it will be worth if you want to sell it later. So keep that in mind.

Types of Domains

When it comes to the different types of domains, .com is king. This is simply because it is the most common, and by far the easiest to remember. If your site is "dogwalking.net" many people will not remember that it is a .net and go to "dogwalking.com" instead. As you can probably tell, this can cause a lot of lost traffic in some cases and is terrible from a branding standpoint.

Another problem with .net, .info, and other top-level domains is that if you create a custom email address using your domain, such as "jim@dogwalking.net," people will also forget the .net when emailing you and send their messages to "jim@dogwalking.com" instead. This can be a huge problem if you use that email address for customer service.

Perhaps the worst thing about a non .com domain name is that it just isn't worth as much as a .com. This is due to the reasons discussed above and simply because a .com is a powerful branding force. If you have a website that is a .net, don't expect it to sell for as much as a .com if you do decide to sell it.

In the end, just make sure you get a .com as your domain. Don't settle for anything else, even if the particular name you want is already taken. Change up the name you were thinking of a bit and keep searching until you find a .com that works for your site.

The SEO Factor

If you're creating your site to make money, you need to do some serious keyword research before you even begin brainstorming ideas for your domain name. This is because you want a domain name with a high amount of search volume but a relatively low amount of competition. While terms that fit these criteria can be hard to find, they do exist.

There are three main ways to do keyword research: estimation, testing, and analytics. Analytics can only be used to gather keyword research if you already have a site set up and analysts installed, so for now we'll concentrate on estimation and testing.

Estimation

Estimation is simply using a keyword research program, such as the Google AdWords Keyword Tool, to see how heavily searched keywords are. This is considered estimation because these tools are not 100% accurate. However, in many cases the tools can give you a good idea of what to expect in terms of traffic.

To use the Google AdWords Keyword Tool, simply go to https://adwords.google.com/o/KeywordTool. Type the keyword you're thinking of having in your domain name into the box and click "Search." You can also refine your

search by selecting Broad, [Exact] and "Phrase" as needed. Here is an example of how that works using the keyword "dog walking."

Broad looks like this when someone types your keyword into Google:

Walking the dog

dog walking classes

dog obedience walking

As you can see, the keyword can be split, as long as it appears.

[Exact] looks like this in Google:

dog walking

This is the exact keyword with no other words added.

"Phrase" looks like this:

dog walking classes

how to dog walking

tips on dog walking

In this case "Phrase" simply ensures that the keyword isn't split up.

While [Exact] is the most refined search option, it may not cover all instances of people searching for your keyword. This makes it better to choose "Phrase" for keyword research purposes in most cases, but once again be aware that the data isn't going to be 100% accurate.

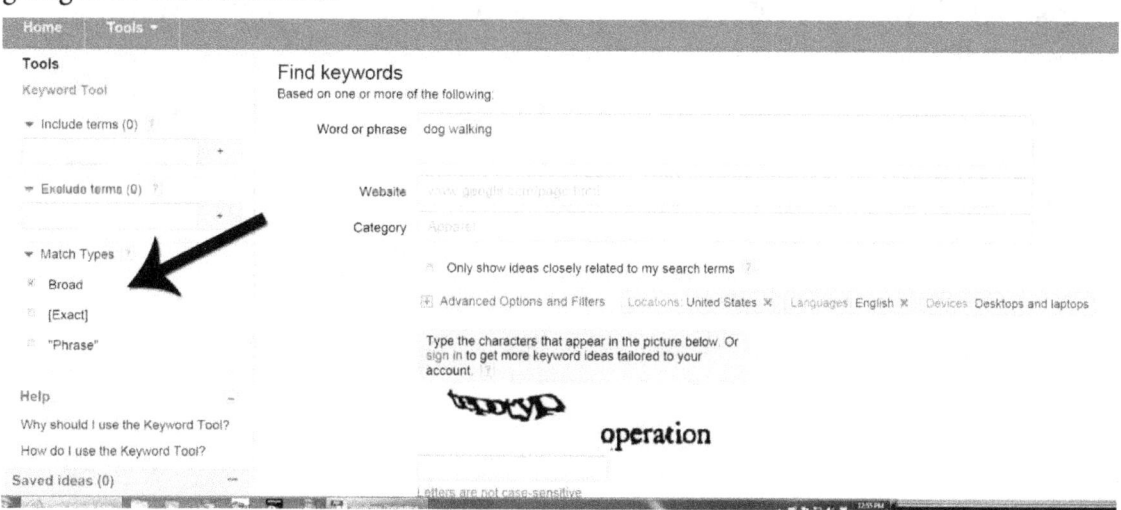

Once you type in your keyword and get the results back, you will notice that not only do you get search data on your keyword, but also a list of other keyword ideas. Take note of these and see if any of them have a particularly high search volume.

You will also notice that search results are calculated for both local and global. If your site is advertising a service that only operates in a local area, such as hairstyling, you want to pay more attention to the local results. If you're selling digital products worldwide on your site, then the global results will be more important to you.

Keyword	Competition	Global Monthly Searches ?	Local Monthly Searches ?
"dog walking" ▾	Low	201,000	90,500
"dog walking rates" ▾	High	2,900	1,600
dog walking rates ▾	High	5,400	3,600
dog walking service ▾	High	18,100	8,100

Once you have found some keywords that have a good search volume, you can then begin checking your competition. You may notice that there is a section in Google AdWords Keyword Tool that says "competition." This is not the competing websites but rather how competitive the AdWords listing is for that term. This is pretty much irrelevant at this point but can give you an idea whether there is money to be made from your keywords, because a lucrative keyword will have plenty of AdWords ads targeting it.

Keyword	Competition
☐ **dog walking** ▾	Medium
☐ **"dog walking"** ▾	Low

To estimate your competition go to Google.com and begin typing in your keywords to see what comes up. Once again you can use Broad, [Exact], or "Phrase" to do these searches. While this is situational, in most cases it can be best to use "Phrase," which is simply your keyword in quotation marks.

Once you type your keyword in and do your search, take note of how many pages come up. Generally speaking, the fewer pages that come up, the easier it will be to rank for that keyword. However, the main factor determining whether or not you can rank on Page 1 for your keyword is the strength of the pages that are already on Page 1. There are ways to measure this, which we'll get into in just a moment.

dog walking	🔍

About 115,000,000 results (0.29 seconds)

Overall, the estimation method isn't perfect, but many people use it because it's free and can be done in a matter of minutes. The other method available to you right now, testing, is much more accurate but does have a few drawbacks.

Testing

If you absolutely demand accurate keyword data then you're going to want to do some actual testing, using Google AdWords because you want Google data. Google is the dominant search engine, after all, and will be responsible for the majority of your organic traffic. Of course, if you don't have a site yet then skip this for now.

To test the search volume of a keyword, you have to sign up for Google AdWords http://google.adwords.com/ and start a campaign. This isn't too complicated, and Google walks you through the process. What you're essentially going to do is run an ad for a day or two and measure the amount of clicks you get. Your ad will show up on the right side of Google searches and consist of a title and a short description.

About 549,000 results (0.30 seconds)

Ads related to **gout triggers**

What Causes Severe Gout? | TreatSevereGout.com
www.treatseveregout.com/
Learn How People Get Severe **Gout**, And Find a Treatment Option Now.

Gout Attack? | gout.com
www.gout.com/
Get Free Tips to Help Manage and Reduce Painful **Gout** Attacks.
What is Gout? - What Causes Gout? - Manage Your Gout.

✔ 9 Surprising **Triggers** of Gout Pain - Health.com
www.health.com/health/gallery/0,,20458446,00.html
Got **gout**? Aspirin, hormones, dehydration, and other factors that can **trigger gout**

Why these ads?   Ads - Why these ads?

Gout Diet & Med Info
www.thegoutmed.com/
Discover a Prescription to Help Manage the Root Cause of **Gout**.

What Causes The Gout
www.ask.com/What+Causes+The
Explore What **Causes** The **Gout**. Satisfy Your Curiosity on Ask.com

Foods That Trigger Gout
www.lifescript.com/

Now, when you're doing this the most important part is to set your budget cap to between $5 and $10 a day, to keep you from running up a massive tab while doing this. Also, $10 to $20 should be more than enough data to tell whether or not a keyword is getting traffic.

Basically, you're going to add up the clicks your ad got and multiply that. So, if you got 60 clicks in one day you'd multiply that by 30 and get 3000, the amount of visitors you'd expect to get in a month.

Remember, there is a small margin of error when using this method due to two factors. The first is the fact that the more competitive keywords have a higher cost-per-click, and $10 to $20 may not cover enough clicks to get a lot of accurate data for you. This can be overcome by some simple mathematics. Let's say your budget for day one runs out and reaches $10 in a 4-hour period. Take that amount and multiply it by

6 to get 24, and calculate what you would have gotten for the day. Now this isn't perfect, but it is close enough in most cases.

The second factor for margin of error is your ad itself. If you're awesome at writing ads you will get more clicks, which is fine. However, if you aren't any good at writing ads you will get fewer clicks, which can skew your results. To compensate for this take time to learn some basic copywriting techniques related to writing AdSense ads. This is very simple and doesn't require a huge learning curve. Not only will this help you get more accurate results when doing keyword research, it will also help you understand how to write attractive titles for your website and web pages so that people click on them.

Also, another word of advice: Don't use the word "scam" in your ad when testing keywords unless it is actually part of your keyword itself. This is because the word "scam" is a very hot word that typically gets a ton of clicks. Using this when testing can really skew your results.

Overall this testing method isn't 100% perfect, but it is a vast improvement over the estimation method in terms of accuracy, because you are actually collecting real data. The only drawback is of course that it does take a bit of time and money to do these tests.

The second part of testing is to identify your competition. You will do this in exactly the same way as the estimation method, only you will take things a bit further using a tool known as SEOmoz Toolbar, which you can get by going to this UR by entering it into your browser.
http://www.seomoz.org/seo-toolbar

With this tool you're going to go and look at all 10 websites on the first page of the search results for your keyword and analyze their statistics. You're going to look at the Page Authority (PA) and the Domain Authority (DA).

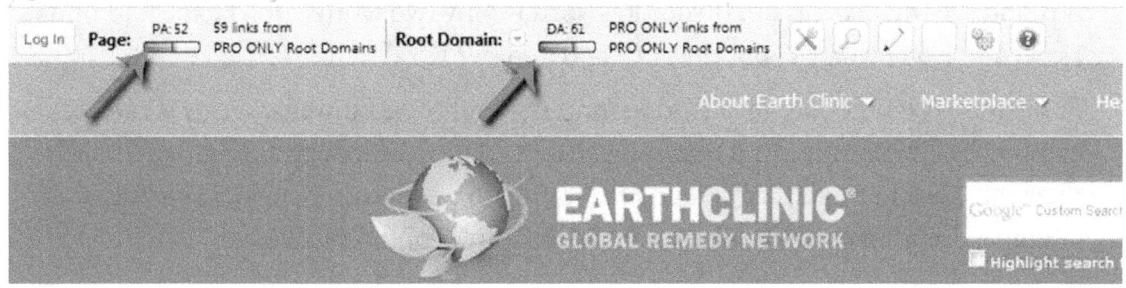

If two or more sites on Page 1 of Google have 40 or fewer in both of these categories, getting your website up onto Google Page 1 should be very easy. If you want, you can do this method before the AdWords test in order to ensure you don't spend money testing keywords that have extremely strong competition.

Regardless of whether you're using estimation or testing, you need to ultimately pick out several keywords that you like, that have a high search volume and low competition. Once you have this list of keywords that you'd possibly like to use in your domain name, it's time to move on to a registrar to purchase the name itself.

Choosing Your Registrar

When it comes to choosing which site to use to register your domain name, there are many options available. However, the two most popular registrars are Go Daddy and Namecheap. As far as price goes either one can be cheaper at any given time just depending on what discounts they happen to have available. Before purchasing a name at either place, do Google searches on "Go Daddy coupon code" and "Namecheap coupon code" to make sure you're getting the best discounts available.

An advantage that Go Daddy has over Namecheap is that more people use it. This means that if you ever sell your domain and/or site you can transfer the domain more easily if your customer is already signed up on Go Daddy. Transferring domains between registrars isn't hard but does take a bit more of a learning curve to do.

Choosing the Right Domain Name

Regardless of what registrar you choose, the purchasing process is basically the same and starts with running a search for your desired URL. Once again I highly suggest you search for a .com.

Basically all you're going to do is type your most preferred keyword into the search box and see what comes up. If your keyword is only two words, don't expect to find it as a .com. Don't worry about this, just add another word to it.

For example, if your keyword is "dog training" and "dogtraining.com" is taken you can try "bestdogtraining," "dogtrainingclasses," "affordabledogtraining," and words like that. Keep in mind that if your site is going to be advertising a local business, adding a geo term can be really beneficial. Examples of that would be:

"memphisdogtraining," "losangelesdogtraining," or "detroitdogtraining." This will help people in your area find you much easier.

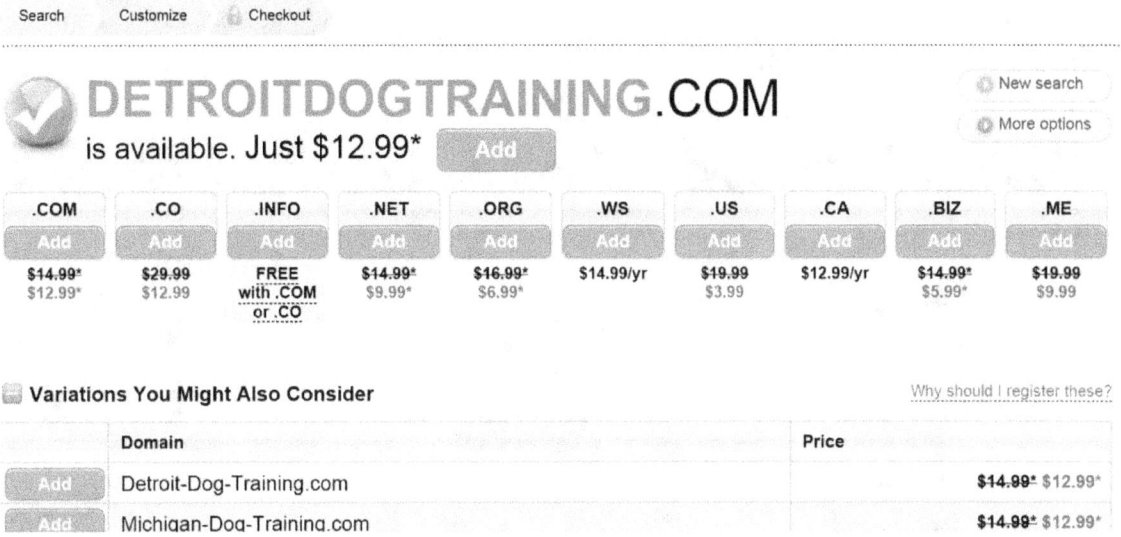

Once you've done a few searches and have found an acceptable .com you can then go through the checkout process. Keep in mind that you will have to renew your domain every year unless you are on a plan in which it is registered for more than one year. You can set your subscription so that your bank account or credit card is billed automatically in most cases. Also, don't forget to use the promo code that gets you the biggest discount.

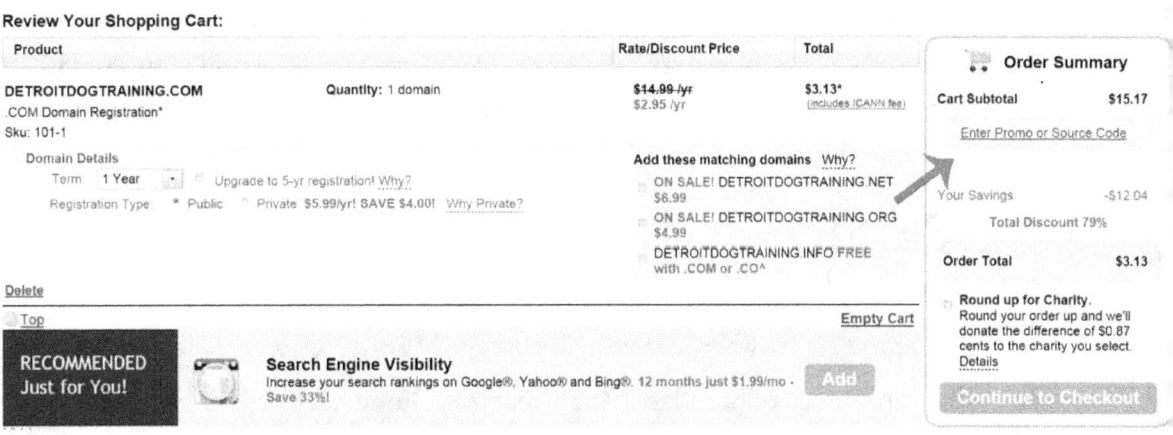

Also keep in mind that you can get something known as "whois guard" when you go through checkout. Whois guard basically protects your identity and allows you to register the site anonymously. It also typically costs a little extra. Whois guard can be

beneficial in some cases but is ultimately up to you. Namecheap has been known to give free whois guard registration at times.

If you are a domain name investor, you should not get whois guard because it can prevent potential customers from being able to find your contact information. Domain investing is beyond the scope of this guide.

Once you are finished purchasing your domain name, it will show up in your control panel on your registrar's website. Sometimes this can take a few minutes, or even hours in some cases, after you make your purchase. You'll be accessing your domain name here later in order to point it to your server once you buy hosting, which is what you'll be doing on Day 2.

Day 1 Recap

Here is what we went over today:

- ↟ The difference between WordPress.com and WordPress.org
- ↟ The importance of brandable, high-search-volume keywords
- ↟ Why .coms are the best top-level domains
- ↟ How to find good keywords using Google AdWords Keyword Tool and the Google search engine (estimation)

- ⚔ How to find good keywords using Google AdWords and SEOmoz Toolbar (testing)
- ⚔ How to register your domain name
- ⚔ How to find promo codes
- ⚔ What whois guard is and why you should consider it

Congratulations on completing Day 1! With an SEO-optimized, highly brandable domain name in your possession, you are well on your way to having an awesome WordPress website. Also, don't forget that domain name you just purchased is an asset with tangible value and should be viewed as such. Domain flipping and investment is an entire industry in and of itself, after all.

Day 2 – Getting Web Hosting

Now that you've chosen a domain name that is both SEO friendly and brandable, you're going to have to purchase hosting, which is essential for WordPress.org based sites. Web hosting is basically renting a web server to host your actual site data on. Alternately, you could purchase your own physical servers, but that would be both expensive and impractical for our purposes.

Today we're going to go over how to purchase hosting, which hosting companies are the most popular, setting your nameservers, and getting WordPress set up on your domain and on your hosting server. This will be a bit more challenging than Day 1, but overall this is pretty simple stuff.

Chapter 3: Purchasing Hosting

There are many different hosting companies to choose from, and you may be overwhelmed at first. It would be impossible for this guide to cover them all, so we'll just be taking a look at two of the most popular, Bluehost and HostGator. These services have a lot in common, but there are a few differences worth noting. Let's see what Bluehost has to offer first.

Bluehost

Bluehost is a great hosting service and one I use personally. It has everything you need to run a WordPress site easily and efficiently. There are two basic plans you can sign up for, Regular and Reseller. Reseller hosting comes in three different varieties on Bluehost and allows you to rent server space to others as a reseller of Bluehost web hosting. Because this isn't really the focus of this guide, we'll just go over Regular hosting.

Regular hosting on Bluehost only comes in one variety (unlike HostGator), but it does have everything you need to create an impressive WordPress site. Here are some of the notable features you get when you purchase Regular hosting.

- 24/7 U.S.-based customer support
- 1-click installs for many programs
- Unlimited disk storage
- Unlimited domain hosting
- Supports international domains
- 3 different web mail solutions
- Unlimited GB of site transfer
- Unlimited add-on domains
- Unlimited parked domains
- Courtesy site backups
- cPanel account control panel
- FTP access

To view the complete list by go to this UR by entering it into your browser
http://www.bluehost.com/cgi/info/hosting_features

Bluehost is also very affordable and is usually $7.95 a month, although there are discounts at times. Also, there are promo codes that you can use for even more discounts. Don't forget to search Google for "Bluehost promo code" before signing up if you decide to go with Bluehost.

Overall Bluehost is a great service for beginners and more experienced users alike when it comes to web hosting. Bluehost also makes installing WordPress extremely easy, as I'll show you in just a little bit. First, let's take a look at the other hugely popular hosting service, HostGator.

HostGator

Like Bluehost, HostGator is an incredibly easy-to-use web hosting service. One notable difference between the two is the fact that HostGator has more plans to choose from, allowing you to pick what you need instead of simply giving you a "one-size-fits-all" plan. Here are some of the different plans available at HostGator.

Hatchling Plan

- Single domain hosting
- Unlimited disk space
- Unlimited bandwidth
- $8.95/month

Baby Plan

- Unlimited domain hosting
- Unlimited disk space
- Unlimited bandwidth
- $9.95/month

Business Plan

- Unlimited domain hosting
- Unlimited disk space
- Unlimited bandwidth

- Free private SSL and SP
- Free toll-free phone number
- $14.95/month

For creating a WordPress site I recommend the Baby Plan, in case you want to add more domains in the future. If you want, you can just get the Hatchling Plan and upgrade to the Baby Plan later if you really don't need unlimited domains right now. You probably also noticed that HostGator prices are a bit higher than Bluehost. While this is true, you can get discounts for your first month and use promo codes as well.

One advantage that HostGator has in the area of price is its "penny hosting" discount. You can obtain this discount by using the promo code 404PAGE. This code subtracts $9.94 from your first month and will get you the Baby Plan for $0.01 and the Hatchling Plan for free. The Business Plan becomes $5.01 for the first month. This discount is great if you're on a shoestring budget and need a bit of time to get your website up and running to make some money.

There is also Reseller hosting on HostGator that comes in five different varieties as well as VSP Hosting and Dedicated Server plans. Because these aren't really important for this guide we won't go over them. Before we move on, let's take a look at some of the features that all standard HostGator plans share.

- 24/7 support
- Instant data backups
- No contract
- 99.9% uptime guaranteed
- Unlimited add-on domains (not available for Hatchling)
- Unlimited parked domains (not available for Hatchling)
- Sub domains
- Free module installation
- Email alias
- Autoresponders
- Mailing lists
- Email forwarding

- ⅄ Latest cPanel
- ⅄ Instant forums
- ⅄ Instant guestbook
- ⅄ 3 email clients
- ⅄ Free Google AdWords $100 credits

To view the complete list by going to this UR by entering it into your browser, http://www.hostgator.com/shared.shtml then click where it says "Compare All Hosting Plans."

I also want to take a moment to explain that last benefit on the bulleted list, the Google AdWords credits. Something really cool about HostGator is that occasionally in the mail you will receive free $100 credits for Google AdWords. These can be used to test out keyword search volume, as we discussed earlier, or to drive traffic to your website once you have it up and running.

Choosing the Right Hosting

As you can tell, both Bluehost and HostGator have their own sets of benefits. While Bluehost is a bit cheaper, it does lack some of the features and plans that HostGator offers. In the end both services are amazing and make setting up and managing a WordPress site incredibly easy.

In the end, which service you sign up for is up to you, and don't forget that there are many other hosting services available in addition to HostGator and Bluehost. Make sure you search for promo codes and discounts regardless of which service you choose, and that the monthly payment plan is set up in a way that you're able to easily manage.

Go to this UR by entering it into your browser to visit <u>Bluehost</u>.
http://www.bluehost.com/

And here to visit <u>HostGator</u>.
http://www.hostgator.com/

Root Domains and Add-on domains

When you purchase hosting you will be prompted to enter a domain name in most cases and will even be offered a free domain sometimes, depending on which hosting company you sign up with. Something very important that you need to remember is that the domain name you sign up with to get web hosting is your root domain, and any domains you add later will be considered add-on domains.

There isn't a big difference between these, but the way you access your root domain is different from how you access add-on domains. This can be confusing when you're trying to upload files if you aren't familiar with it. Later, when we're discussing how to upload files, I will go over how to access each of these.

Chapter 4: Setting Nameservers

Once you have both hosting and a domain name, you will then have to set your nameservers so that your domain shows up on your hosting. In most cases this is incredibly easy and only takes a few minutes to do. In some cases your root domain will show up on your hosting server automatically if you purchased that domain (or got it for free) through your hosting company. All add-on domains will need to have their nameservers set, though.

The first step to setting your nameservers is to figure out what your nameservers are. Nameservers are two number/letter combinations that will be given to you in one of the first emails you're sent after signing up for hosting. If for some reason you can't find that email your nameservers should be located somewhere in your cPanel. Here is an example of what a typical nameserver looks like.

ns.123.hostgator.com

ns.124.hostgator.com

Of course the numbers will be different for you, but this is basically what nameservers look like. Once you have your nameservers it's time to go into the account you have with your registrar and type them into the designated area.

Go Daddy is known for their somewhat confusing interface that they tend to change a lot. Basically what you're going to do after logging in is click "My Account" and then "Account Summary." Find the domain you just purchased, and then click on it to bring up a new screen.

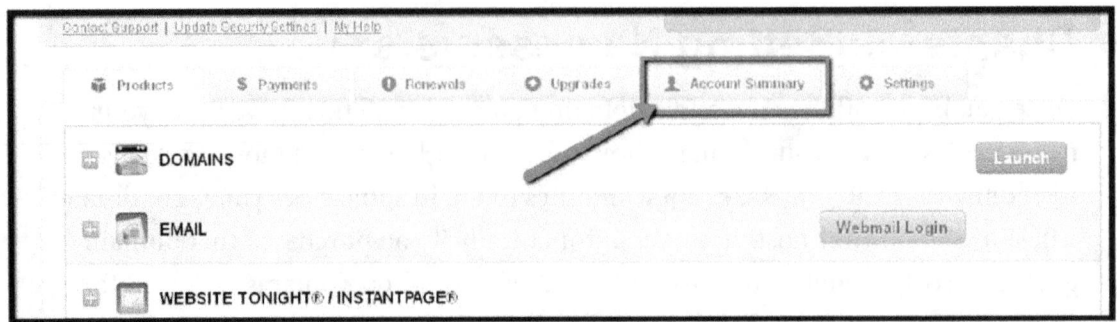

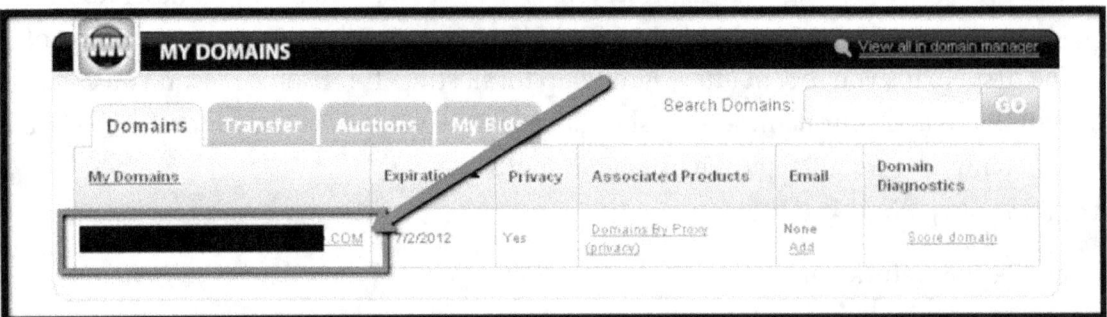

On the new screen click on "set nameservers" and you get a pop-up window. In this window select the button next to "I have specific nameservers for my domains" and enter your two nameservers in the first two boxes below.

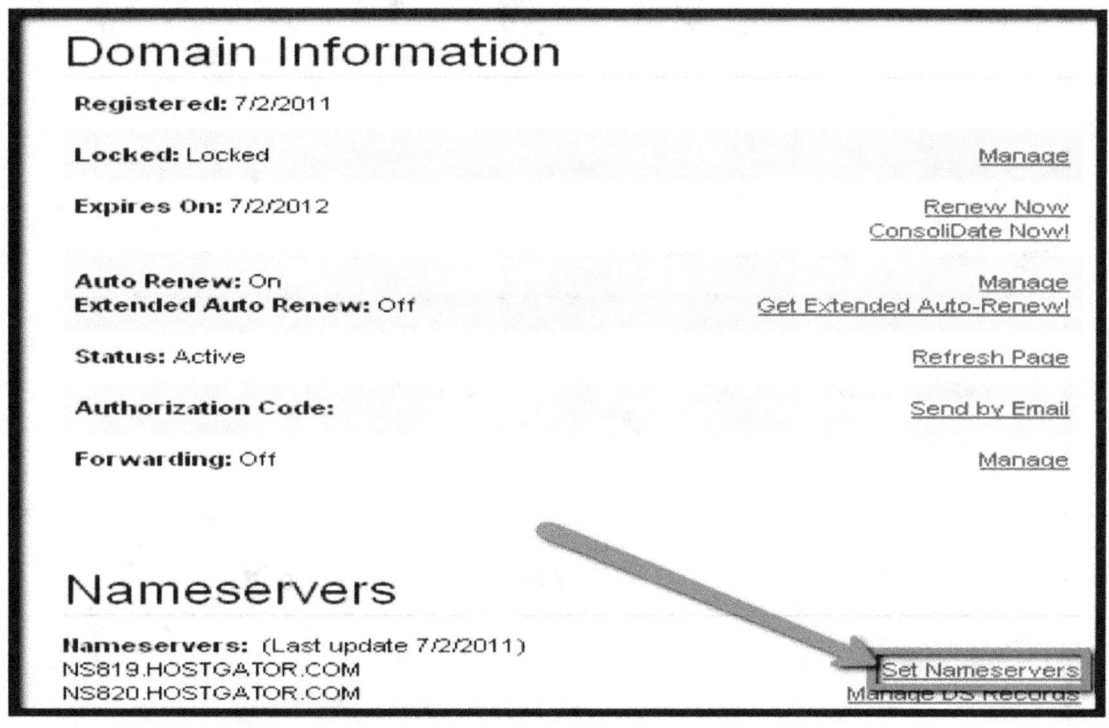

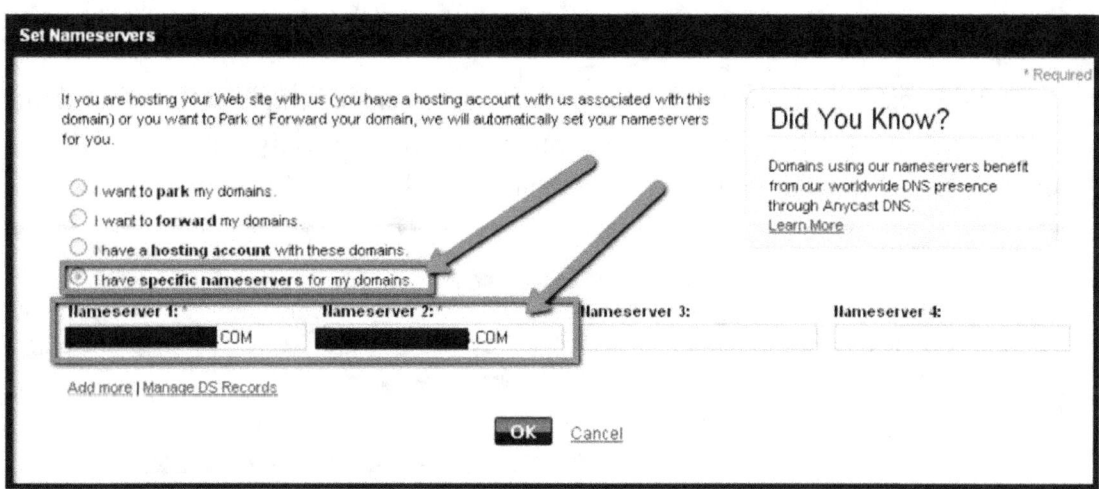

For Namecheap, log in and you will be taken to your user page. On the main page, just hover your mouse over the "My Account" tab, and then click where it says "Manage Domains." Now click your domain to open a new page.

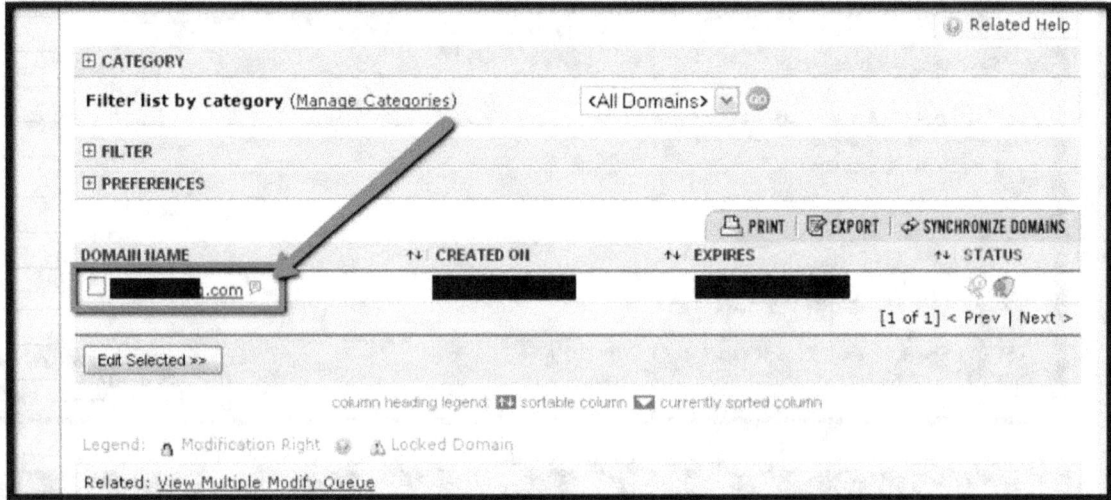

On this new page click where it says "Domain Name Server Setup" on the left and the nameserver page will come up. Click the bubble that says "Specify Custom DNS Servers" then enter your nameservers in the first two boxes and save changes.

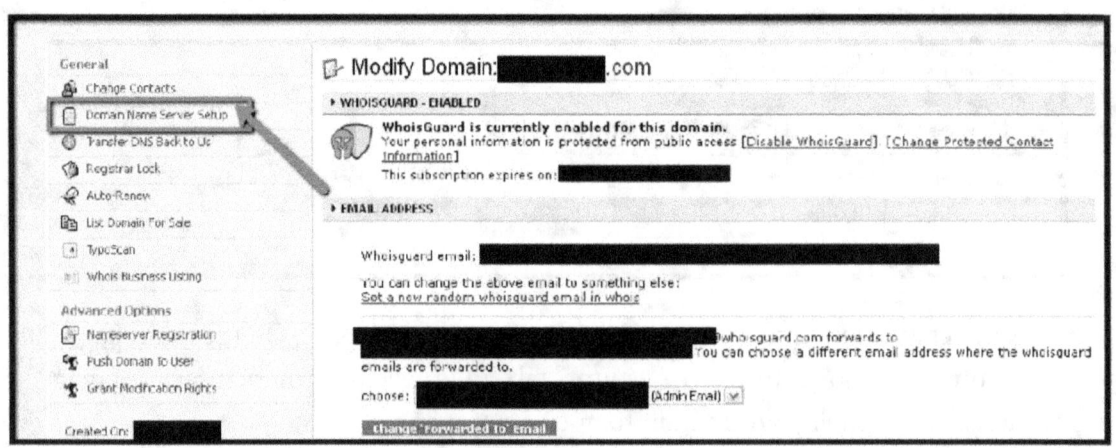

When setting nameservers it usually takes a few minutes for your domain to show up in your hosting cPanel. In some cases it can take up to 72 hours. If it takes longer than that, you should verify that you entered the nameservers correctly, and then contact customer support if you did.

Once your domain is showing up in your cPanel you can then install WordPress on it and begin building your website.

Chapter 5: Installing WordPress

Installing WordPress is going to be different depending on who you have web hosting with. In most cases, such as with Bluehost and HostGator, installing WordPress is incredibly simple and will take only a few minutes. There is some important information you need to be aware of when setting this up, such as your admin name and subdomain. I'll walk you through how to do this with Bluehost and HostGator.

Installing WordPress on Bluehost

To install WordPress on Bluehost simply sign in to your cPanel and scroll down to where it says "Software/Services" and click on the WordPress icon. This will bring up a new page where you simply need to click on "Install."

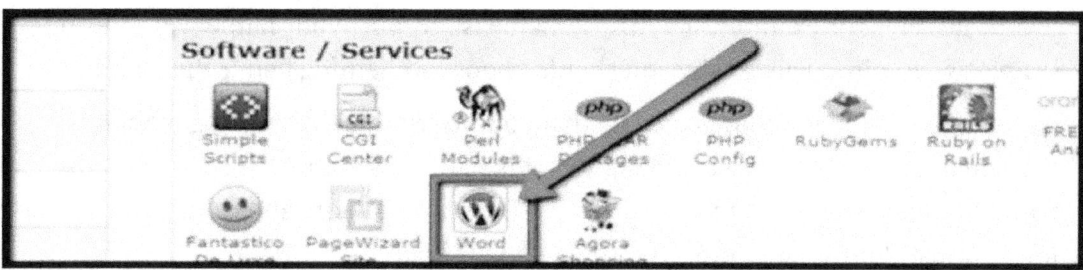

This will take you to another page where you must select the version of WordPress you want to install. Select the latest version. Now indicate where you want WordPress installed. The easiest way to do this is to leave this field blank and install WordPress on the root directory. If you want it in a subdirectory, type what you want to call it into the box.

For example, if your domain name is hockeyfans.com and you type in "database" WordPress will be installed on "hockeyfans.com/database." In most cases this is not recommended.

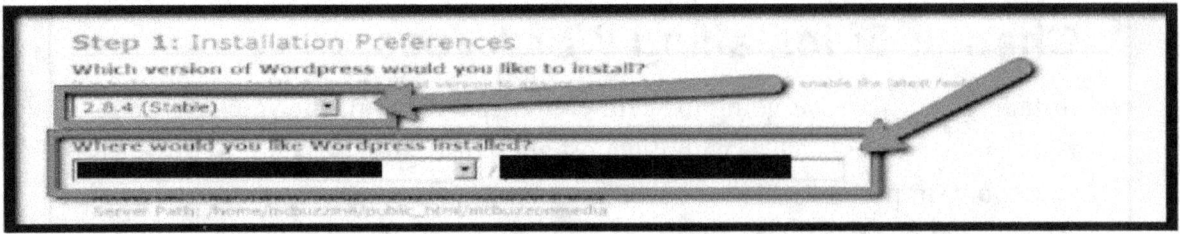

Once that is done go down to where it says "Advanced Options" and open up that section by clicking "Click here to display." Here you will enter the title of your site that you can change later if you want. This will appear in the header of your site for now.

You will also need to assign your username and password. Default username is "admin" but I recommend you change it to something else. Not only will you use your username and password to log in to your WordPress control panel, the username will also show up as the post author in some themes as well as in the comments section if you post there. For example, if your username is "admin" your name will show up simply as "admin." This is why you should choose something better than admin.

Something to keep in mind is the fact that your username that you log in with is permanent. However, you can change what is known as your "display name," the name that shows up on your site, later on. We'll discuss more about this a bit later, but for now just choose something you think sounds good.

Keep "Automatically create a new database" selected and then read the terms and conditions. Once you've done that check the box and then click "Complete."

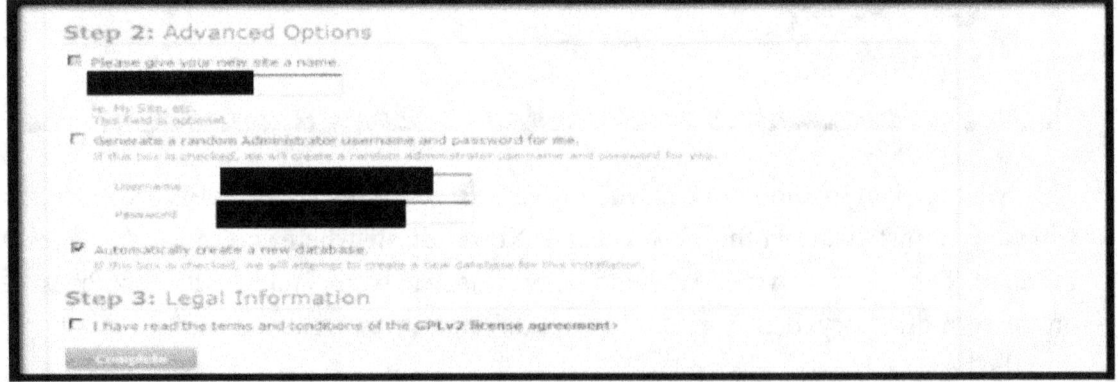

Another page will now open up and WordPress will install. This takes only a few seconds, and once it is done you get a link to your site as well as a link to your WordPress control panel and your login information. Remember, you can always

access your control panel by typing your URL followed by "/wp-admin." to bring up the login screen.

As you can see, installing WordPress on Bluehost is pretty easy. Here is how to install WordPress on HostGator.

Installing WordPress on HostGator

To install WordPress on HostGator, log in to your cPanel and scroll down to the icon that says "Fantastico De Luxe," which looks like a blue smiley face. Click that and you'll be taken to a new page.

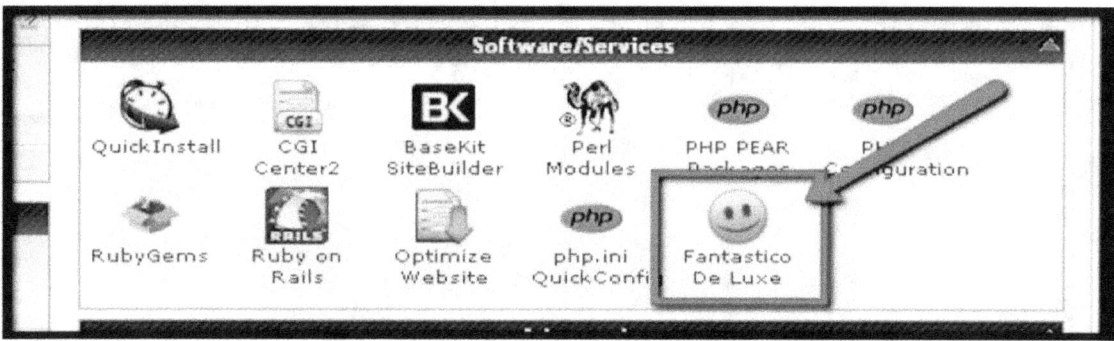

On this page check out the column on the left and click where it says WordPress, under "Blogs." A new section will open up on the right, and there will be a link that says "New Installation." Click that to move on to the next step.

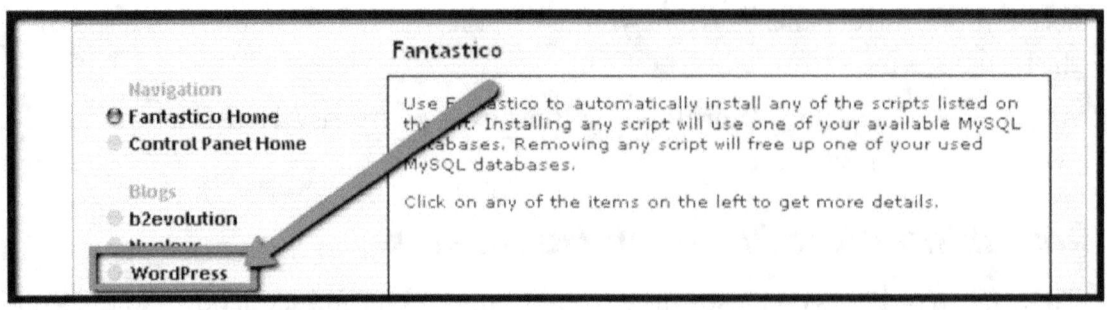

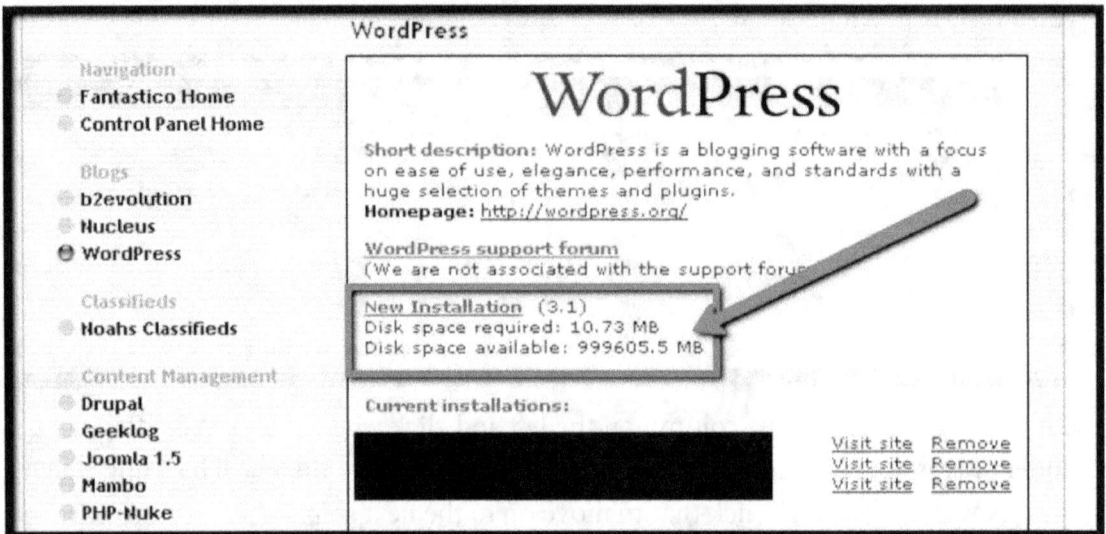

Use the drop-down menu to select the domain you want to install WordPress on. Leave the box for the directory blank unless you want to install WordPress on a subdomain as we discussed earlier. Leaving this blank is recommended in most cases.

Now enter your admin name (username) and password. Once again, the admin name you choose is permanent, but you will be able to change your display name later.

Moving on, choose your admin nickname (your display name) and your admin email. Your admin email will be the email address that you receive updates from WordPress on. You can use an existing email address or create one that exists on your domain, such as "admin@hockeyfans.com" for example.

Keep in mind that this email will get notifications on things such as users posting comments on your site, so it can be flooded fairly quickly in some cases. For this

reason I would recommend not using an existing email account and instead creating a new one.

Now choose your site name and description. This will be the title and tagline that appear in your website's default header. You can choose to change these later if you want.

Once you're finished click "Install WordPress" and you're good to go. You can access your site by typing your domain name into the URL bar, and you can access your control panel login page by adding "/wp-admin" to the end of it, such as "www.hockeyfans.com/wp-admin."

As you can tell, installing WordPress on HostGator is just as quick and easy as it is on Bluehost.

Day 2 Recap

Here is what we went over today.

- What web hosting and servers are, and how they work
- That there are different web hosting companies to choose from
- Detailed information about Bluehost
- Detailed information about HostGator
- There are promo codes and discounts available for hosting; search for them on Google before signing up
- The difference between add-on domains and root domains
- What nameservers are and how to locate them
- How to go into your registrar account and set your nameservers
- It can take up to 72 hours before your domain shows up in your hosting cPanel after setting nameservers
- How to install WordPress on Bluehost and HostGator
- Your username is permanent, but you can change your display name
- How to access your WordPress control panel by adding "/wp-admin" to the end of your URL

Good job on getting your hosting set up and pointing your nameservers to it. Day 2 was a bit more technical than the previous day but overall still pretty simple. Always remember, if you are ever having any trouble with your web hosting account, contact customer service. Most companies have 24/7 support and can get back to you very quickly.

Day 3 – Setting Up WordPress

Today will be your first day actually logging in to WordPress and getting to know how to use it. I'll teach you the basic functions of the WordPress control panel and let you know which features are the most important. We'll also be going over how to create categories and sidebar links, how to use widgets, how to acquire and upload custom themes, and more.

As you can tell, we're going to be covering **a lot** of stuff today. The good news is that most of this is easy to understand, and I'll walk you through the more challenging parts like using FTP to upload files to your hosting server.

Chapter 6: Logging In and Updating WordPress

Logging in to WordPress is very simple once you have it installed on your domain name. The first thing you do is type in your URL followed by "/wp-admin" and you will get your login page, where you enter your username and password.

Username

Password

☐ Remember Me   Log In

Lost your password?

When you do this you have the option of checking the little box that says "remember me" so that when you come back to this page in the future you will already be logged in. This is obviously only advised on computers that are only used by you. Checking this box on shared computers or computers at a library or other public place presents a huge security risk.

If by chance you lose your password you can click the link that says "Lost your password?" and you will be given the opportunity to enter your username or email. You will then be sent an email allowing you to create a new password.

If by chance you forget your username *and* email you'll have to contact support to help you out. You can view the support page for this by going to this UR by entering it into your browser

http://en.support.wordpress.com/contact/

You'll have to click on the buttons that say "I didn't find the right answer" a couple of times before the support form comes up.

Once you get logged in the very first thing you're going to want to do is update WordPress. There will most likely be a yellow bar across the top of the control panel prompting you to do this. Click "Please update now" and then click "Update Automatically" on the next page. WordPress will then update to the latest version.

WordPress 3.4.1 is available! Please update now.

 # Dashboard

There may also be some plugin and theme updates for you to do as well. Once again these are very simple, and a few clicks of the mouse will have you good to go. Whenever there is an update it appears on the left side of the black upper toolbar.

 **Kindle and PDF Books**  9 81

 WordPress 3.4.1 is available!

When you're logged in you can navigate away from the control panel and even close the browser, then come back to the control panel without having to log back in if you have cookies enabled in your browser. If you click away the tab or browser window for the control panel and don't return for an extended period of time, you will have to log back in, though.

You can log out at any time by mousing over the tab in the upper right hand corner that says "Howdy, [your username]" and then clicking on "Log Out" on the drop-down menu.

Sign In

Howdy, Lambert

Screen Options ▼   Help ▼

Chapter 7: Control Panel Basics

Now we're going to go over the basic function of most of the WordPress control panel. If something isn't mentioned here it is most likely because it will be discussed in greater detail later. Also, as we go through this chapter I'll be denoting which parts you should pay extra special attention to by writing (Very Important) next to them. These are the sections that you will really need to understand in order to build your website.

Edit Profile

The first thing you're going to want to do when you first log in to your control panel is to edit your profile. You can access your profile by mousing over the tab that says "Howdy, [your username]" that was just mentioned and then clicking "Edit My Profile."

Here you will have the option to change your admin color, enable keyboard shortcuts, enable/disable the toolbar (the black bar across the top) when viewing your actual site, and edit your contact information. Your profile also allows you to fill out your biographical information if you want to, as well as change your password.

Another important thing you can do here is to change your display name. You do this by entering what you want your display name to be in the field under "Name" that says "nickname." Then go down to the box that says "Display name publicly as" and select from between your username and nickname.

Once you are done with your profile click "Update Profile" at the bottom.

 Profile

Personal Options

Visual Editor ☐ Disable the visual editor when writing

Admin Color Scheme

◎ Blue

◉ Gray

Keyboard Shortcuts ☐ Enable keyboard shortcuts for comment moderation. More information

Toolbar ☑ Show Toolbar when viewing site

Name

Username lklein *Usernames canno*

First Name Lambert

Last Name Klein

Nickname *(required)* ⟶ lklein

Display name publicly as ⟶ Lambert

Other Toolbar Options

Two more things that are located in the upper right hand corner of the black toolbar up top are the Screen Options and Help tabs. Screen Options allows you to alter the display of your control panel, including how many columns are on the page. Help is, as its name implies, what you click if you don't understand something.

Under the Help tab are two options that appear when you click on it, Documentation on Dashboard, which basically explains everything in the control panel like I'm doing, and Support Forums where you can sign up and discuss things with fellow WordPress users.

Howdy, Lambert

Screen Options ▾   Help ▾

Howdy, Lambert

een you

ss to all

et help for

For more information:

Documentation on
Dashboard

Support Forums

Help ▲

On the left-hand side of the black toolbar are several more options. The first is a WordPress logo that gives you the following options when moused over:

- About WordPress – info on the latest version of WordPress
- WordPress.org – a link to the main WordPress.org website
- Documentation – a link to information on how to use WordPress (very handy if you are a beginner)
- Support Forums – already explained
- Feedback – a link to the feedback section of the WordPress forums

Next to the WordPress logo you'll see the name of your website. Clicking this, or the drop-down tab that says Visit Site, will simply take you to the main page of your site. The little speech bubble notifies you of comments awaiting moderation while +New tab is just a shortcut to create a new Post, Link, Page, User, or add something to the Media Library.

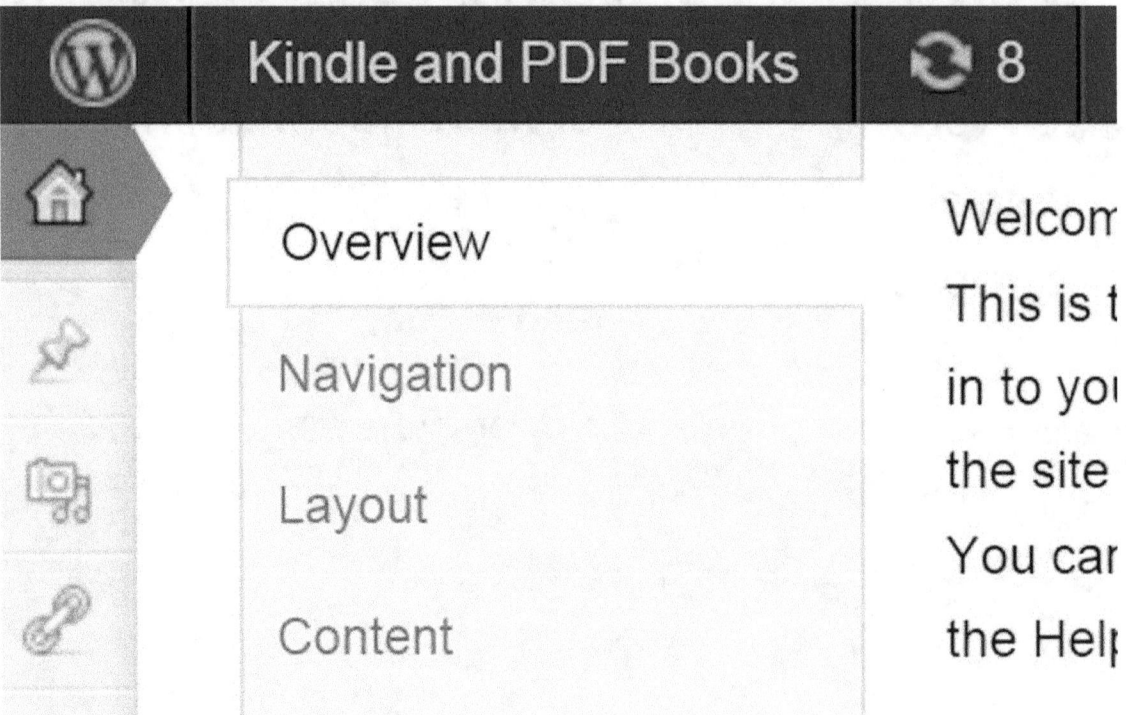

As of right now most of these options aren't going to be needed though the Support Forums, and Documentation may come in handy in the future if you're trying to do something beyond the scope of this guide.

Also remember that if you need to update your plugins, or if you need to update your current version of WordPress, those notifications will appear in the black toolbar as well.

Your Dashboard

The Dashboard is the main page of your control panel and can be accessed at any time by clicking "Dashboard" in the upper left section of the main menu bar. Beneath the Dashboard tab are two options, Home, which takes you to the Dashboard same as clicking Dashboard itself, and Updates, which allows you to update WordPress when needed.

One thing to keep in mind about the menu bar on the left is that suboptions for each tab can be viewed by mousing over each tab. However, once a tab is selected its suboptions will display below it.

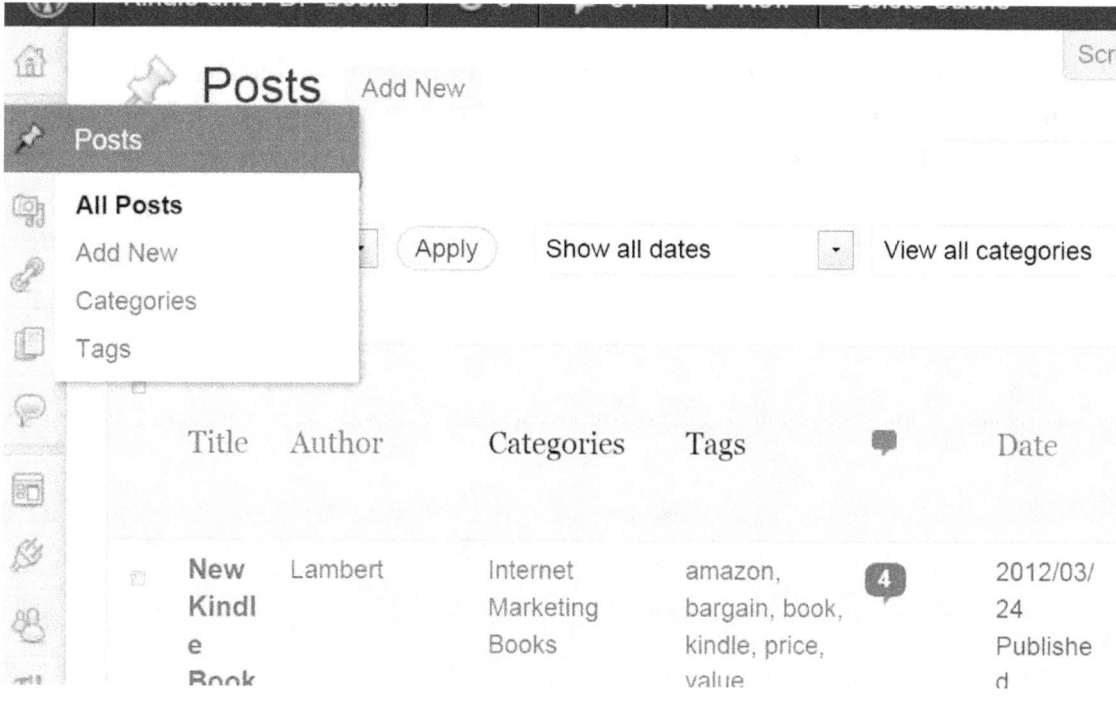

On your Dashboard you will see a variety of information regarding your website under the "Right Now" section on the left. Info that displays includes details on how many posts, pages, categories, and tags under Content as well as information on user comments under Discussion.

To the right of that is the QuickPress section, which allows you to quickly add a post instead of having to go through the Post process by using the Post tab on the left. This can be handy but lacks many of the features that you get when using the actual Post tab.

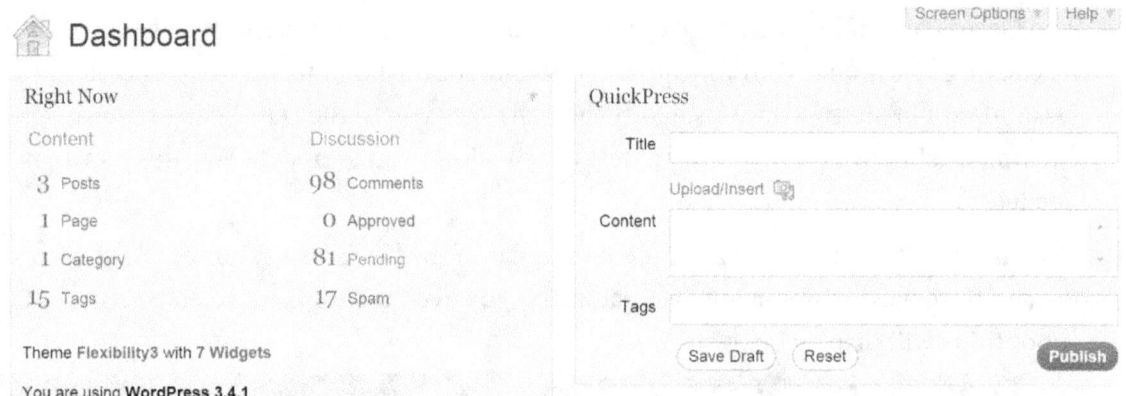

Below Right Now are three more sections, Recent Comments, which shows recent comments, Incoming Links, which shows other blogs that have linked to your website, and Plugins, which gives a quick overview of what is going on in the world of WordPress plugins.

Recent Comments

 From ro filter on WordPress Domination – Beginner to Ninja # *[Pending]*

Whoa! This blog looks exactly like my old one! It's on a completely different topic but it f

 From Jasa SEO on WordPress Domination – Beginner to Ninja # *[Pending]*

I think other site proprietors should take this website as an model, very clean and magn
and ...

 From Philip Virzi on WordPress Domination – Beginner to Ninja # *[Pending]*

G'day, only just passing through and thought i'd provide you with encouragement regard
put in your ...

Approve | Reply | Edit | Spam | Trash

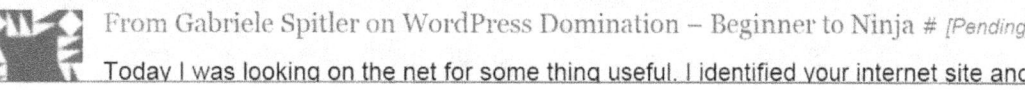 From Gabriele Spitler on WordPress Domination – Beginner to Ninja # *[Pending]*

Today I was looking on the net for some thing useful. I identified your internet site and v

Do not rely on Incoming Links for analytics data once you start doing off-page SEO and building backlinks. There are more accurate programs and plugins available for that.

On the right-hand side of the Dashboard under QuickPress are several sections. Recent Drafts lists recent drafts of posts that you have created but have not actually published, WordPress Blog shows info from the official WordPress blog, and Other WordPress News is self-explanatory.

Recent Drafts

There are no drafts at the moment

WordPress Blog

Event Organizers Unite! July 13, 2012

I'm happy to announce the formation of a new official contributor group withi organizers of in-person events that promote WordPress. Though there are h organizing WordCamps, WordPress meetups, hackathons, free classes and all happening locally there was nev […]

WordPress 3.4.1 Maintenance and Security Release June 27, 2012

WordPress 3.4.1 is now available for download. WordPress 3.4 has been a flying off the shelf — 3 million downloads in two weeks! This maintenance re

Overall the Dashboard has some handy info on it, but truthfully you won't be spending a lot of time going over it. As previously mentioned there are more accurate analytics programs out there for gathering data on your website, and QuickPress is pretty useless in most cases unless you're just blogging for the fun of it. Although the Dashboard is the main page of your control panel, you won't be spending most of your time here.

Posts (Very Important!)

Clicking or mousing over the Posts tab under Dashboard on the menu to the left grants you access to several options. This is going to be one of your most-used sections in your WordPress control panel, because this is where you will upload and publish much of your new content to your website.

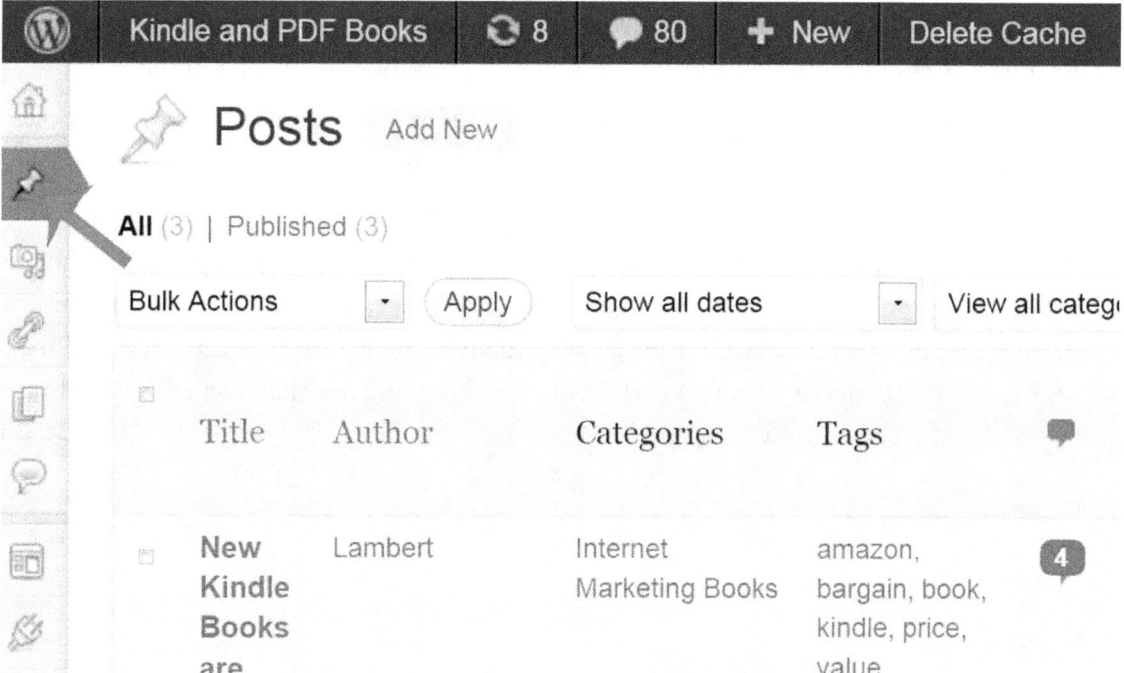

Clicking on "Posts" takes you to the posts page, which lists all of your published posts and drafts. These are posts that have been written but not published. Mousing over the title of each of your posts grants you several options: Edit, Quick Edit, Trash, and View. Edit takes you to the main editing/post creation page, Trash moves the post to the trash, and View allows you to view the post on your actual website.

Clicking on a post title takes you to the edit screen, which will be explained later when we discuss creating posts.

Quick Edit gives you fast access to several editing options such as Title, Date, Category, Tags, and more. This makes Quick Edit useless for editing the actual content but very efficient for editing specific data about the post itself. Click "Update" when you're done with a quick edit or "Cancel" to remove the Quick Edit screen.

You will also find other options on the Post page such as Bulk Actions, which allow you to Edit or Trash multiple posts at once. Keep in mind that when doing a Bulk Edit your options are very limited.

You can also filter your posts by their post dates and categories if you want. This can make it easier to find certain posts you're looking for sometimes.

The Search Posts option in the upper right hand corner allows you to quickly search for posts. Keep in mind that this option only searches the post titles, not the body.

Below the search box are two more options that allow you to configure how you view the posts page: list view (default) and excerpt view, which shows a brief excerpt of your post under each title.

Next to each individual post there will be information displayed showing the author, category, tags, number of comments, and the date. You can click on the author name to view all posts by that author, the category to view all posts in that category, and the tags to view all posts that share a certain tag. Clicking on comments will take you to a page allowing you to view the comments for that post.

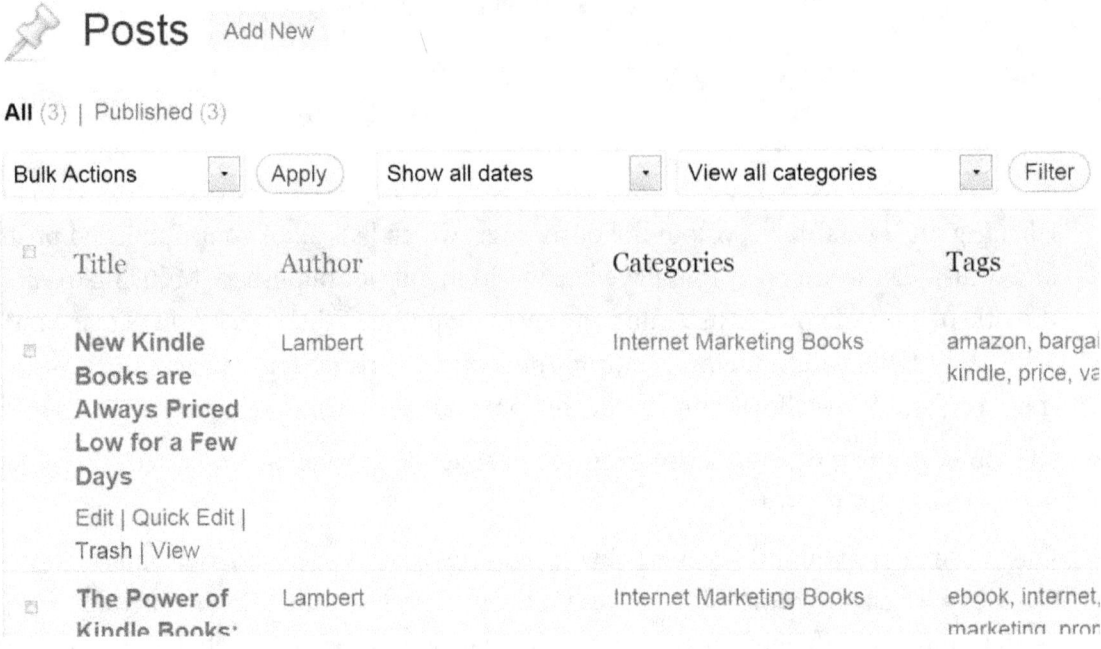

Categories	Tags	💬	Date
Internet Marketing Books	amazon, bargain, book, kindle, price, value	4	2012/03/24 Published

Underneath the All Posts tab is the Add New tab. Clicking this will take you to the post creation/editing page. We'll get into that a bit later.

Below Add New is the Categories tab. This tab opens up a page allowing you to edit and create categories. Categories are important on WordPress because they allow your visitor to easily navigate your website and access similar posts and pages that are related to one another.

Overall you probably won't be using the Category tab very often. Categories are more easily created when you create posts. If you do need to manage your categories, this is the place to do it.

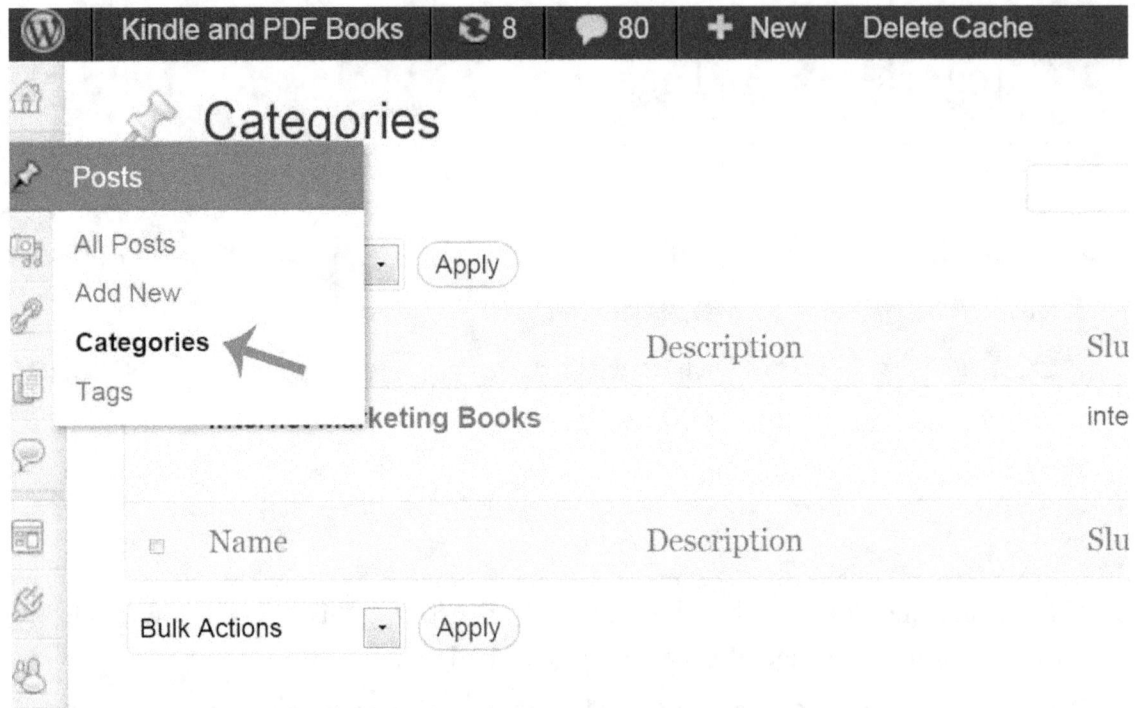

Adding a new category consists of creating its name and choosing a "slug," which is basically a URL-friendly name if you need one. In most cases the slug will simply be the category name in lowercase letters with hyphens between each word. You can also make a new category the child category of an existing category by selecting the "Parent" drop-down menu. In most cases this is unnecessary.

Beneath that is a field where you can write a description for your category. This is mostly unnecessary as well, and most themes will not show the description by default, although some will.

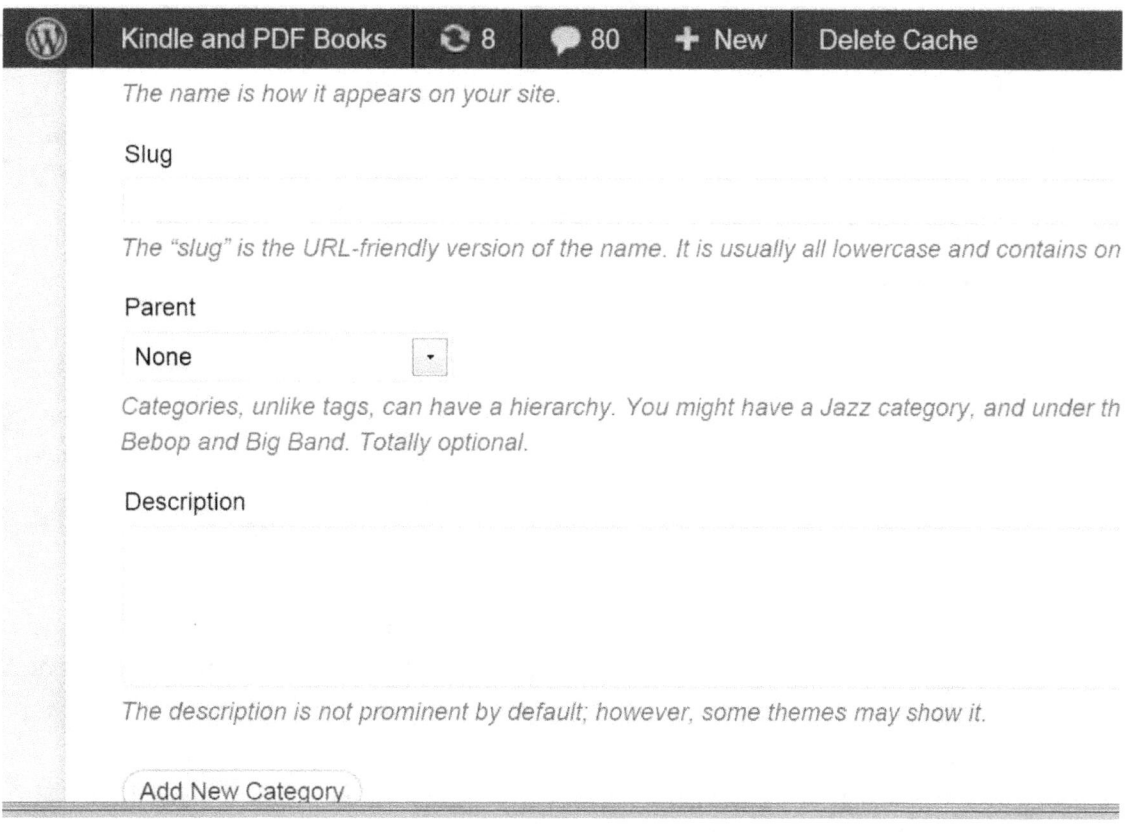

The name is how it appears on your site.

Slug

The "slug" is the URL-friendly version of the name. It is usually all lowercase and contains on

Parent

None   ▾

Categories, unlike tags, can have a hierarchy. You might have a Jazz category, and under th
Bebop and Big Band. Totally optional.

Description

The description is not prominent by default; however, some themes may show it.

Add New Category

To the right is an area where you can use Bulk Actions to delete multiple categories if you need to. There is also a search box allowing you to search for categories by name.

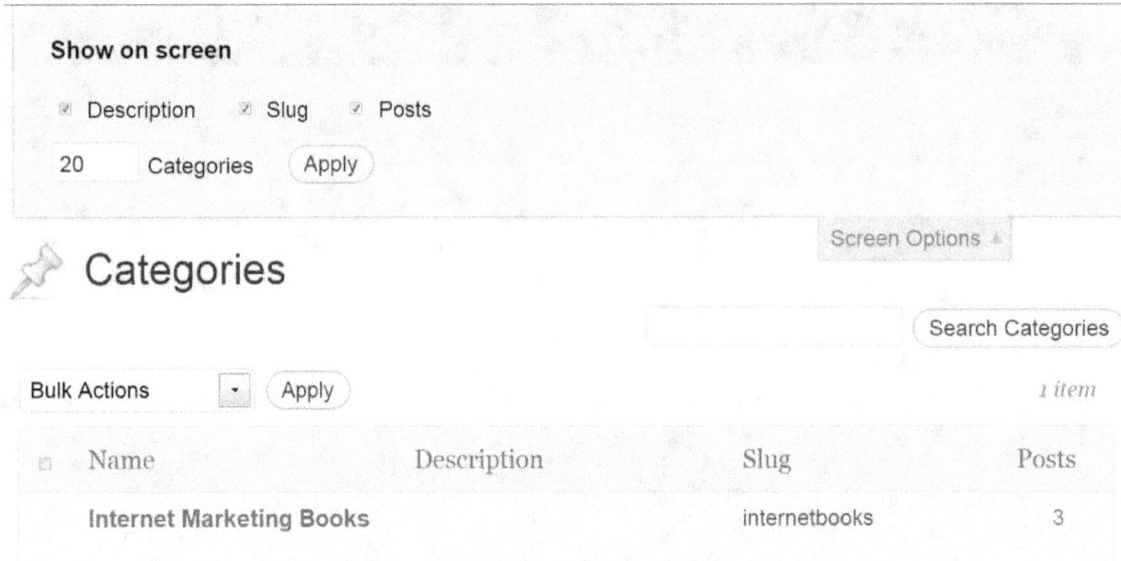

In addition, you can mouse over each category for more options: Edit, Quick Edit, Delete, and View. Edit allows you to edit your category on a screen similar to the one used to create categories. Quick Edit allows you to quickly edit a category's name and slug, while View takes you to a page on your website where all posts in a specific category are shown. You can also click on the number under Posts to view all posts in a category. Delete will of course delete the category

The Tags tab is very similar to the Categories tab in many ways. When you click on it a page opens that allows you to create new tags and edit existing tags. You won't be using this much since you will, more often than not, be creating tags as you create posts.

Tags are basically terms you apply to your posts that you want search engines to associate them with. We'll talk about this a bit later when we get into SEO. For now just know that you can create and edit tags here.

Tags

🖼 Media

🔗 Links

📄 Pages

💬 Comments **80**

🖼 Appearance

🔌 Plugins **6**

👥 Users

🔧 Tools

⚙ Settings

🖼 Contact

◀ Collapse menu

wordpress

Add New Tag

Name

The name is how it appears on your site.

Slug

The "slug" is the URL-friendly version of the name. It is usually all lowercase and contains only letters, numbers, and hyphens.

Description

advance

amazon

bargain

beginner

book

ebook

instructions

Media

Under the Posts tab is the Media tab. This section allows you to upload media files such as images, audio files, video files, and more. In most cases you will be adding these files as you create your posts and pages, but if you ever need to upload a bunch of files all at once, this is where you do it.

The main page of the Media tab shows all the items in your media library and allows you to edit them. Mousing over each file presents you with the options: Edit, Delete Permanently, and View. Delete Permanently and View are self-explanatory, while Edit opens a new page and allows you to change basic info such as the name, description, and URL of the file. You can also access some advanced editing features by clicking on the Edit button on the new page that opens up.

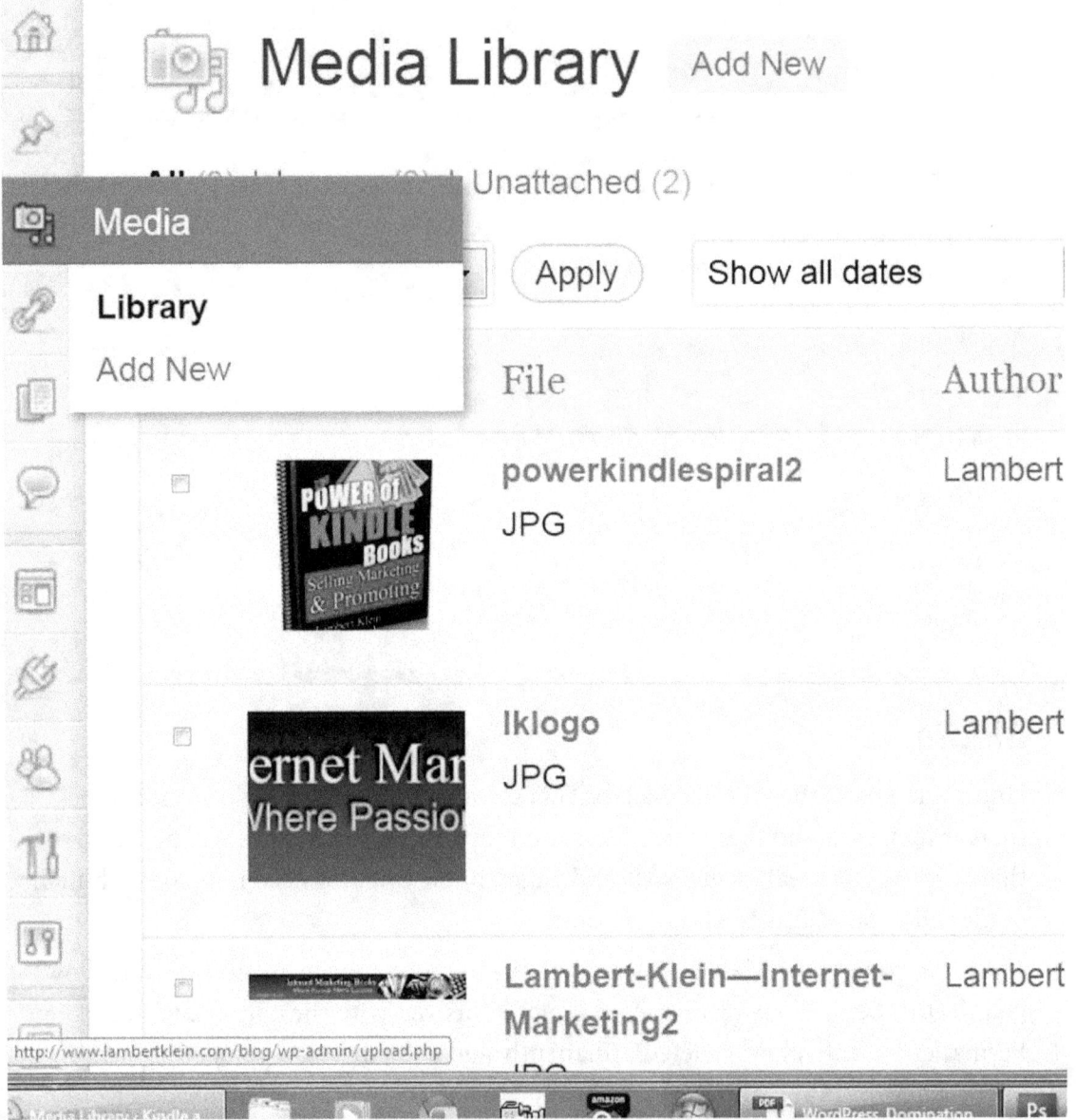

You can also do bulk deletes on the Main page, filter the page by date, and use the search box to find specific files.

You can click on the posts that each media file is attached to, as well as view pending comments on each file.

Below the "Library" tab in the menu to the left you'll find the Add New tab. This opens a new page that allows you to add new media files using the "Select Files"

button or by dragging and dropping them into the field. In most cases you will be adding files per post instead of here.

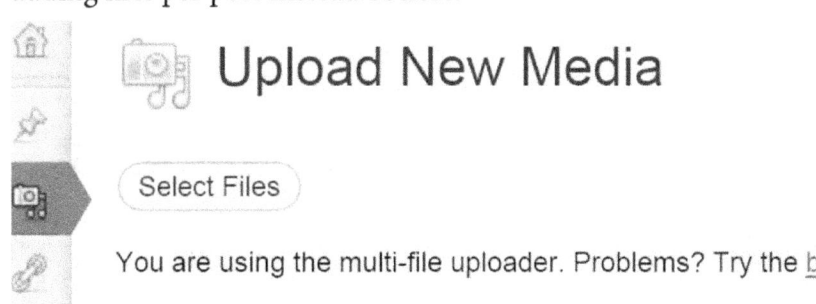

Upload New Media

Select Files

You are using the multi-file uploader. Problems? Try the browser uploader instead.

Maximum upload file size: 10MB. After a file has been uploaded, you can add titles

Links

This tab, which appears beneath Media, allows you to manage some of the links on your site. For the most part this section is irrelevant, as there are better ways to add links if you need to. The only major exception would occur if you decide to charge people to link your site to theirs in the future, in which case the Links tab can be a handy way to create and manage these links.

Pages (Very Important)

The Pages tab under Links allows you to create and manage your website's pages. Pages are different from posts, and we'll get into that a bit later, but for now just think of "pages" as pages on your website like "About," "Privacy Policy," "Contact," and stuff like that. Clicking the Pages tab opens a page that allows you to create and manage pages like these.

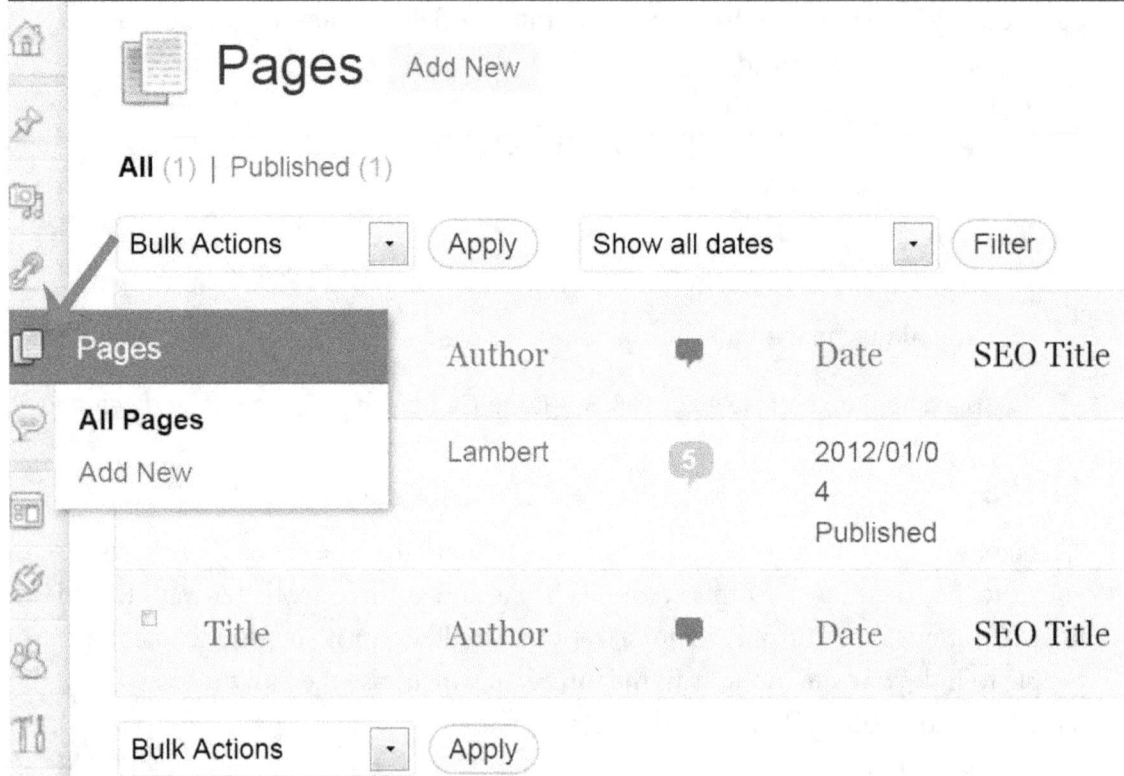

To view and edit your page select the All Pages tab. This opens a page that looks very similar to the All Posts tab, and they function virtually the same. Mousing over a page gives you the same options: Edit, Quick Edit, Trash, and View. The bulk actions, filter, and search bar are all the same as well.

Clicking on a page title or the "Edit" option takes you to the page editor/creator, which is also pretty much identical to the post editor/creator. Clicking Add New under the All Pages tab also takes you here.

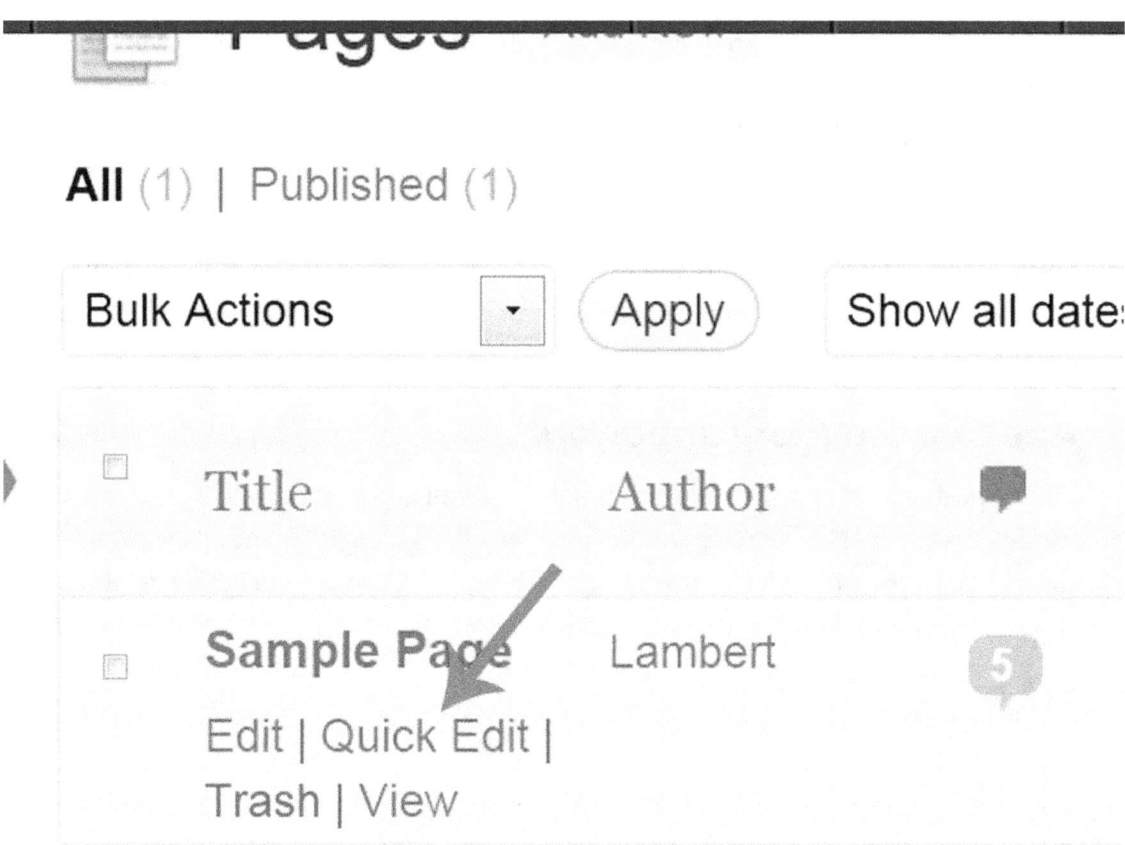

One important thing to remember about pages is that, unlike posts, when you create a page it typically shows up in the navigation bar on your website. This can be disabled by editing the CSS in order to create hidden pages, but it's easier to just use the Exclude Pages plugin.

http://wordpress.org/extend/plugins/exclude-pages/

Also keep in mind that there can be parent and child pages in addition to standalone pages. This is great for situations in which you need certain pages to belong to a certain category or section of your website.

Comments

The comments section is where you can manage the comments you get on your website's posts if you allow them. This section is virtually identical to previous sections of the Dashboard, so we're not going to spend too much time on it. Comments awaiting approval will show up in this section.

An interesting thing you can do here is view the IP address of the person who made the post and their email address. Mousing over the comment gives you more options: Unapprove/Approve, Reply, Edit, Quick Edit, Spam, and Trash. Selecting "Spam" will save spam comments in your database to help spam blockers block spam more easily in the future.

You actually can go in and edit other people's comments. This isn't advised though, and if someone makes a comment you don't like you should simply delete it if you feel the need to do that.

Appearance (Very Important)

The Appearance tab is a very important tab, as it will allow you to access options to configure your theme. Clicking on the tab opens the Manage Themes page, which allows you to control which theme is currently active on your website. By default WordPress comes with two themes, Twenty Eleven 1.3 and Twenty Ten 1.3. These themes are decent, but you should get something better. We'll discuss getting custom themes a bit later.

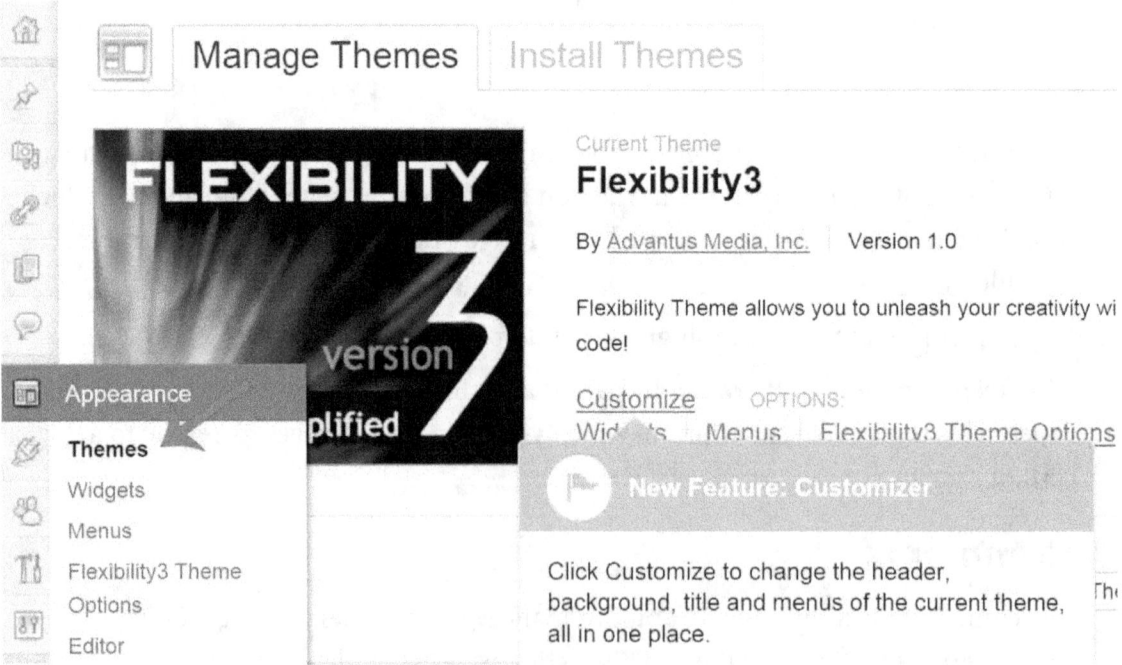

Any custom themes you install will appear on the Manage Themes page as well, with your active theme appearing at the top. The options available to you will depend on what theme you're using.

On this page you can also click on the Install Themes tab up top to access a new page in which you can install new themes, among other things. The default page is the Search page that allows you to search for new themes to use. I feel it's more efficient to use Google or another search engine to find new themes to use.

Next to "Search" is "Upload," which allows you to upload themes from your hard drive. You can also upload themes via a FTP program like Filezilla. We will go over this later.

The next option is "Featured," which will allow you to choose from some featured custom themes that WordPress is promoting. Next to this is "Newest," which features the newest themes available. Lastly there is "Recently Updated" which, as its name implies, shows recently updated themes.

Widgets (Very Important)

Under the Appearance tab to the left you will find Widgets, when you have Appearance selected or if you mouse over Appearance. Clicking on Widgets allows you to basically insert custom fields into your website, most of them in the sidebars.

There are many different Widgets, and since the Widgets page gives a description of each one I'm not going to go over what each one does here.

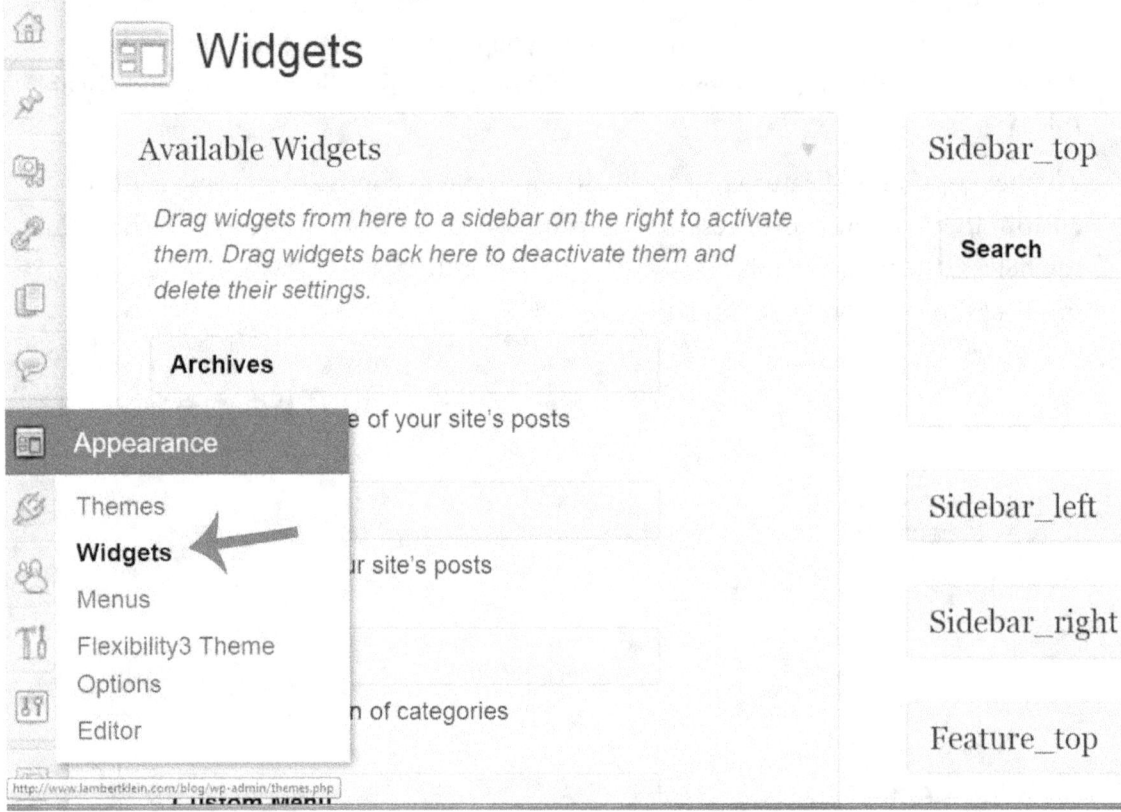

On the Widgets page you will also see a section to the right that has several fields such as Primary Widget Area, First Footer, and more. The options you have available in this section are determined by your theme, and using a custom theme can grant you a completely different set of options.

To add a Widget to your website, simply drag the one you want from the selection of widgets to the area that you want it to appear in. For example, if you want an RSS widget to appear in the top sidebar, click on RSS and drag it over to Secondary Widget Area.

Once you do this you will notice that new options become available. These options will be different depending on which widget you use. Most of these options are self-explanatory and easy to understand. Once you've chosen the options you want and have filled out the information, click "save" to save your widget, and it will appear on your website in the area you chose.

Sidebar_top

ate them and delete their settings.

Search

Categories

A list or dropdown of categories

Meta

Log in/out, admin, feed and WordPress
links

Sidebar_left

Recent Posts

Sidebar_right

The most recent posts on your site

Recent Posts: Current Topics

Tag Cloud

Your most used tags in cloud format

Text: Kindle Books

Tag Cloud: Topics

Text: Contact

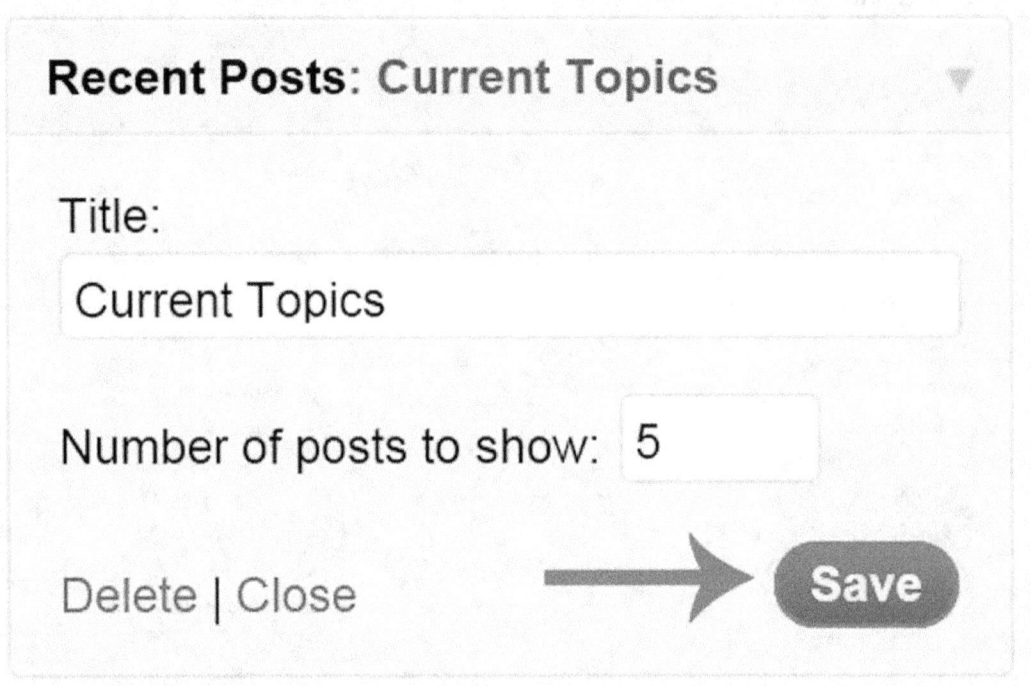

The Text widget is special because not only does it allow you to enter text, it also allows you to enter HTML, which opens up a lot of opportunities for customization, such as adding social like buttons, opt-in forms, and more.

Text: Kindle Books

Pre   Title:

Kindle Books

Kindle Books</h3>
    <div class="aligncenter">
    <p><a href="http://www.amazon.com/dp/B007LS0TLE" target="_blank"><img src="../images/wpdomination-redbar200.jpg" width="200" height="266" alt="WordPress Beginner to Ninja" /></a>
    Just Released!</p>
    </div>
    <p>
</p>
    <div class="wasocial_facebook_like">
    <div id="fb-root"></div>
    <script src="http://connect.facebook.net/en_US/all.js#xfbml=1"></script>

☐ Automatically add paragraphs

Delete | Close   **Save**

To delete a widget simply click on it to open it up, then click delete. You can also simply drag the widget back out of the area, if you want.

Menus

Underneath the Widgets tab you will find Menus. This tab simply opens up a page that shows your Links, Pages, and Categories. It also allows you to create custom menus, if you'd like. Overall this section isn't that important unless you want to create a new menu.

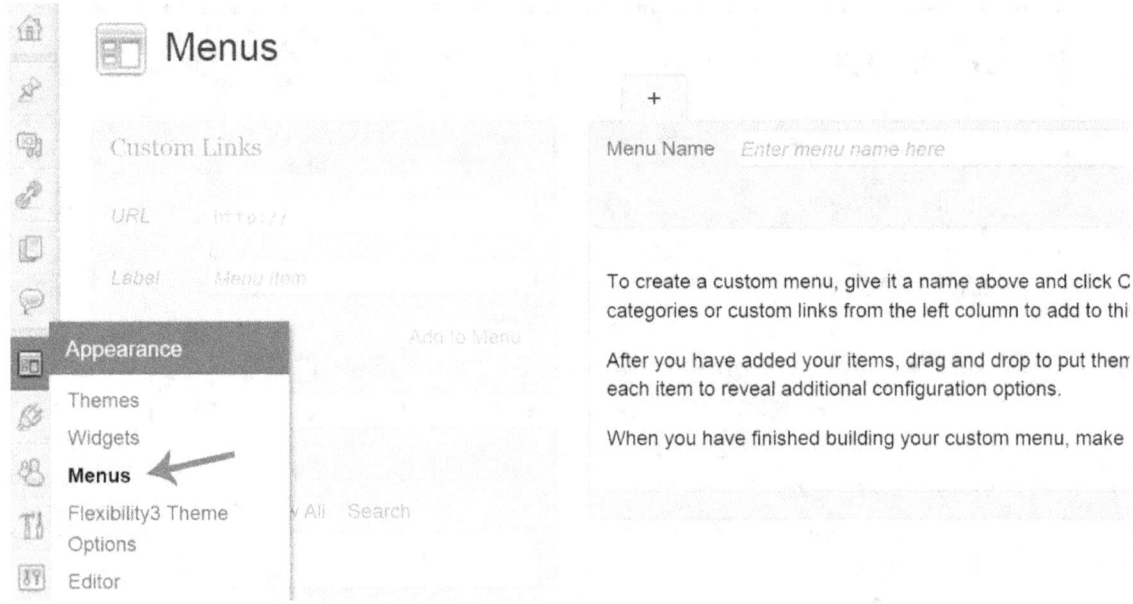

Also note that certain custom themes will have their own options available. In most cases these options will appear beneath the Menus tab, but in some cases they can appear elsewhere, it just depends on the theme you're using.

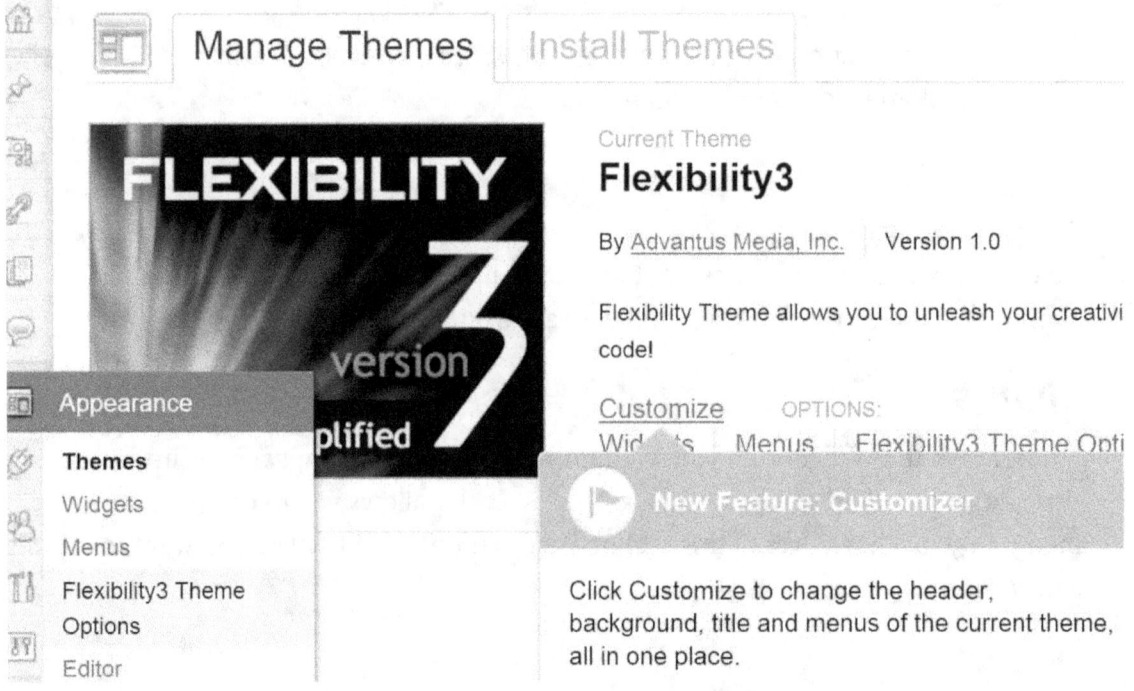

Next are the Header and Background links. Sometimes having a custom theme installed will cause these to disappear, and you'll have to install your header and background through the theme configuration settings.

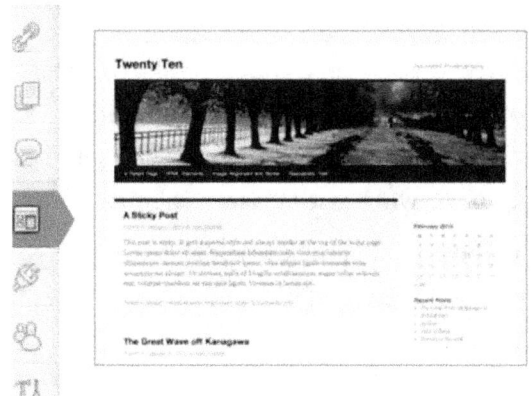

Current Theme

Twenty Ten

By the WordPress team   Version 1.3

The 2010 theme for WordPress is stylish, customizable, si — make it yours with a custom menu, header image, and t Twenty Ten supports six widgetized areas (two in the sidel footer) and featured images (thumbnails for gallery posts a images for posts and pages). It includes stylesheets for pri Visual Editor, special styles for posts in the "Asides" and "C and has an optional one-column page template that remov

There is a new version of Twenty Ten available. View v or update now.

Customize   OPTIONS:
Widgets   Menus   Header   Background

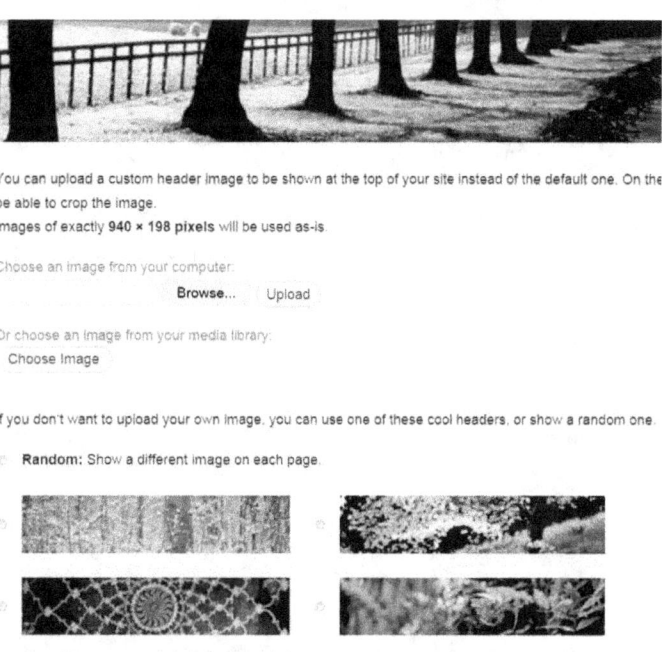

You can upload a custom header image to be shown at the top of your site instead of the default one. On the be able to crop the image.
Images of exactly **940 × 198 pixels** will be used as-is.

Choose an image from your computer:
                              Browse...   Upload

Or choose an image from your media library:
  Choose Image

If you don't want to upload your own image, you can use one of these cool headers, or show a random one.

  Random: Show a different image on each page.

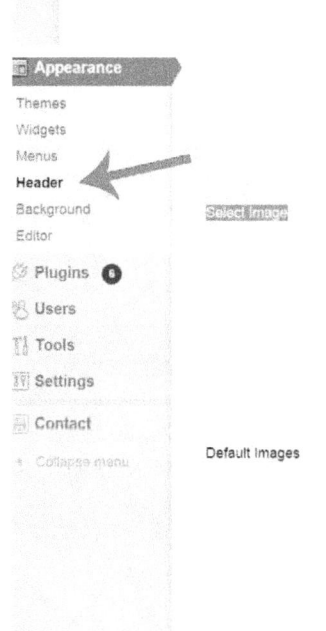

Select Image

Default Images

Appearance
Themes
Widgets
Menus
Header
Background
Editor

Plugins
Users
Tools
Settings
Contact
Collapse menu

The final tab underneath Appearance is the Editor tab. This allows you to actively edit the CSS of your theme to change the appearance. If you don't understand CSS, you should leave this alone as you could mangle your theme pretty badly if you get in there and start messing around with stuff.

There are certain things that can be done here even if you don't understand CSS, such as configuring your website to show excerpts of posts on your main page instead of complete posts. Little tricks like this are handy to know, and in some cases you will be expected to edit CSS in order to get certain plugins to work with certain themes.

Also don't forget that you can edit any theme you have installed on WordPress, not just your active theme, by using the theme selector to the right.

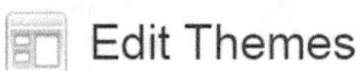 Edit Themes

Twenty Ten: Stylesheet (style.css)

```
/*
Theme Name: Twenty Ten
Theme URI: http://wordpress.org/
Description: The 2010 theme for WordPress is stylish, cus
yours with a custom menu, header image, and background. T
in the sidebar, four in the footer) and featured images (
images for posts and pages). It includes stylesheets for
styles for posts in the "Asides" and "Gallery" categories
that removes the sidebar.
Author: the WordPress team
Version: 1.3
License: GNU General Public License
License URI: license.txt
Tags: black, blue, white, two-columns, fixed-width, custo
comments, sticky-post, translation-ready, microformats, r
*/
```

Select theme to edit: Twenty Ten Select

Templates

404 Template

Plugins (Very Important)

The next tab in the menu to the left is Plugins, and this is where you can manage, search, and install plugins for your site. Plugins are basically programs that perform specific functions on your site, such as catching spam, making navigation easier, and much more.

Also notice that if you need to update a plugin, a little black circle will appear next to the Plugins tab with a number in it. The number is the number of plugins that require your attention.

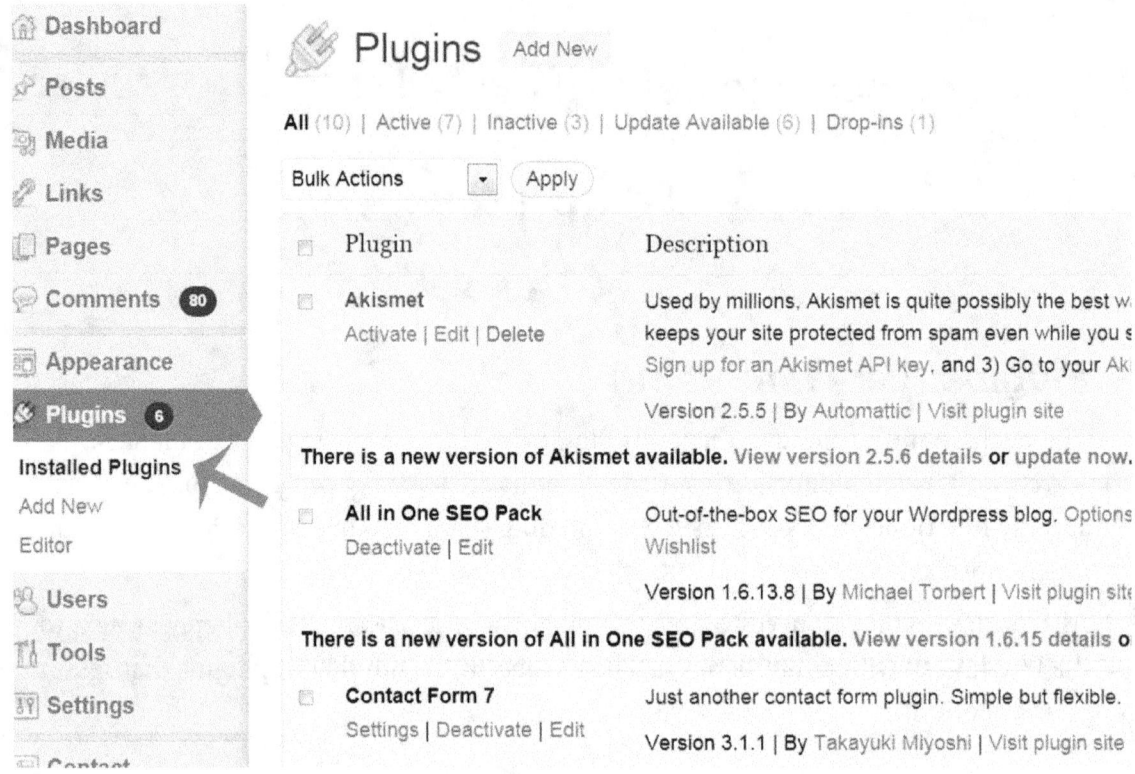

By default you start with two plugins: Hello Dolly and Akismet. Hello Dolly simply displays random lyrics from the famous song sung by Louis Armstrong, while Akismet filters spam. Hello Dolly can be deleted because it is functionally useless. Akismet now requires you to go through some stuff such as registering and receiving an activation code to use, so keep that in mind. There are other spam filter plugins available, should you decide to delete Akismet.

To delete a plugin you must first deactivate it. You can do this by clicking the deactivate option underneath it. You can also edit the code of most plugins, but this is not advised unless you have a very thorough understanding of this sort of thing. Otherwise you will probably just end up making your plugin nonfunctional.

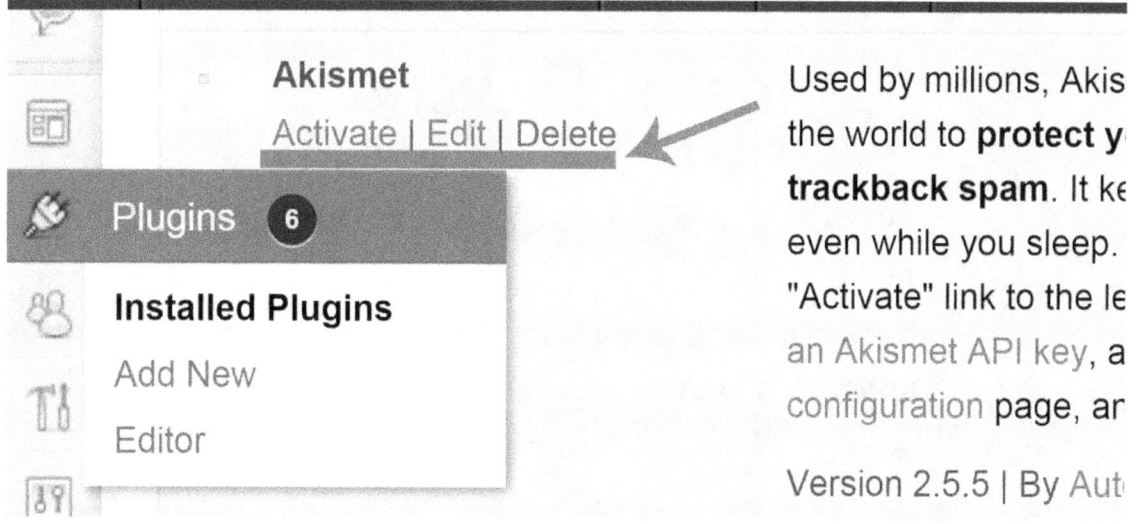

Keep in mind that some plugins will have a "Settings" option that allows you to configure them. In some cases this will appear down next to the Delete and Edit options, but in other cases it will appear in a completely different section of the WordPress control panel. It just depends on the plugin. Many plugins' options show up in the Settings tab in the main menu on the control panel.

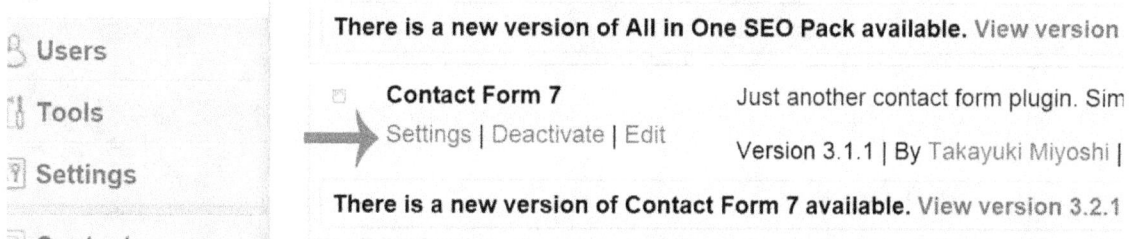

To find new plugins you can either search for them in Google or another search engine, then upload them via FTP, or you can simply click Add New and do a search for the plugin you're looking for and install it through your control panel.

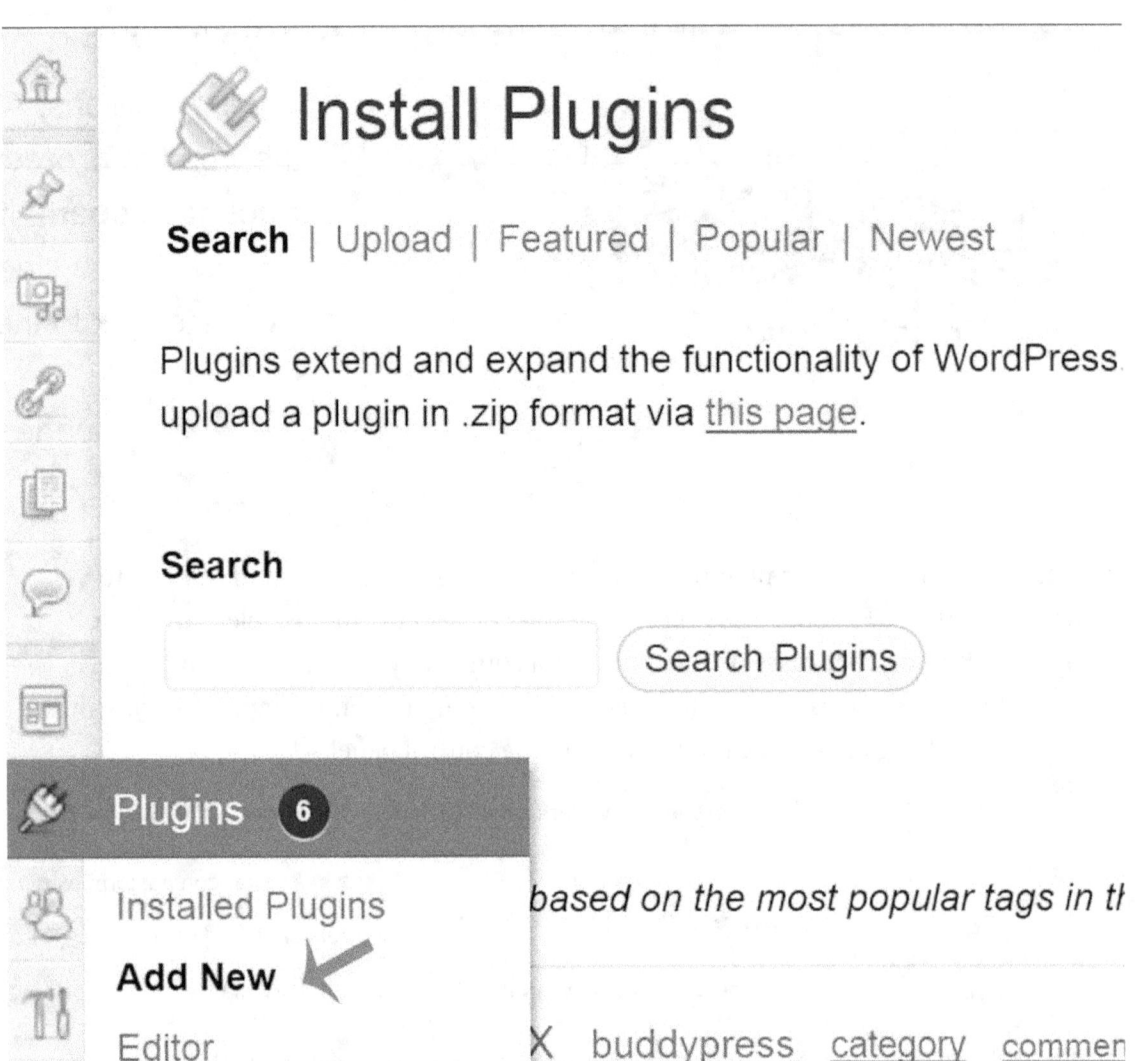

Install Plugins

Search | Upload | Featured | Popular | Newest

Plugins extend and expand the functionality of WordPress. upload a plugin in .zip format via this page.

Search

Search Plugins

Plugins 6

Installed Plugins   *based on the most popular tags in th*

Add New

Editor   X buddypress category commen

While installing via your control panel is the easier way to do things, occasionally it can be hard to find the plugin you want using the search option.

When you do a search, a new page will come up listing several plugins that match your criteria. You'll be able to get more details on the plugin, install it right away, and check the rating the plugin has. Make sure you read the description to verify that a plugin is what you are looking for before installing. If you install a plugin that you don't want or need, simply deactivate it and delete it.

Users

The next tab is the Users tab. This allows you to manage your profile and add new users to your site. Adding a new user is handy in two ways. First, it allows you to create another profile for yourself that you can use to post under different usernames if you wish.

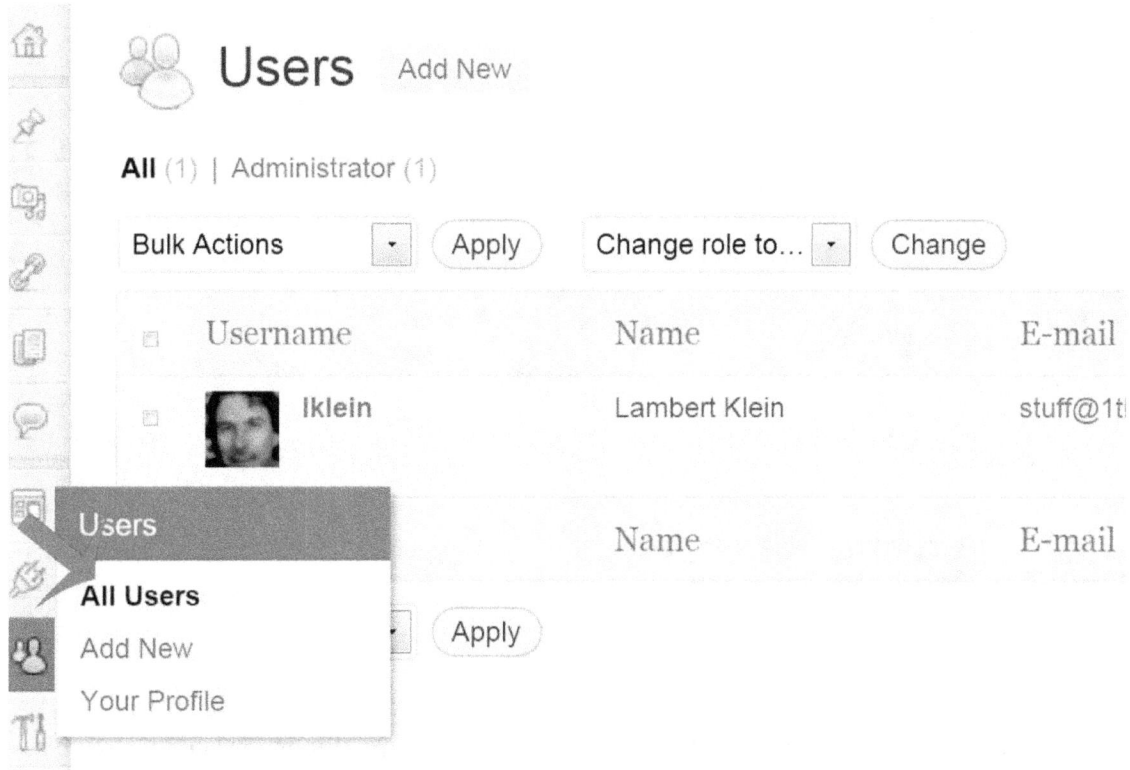

The second thing you can do is create special user accounts for others if you need to let someone else have access to the control panel but don't want them to have full administrative control over the site. Clicking "Add New" will take you to the page where you can create a new account, and at the bottom you will see a drop-down menu that allows you to determine what privileges the user will have. This is incredibly handy if you're outsourcing content creation or hiring someone to change the layout of your site.

Add New User

Create a brand new user and add it to this site.

Username *(required)*

E-mail *(required)*

First Name

Last Name

Website

Password *(twice, required)*

Tools

The Tools section is where you'll find tools that do various things for WordPress. By default you'll have Press This, which allows you to quickly and easily take content from the web and publish it on your site. This can be handy if you're creating a content curation site.

The other tool you get is Categories and Tags Converter. This simply allows you to convert tags to categories and vice versa.

Below the main tab you'll find two more tabs, Import and Export. Import allows you to import a variety of things onto your site, such as Blogger blog posts, Tumblr posts, and more. This can be handy if you want this information to be reposted on your WordPress site.

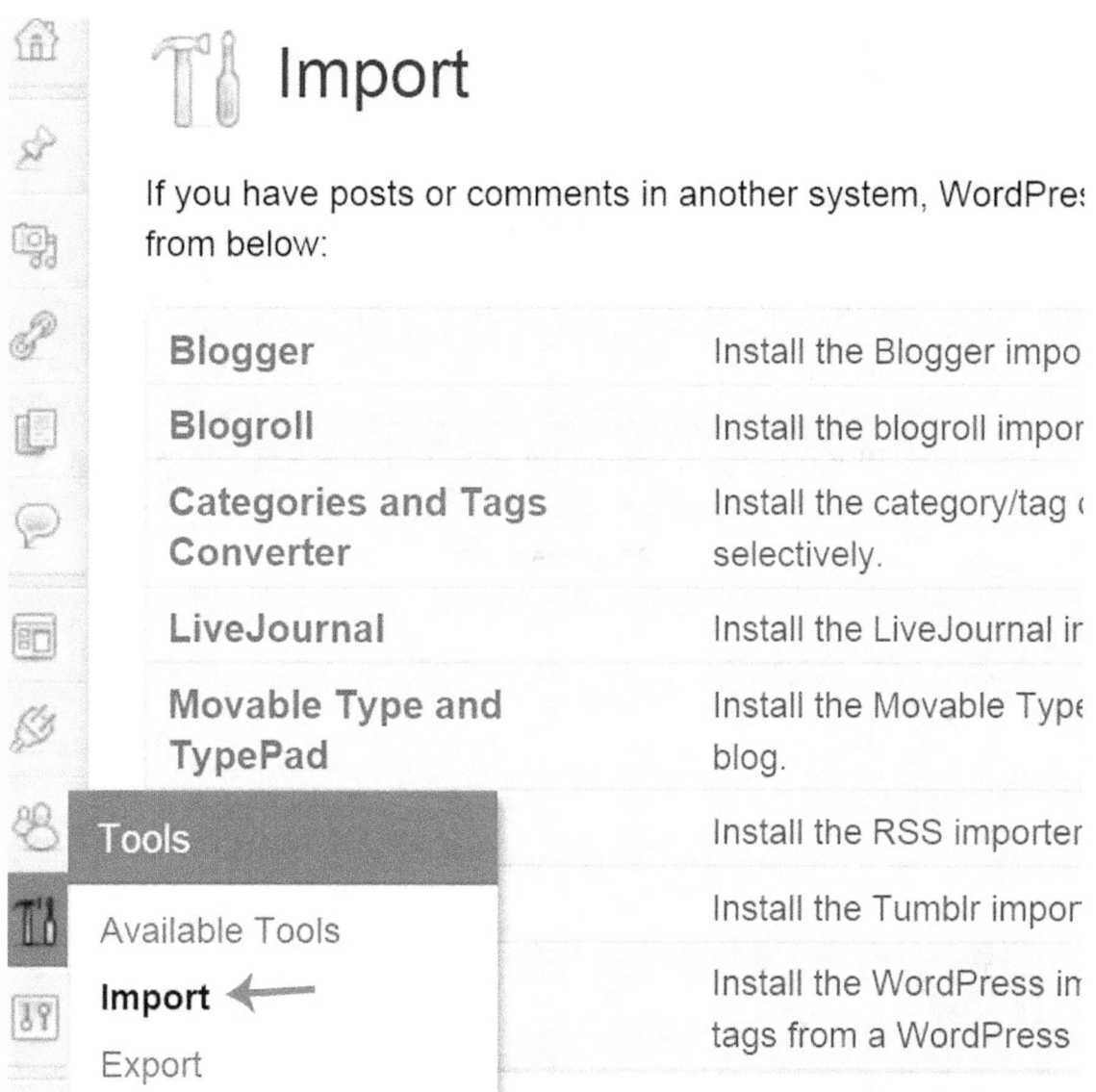

Import

If you have posts or comments in another system, WordPres from below:

Blogger	Install the Blogger impo
Blogroll	Install the blogroll impor
Categories and Tags Converter	Install the category/tag selectively.
LiveJournal	Install the LiveJournal in
Movable Type and TypePad	Install the Movable Type blog.

Tools

Install the RSS importer

Install the Tumblr impor

Available Tools

Install the WordPress in

Import ←

tags from a WordPress

Export

Export allows you to export various bits of data such as pages, comments, and more as an XML file. Once you export your data you can then import it onto another WordPress site.

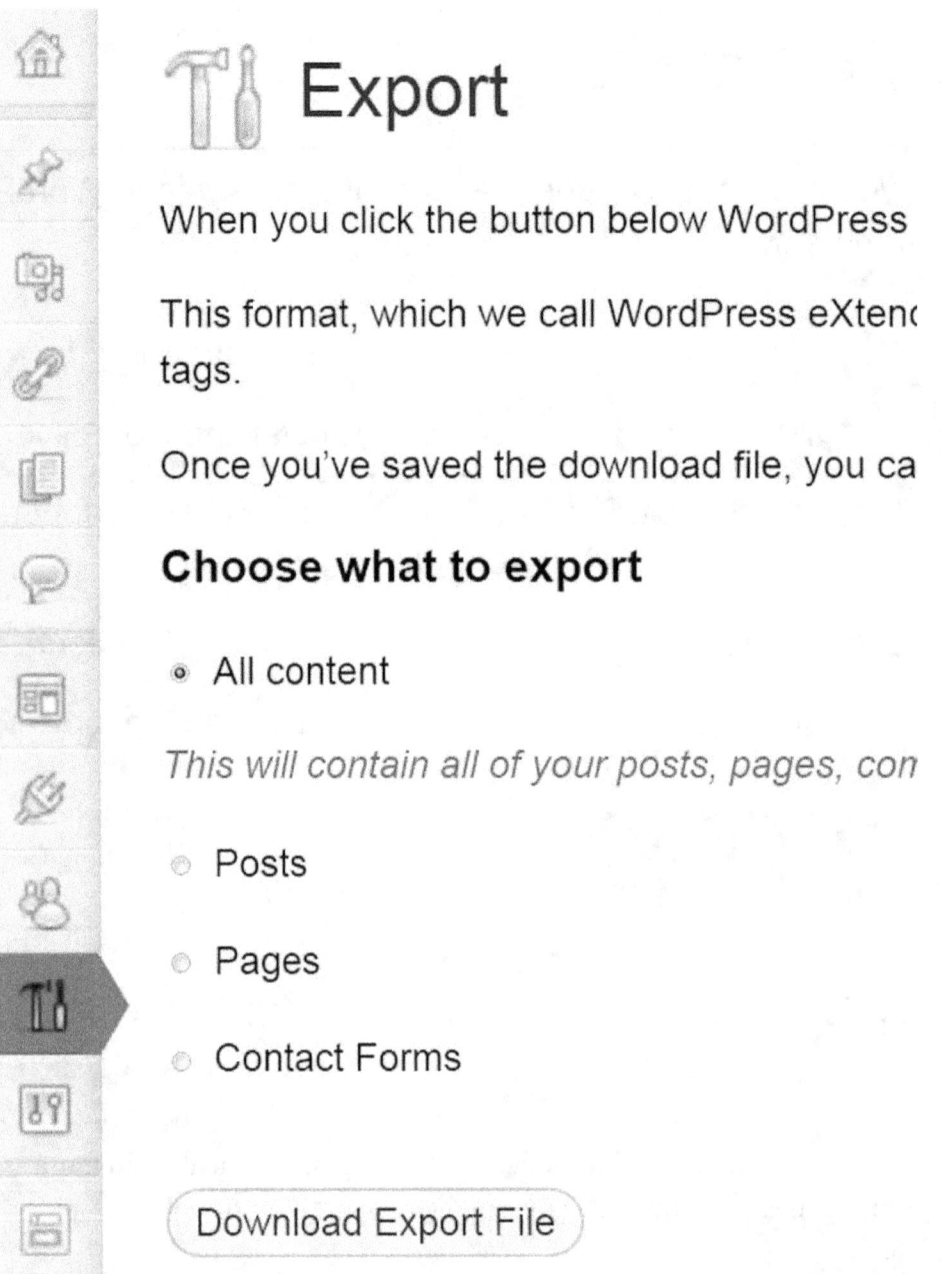

Export

When you click the button below WordPress

This format, which we call WordPress eXtend tags.

Once you've saved the download file, you ca

Choose what to export

◉ All content

This will contain all of your posts, pages, con

○ Posts

○ Pages

○ Contact Forms

(Download Export File)

Also be aware that some of your plugins will have their settings and options show up here in the Tools section. If you install a plugin and its options don't show up in the Plugins section, check here and in the Settings tab below.

Settings (Very Important)

The final tab in the left menu is the Settings tab. This tab allows you to change many of the fundamental properties of your website. Most of this comes down to personal preference, although there are a few things you're going to want to do a certain way for SEO purposes and that will be explained a bit later.

The first sub-tab is General, which allows you to change things such as your site's title, date, and time, email address, and much more. Everything here is pretty self-explanatory, but just make sure your time zone is set correctly, as this can impact how certain plugins work if they require a cron job.

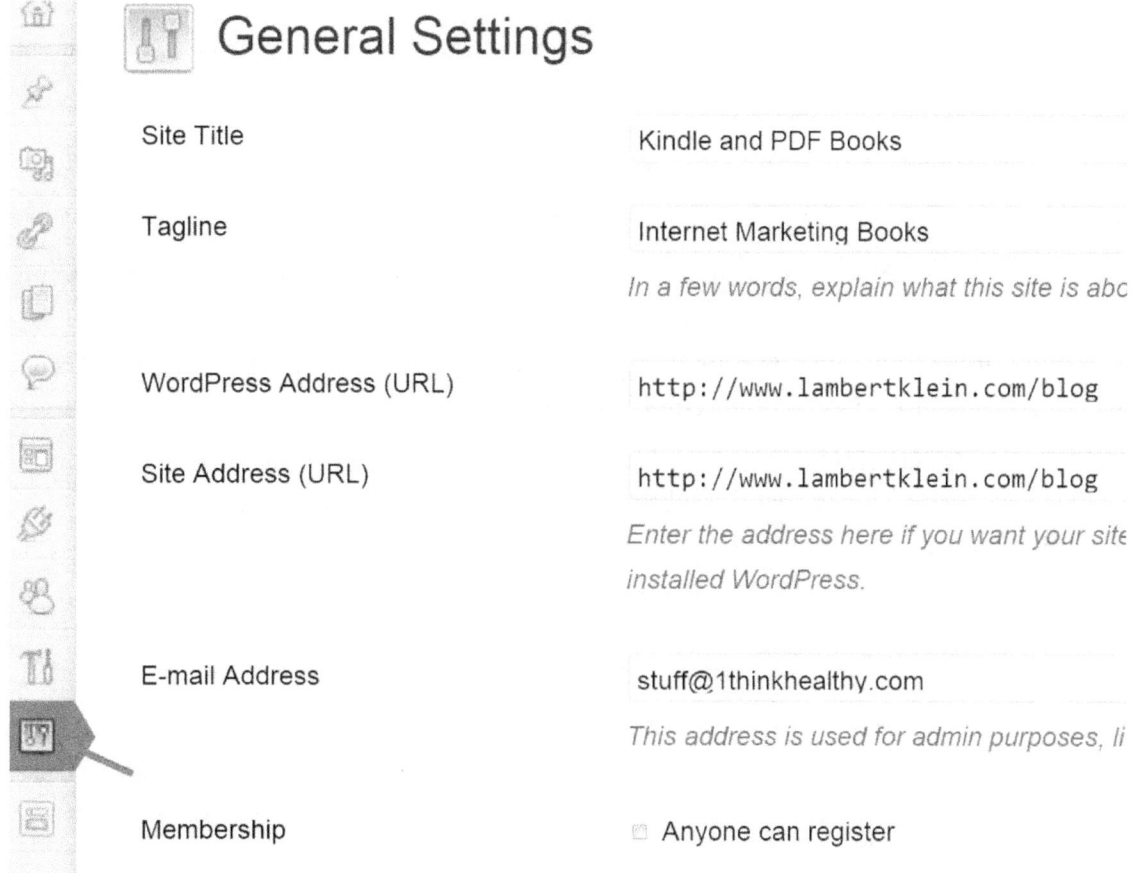

The next subtab is Writing, which allows you to configure some options that affect the creation of your posts. Everything here is also explained on the page.

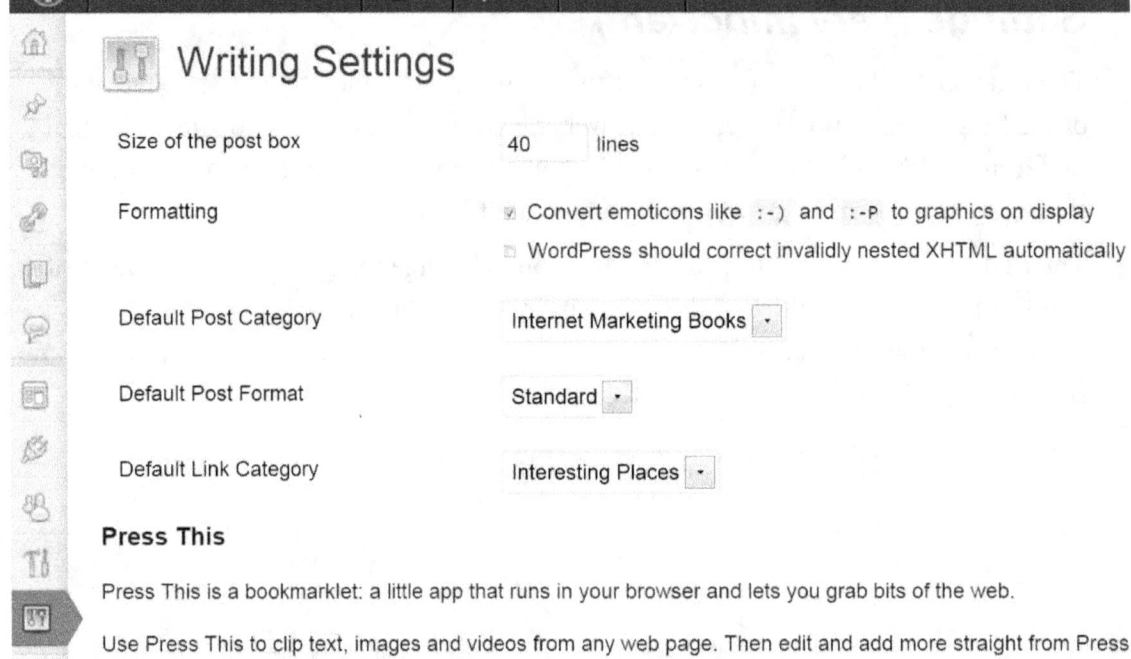

The next sub-tab is the Reading tab. This section is going to be very important when it comes to configuring how your website's posts display. The first option allows you to choose to display either your blog posts or a static page as your home page. This really comes down to personal preference, and we'll go into this in more detail later.

You can also configure how many blog posts your "posts page" (by default your main page) displays. This is great for editing your site to ensure that you don't have a ridiculous number of posts displayed on your main page.

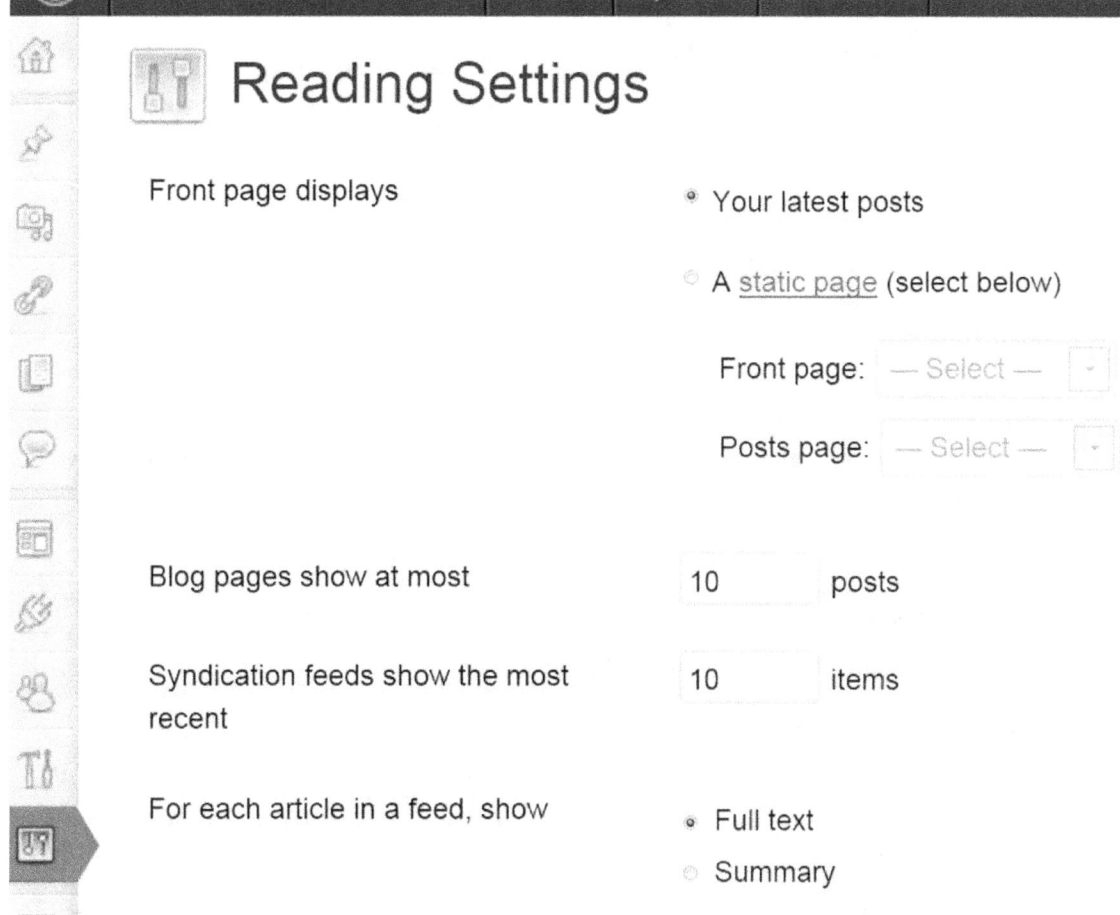

Reading Settings

Front page displays	⦿ Your latest posts
	○ A static page (select below)
	Front page: — Select —
	Posts page: — Select —
Blog pages show at most	10 posts
Syndication feeds show the most recent	10 items
For each article in a feed, show	⦿ Full text
	○ Summary

The next sub-tab is the Discussions tab. This page allows you to configure various things having to do with the comments on your site. There is nothing particularly important here.

Next is the Media subtab. This section allows you to configure a few things that have to do with your media files, such as image thumbnail size and other things. Once again, this is simply a matter of personal preference.

The next sub-tab is Privacy. This allows you to set whether or not search engines can index your site. **Make sure that this is turned on**! If the search engines can't index your site then you won't appear in the search results and won't get organic traffic.

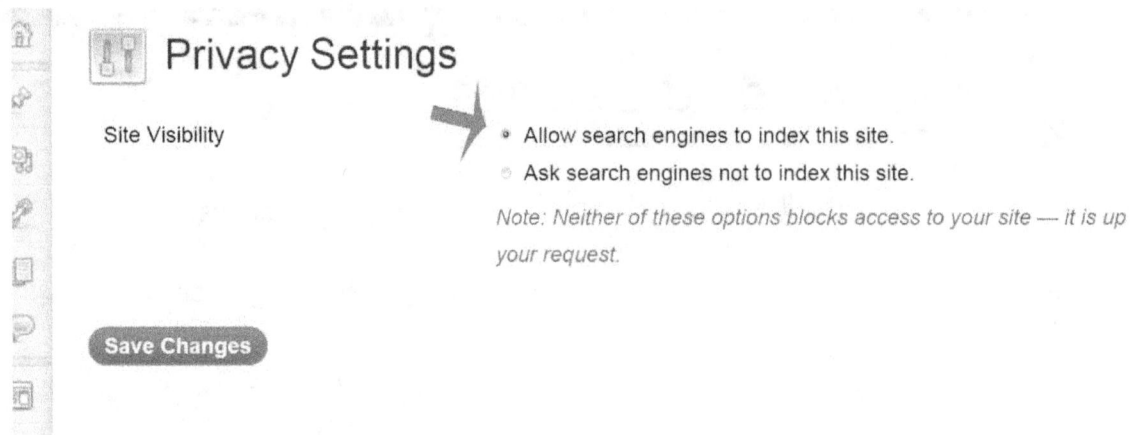

Privacy Settings

Site Visibility

• Allow search engines to index this site.
○ Ask search engines not to index this site.

Note: Neither of these options blocks access to your site — it is up your request.

Save Changes

The Permalinks sub-tab allows you to configure how your URL extensions display. For example, a page can display as

www.hockeyfans.com/throwback-jerseys

www.hockeyfans.com/2012/03/throwback-jerseys

www.hockeyfans.com/p=1

The way you set this up is **very** important for SEO. There is an entire chapter coming up dedicated to making sure you set up your permalinks correctly and why you're going to do it that way.

After permalinks you will usually see any settings for plugins you have that appear in this section. Under that you'll find a little button that says "Collapse menu" that will simply move the left-hand menu to the side and out of the way if you need that.

Chapter 8: Setting Permalinks

As promised, this is the chapter dedicated to setting your permalinks and explaining why it is so important. This is one of the most fundamental parts of on-site SEO, and botching this can cripple your efforts to rank in Google and other search engines. The good news is that this is very easy to implement.

By default your permalinks are set to "?p=123" and this setting will cause your entire page and post URLs to be displayed as the extension "/p=1" or whatever page number it happens to be. This is terrible for SEO because "/p=1" tells the search engine spiders that crawl your site absolutely nothing about your page or post.

You want your URL extensions to give an indicator of what your post or page is about so that it can rank for those keywords in Google and other search engines. For example, the URL "www.hockeyfans.com/throwback-jerseys" tells the search engine spiders that the page/post is about throwback jerseys. This will help the site to rank for that term.

To set up your site to display URLs like this, go to the Permalinks subtab under Settings and go down to where it says Custom Structure. Click that bubble and enter this:

%postname%

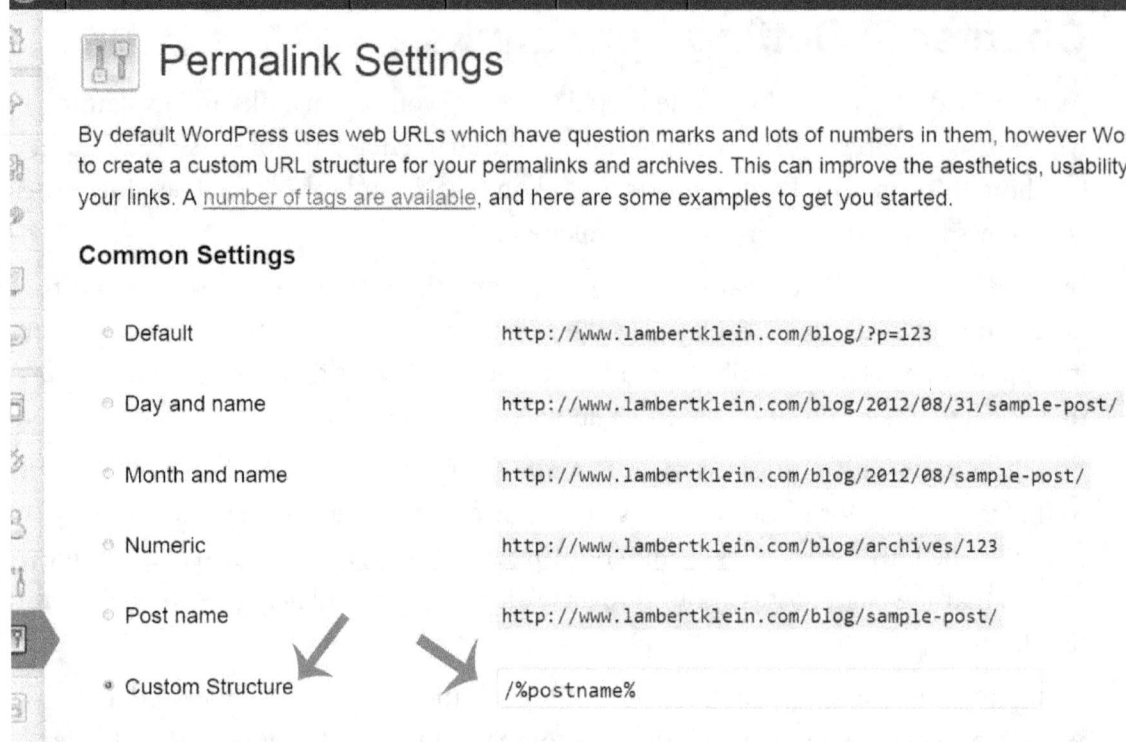

Permalink Settings

By default WordPress uses web URLs which have question marks and lots of numbers in them, however Wor to create a custom URL structure for your permalinks and archives. This can improve the aesthetics, usability your links. A number of tags are available, and here are some examples to get you started.

Common Settings

○ Default	`http://www.lambertklein.com/blog/?p=123`
○ Day and name	`http://www.lambertklein.com/blog/2012/08/31/sample-post/`
○ Month and name	`http://www.lambertklein.com/blog/2012/08/sample-post/`
○ Numeric	`http://www.lambertklein.com/blog/archives/123`
○ Post name	`http://www.lambertklein.com/blog/sample-post/`
● Custom Structure	`/%postname%`

Doing this will cause the name of your post or page to show up as the URL extension, not "/p=2" or something like that.

This also makes choosing your post titles wisely very important. Because you want your keywords in your URLs, you have to also make sure they're in your post titles. Because this is such a fundamental part of successful WordPress SEO, I encourage you to do this right now so that you don't forget.

Chapter 9: Creating Categories and Sidebar Links

You should familiarize yourself with how to create categories and sidebar links. These features will show up in your sidebars using widgets and are pretty easy to configure.

Categories

Categories are basically just a way of organizing your posts and making navigation a bit easier for your views. For example, you may have a category on www.hockeyfans.com called "Highlights" that contains all posts related to game highlights. You could also have a category called "Red Wings" if you want to group all posts about the Red Wings.

Keep in mind that a post can fall into more than one category. For example, if you're making a post about the highlights of a Red Wings game, you can place that into both of the previously mentioned categories.

To create categories you can click the Posts tab, then click the Categories sub-tab. Here you can create the title, slug, and description of new categories as well as edit existing categories like we talked about earlier.

Keep in mind that you don't have to create all of your categories all at once here, and you can create them on the go as you make new posts. To do this, click on Add New under the Posts tab to begin creating a new post. Scroll down and you will see the Categories box on the right. Here you get to select what category your post falls into as well as create a new category if you want. You can also view your most-used categories by clicking the Most Used tab.

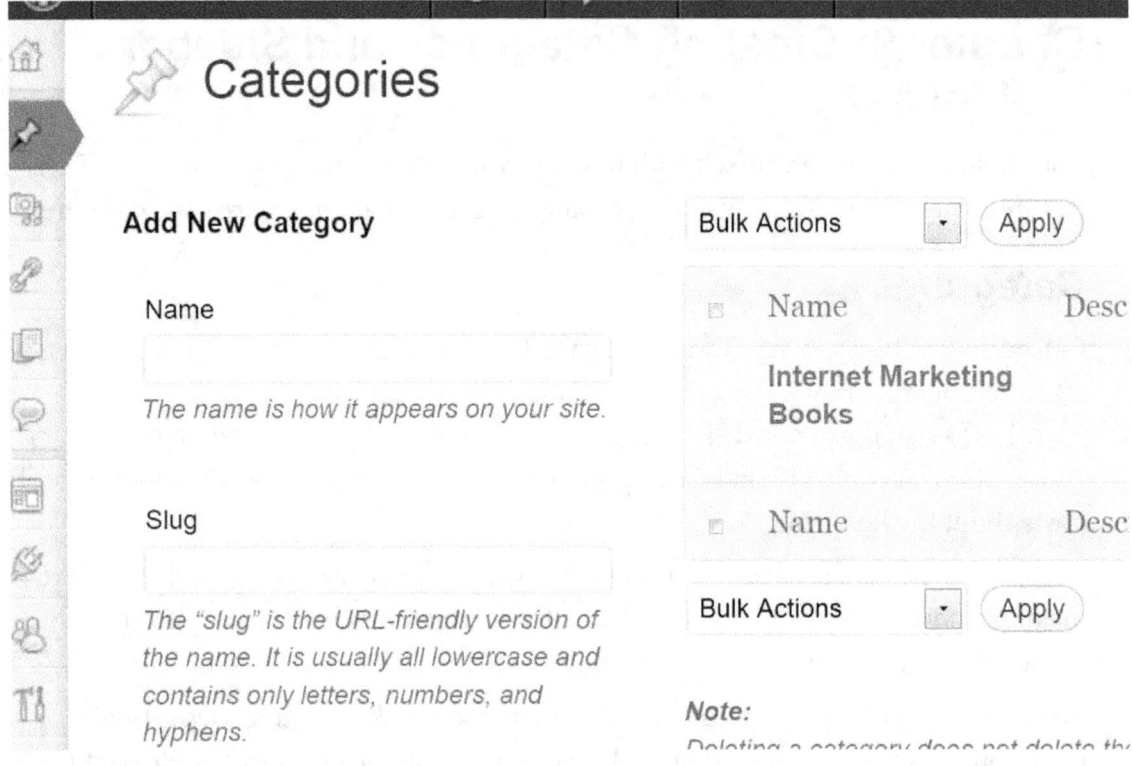

Sidebars

You are also going to want to ensure that your categories show up in your sidebar links. You do this by creating a categories widget in the Widgets section. Other links that you will definitely want to have in your sidebar are your archives, which allow viewers to access older posts.

You can also link viewers to other things in the sidebar such as recent posts, recent comments, other web accounts you have such as Facebook, and other people's blogs/websites if they're paying you to advertise for them.

Because creating these sidebar links is done using widgets, we'll discuss that next.

Chapter 10: Using Widgets

We've already gone over a lot about widgets, but I'm going to walk you through the creation of a few of them just to help you get the hang of it. The first widget you're going to create is the Categories widget, which will list links to all your categories.

The first step is simple. Go to Appearance, then click on Widgets. Once you're in the widgets section you need to think about which section you're going to place your Categories widget in. The most common choice would be Primary Widget Area, but because it is likely that there is a Categories widget in there by default, let's put it in another area. If you have a custom theme already installed there may be other options too. In the end this is a matter of personal preference.

Once you've made up your mind, go get the Categories widget and drag it over to the section you want it to appear in. This will bring up some new options.

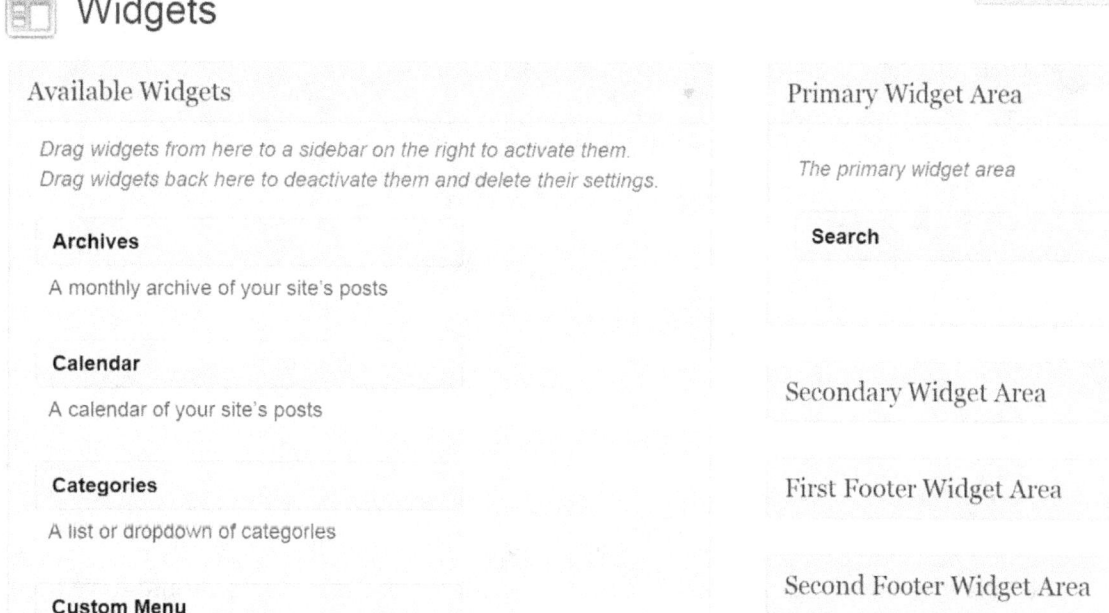

The title will be the title of the widget, and I'd recommend just using "Categories." The "Display as drop-down" option will make the widget display as a drop-down menu that must be selected in order to see the categories. This is only good if you are really cramped for space on your website. "Show post counts" will show the number of posts in each category and "Show hierarchy" will cause the categories to display with

the child categories underneath the parent categories, if you have created parent and child categories.

Once you're done click "Save." Now click on your website's title in the upper-left corner on the black toolbar to make sure the widget is displaying the way you want it to. If it isn't, go back and try again. Sometimes you have to play around with it for a while before you get it displaying the way you want it to.

The next widget we're going to create is the Tag Cloud widget. Tag Cloud is a widget that displays all of your tags in the sidebar. This is good for SEO because these tags will show up on every single page and post of your website to help the spiders rank your pages for more keywords.

Once you have an idea of which sidebar section you want your tag cloud to go in, drag the Tag Cloud widget over to it. Once again, new options will appear.

You can create the title of your tag cloud here as well as change it from displaying tags to displaying categories. This isn't recommended, as your categories should have their own widget. Once you're done click "Save" and then check your site to see if the widget is displaying how you want it to.

Overall using widgets is very easy but can take some getting used to in order to make sure they're displaying where you want them to. Also, configuring how your widgets

look on your site can be a bit like fitting together the pieces of a puzzle sometimes. Just play around with widget creation a while, and you'll soon get the hang of it.

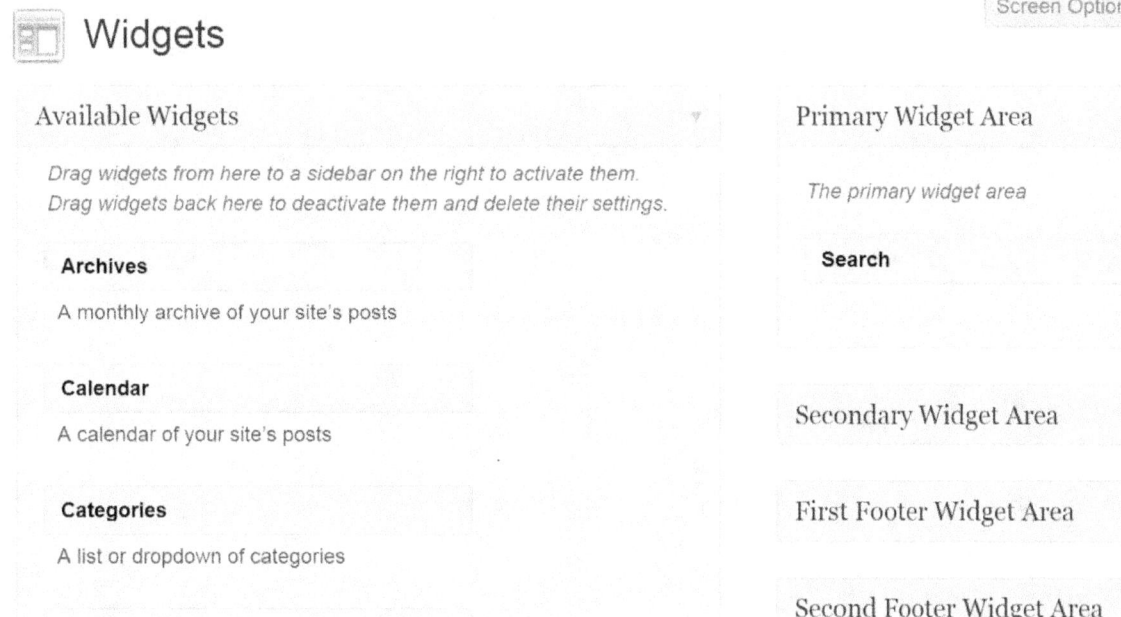

Widgets

Available Widgets

Drag widgets from here to a sidebar on the right to activate them.
Drag widgets back here to deactivate them and delete their settings.

Archives

A monthly archive of your site's posts

Calendar

A calendar of your site's posts

Categories

A list or dropdown of categories

Custom Menu

Primary Widget Area

The primary widget area

Search

Secondary Widget Area

First Footer Widget Area

Second Footer Widget Area

Chapter 11: Setting Up Themes

When you first install WordPress your default theme is going to be Twenty Ten. Twenty Eleven will also be installed (after updating to the latest version of WordPress) and can be activated from the Themes tab. These themes are decent, but there are better themes available. In some cases you're going to want to get a particular theme that is based around your business model, such as an AdSense theme for Google AdSense.

Getting a Theme

As we briefly touched on earlier, there are several ways to go about getting new themes. You can browse themes from your WordPress control panel by clicking the Install tab on the Themes page. You can then browse a variety of themes by clicking on the options there.

The other way of getting themes is to look for them on Google or another search engine. Using a search term such as "WordPress themes" or "free WordPress themes" is a great way to search. Also keep in mind that not all themes are free, but just because a theme must be purchased doesn't necessarily make it superior to a free theme.

These themes will have to be downloaded to your hard drive, then uploaded to WordPress using a FTP client. We'll discuss that in the next chapter.

When choosing a theme try to pick something that fits your website. Also, remember that you can go back and change your theme later if you feel like it. If you're having trouble picking a theme for your site, try browsing around and checking out what similar sites are using.

Two popular themes that work well for a variety of websites are Thesis http://diythemes.com/ and Flexibility http://www.flexibilitytheme.com/ . Go to these URLs by entering them into your browser to check them out. They're great all-around themes that can be used with a variety of monetization methods. This makes them a good choice to start with if you haven't yet decided how you're going to monetize your site. I recommend getting at least one of them (Flexibility is free), because I'll be walking you through how to use FTP to upload a theme in the next chapter.

Activating and Editing Themes

Once you upload a theme it can be activated from the Themes page by selecting the Manage Themes tab. Then click on the "Activate" option.

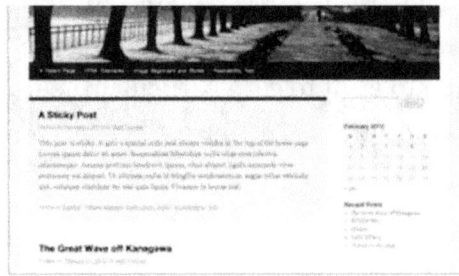

By the WordPress team   Version 1.3

The 2010 theme for WordPress is stylish, customizable, s menu, header image, and background. Twenty Ten suppo footer) and featured images (thumbnails for gallery posts includes stylesheets for print and the admin Visual Editor, categories, and has an optional one-column page templat

There is a new version of Twenty Ten available. View '

Customize   OPTIONS Widgets   Menus   H

Available Themes

Flexibility3
By Advantus Media, Inc.

Activate   Live Preview   Details   Delete

Twenty Eleven
By the WordPress team

Activate   Live Preview   Details   Delete

Your active theme will appear up above the other installed themes. Depending on what theme you have installed, you may get some extra configuration options.

New theme activated. This theme supports widgets, please visit the widgets settings screen to configure them.

Current Theme
Flexibility3

By Advantus Media, Inc.   Version 1.0

Flexibility Theme allows you to unleash your creativity without having to know code!

Customize   OPTIONS   Widgets   Menus   Flexibility3 Theme Options

Most themes allow you to install a custom header, which you should do as soon as possible to make your site look more professional. Most themes will also allow you to upload a background if you'd like to. Additionally you can go into the actual CSS and configure a theme from there, as we discussed earlier. Once again, don't do this if you don't understand CSS.

Because different themes have different options and settings, this is something you will have to play around with and figure out on your own. Generally speaking, there are several guidelines to follow when configuring your theme.

- Keep the layout clean and simple
- Don't add pointless widgets and images
- Don't add a distracting background
- Add a professional-looking header
- Choose an attractive color scheme (colorschemedesigner.com can help)

Choosing and configuring a WordPress theme takes more than just technical knowhow, it also takes an understanding of basic graphic design. If you're having trouble and just can't get your theme and layout to look right, don't forget that you can outsource this. Most web designers don't charge a lot just to quickly configure a theme for you. Header design and your background graphic can also be outsourced easily using Fiverr.com.

Chapter 12: File Uploading Using FTP and cPanel

While themes and plugins can be uploaded directly from the WordPress control panel, there may come a time when you have to upload the file from your hard drive and directly into your hosting account. There are generally two ways to do this: FTP (file transfer protocol) and using the cPanel itself.

The Difference Between Root Domains and Add-on Domains

While there is very little fundamental difference between a root domain and an add-on domain, the file path you use to access each of these is different. Just to be clear, the very first domain that you install your web hosting server on is the root domain. Any domains you install after that are add-on domains.

cPanel

Using the cPanel will be different for each hosting company, so I'm not really going to get into that. In most cases though you will have to access your domains via your cPanel and then get into the Public HTML folder. If you're really struggling to upload files through your cPanel, try looking up tutorials online, particularly on YouTube. Alternately you can just do it using FTP, which is much easier.

While getting into your files via cPanel is going to be different depending on what host you have, you typically want to try to find a file manager and open that up. Here are the different file paths for your root domain and add-on domains.

Root Domain:

root/ → public_html → wp_content → themes

Add-on Domain:

root/ → public_html → [name of add-on domain] → wp_content → themes

Remember, this is just an example, and different hosting services may have different file paths. If you're having trouble figuring out the file path for your web hosting, contact customer support and they'll help you out.

FTP

File transfer protocol (FTP) allows you to quickly and easily upload files to your website using an FTP program. I recommend Filezilla, which you can download for free by going to this UR and entering it into your browser http://filezilla-project.org/

Filezilla is easy to use, but I'll walk you through how to upload a theme to your WordPress site. The first thing you need to do once you get Filezilla installed on your computer is to connect to your web hosting server. You do this by entering the following information:

- ⋏ Host – Your server's IP address or your root domain name
- ⋏ Username – Your username used to log in to your cPanel
- ⋏ Password – Your password used to log in to your cPanel
- ⋏ Port – You only need to enter this if it is *not* the default port. In most cases you can just leave this blank.

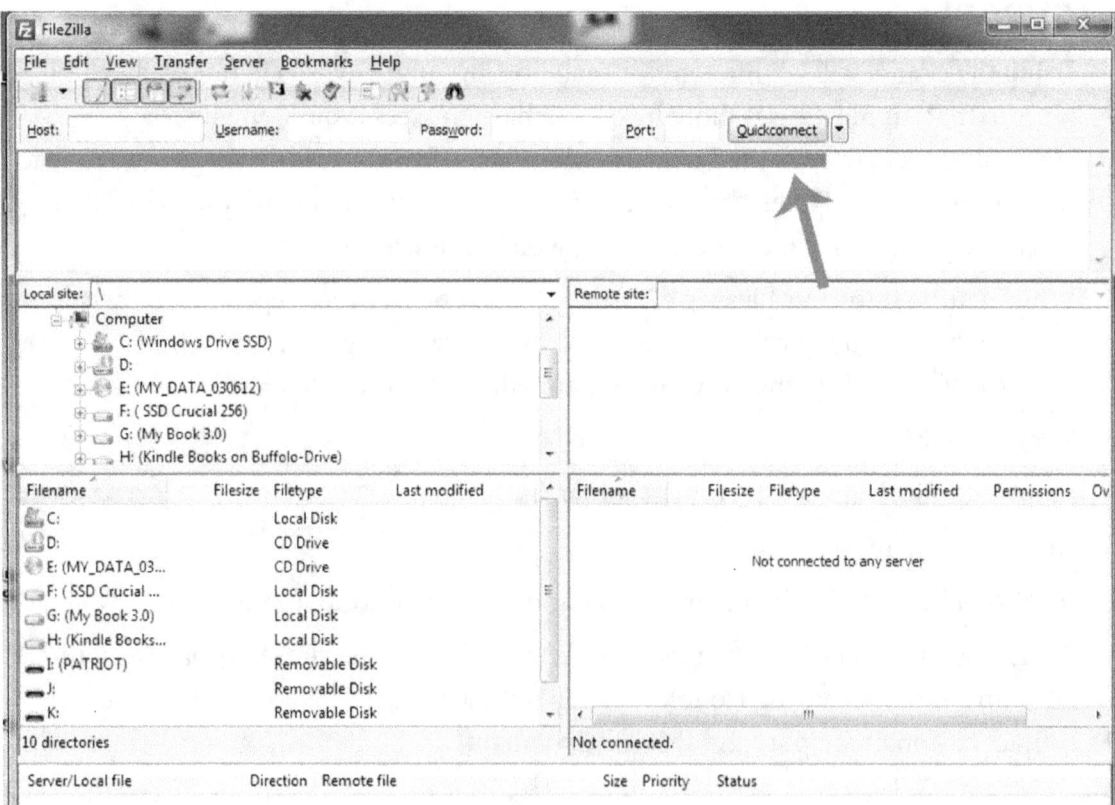

If you don't know your hosting server's IP address, it can usually be found on the main page of your cPanel. If you can't find it there, check the first email that your web host sent you that had your nameservers in it. Your IP address should be in there as well in most cases.

An alternate method of entering the "Host" info is to enter the root domain on which the server is connected to. For example, if when you first signed up you connected your web hosting to the domain cats.com then you can enter cats.com in the host field.

Remember, this only works for the root domain that your hosting is connected to, not necessarily the domain your website is on. For example, if your root domain is cats.com but the domain you're building your WordPress site on is hockeyfans.com you can't use hockeyfans.com to access your hosting server via FTP, because it is an add-on domain, not the root domain.

Once all the info is entered click "Quick Connect" and Filezilla will hook up to your hosting server, giving you access to all the files found there. Now what you're going to do is get into the files for the domain you're building your WordPress site on. I'll go over how to do this for add-on domains first because it is slightly more complicated.

Below the connection data area you'll see four fields. The two on the left are files on your computer. The two on the right are files on your hosting server. The ones on top help you navigate, while the larger ones on the bottom are for transferring specific files. For this example we'll be transferring a theme from your computer to the hosting server.

The first thing you need to do is go into the files on the left and locate the WordPress theme you downloaded. Once you've found your theme the specific folder containing all the files should appear in the lower-left box. Make sure the file is unzipped if you downloaded a zipped file.

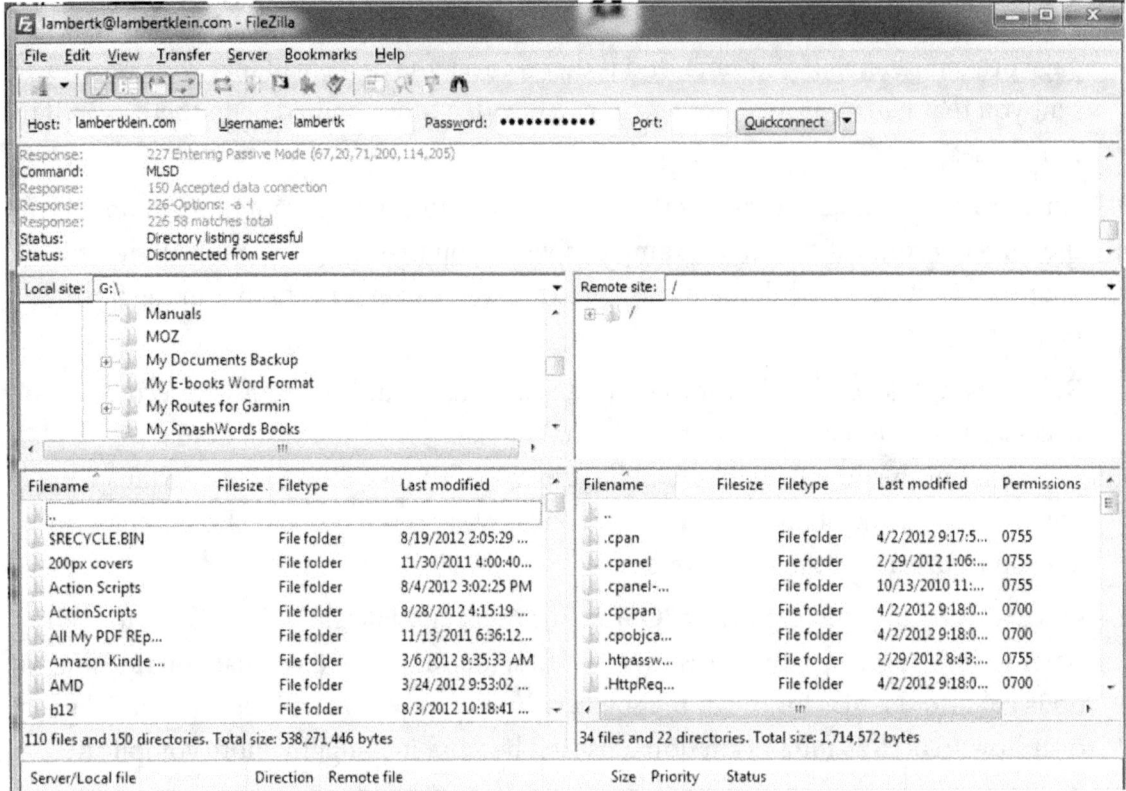

After you find your theme go to the upper-right area and click the folder found there that is labeled "/". This should open several subfolders in the lower-right area as well as in the upper area. Ignore the folders in the lower area for a moment and concentrate on the folders in the upper area. Scroll down and you should see a folder labeled "public_html." Double-click that.

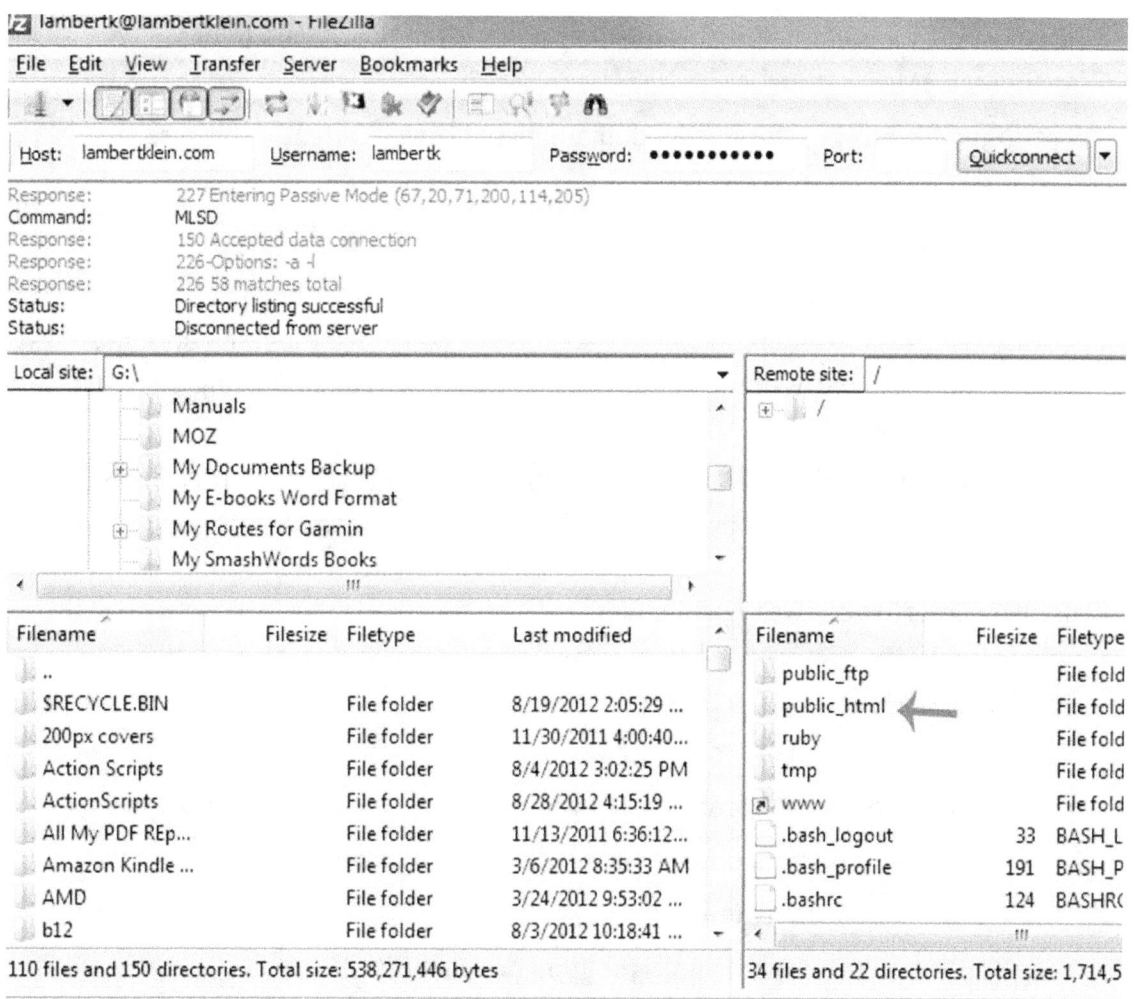

Once you're in this folder you should see more folders. Find the one that is labeled with the domain name you're building your WordPress site on, and click that. More folders will appear, and find the one that says "wp-content" and click that. More folders will appear, and find the one that says "themes" and click that. Also take note of the folder that says "plugins" here, as you will need to use that folder to install plugins later.

Once you are in the themes folder you can upload your theme. Right click on your themes folder and select "Upload." This will upload your theme into the theme folder on your file hosting. That's all there is to it.

Just to recap, for add-on domains the file path to get to the themes folder in your hosting server is:

root/ → public_html → [the add-on domain name] → wp-content → themes.

The file path for root domains is:

root/ → public_html → wp_content → themes

Keep in mind that this might not be exactly the same for every hosting service. If your hosting is drastically different from the steps outlined here, try looking up some tutorials on YouTube, visiting the forums if there are any, or contacting customer support if you have to.

In addition to using the Quick Connect feature on Filezilla you can also configure specific connection profiles by clicking File then Site Manager. This is good if you will be sharing Filezilla or your computer with others and want to make sure that no one else has access to your web hosting files.

Day 3 Recap

Here is what we went over today.

- ⅄ How to log in to WordPress using your domain name and "/wp-admin"
- ⅄ All of the basic functions of the WordPress control panel
- ⅄ The difference between posts and pages
- ⅄ How to set your permalinks for good on-site SEO
- ⅄ What categories are and how to create them
- ⅄ How to use widgets
- ⅄ How to acquire and set up your theme
- ⅄ The difference between uploading files using FTP and your cPanel
- ⅄ The difference between root domains and add-on domains
- ⅄ How to upload files using Filezilla

We covered a lot of information today, and it may seem like a lot to take in if you're a beginner. For now you should concentrate on becoming comfortable with the following aspects of WordPress:

- ⅄ Posts

- Pages
- Appearance
- Plugins
- Widgets
- Settings

Don't be afraid to play around with these a bit and get used to how they work. We'll be going into more detail on how to create pages and posts a bit later, as well as how to install plugins. WordPress is very easy to use once you familiarize yourself with its basic functions.

Day 4 – Enhancing WordPress

Now that you have a general understanding of how WordPress works and how to use its basic functions, we can concentrate on some of the intermediate/advanced functions of this platform. While WordPress is a very powerful platform right out of the box, these functions are going to help you take it to the next level.

We're going to cover how to install and use plugins, which plugins are best for your site, how to create and manage pages on your site, what security measure you should take to protect your site, and the basic on-site SEO you should be doing to make sure your site is indexed by Google and other search engines. While we will be going over less stuff today than we did yesterday, much of this will be more challenging and will require you to adequately understand what we went over yesterday.

Chapter 13 – Plugin Installation

The easiest and most popular way to enhance your WordPress site is to add plugins. As mentioned before, plugins are simply programs that you upload to your site that do different things. There are thousands of plugins available that do *many* different things. Before we get into which plugins are the best for your site, I'm going to walk you through how to install them.

Installing Through WordPress

The fastest and easiest way to install a plugin is through the WordPress control panel. To get started, click on the Plugins tab on the left-hand menu. The default page that opens will be the one showing your installed plugins. Click on the "Add New" subtab.

In the search box type "Google XML Sitemaps," then click search. A list of plugins will come up, and Google XML Sitemaps should be at the top or somewhere near it. This plugin basically helps search engines like Google and Bing to index your site easier.

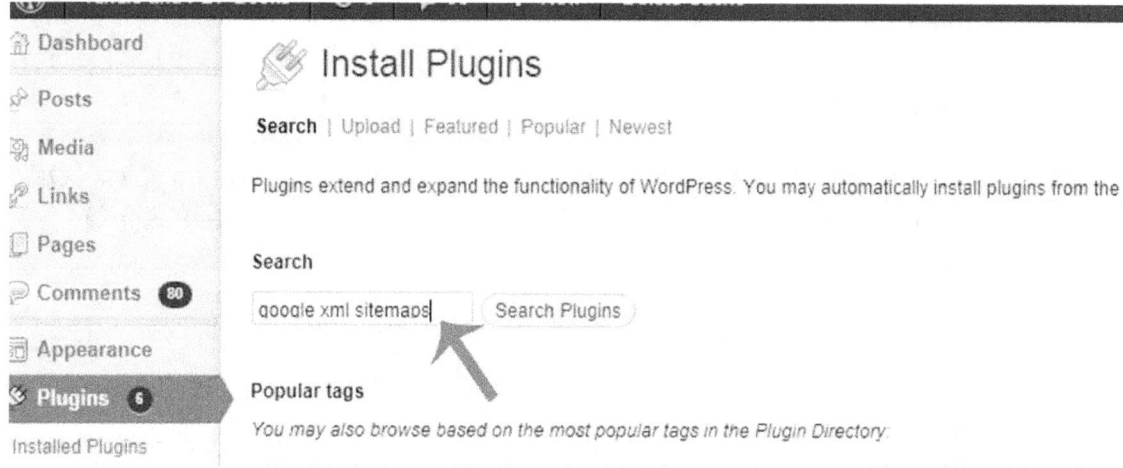

Install Plugins

Search | **Search Results** | Upload | Featured | Popular | Newest

Keyword ▾ | google xml sitemaps | (Search Plugins) | *72 items*

Name	Version	Rating	Description
Google XML Sitemaps Details | Update Now	3.2.8	☆☆☆☆☆	This plugin will generate a speci search engines like Google, Bin better index your blog. With sucl for the crawlers to see the comp retrieve it more efficiently. The p WordPress generated pages as Additionally it notifies all major s
Better WordPress Google XML Sitemaps	1.2.1	☆☆☆☆☆	With BWP GXS you will no long 50,000 URL limit or the time it ta generated. This plugin is fast, cc and can be extended via your ve

Click on "Install Now" and a window will pop up asking for confirmation. Click "OK" and the plugin will install. A new page will open up, and click "Activate Plugin" to activate the plugin.

☐	**Google XML Sitemaps** Activate | Edit | Delete	This plugin will generate a special XML sitemap whi engines like Google, Yahoo, Bing and Ask.com to bι Version 3.2.8 | By Arne Brachhold | Visit plugin site

Now the plugin is installed and activated. Google XML Sitemap's settings/options page is located in the Settings tab on the left. Because this plugin pretty much works the way it is supposed to right out of the box, you don't really need to configure it or mess with anything.

Many of these plugins will have an option for you to donate to the creator. Because the creator is giving the plugin away for free, it's always nice to support the plugin you like

by giving a little back to the creator if you can. Even donating $1 can make a difference.

Google XML Sitemaps
Deactivate | Edit

This plugin will generate a special engines like Google, Yahoo, Bing

Version 3.2.8 | By Arne Brachholc
Support | Donate ◀━━━

Installing Plugins Using FTP and cPanel.

In addition to installing plugins through WordPress, you can also do it through FTP and cPanel, just like with themes. In fact, this is absolutely no different from how you do it when you install a theme, so I'm not going to go over this again. Here is the file path you will use, and the only difference is that you're going to put the plugin in the plugins folder, not the themes folder.

For Add-on Domains:

root folder/ → public_html → [the add-on domain name] → wp-content → plugins.

For the Root Domain:

root folder/ → public_html → wp-content → plugins

In most cases it is much easier and faster to install plugins through WordPress, but if you download a plugin from a website or if you buy one (not all plugins are free), you will have to use FTP or cPanel. Certain plugins don't show up in the WordPress plugins search, so downloading them then uploading them like this is a must in this case.

Chapter 14 – Recommended Plugins

With so many plugins to choose from it can be easy to end up installing a ridiculously huge amount on your site. While there is nothing wrong with having a lot of plugins, you can streamline things a bit by making sure you get the ones that are going to benefit you the most.

Also, the nature of your site will impact what plugins you choose. However, there are certain plugins that are practically essential regardless of what kind of site you're building. Here is a list of some of my recommended free plugins and what they do. The ones that I consider essential will be marked as such.

Zemanta

Zemanta is a plugin that actually installs into your browser and must be downloaded outside of WordPress. Despite this, Zemanta actually functions inside your WordPress control panel when you open the post page to edit or create a new post.

Zemanta provides you with content recommendations and allows you to easily add a variety of things to your post, such as pictures and related articles. It also allows you to easily create text-based links, and it recommends tags that you can add to your post just by clicking on them.

To get Zemanta for free. Go to this UR by entering it into your browser http://www.zemanta.com/

Automatic SEO Links

This plugin allows you to quickly and easily turn any word or phrase into a link in your text. It also allows you to set links to "nofollow" if you want, and it only links the first word in each post so your entire post isn't spammed up with links. To configure it, check out the Automatic SEO Links subtab in the Settings area of the left-hand menu on the control panel.

This plugin can be found using the WordPress plugin search function and can be installed from there. Or you can get the plugin by going to this UR by entering it into your browser.

http://wordpress.org/extend/plugins/automatic-seo-links/

SEO Friendly Images

Images on your site can also be a great way to attract visitors through places such as Google Images and Yahoo Images. This plugin makes sure that the images on your site have the correct tags so that they are properly indexed by search engines. The options for this plugin can be found under the Settings tab in the control panel main menu.

SEO Friendly Images can be found and installed by using the WordPress plugin search function. Alternately, you can get the plugin by going to this UR by entering it into your browser.
http://wordpress.org/extend/plugins/seo-image/

SEO Tag Cloud Widget

If you plan to use a tag cloud on your site, you should definitely pick up this plugin. Tag clouds are sometimes not read correctly by search engines, but this plugin will ensure that your tag cloud is converted into an easily read HTML code so that search engines pick it up more easily.

You can find and install this plugin using the WordPress plugin search function. Alternately, you can get this plugin by going to this UR by entering it into your browser.

http://wordpress.org/extend/plugins/seo-tag-cloud/

SEO Title Tag

This SEO plugin helps to identify tags on your site to search engines so that they're better indexed and ranked. It can be used to add tags to your posts, pages, main page, and any URL that exists anywhere on your site. The options for this plugin can be found in the Settings section in the menu to the left.

SEO Title Tag can be found and installed using the WordPress plugin search option. You can also get it by going to this UR by entering it into your browser.
http://wordpress.org/extend/plugins/seo-title-tag/

Slick Social Share Buttons

There are a variety of ways to add share buttons for Facebook, Google +1 and more to your website, but this plugin makes it fast and easy. Slick Social Share Buttons creates a social share button bar that can be customized in a variety of ways and configured to show up on the pages you specify.

The best thing is that it scrolls with the page itself so that even when visitors scroll down it's still visible. To access the configuration options for this plugin, click the new tab that appears under Settings in the WordPress control panel main menu.

Slick Social Share Buttons can be found and installed using the WordPress plugins search function. Or you can by go to this UR by entering it into your browser to get it. http://wordpress.org/extend/plugins/slick-social-share-buttons/

Subscribe to Comments

This plugin is great for getting visitors to return to your website if you encourage comments. Subscribe to Comments allows visitors to subscribe to the comments section on your posts. When a new comment is added the visitor receives an email alert. This plugin is highly recommended for content-heavy sites and blogs. The options for this plugin can be found in the Settings tab on the WordPress main menu.

You can find and install Subscribe to Comments by using the WordPress plugin search function or by going to this UR by entering it into your browser.. http://wordpress.org/extend/plugins/subscribe-to-comments/

Personal Favicon

This plugin makes managing your website's favicon (the little symbol next to the URL) incredibly easy. While this plugin may not be essential, it is **highly** recommended because your favicon is important for branding purposes. The options for this plugin will be located in the Settings tab in the WordPress main menu.

Personal Favicon can be found and installed using the WordPress plugin search feature. You can also get this plugin by going to this UR by entering it into your browser.

 http://wordpress.org/extend/plugins/personal-favicon/.

SEO Ranker Report

Manually keeping track of which pages and posts on your site are ranking well in Google can be a major chore. This plugin allows you to keep track of your website's posts and pages rankings based on keywords. In fact, you can configure this plugin to track data from any URL you want.

It should be noted, however, that many people using HostGator have been unable to get this plugin to work due to errors. The options for this plugin are found in their own unique tab that will show up under the Settings tab in the WordPress main menu.

You can get SEO Ranker Report by using the WordPress plugin search option or by going to this UR by entering it into your browser. http://wordpress.org/extend/plugins/seo-rank-reporter/.

WP-PageNavi

This plugin adds a stylish page navigation area at the bottom of your website that is fully customizable. If you run a blog or website that has many different areas and categories, this plugin can help make navigation a lot easier for visitors. The options for WP-PageNavi can be found in the Settings area of the WordPress menu.

This plugin can be found and installed using the WordPress plugin search function or by going to this UR by entering it into your browser. http://wordpress.org/extend/plugins/wp-pagenavi/.

Google Analyticator

This handy plugin allows you to check your Google Analytics data directly from your WordPress dashboard instead of having to go to Google Analytics to check it each time. While this isn't essential, it can save you a lot of time. The configuration options for this plugin can be found in the Settings tab on the WordPress main menu. Look for "Google Analytics," not "Google Analyticator."

You can get Google Analyticator by using the WordPress plugin search option or by going to this UR by entering it into your browser. http://wordpress.org/extend/plugins/google-analyticator/.

Breadcrumb NavXT

This plugin is great for optimizing your on-page SEO. It provides a link chain at the top of each post linking viewers back to where they came from. For example, if they are on a post titled "Dog Walking" in the category "Dog Behavior" the breadcrumb trail will read something like "Home → Dog Behavior → Dog Walking." This is also great for helping your viewers to navigate your site.

This plugin has a ton of options that you can customize and that can be found in the Settings tab in the WordPress control panel menu. I would recommend clicking the General tab and changing the Home Title to the actual name of your site. This will cause the word "Home" to be replaced in the trail with the name of your site, which is more SEO-friendly.

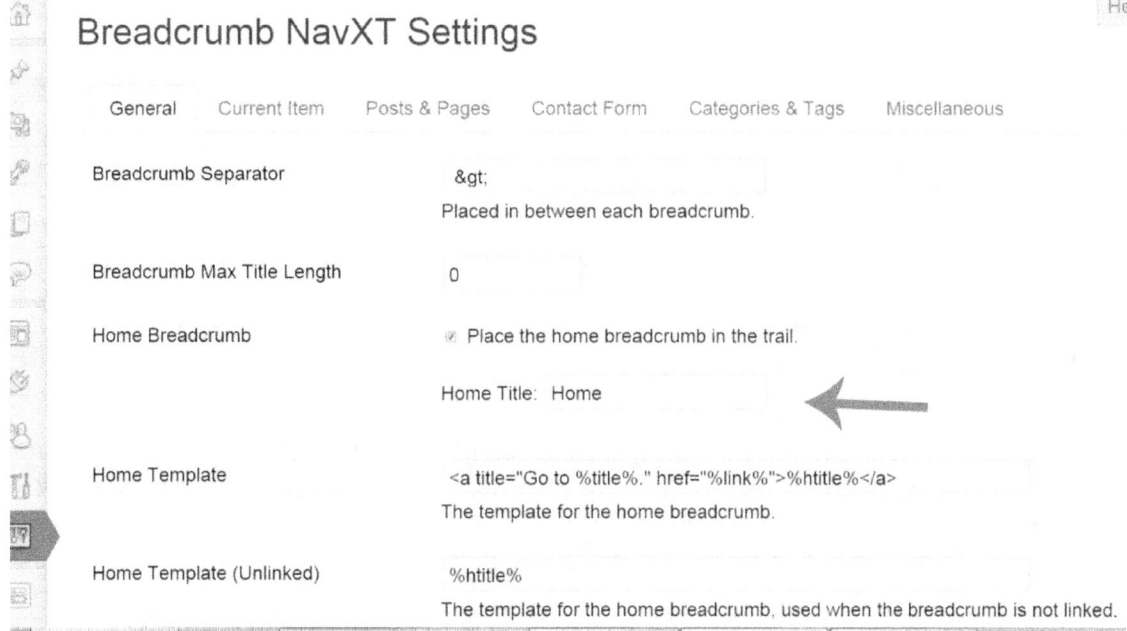

Something you have to keep in mind when using this, and the reason I didn't list this plugin as "essential," is that you have to insert some CSS code to get it to work in most themes. The code you use is:

```
<div class="breadcrumbs">
    <?php if(function_exists('bcn_display'))
    {
        bcn_display();
```

```
  }?>
```
</div>

In most cases this should be inserted in the Single Post (single.php) section of the Editor section in the Appearance tab of the WordPress control panel.

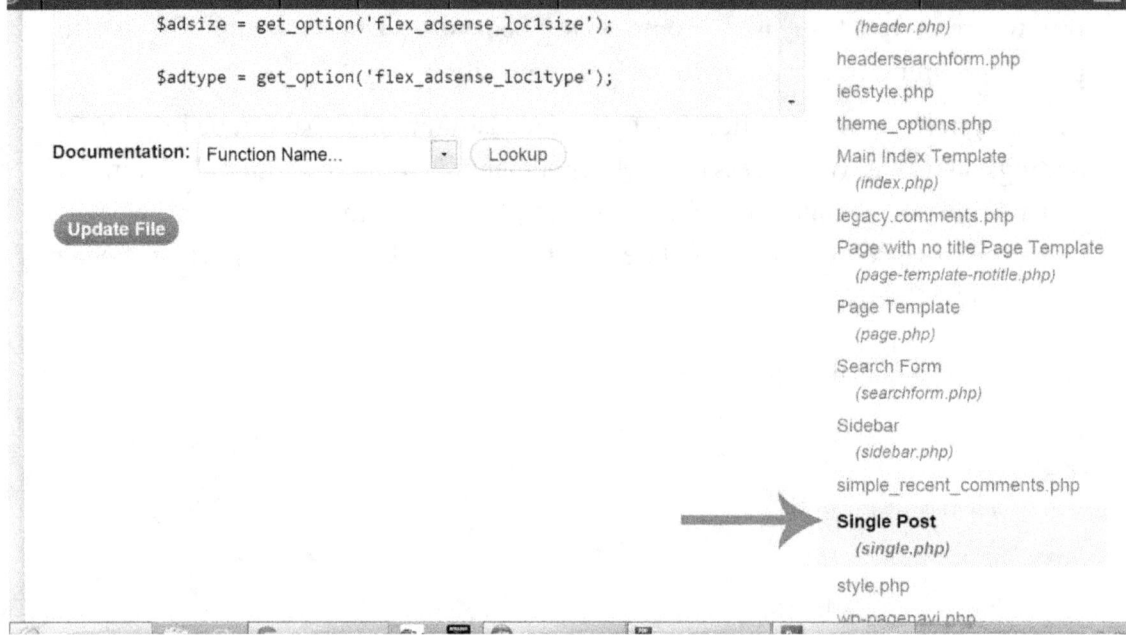

Where you insert this code will determine where the navigation is displayed. I like to do it either above the title or just below the post date.

There are also ways to edit the code itself to change the font, make the trail appear in multiple places, and more, but doing so is different for each theme. If you are interested in doing this I suggest looking up resources on Google or in YouTube, depending on what theme you are using.

Remember, this can seem complicated if you have never done CSS. If you aren't confident that you can do this without screwing up your theme, either get someone else to do it, look up some tutorials on YouTube for help, or just don't bother with it.

You can get this plugin by using the WordPress plugin search function or by going to this UR by entering it into your browser.

http://wordpress.org/extend/plugins/breadcrumb-navxt/.

WordPress Related Posts (Essential)

This plugin adds a list of related posts at the bottom of each post you create. This is great for SEO as well as encouraging visitors to visit multiple pages on your website, which is one of the keys to beating Google's Panda update. Just about any site imaginable can benefit from this. The options for this plugin will be found in the Settings tab and be listed as "Related Posts."

You can get WordPress Related Posts by using the WordPress plugin search function or by going to this UR by entering it into your browser. http://wordpress.org/extend/plugins/wordpress-23-related-posts-plugin/.

WP Super Cache (Essential)

Providing your visitors with a good user experience is another key to defeating Panda, and if your site loads really slowly you're going to be in trouble. This plugin helps to ensure that your website loads quickly regardless of how much traffic you're getting by keeping a cached version of your site in the browser. The options for WP Super Cache can be found in the Settings tab in the WordPress main menu.

You can get WP Super Cache by using the plugin search function in the WordPress control panel or by going to this UR by entering it into your browser. http://wordpress.org/extend/plugins/wp-super-cache/.

Google XML Sitemaps (Essential)

We already went over this one. Google XML Sitemaps generates a sitemap to help your website be indexed more easily by search engines like Google. No matter what kind of site you're building you *must* get this plugin. The options for this plugin can be found in the Settings tab on the main menu.

Google XML Sitemaps can be found and installed using the WordPress plugins search function or downloaded by going to this UR by entering it into your browser. http://wordpress.org/extend/plugins/google-sitemap-generator/.

All in One SEO Pack (Essential)

There are many SEO plugins out there, but this is probably the most popular free one. All in One SEO Pack works to help optimize each page and post, as well as your

website as a whole. Just don't forget to configure it after you've installed it, or it will be functionally useless. The configuration options can be found in the Settings tab on the main WordPress menu.

All in One SEO Pack can be found using the WordPress plugin search option and installed through the control panel. Alternately, you can get the plugin here http://wordpress.org/extend/plugins/all-in-one-seo-pack/.

Contact Form 7 (Essential)

Regardless of what kind of site you're building, you're going to need to give your visitors a way to contact you. Contact Form 7 allows you to not only put a contact form on your Contact page (or anywhere you desire), it also allows you to edit and customize your contact form. The options for Contact Form 7 are listed in the plugins page under the plugin name and are labeled "Settings."

Contact Form 7 can be found by using the search function in WordPress and can be installed directly from the control panel. You can also get it by going to this UR by entering it into your browser http://wordpress.org/extend/plugins/contact-form-7/.

Really Simple Captcha (Essential)

This plugin is recommended to keep bots from relentlessly spamming your email address through your contact form. This plugin adds a captcha form that visitors have to complete in order to contact you. Really Simply Captcha was developed by Takayuki Miyoshi, the same individual who created Contact Form 7, and is intended to work with it.

To get this plugin to work you have to go into the settings for Contact Form 7 and click on the drop-down menu that says "Generate Tag" and select "Captcha."

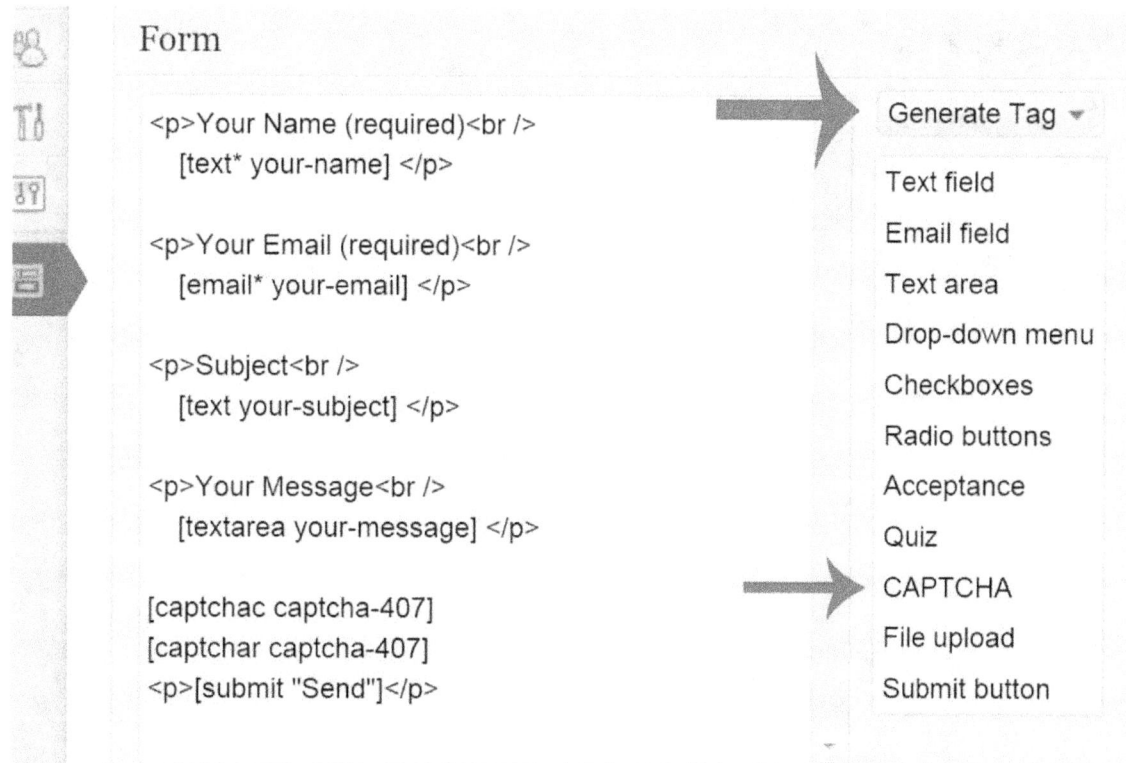

Form

```
<p>Your Name (required)<br />
   [text* your-name] </p>

<p>Your Email (required)<br />
   [email* your-email] </p>

<p>Subject<br />
   [text your-subject] </p>

<p>Your Message<br />
   [textarea your-message] </p>

[captchac captcha-407]
[captchar captcha-407]
<p>[submit "Send"]</p>
```

Generate Tag ▾

Text field

Email field

Text area

Drop-down menu

Checkboxes

Radio buttons

Acceptance

Quiz

CAPTCHA

File upload

Submit button

You then copy and paste the two bits of code at the bottom over into the field to the left just before the last tag.

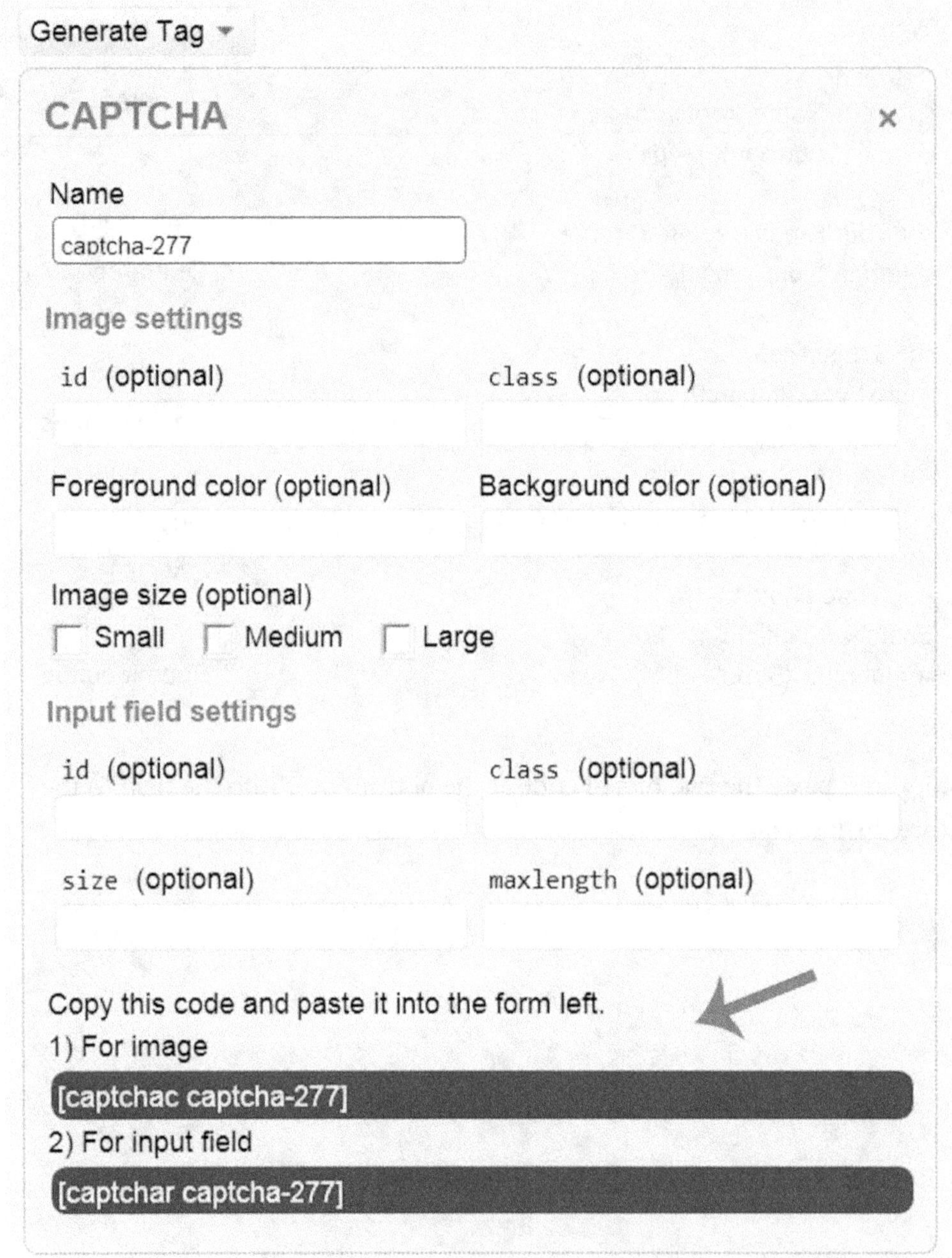

Generate Tag ▼

CAPTCHA   ✕

Name

captcha-277

Image settings

id (optional)

class (optional)

Foreground color (optional)

Background color (optional)

Image size (optional)
☐ Small   ☐ Medium   ☐ Large

Input field settings

id (optional)

class (optional)

size (optional)

maxlength (optional)

Copy this code and paste it into the form left.

1) For image

[captchac captcha-277]

2) For input field

[captchar captcha-277]

```
<p>Your Name (required)<br />
    [text* your-name] </p>


<p>Your Email (required)<br />
    [email* your-email] </p>


<p>Subject<br />
    [text your-subject] </p>


<p>Your Message<br />
    [textarea your-message] </p>


[captchac captcha-407]
[captchar captcha-407]
<p>[submit "Send"]</p>
```

Really Simple Captcha can be found through the plugin search function on WordPress and can be installed from there. You can also get it by going to this UR by entering it into your browser.

http://wordpress.org/extend/plugins/really-simple-captcha/.

Akismet (Essential)

Akismet comes already installed on WordPress and is a spam blocker. To activate it, you have to go to the plugin page, click "Activate," then click the link where you go to get your API key. There are paid versions with more options, but the free version is fine. Once you get the key, click the link in the yellow bar at the top on your WordPress control panel that prompts you to enter it. Once you enter the key you're good to go. Akismet will have its own configuration link in the Plugins tab on the WordPress main menu.

Choosing the Right Plugins

While some plugins work well with pretty much any site and are essential for good SEO, blocking spam, and other functions, your plugin selection will largely depend on the type of site you're creating. Some plugins are designed to enhance blogs, and others to enhance affiliate sites. Consider what functions you need on your site and choose your plugins accordingly.

Chapter 15: Creating Pages

One of the first things you are going to want to do on your WordPress site is to create several pages. While you can create as many pages as you want for whatever purpose you want, it is recommended that you start by creating an About page, Contact page, and Privacy Policy. Something to keep in mind about pages is that they will show up in your navigation bar unless you make them hidden, which I'll go over in just a moment.

About

Your About page is going to be the page where you explain a bit about who you are, what your site is all about, and any other essential info you feel your visitors need. Depending on the type of site you're creating, you may want to put a picture of yourself here, because having a picture of yourself will increase your trust and credibility among your visitors.

To create your About page, click the pages tab in the WordPress control panel and then select Add New. This will open the page creation page.

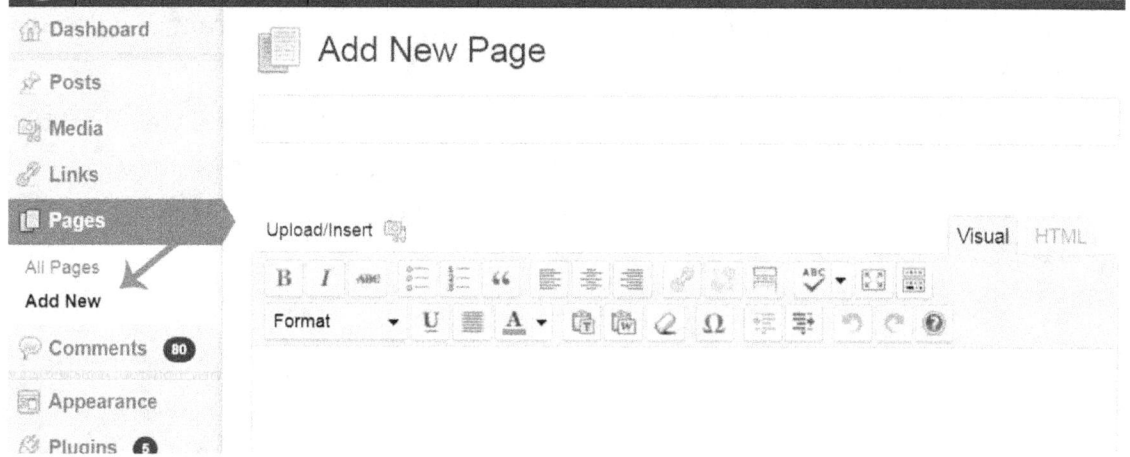

Creating a page here is as simple as adding a title, then entering the text you want. You can also add pictures if you need to by clicking the Add Media button. When you're writing don't forget that you have access to a variety of tools in the text toolbar, such as bold, underline, block quote, add hyperlink, and more.

Also of note is the HTML tag. You can click this if you want to enter HTML information in your page, such as different fonts and text sizes. You can also use HTML to insert pictures that are hosted at a separate location.

If you are having trouble figuring out how to create your About page, then go to this UR by entering it into your browser. http://www.lambertklein.com/about.html to take a look at mine and get an idea of how it should look and what info should be included. Remember, there is no set formula for your About page, just make it unique and suited to your site and your personality. It also pays to provide a contact link on your About page.

Once you have finished writing your page, you can do three things: save your draft to work on later, preview your page in a new tab or window, and publish your page immediately. I would recommend previewing your page before publishing, just to make sure it looks right.

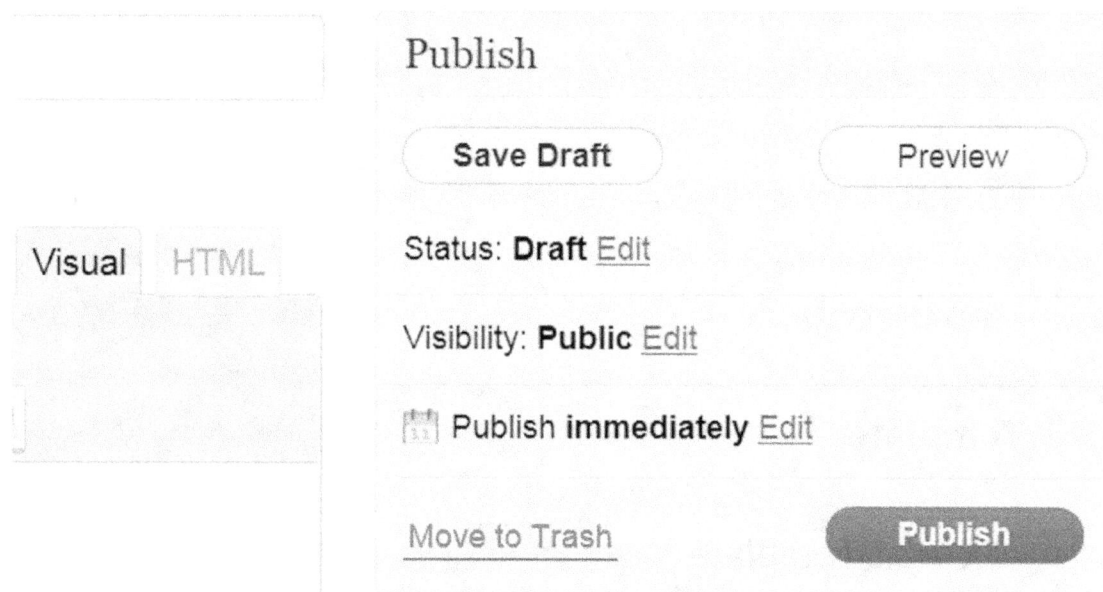

There are a few other things you can do before you publish your page, such as assigning a parent page or changing the template to remove the sidebar. For SEO purposes it is recommended that you leave the sidebar. This is especially true if you have advertisements in your sidebar.

There is also an option that says "Set Featured Image," which attaches a thumbnail image. This is practically useless for pages but can be useful for posts in some cases. It must be mentioned though that this feature doesn't work well with some themes, including the default Twenty Ten theme, thus requiring you to edit some CSS to make it work. If you are having trouble getting it to work with your theme, then go to this UR by entering it into your browser

http://codex.wordpress.org/Post_Thumbnails
to visit the WordPress support page on it.

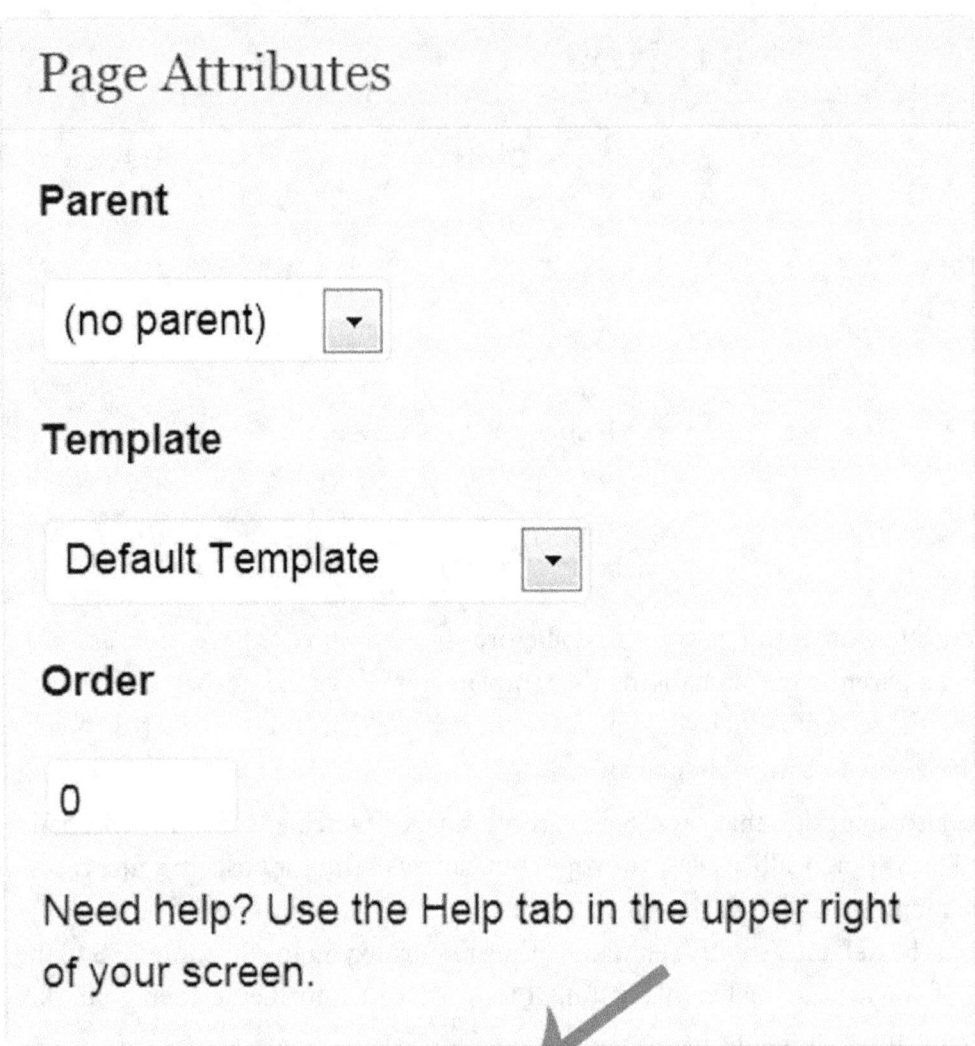

If your theme supports it, then Featured Image button would show up here.

Contact

This is the page where you provide your contact information. It's completely up to you how much info you provide, but you should at least have a contact form, as

mentioned previously. Don't forget to make sure your Captcha plugin is activated so you don't get flooded by spambots. Once the page is set up to your liking, preview and publish it.

Privacy Policy

Having a privacy policy is just standard procedure for most sites, and it would be wise to incorporate one into your site as well. Creating a privacy policy page used to be as simple as installing a plugin, but there are no longer any functional privacy policy plugins, to my knowledge. Instead what you can do is search Google for privacy policy templates to use instead.

For a generic template that works with just about every website. Go to this UR by entering it into your browser.

http://www.inixmedia.com/2010/03/free-privacy-policy-sample-template-for-a-new-website/. Just be sure to edit certain parts of it to suit your particular site.

To create a more customized privacy policy you can go to www.freeprivacypolicy.com. This site will allow you to create a highly customized privacy policy for free, but you're going to have to go through some stuff to get it.

You will have to input your email address once you create the policy, then you will be shown some upsells. These are unnecessary, and I don't encourage you to buy these unless you really need them for some reason. You will then be emailed a username and password as well as a link allowing you to access your privacy policy. It will be in both text and HTML, so you can enter it either way when you create this page.

Overall, www.freeprivacypolicy.com is a great way to get a very customized privacy policy for free as long as you're willing to put up with the fact that they're going to put you on their mailing list and try to sell you a bunch of stuff.

Sneeze Pages

A sneeze page is simply a page that has links to multiple posts on it. It could be titled something like "Hottest Articles," "Breaking News," or "Most Popular Blog Posts." The purpose of a sneeze page is to drive visitors deeper into your site, because most won't bother clicking on your Archives section in the sidebar if you use one.

Also, while sneeze pages are great, you can also incorporate sneeze page elements into other sections of your blog. For example, you could create a "sneeze widget" that features some of your most popular posts in the sidebar. You can also configure your excerpts on the main page to feature two or three links in addition to the thumbnail and description, turning them into mini sneeze pages in a way.

The thing to remember about a sneeze page is that you want to give it a really catchy, interesting title. No one is going to click on a sneeze page or widget if you label it something like "Older Posts." Make the title interesting like the examples given earlier.

Other Pages

Depending on what type of site you're creating, you may want to add other pages as well. If your site is based on selling a service, you can add a page to describe different aspects of it. If you're selling products, you can have a different page for each product category. The possibilities are endless, and ultimately it's up to you to decide what pages you need to create.

Two types of pages that you may need to consider are a Terms of Service page and a Terms of Use page. These are useful if you're running a business (such as a membership website) directly from your website and visitors need to be aware of certain things.

Parent and Child Pages

If you're creating a website in which you're going to have multiple pages listed under the same category, you can assign them to a parent page. In a way this functions somewhat similarly to how you would assign posts to a post category.

A good example of this would be if you want to group your Privacy Policy, Terms of Service, and other legal pages together in your navigation bar. What you would do is create the page that you want to be the parent page first, then as you create your other pages, you would select the option to assign them to your first page as a child page. You can find this feature by scrolling down and looking on the right side of the screen in the page creation page.

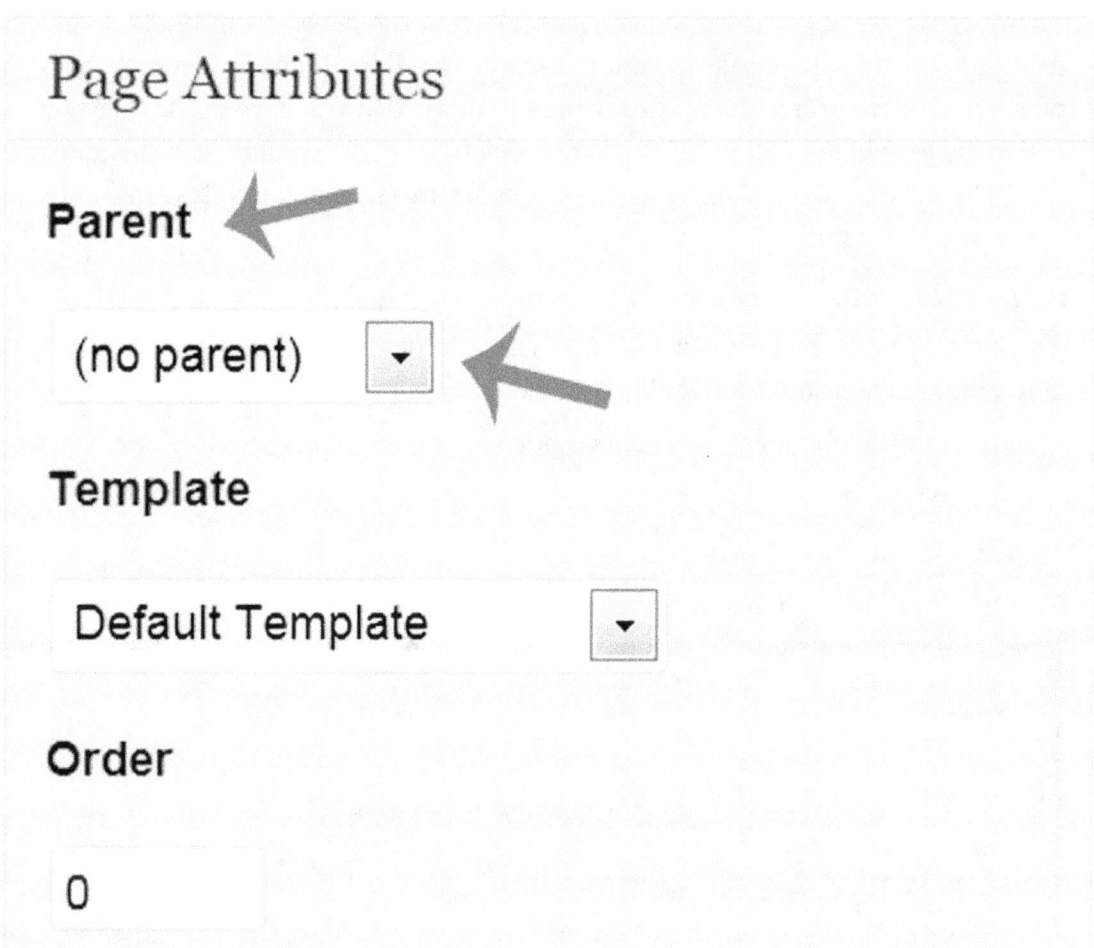

One thing to keep in mind is that the parent/child page system is **not** to be used to replace the categories/posts system. This is because you want your categories to appear in the sidebar for SEO. The parent/child page system should really only be used to save space on the navigation bar.

Hidden Pages

Sometimes you may want to have pages on your website that are hidden. A good example of this is a download page where people who purchase your products go to make their downloads. You obviously don't want this on the navigation bar, or people will be downloading your products for free.

There are two ways to create hidden pages. The first is relatively simple and involves using FTP to upload the page to your add-on or root domain folder, depending on which one you're using. The only drawback to this is that you have to use HTML to create the page in the first place. If you're going to do this, I would recommend using an HTML editor such as nvu. You can get nvu for free by going to this UR by entering it into your browser.

http://net2.com/nvu/download.html.

There is also a bit of code you will need to add in order to make sure that these pages aren't indexed by search engines like Google. The code is

<meta content="nofollow,noarchive,noindex"

name="robots" />

<meta content="never" name="revisit" />

This typically goes right below the </title> tag.

```
 1.  <!DOCTYPE html PUBLIC "-//W3C//DTD XHTML 1.0 Transitional//EN" "http://w
 2.  <html xmlns="http://www.w3.org/1999/xhtml">
 3.  <head>
 4.    <meta content="text/html; charset=utf-8"
 5.    http-equiv="Content-Type" />
 6.    <title>Thank You!</title>
 7.    <meta content="nofollow,noarchive,noindex"
 8.  name="robots" />
 9.    <meta content="never" name="revisit" />
10.    <link type="text/css"
11.    rel="stylesheet" href="style.css" />
12.  </head>
13.  <body>
```

Also make sure that you give the HTML file a unique, hard-to-guess name like "Special-Offer-Download83925783275" or something like that so people won't be able to figure out how to get to it easily.

Another thing you must be aware of when doing this is that in addition to the HTML file, you must also upload any CSS style sheets and images associated with the HTML. These all go in the domain name folder with the HTML file.

In any event, if you use FTP the file path will be "root/ → public_html → domain name folder" for add-on domains and "root/ → public_html" for the root domain.

If you want to hide pages you create in WordPress the easy way, simply search and install the PC Hide Pages

http://wordpress.org/extend/plugins/pc-hide-pages/
plugin from the WordPress Plugins section. This will not only make selected pages hidden but also hide them from search engine spiders. This will ensure that they aren't indexed and can't be accessed through Google and other search engines.

Another option if you want to keep pages off of your navigation bar but still public is the plugin Exclude Pages. You can grab it by going to this UR by entering it into your browser
http://wordpress.org/extend/plugins/exclude-pages/
to get this one.

Creating a Static Home Page

The main page of your website can come in one of two different varieties: Static and Latest Posts. By default your home page will show your latest blog posts, and if you decide to go with this format make sure that you are using the "Insert More Tag" button to show only an excerpt on the home page. You're also going to want to limit how many posts are shown by clicking Reading under the Settings tab in the main WordPress menu.

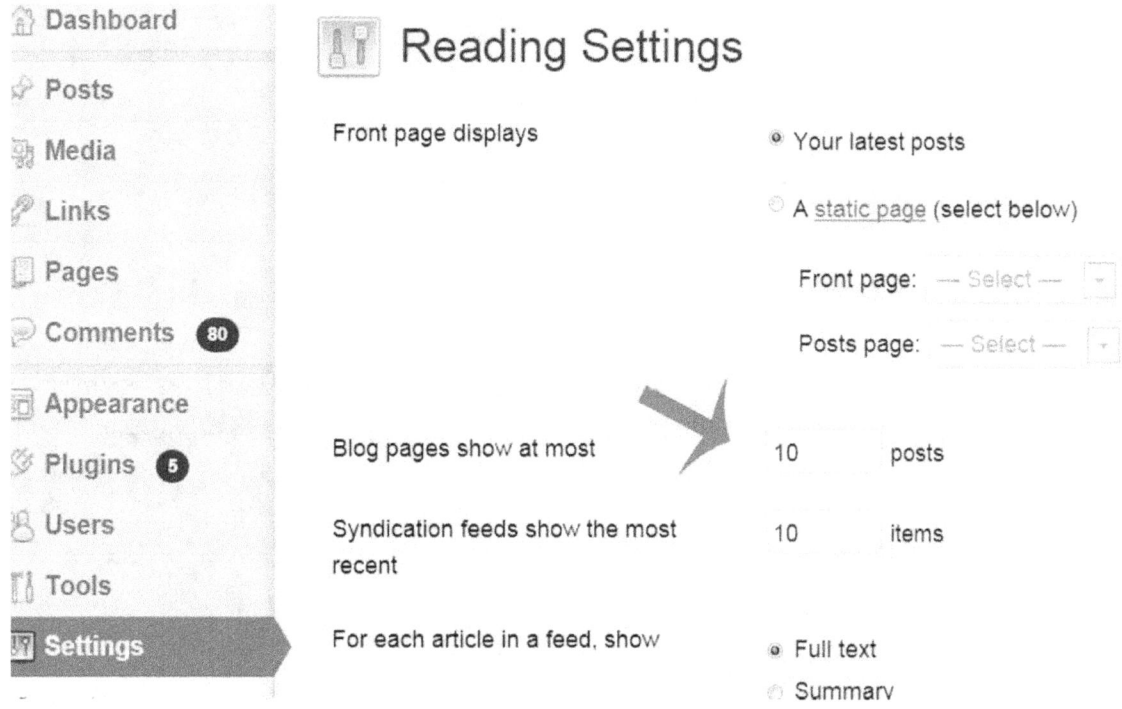

To create a static home page simply click on Reading in the Settings tab and take a look at the page that opens. The first thing on the page is two bubbles. The first is "Your latest posts" and the second is "A static page." Select the second one to make your home page a static page.

Now what you have to do is go down to the drop-down menu below and select which page you want to be your static home page. The page that you select will then be listed as "Home" in the navigation menu on your website. You also need to select what page your posts will be displayed on.

 # Reading Settings

Front page displays
- ○ Your latest posts
- ◉ A static page (select below)

Front page: Sample Page ▾

Posts page: — Select — ▾

Blog pages show at most   10   posts

Syndication feeds show the most   10   items
recent

Whether or not you have a static home page is completely up to you. However, if you're creating a blog it is usually best to keep your latest posts as the home page.

Chapter 16: WordPress Security

One of the worst fears of anyone who runs a website is having their site hacked. This can lead to lost data, corrupted files, Trojans, and malware entering your computer and many other undesirable outcomes. The good news is that protecting your WordPress website isn't hard as long as you employ smart online and offline security practices.

Limiting Access

As with many things, prevention is the key when it comes to protecting your WordPress site. As we touched upon earlier you shouldn't be accessing your WordPress site from public computers if you can help it, and you should certainly never set your username and password to "remember" for any public or shared computers.

It is also a good idea to make sure you log out of your WordPress account once you're done using the control panel if you use a shared computer. This will prevent anyone else from gaining access by using your cookies. This is also highly recommended if you access your control panel using a mobile device or phone that could potentially fall into the wrong hands.

Computer Vulnerabilities

All the WordPress security in the world isn't going to do you any good if your computer is infected with malicious software or compromised by a hacker. Make sure your computer always has the latest antivirus and malware protection available, and make sure that it is always up to date. Also ensure that you perform scans regularly. Remember, anyone who gets into your computer can potentially get into any of your online accounts such as WordPress, Facebook, and more as well as your WordPress sites.

Updating WordPress

WordPress.org's built-in security is pretty robust, but like any security system it must be updated regularly, or new and improved malicious software can get through. Make

sure that you regularly check the control panel of your WordPress sites so that you can update them as soon as an update becomes available.

Web Server Vulnerability

If your hosting server becomes compromised then your WordPress sites are as good as compromised as well. The good news is that practically every hosting company out there has exceptional security features. However, you have to do your part too.

Avoid logging in to your cPanel from public computers, and always log out on shared computers just like you do for your WordPress control panel. Changing your password frequently can also be a good idea.

Keep in mind that if you are on a shared server (most web hosting plans fall into this category unless you specifically get dedicated hosting), your data can be more easily compromised. Luckily most big companies like HostGator and Bluehost have excellent security measures.

If you purchase reseller hosting (from a private individual, not a web hosting company), you need to speak with the server administrator beforehand to make sure that you understand what security measures are in place and what precautions you should take. This is especially true if the reseller hosting is from a lesser-known company.

Overall, protecting your web server is actually more important than protecting your WordPress site itself. This is because if someone gets into your hosting, they could gain access to every site stored on that hosting server, which could lead to catastrophe.

Network Vulnerability

If you are on a LAN or are part of a cloud computing network, make sure you are familiar with the security systems in place. While most cloud computing companies have ultra-secure networks, LANs and other public computing networks may not. This makes it very easy for your passwords and other sensitive information to be intercepted. Don't access your WordPress account or web hosting account if you are unsure of a network's security level.

FTP Vulnerability

FTP presents another possible security breach because it accesses your server directly. Many FTP clients, such as Filezilla, can be configured so that you must input a password in order to access a server by configuring separate profiles for separate web servers. This is a must on shared computers. Also, Quick Connect absolutely should not be used on shared computers, because anyone can access servers that have been typed in previously if you forget to delete the history.

Also, FTP clients should not be used while connected to networks with anything less than exceptional security, because your entire server data will be exposed when you access the hosting server. This could lead to a sever compromise by someone on the network or an external computer.

File Permissions

Some files on your WordPress site are write accessible by your web server. What this basically means is that your web server can access these files and alter them. In some cases this is necessary for the function of your website, but certain files should never be write accessible. Here is a quick list of files that you should make sure are only writeable by your user account.

- The root directory (except .htaccess if you want WordPress to automatically configure rewrite rules for you)
- /wp-admin/
- /wp-includes/
- /wp-content/plugins/

It should be noted that /wp-content/ itself should be writable.

You can change file permissions directly from your hosting server through your cPanel in most cases, or you can use an FTP client to do it as well. In Filezilla you can do this by accessing your server and bringing up the file you want to change permissions for. Right-click the file and select "File Attributes." A little window will pop up with your permissions. Make sure that "Write" for Group and Public is disabled, then click OK. Do this for all the files above and any others you don't want to be rewritable.

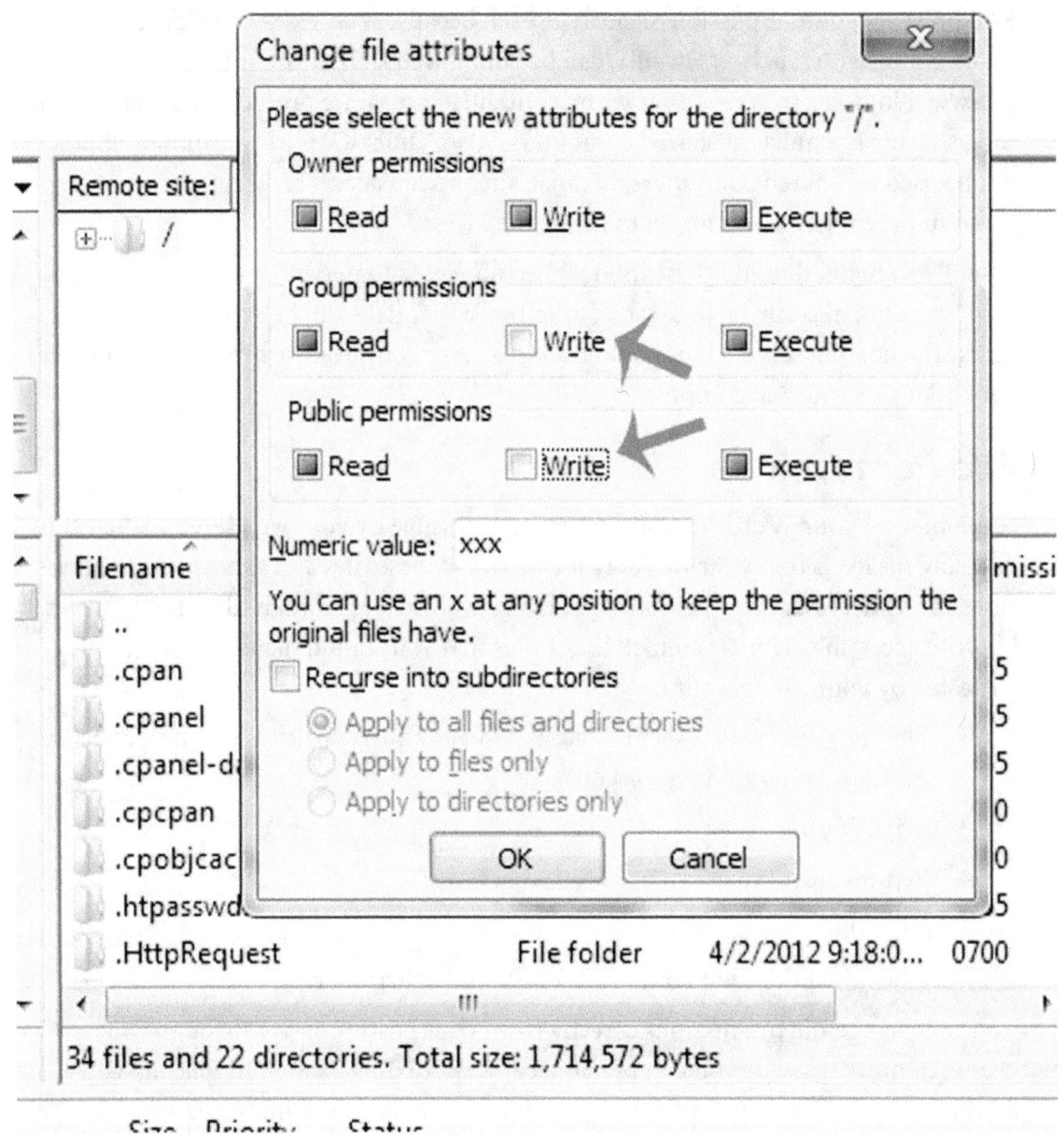

Firewall Plugins

You can further deter potential hackers by installing firewall plugins on your WordPress site. While this can be overkill in many cases, considering WordPress

already has very tight security, you can still do it if it will help you feel better about your website's security.

WordPress Firewall 2
http://wordpress.org/extend/plugins/wordpress-firewall-2/
 and cloudsafe365_for_WordPress
 http://www.cloudsafe365.com/how-it-works/
 are two popular firewall options.

Plugins that Need Write Access

There may come a time when you download a plugin that says it needs write access to files that you have disabled write permissions for. In this event you need to make absolutely sure you trust the plugin publisher and that it isn't going to do anything malicious to your system. If you are unsure about the plugin, check the code to make sure it doesn't contain anything threatening, or get someone who understands code to check it for you.

SQL Database Security

If you are going to have multiple WordPress sites, a good security measure is to install each one on a different database managed by a different "user." What I mean by user is the fact that when you create a database you have to create a user profile that will be identified by a username and password. This will ensure that if someone does hack into one of your WordPress sites they won't automatically have access to the others.

You create a database by going into your hosting account and creating what is known as a MySQL database for each additional WordPress site you want to install. While I can't do a walk through for every single hosting company out there, I will briefly walk you through how to do this on HostGator so you can get an idea of how this is done.

First go into your cPanel and select the icon that says MySQL Database.

Databases

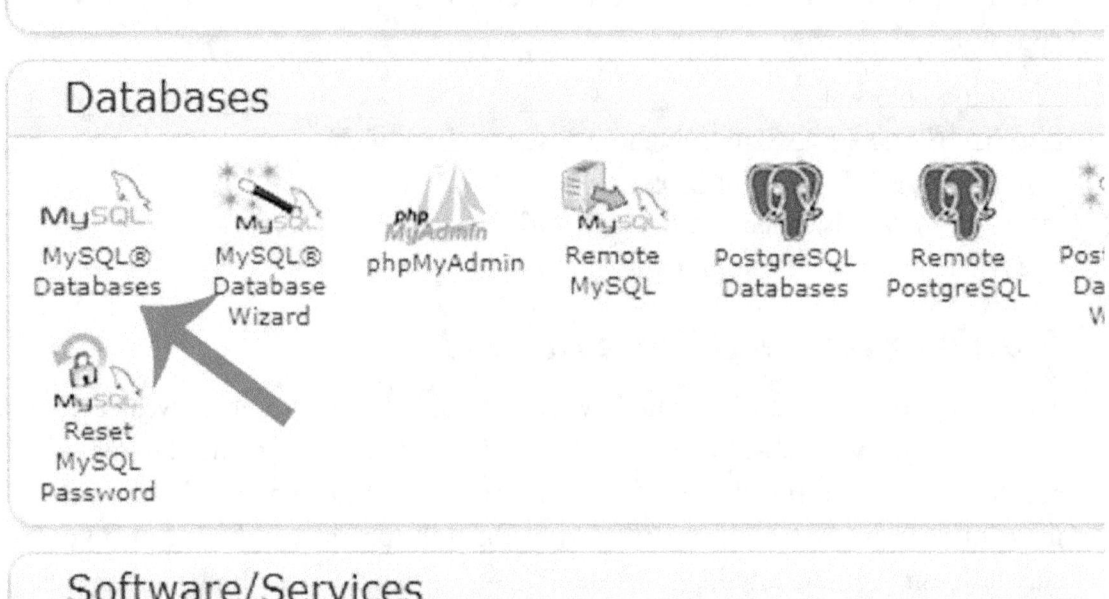

Software/Services

Enter the database name, then click "Create Database." Now you will have to create a user for the database by entering a username and password below.

Create New Database

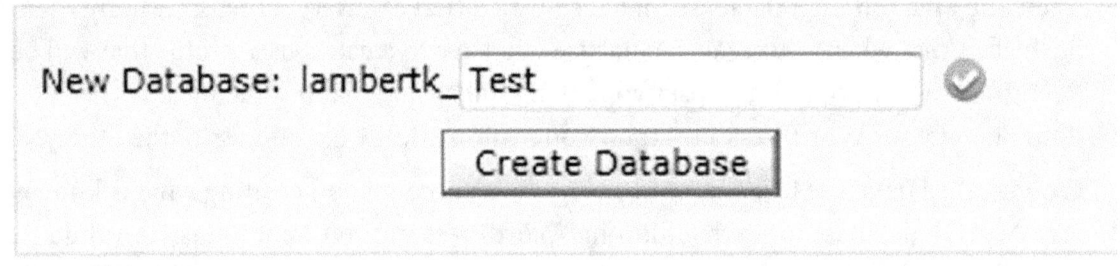

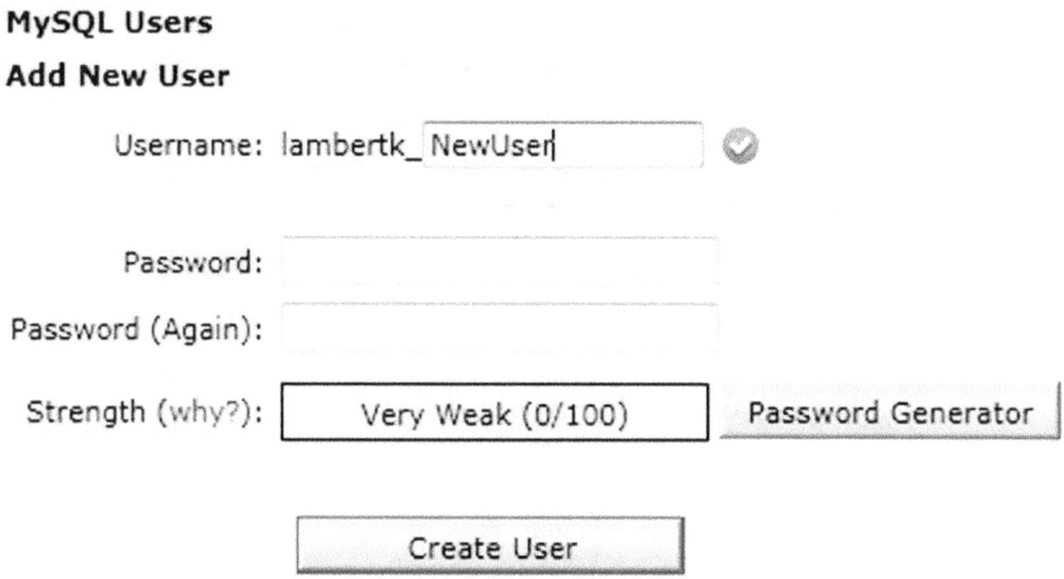

MySQL Users

Add New User

Username: lambertk_ NewUser ✓

Password:

Password (Again):

Strength (why?): Very Weak (0/100)   Password Generator

Create User

Once that is complete you're going to have to add that user to the database. Remember, you can add a single user to multiple databases, but that would defeat the purpose because you want each WordPress site to be managed by a different username and password.

To add a user to a database, simply select the user you want from the drop-down box and the database you want from the drop-down box under it, then click "Add."

Create User

Add User To Database

User: | lambertk_NewUser ▾ |

Database: | lambertk_Test ▾ |

| Add |

A new screen will pop up prompting you to give permissions. It is recommended that you give all permissions to the user by clicking the box at the top that says "All privileges." Once you're done click "Make changes."

Another way you can do this is to use the SQL Database Wizard, which you may find easier.

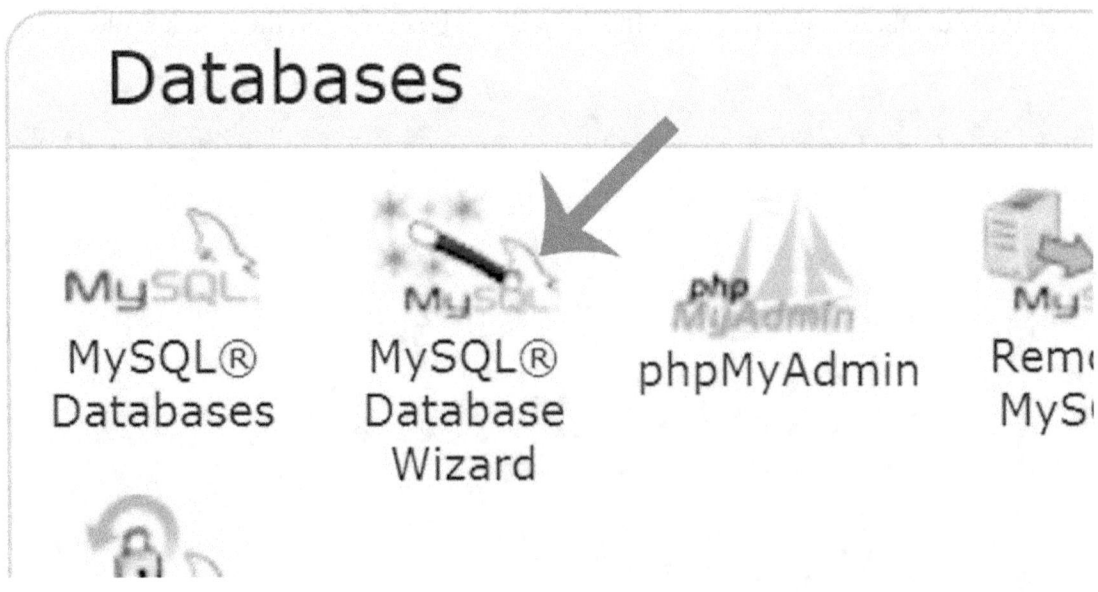

Databases

MySQL® Databases   MySQL® Database Wizard   phpMyAdmin   Rem(
                                                                        MyS(

Once this is done you now have a database that you can install your WordPress site on. This is somewhat technical but isn't hard at all. What you first need to do is locate your wp-config.php file for your WordPress site. Once again you can use either an FTP program or your cPanel. The file path will also be different for the root domain and add-on domains.

Important: Do not confuse wp-config.php with wp-config-sample.php that is located directly above it.

Root Domain Path:

root/ → public_html (you then have to look in the subfiles for this folder)

Filename	Filesize	Filetype	Last modified
.htaccess	246	HTACCESS...	8/31/2012 6:29:...
index.php	395	PHP Script	8/31/2012 2:57:...
license.txt	19,929	Text Docu...	8/31/2012 2:57:...
readme.html	9,177	HTML Doc...	8/31/2012 2:57:...
sitemap.xml	2,035	XML Docu...	9/1/2012 2:38:3..
sitemap.xml.gz	698	GZ File	9/1/2012 2:38:3..
wp-activate.php	4,264	PHP Script	8/31/2012 2:57:...
wp-app.php	1,354	PHP Script	8/31/2012 2:57:...
wp-blog-header.php	271	PHP Script	8/31/2012 2:57:...
wp-comments-post.php	3,522	PHP Script	8/31/2012 2:57:...
wp-config-sample.php	3,177	PHP Script	8/31/2012 2:57:...
wp-config.php	3,519	PHP Script	3/23/2012 9:36:...
wp-cron.php	2,726	PHP Script	8/31/2012 2:57:...
wp-links-opml.php	1,997	PHP Script	8/31/2012 2:57:...
wp-load.php	2,341	PHP Script	8/31/2012 2:57:...
wp-login.php	29,084	PHP Script	8/31/2012 2:57:...
wp-mail.php	7,712	PHP Script	8/31/2012 2:57:

Add-on Domain Path:

root/ → public_html → [the name of your domain] (you then have to look in the subfiles for this folder)

Remote site:	/public_html/blog

```
    ?  ajxlightbox4_files
    ?  ajxlightbox5_files
    ?  ajxlightbox6_files
    ?  ajxlightbox_files
    ?  bin-dl
⊞      blog
    ?  cam
```

Filename	Filesize	Filetype	Last modified
.htaccess	246	HTACCESS...	8/31/2012 6:29:...
index.php	395	PHP Script	8/31/2012 2:57:...
license.txt	19,929	Text Docu...	8/31/2012 2:57:...
readme.html	9,177	HTML Doc...	8/31/2012 2:57:...
sitemap.xml	2,035	XML Docu...	9/1/2012 2:38:3...
sitemap.xml.gz	698	GZ File	9/1/2012 2:38:3...
wp-activate.php	4,264	PHP Script	8/31/2012 2:57:...
wp-app.php	1,354	PHP Script	8/31/2012 2:57:...
wp-blog-header.php	271	PHP Script	8/31/2012 2:57:...
wp-comments-post.php	3,522	PHP Script	8/31/2012 2:57:...
wp-config-sample.php	3,177	PHP Script	8/31/2012 2:57:...
wp-config.php	3,519	PHP Script	3/23/2012 9:36:...
wp-cron.php	2,726	PHP Script	8/31/2012 2:57:...
wp-links-opml.php	1,997	PHP Script	8/31/2012 2:57:...

Once you have accessed the right folder, right-click the wp-config.php file and open it in a text editor if you're using FTP. If you are using your cPanel, you will edit the file in a new browser tab or window in most cases.

146

There are three sections of this file you need to edit: DB_NAME, DB_USER, and DB_PASSWORD. Simply change these values to your database name, username you created for it, and the password you created when you made the SQL database earlier.

```
//Added by WP-Cache Manager

define('DB_NAME', '_____');  /** MySQL
database username */
define('DB_USER', '_____');
/** MySQL database password */
define('DB_PASSWORD', '_____');
/** MySQL hostname */
define('DB_HOST', 'localhost');

/** Database Charset to use in creating database
```

Once you have changed the data, save the file. Now your site will be attached to the database. Keep in mind that in some cases you may be prompted to install WordPress once again when you try to visit the site or login page in your browser. Just fill in the required information and WordPress will be ready to be used again.

It is recommended that you do the editing of the wp-config.php file through FTP so that you can save a copy of this file to your computer before you begin editing. This way if you screw something up you can delete the messed-up file and upload the original. You can then try again.

Keep in mind that a WordPress site should be installed on a new database before you begin doing any work on it. This is because a new database will have no data on it. If you create a new database for an existing WordPress site and edit the wp-config.php file, the old data will remain in the database that was automatically created when you first installed WordPress. The original database will usually be something like "[your webhosting log in name]_wrdpr1" or "[your web hosting login name]_wrdpr2."

If you have multiple WordPress sites already created, you can simply check their wp-config.php file to see which databases they are each connected to. You can then add a unique user and password to each instead of having to create a brand new database for each one. This will allow you to keep your data and not have to rebuild each site from the ground up.

Back Up Your Data

In the event that your WordPress site or host server becomes compromised, you want to ensure that your data is backed up. Backing up your data regularly can be a great way to prevent a catastrophic loss of data if you are compromised. There are several plugins that can help you back up your data, such as Online Backup for WordPress http://wordpress.org/extend/plugins/wponlinebackup/
and EZPZ One Click Backup
http://wordpress.org/extend/plugins/ezpz-one-click-backup/.

You should also back up your SQL Databases if you are using multiple databases for multiple sites. This can help to protect against data loss as well.

Monitoring

If you really want to stay on top of things, you can actively monitor your website's logs for hacking attempts, your files for any suspicious changes, and even use a web-based integrity monitor to monitor your site externally. This level of security can be somewhat complicated to those who are unfamiliar with how these things work. Fortunately, you don't usually need to go so far as to constantly monitor your files and data for intrusion attempts, so long as you're smart about your website and server security.

Stopping Spam

When it comes to blocking spam in your comments section, Akismet is the most preferred spam-blocking plugin. It comes with WordPress, but you have to go to their site to get the API key, as mentioned in the plugins section.

To keep your contact form from being spammed, make sure you're using a captcha plugin. Really Simple Captcha is recommended, especially if you are using Contact Form 7.

Chapter 17: Website SEO

SEO for your website is incredibly simple yet also one of the most important things you're going to have to do to ensure that your site ranks well in the search engine results. Let's go over the key components of website SEO.

Domain Name

The domain name of your website is where your SEO begins, as we discussed earlier. Your domain name should preferably be a keyword phrase that has a high search volume, low amount of competition, and be composed of two to three words. This will help to ensure that the search engine spiders that crawl your site understand what it is about, and rank it accordingly. Also, because your root domain shows up on every single page and post of your website in the URL, it's one of the most powerful forms of SEO for your site as a whole.

Title and Tag Line

Your title and tag line show up by default in your WordPress site's header. When you install a custom header they disappear for most themes, while with some themes you will have to set your configuration to not show them. The thing to remember is, just because they aren't visible in your header doesn't mean they aren't important.

You can set your title and tag line by going into the Settings tab on the control panel menu and clicking on "General."

General Settings

Site Title	⟶	Kindle and PDF Books
Tagline	⟶	Internet Marketing Books

In a few words, explain what this site is about.

WordPress Address (URL)	http://www.lambertklein.com/blog
Site Address (URL)	http://www.lambertklein.com/blog

Enter the address here if you want your site homepage to installed WordPress.

E-mail Address	stuff@1thinkhealthy.com

This address is used for admin purposes, like new user no

Make sure that both your title and tag line contain the same keywords as your domain name or related keywords. Because this is technically a part of your header, whether they are visible or not, your title and tag line will be showing up on every page and post as well.

Meta Tags

Meta tags are another way to help search engines recognize what your site is about and rank it accordingly. The easiest way to do meta tags is to use the All in One SEO plugin mentioned earlier. It will allow you to enter information such as your home page's title, description, and a list of related keywords.

I enjoy this plugin and have made a donation:	☐
Plugin Status:	⦿ Enabled ○ Disabled
Home Title:	Kindle and PDF Books
Home Description:	Internet Marketing Books
Home Keywords (comma separated):	wordpress,books,pdf,kindle,inte
Canonical URLs:	☑
Rewrite Titles:	☑
Post Title Format:	%post_title% | %blog_title%

This is a great way to optimize your home page for search engines. All in One SEO also allows you to do this for individual pages and posts, but we'll get into that a bit later.

Breadcrumb Navigation

As mentioned before in the plugins section, having breadcrumb navigation on your site is a great way to appeal to the search engines by basically adding even more

keywords to each post in the form of navigation links. Additionally, this improves the internal linking structure of your site, which appeals to the search engines as well.

As previously mentioned though, getting breadcrumb navigation plugins such as Breadcrumb NavXT to work can be a chore, depending on what theme you're using. If you are having trouble getting breadcrumbs to work with your theme, search online for resources that can help.

Sitemaps

A sitemap is basically a map of your site formatted in a way that is appealing to crawlers that the search engines use to index websites, posts, and pages. This aspect of SEO can be easily taken care of by installing the Google XML Sitemaps plugin.

Tag Cloud

A tag cloud is a widget that is displayed on your site that lists all of your most common tags. There has been somewhat of a controversy over whether or not tag clouds help SEO, and whether or not you should use them at all. Generally speaking there is nothing wrong with using tag clouds, so long as you don't overdo it. Having too many tags in the tag cloud can appear as "keyword stuffing" and have a negative effect on how search engines rank your site.

Another thing about tag clouds is that while they do enhance the internal linking structure of your site, they do it in a somewhat random way. This gives you practically no control over what pages and posts your "SEO juice" is going to.

If you do choose to use tag clouds, make sure you're using a plugin such as SEO Tag Cloud Widget to assure that your tag cloud is easily read by search engines. Also make sure that you are placing your tag cloud down at the bottom of your sidebar so that you aren't taking up space that could be used for other purposes, such as opt-in forms or advertisements.

WWW Redirect

There is an issue with search engines counting the www version of your URL and the non-www version as two separate pages. This can lead to duplicate content issues, which could cause your site to be penalized in the search engines.

To correct this problem, simply go into your Settings and go into "General." Now set your Site Address (URL) to http://www.yourdomain.com. This will ensure that all non-www versions are redirected to the www version.

Day 4 Recap

Here is what we went over today.

- How to install plugins through WordPress
- How to install plugins using FTP
- Plugins can also be installed through your cPanel
- Recommended plugins
- How to create pages
- How to create hidden pages
- How to create child pages
- What pages are commonly used (Privacy Policy, etc.)
- How to protect your WordPress account and web server from being compromised
- How to back up your data
- How to use SQL databases to protect multiple websites on the same server
- How to stop spam
- How to optimize your on-page website SEO

Some of the things we discussed today were relatively simple and straightforward, whereas others were much more complex. For certain tasks that depend on what hosting company you're using and what theme you have installed, I would once again suggest looking up resources using Google and YouTube. From this point forward I will assume that you have downloaded and installed all the plugins I listed as essential.

Day 5 – Content Creation

Thanks to what you learned yesterday and the day before, you should now have your WordPress site not only set up but also enhanced with plugins, essential pages, categories, a good theme, and any security precautions you wanted to take. Basically the only thing your site should lack at this point is content and a monetization method.

Today we're going to cover adding content to your site as well as how to do proper SEO for your posts and pages. We'll also discuss how to handle your comments section and provide a good user experience for your visitors. All in all, today should be a very short and easy day for you.

Chapter 18: Creating Posts

The majority of the content that you add to your site will be done by creating posts. This allows you to create web pages on your site that contain text, images, video, and even audio files. You also have the option to set the posts you create to be published at a later date if you'd like. There are many different things you can do on the post creation page.

Understanding the Posts Page

Creating posts on WordPress is incredibly easy. Just click on the Posts tab in the control panel menu, click "Add New" and you will bring up the post page.

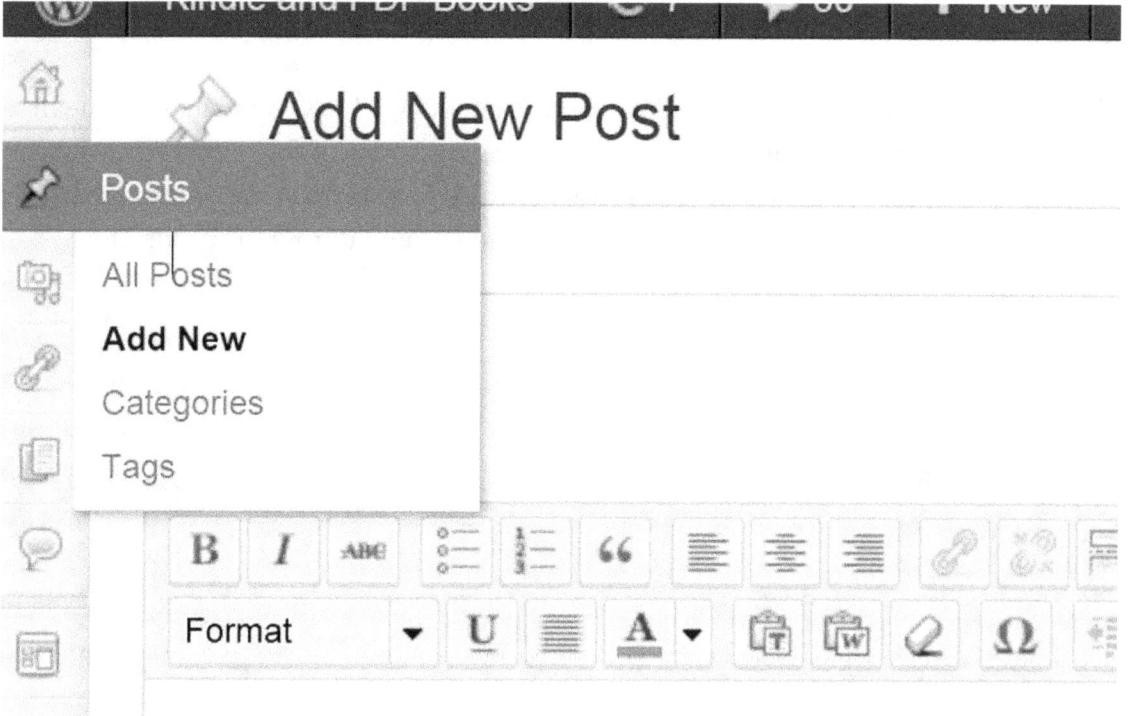

Here you will enter your title and any content you want in the text area. Keep in mind that there are two ways to view the text area, Visual and HTML. Visual is great for most posts you'll be making, while HTML is generally only used to enhance your post in various ways, such as changing the font or text size.

There are also several buttons available on the toolbar here. Most are self-explanatory and will say what they do when you mouse over them. Block quote is a feature that allows you to select a portion of text to appear in a gray block (depending on your theme) while italicized and indented. The gray block won't show up in the text editor here, you'll have to either preview or publish your post to see it. That is, if your theme is capable of showing it.

The Insert More Tag is an incredibly handy feature that allows you to insert a line that cuts off how much of your post will show on the main page of the site if you have your blog posts as the main page. It used to be that you'd have to do some complicated CSS stuff or download a plugin to do this, but now you can do it from the post editor.

Home   Sample Page

Posted on March 15, 2012 by admin

Testing Continue reading →

Posted in Uncategorized | Leave a comment | Edit

The Kitchen Sink button can be clicked in order to show additional options on the toolbar. Click it again to hide the extra options.

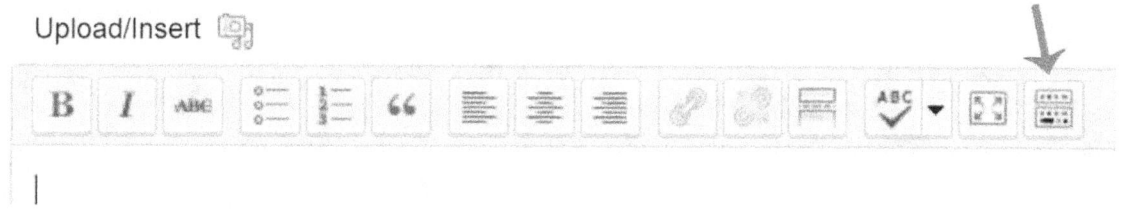

The "Paragraph" tab will allow you to choose some formatting options such as headers and default text, and "Align Full" will adjust the alignment of your paragraphs so that they look better.

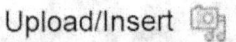

You will also find options that allow you to paste in plain text as well as text from Microsoft Word. This can be handy if you prefer to type out your posts in MS Word first. Keep in mind that your formatting options will not be kept when you do this.

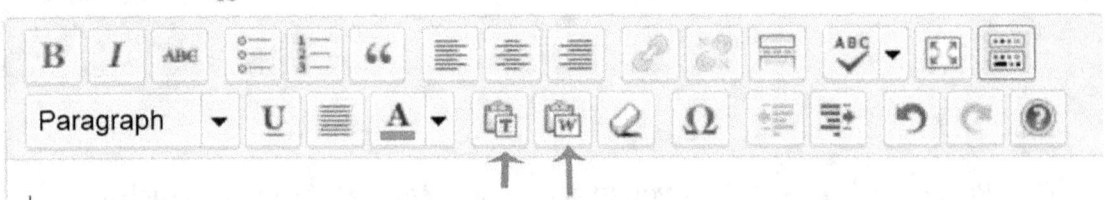

Also available here is a custom character button that allows you to insert symbols such as © if you want. You can also use the indent and out-dent buttons to mimic the effect of a tab key.

Once you have created your post there are several things you can do. If you look to the right you will see a few different options to choose from. "Publish" immediately allows

you to publish your post, "Preview" gives you the opportunity to see what your post will look like, "Save Draft" will save the post as a draft, and "Move to Trash" will move the post to the trash can.

There are also options to change the status, visibility, and the date. Click on "edit" to open these. The status of a post can be set to Draft and Pending Review. Draft will allow you to come back and edit the post later while Pending Review is good for allowing you to check over posts that have been created by hired help if you outsource your content creation before publishing them.

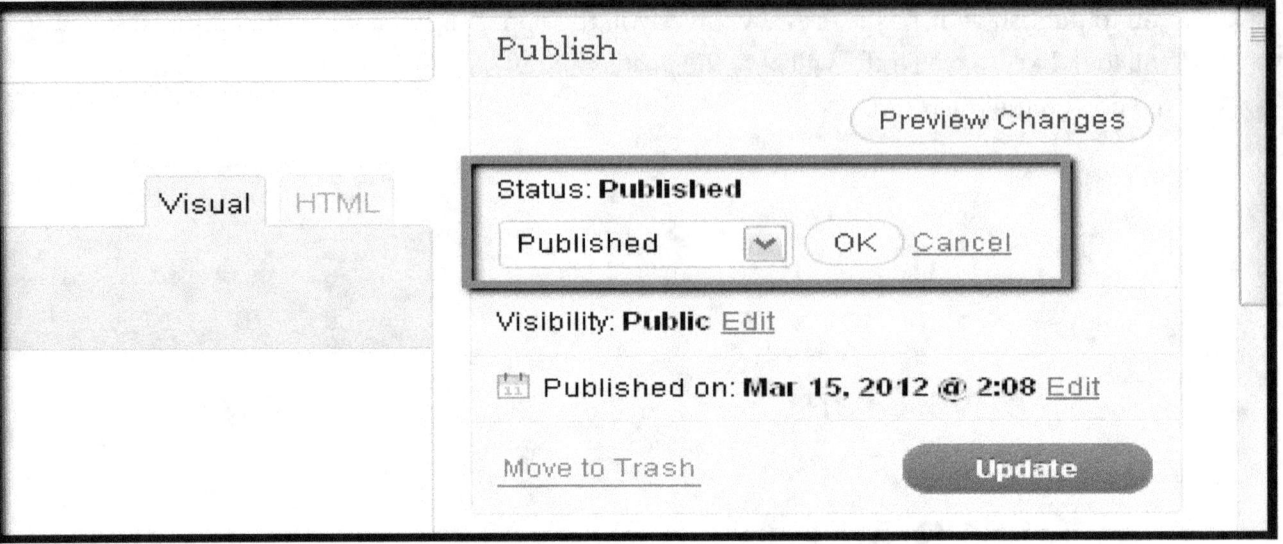

"Visibility" allows you to set who can and can't view your post and to stick the post to the front page if you wish. Generally speaking, "Public" will be your choice here. The "Password Protected" option can be great for making posts and areas of your site that are only accessible to certain people. This is particularly useful if you have a special paid membership section on your site.

Publish

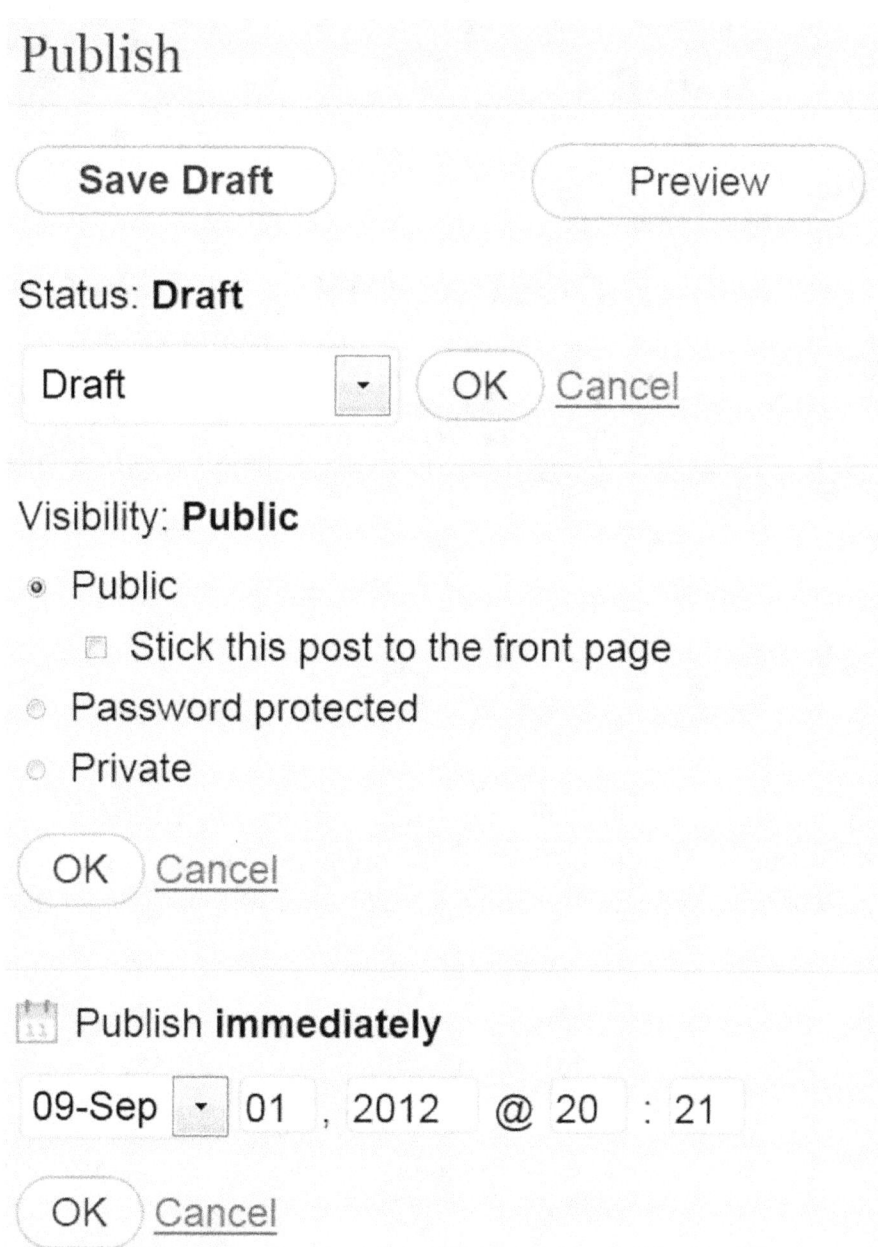

Save Draft　　　　Preview

Status: **Draft**

Draft　　　▾　OK　Cancel

Visibility: **Public**

- ⊙ Public
    - ☐ Stick this post to the front page
- ○ Password protected
- ○ Private

OK　Cancel

📅 Publish **immediately**

09-Sep ▾ 01 , 2012 @ 20 : 21

OK　Cancel

The date allows you to either publish your post immediately or set a time for it to be published in the future. This is good for situations in which you want to drip-feed content to your viewers. When you come back to edit a post that has already been published, you can use this option to edit the date the post was published.

Visibility: **Public**

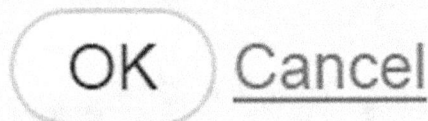 Public

⬜ Stick this post to the front page

⊙ Password protected

⊙ Private

(OK) Cancel

Before you publish your post you're going to want to do a few things first. Scroll down and you will see All in One SEO below the text box. Take a moment to enter your title, description, and keywords in the fields. This will drastically improve your SEO for the post.

📅 Publish **immediately**

| 09-Sep | ▾ | 01 | , | 2012 | @ | 20 | : | 21 |

(OK) Cancel

Move to Trash

Publish

All in One SEO Pack

Upgrade to All in One SEO Pack Pro Version

Title:

0   characters. Most search engines use a maximum of 60 chars for the title.

Description:

0   characters. Most search engines use a maximum of 160 chars for the description.

Keywords (comma separated):

Disable on this page/post: ☐

Next scroll down further and look to the right. You'll see boxes that allow you to choose your categories and set your tags. You can choose from categories and tags that already exist or create new ones if you feel the need.

Categories

All Categories	Most Used

☐ Internet Marketing Books

+ Add New Category

Tags

(Add)

You may also want to add a media file to your post, and that's where the Add Media button comes in. Clicking it opens a box that allows you to drop files in or browse your computer for them. Once you've uploaded a file you can then access it in the

Media Library tab. An alternate way of doing this is to click the "From URL" tab. This will allow you to link in a media file from an external source.

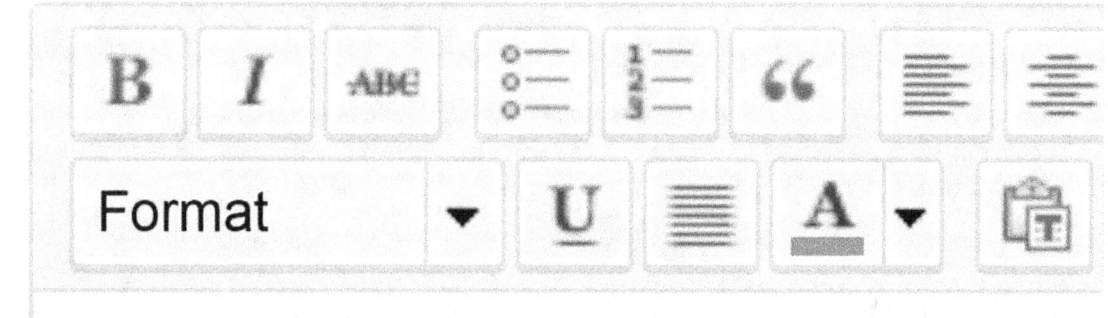

Add Media

From Computer   From URL   Media Library

Add media files from your computer

(Select Files)

You are using the multi-file uploader. Problems? Try the browser uploader instead.

Maximum upload file size: 10MB. After a file has been uploaded, you can add titles and descriptions.

Once you have a media file uploaded, or have selected one from an external source, you can edit how the file displays. For SEO purposes, you should set the title and alternate text to keywords that have to do with the image and post you're creating. You can also fill out a brief description, which is also good for SEO if you put your keywords in it. If you add a caption, it will display underneath the picture. The title will display when someone mouses over it once your post is published.

Once you've entered that information, select the alignment and size of the image. You may have to play around with this a bit to get it just right.

(Edit Image)

| Title | * | appleImage2 |

Alternate Text

Alt text for the image, e.g. "The Mona Lisa"

Caption

Description

Link URL   http://www.lambertklein.com/blog/wp-content/uploads/2012/09/

(None) (File URL) (Attachment Post URL)

Enter a link URL or click above for presets.

Alignment   ○ ▪ **None**   ⊙ ▪≡ **Left**   ○ ▪≡ **Center**   ○ ▪≡ **Right**

Another feature of the Add Media function is that if you click on the button again after adding a picture, you will see a new tab labeled "Gallery." This tab will allow you to check out recently added images and the title and other information you gave them.

Once you have inserted as many pictures as you want and your post is 100% complete, click the preview button to see how it looks. If everything is fine, click the publish button to publish your post on your website. That's all there is to creating posts.

As you can tell, this is very similar to how you create pages but with a few extra options. Try playing around with this a bit until you get the hang of creating posts.

Formatting

When you create a post to publish online you have to take several things into account. First of all you need to understand that people online have *very* short attention spans. To deal with this you need to ensure that your content is broken up into short, easy-

to-read paragraphs. If visitors see a huge block of text when they click on one of your posts, they're going to hit the back button pretty fast.

Also break up sections of your posts with bolded subheadings, similar to the way I do things here in this guide. People online tend to scan, not read, and bolded subheadings and bullet points will give them something to lock on to and focus their attention on.

Also keep in mind that up to 50% of your visitors may not even scroll down the page when they click on a post. This makes it imperative to have any important links "above the fold" in your posts.

When it comes to adding pictures to your posts, don't overdo it. Pictures should be used to enhance a post, and using too many will just be a distraction. If a picture doesn't have a clear purpose, then it doesn't belong in your post.

Chapter 19: Content SEO

When you create content for your website you also want to make sure that it is SEO optimized so that it will be picked up by the search engines. You see, not only are your website's main page/URL crawled by search engine spiders and ranked, but your individual posts and pages are as well. This makes it important to have good SEO on each page and post.

It is unwise to build sites centered around just one keyword, because of the debut of Google's Panda update. You should make your posts centered around keywords that are related to the keyword you used in your domain name. For example, if your domain is "dogtraining.com" your posts could target keywords such as "dog obedience classes," "dog walking," and more. It also pays to do good keyword research to ensure that you're targeting high search volume/low-competition keywords.

Your Title

For pages, don't worry about the title. It should be created for ease of user navigation, not SEO. For posts, however, you do need a good SEO title. This means writing a title that not only includes your keywords, but also makes use of copywriting techniques. Copywriting is the art/science of getting people to take action. In this case, it means clicking on your title when your posts come up in the search engines.

Several examples of title elements that get clicks online are:

"How to..."

"The Secret of..."

"5 Powerful Ways to..."

"The Top 10 Best Cures for..."

Here are some examples of complete titles that get clicks:

"7 Ways to Cure Gout Fast!"

"The Secret to Getting Your Ex Back! Guaranteed!"

"The Top 10 Songs of 2011"

"Warning! Could Your Tap Water Be Deadly?"

"3 Dirty Psychological Tricks to Date Any Girl"

"5 Ways Your Cable Company is Scamming You!"

To fully understand the art of writing titles for the web that get clicks, I recommend going to Copyblogger.com
http://www.copyblogger.com/.
 You can get it by going to this UR by entering it into your browser.
http://www.copyblogger.com/magnetic-headlines/
to view a page that deals specifically with this topic.

You actually can add an SEO-friendly title to a page by using All in One SEO. Just make the main title field at the top navigation friendly, and then enter a keyword and SEO-friendly title in the All in One SEO box below the text field.

Also, you may have heard something about "H1" tags and things like that. On WordPress your post/page title counts as the H1 tag. If you want you can also add an H2 or H3 tag in your post, but this is not necessary and won't have that big of an impact on SEO.

Keyword Density and Placement

Years ago it used to be that the more keywords you had in your posts, the better, and this led to what was known as "keyword stuffing." These days, keeping your keyword density at around 1% to 4% is fine in most cases. In fact, if your density for a keyword is too high, Google will actually penalize you for that.

In addition to density, you also need to have your keyword in certain areas of your post. The most important is the first sentence. This is because the first sentence or two is going to be used in the description of your post when it appears in Google and other search engines, causing them to place more emphasis on this area.

Some people also claim that it helps to have your keyword bolded as well, and it certainly doesn't hurt, especially if you are including it in an H2 or H3 tag. Italicizing your keyword can help too. Just make sure you're not overdoing it with the formatting, because you don't want your post to look ridiculous with tons of bolded, italicized, underlined, and highlighted words.

While each post should center around one main keyword, you should also sprinkle in several related keywords. This is known as LSI and is used by Google search algorithms. For example, if the main keyword for your post is "dog walking" you

could add in words like "dog training," "dog breeds," "dog collars," "leashes," "obedience," and more. Generally speaking, these related keywords should happen naturally as you write your content.

Picture SEO

Using the WordPress Media options, you can give your pictures titles, captions, and descriptions, as we discussed earlier. If you're going to add pictures, take the time to make sure you're doing this for each of them, as the search engine crawlers do check images in addition to text, after all. This also gives them a better chance of showing up in places like Google Images, which can lead to additional traffic.

As mentioned before, the SEO Friendly Images plugin can help boost your picture's impact on your website's SEO.

Related Posts

Using the WordPress Related Posts plugin, you can have each post link to several other related posts. The links will be listed down at the bottom, and this is great for both SEO and internal linking structure. Additionally, it also encourages your visitors to visit additional areas of your site and spend more time on your site, two important factors for beating Panda.

Tags

Tags are simply a way of helping search engine crawlers to identify what your site is about and rank it accordingly. Keywords related to your site are the best tags to use, of course.

When you create a post, add tags but don't overdo it. Also don't forget to use All in One SEO to add keyword tags.

Chapter 20: Getting Comments

If your website is set up like a blog, or another content-heavy type of site, you want to encourage user participation as much as possible. The more visitors that interact on your site the better, and one of the main ways to get people involved is by allowing them to leave comments on your posts.

The thing is, in many cases people may not care enough to leave comments on your posts, regardless of how well written they are. Statistically speaking, 90% of viewers are "lurkers" and don't participate at all. Only 9% will occasionally comment, and only about 1% of visitors will actually comment on a regular basis. Here are some techniques you can use to encourage people to post comments on your site.

Tell Visitors to Leave Comments

The most straightforward method of getting people to comment on your posts is to simply tell them to. Most people don't want to bother thinking for themselves, and if you actively tell people to comment on your posts you'll increase the number of people who do in most cases.

Giving Visitors an Incentive

Sometimes to get people to comment you have to give them a bit of an incentive. Try having a contest in which the person who leaves the most unique, helpful, or insightful comment gets a free gift or something special. It could be a free mini report, a free copy of an eBook you have, or maybe a small gift certificate if your site is an online store or Amazon affiliate site.

Another method of rewarding people who comment is praising them. You can do this simply by leaving a comment of your own and telling someone that you enjoyed their comment, or by quoting their comment in another post. If you really want to go the extra mile, you can even email the person and let them know how much you enjoyed their comment.

Don't Make Visitors Log In to Comment

People online don't like to jump through hoops to do something, and that applies to leaving comments as well. Most visitors will not even register, let alone comment on

your site, if you expect them to do this. Make sure you keep your comments section as easy to use as possible so that it appeals to a wider range of people.

Mind Your Behavior

Something that can turn off lurkers and keep them from leaving a comment is the fear of being called out by you publicly. Never lash out at your commenters or visitors, and always appear humble and friendly. If people think that there is a possibility of your going ballistic on them for leaving a comment, fewer people will comment.

In the event that a commenter calls you out on something or flames you, don't retaliate. If you made a mistake own up to it, and if you didn't simply ignore the flamer or block them. Also be aware of people who may try to troll you in the comments, which is to say, intentionally provoke you. It can be hard to spot a troll at times, but if you think someone is trying to make you mad on purpose don't fall for their tricks.

Good Moderation

If you want people to comment on your posts, make sure that your comments section is kept clean and civil. While there is nothing wrong with people expressing alternate opinions, it can get out of hand if people start flaming one another and being rude in general. Keeping your comments section under control will encourage more people to participate.

Ask Questions

Another great way to get people to comment is to ask readers a question at the end of your post and direct them to leave their answers in the comments section below. This almost always works to help you get more comments because people like to appear knowledgeable.

Interact with Your Visitors

You can comment on your own posts, and this is a great way to interact with your readers and converse with them. This will also signal to lurkers that you are willing to respond to comments and answer any questions they may have. Try to make sure you respond to at least one comment per post you make.

Start a Forum

If you notice that your site is getting a ton of activity in the comments sections on your posts, you may want to consider creating a forum so that your readers will have a more organized area where they can chat with one another and interact with you personally.

There are several plugins that allow you to create a forum on your WordPress site, with WP-Forum Server being one of the most popular http://wordpress.org/extend/plugins/forum-server/.
Other popular choices are bbPress http://bbpress.org/ and Simple:Press http://simple-press.com/.

Chapter 21: User Experience

When you create content for your website you want to focus on creating a positive user experience for all of your visitors regardless of what kind of site you're building. First and foremost your content needs to be useful and provide value to your visitors. Not only will this encourage repeat visits, but it will also make your site look good in the eyes of Google and other search engines.

Every time you create a post or page make sure you ask yourself: Is this useful to the visitor? You want to provide as much value as possible but without "giving away the store" if you are selling something. There are different strategies for this for different models of monetization, and we'll get into that in a bit.

Zemanta

One way of enhancing your content is by using the plugin Zemanta that we went over earlier. This plugin is interesting because it installs into your web browser but functions in your WordPress control panel when you create a post or page.

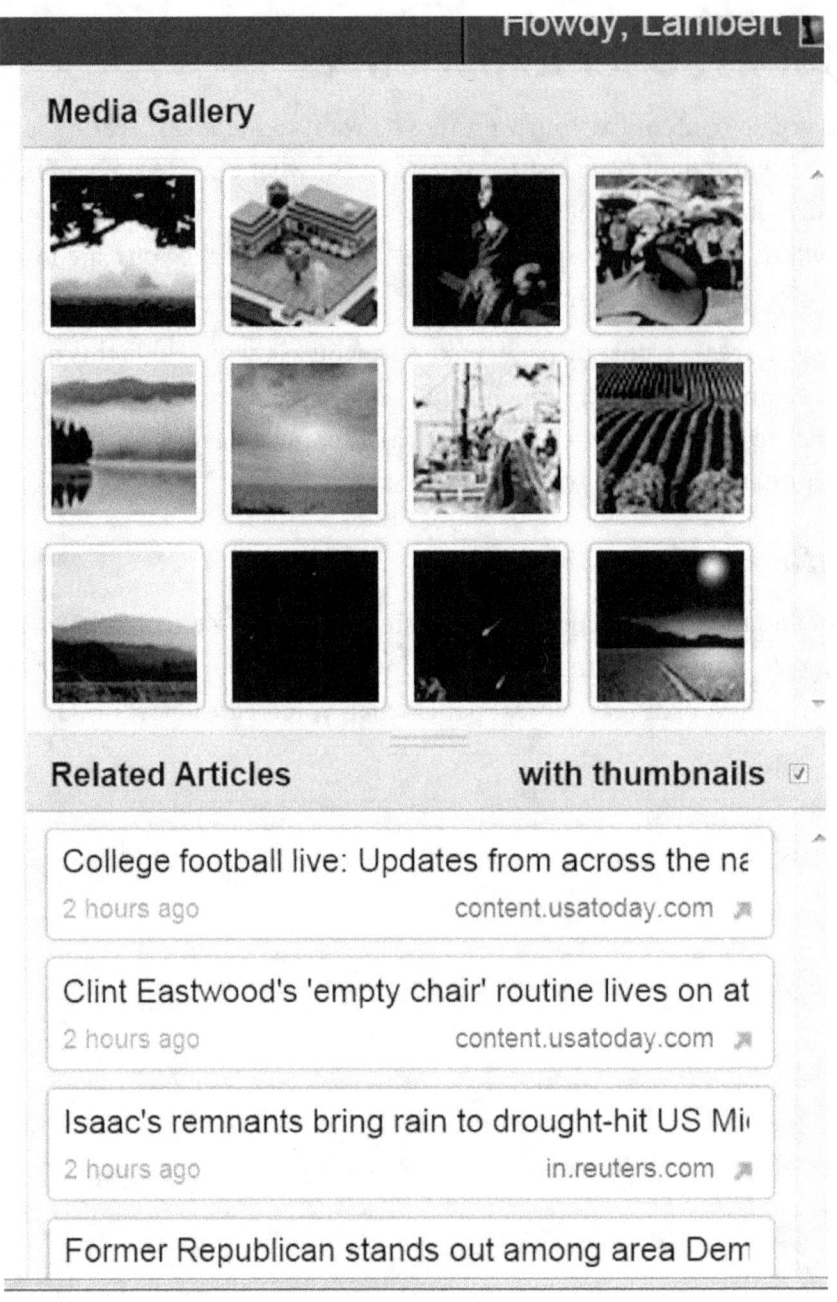

Zemanta is basically a content suggester, or rather, it suggests additional content to supplement what you've already written. For example, if you write a post on dog training, Zemanta will suggest pictures, related articles, and keywords that are related to dog training. It even allows you to turn certain keywords in your post into links to

external content sources. If you're focusing on keeping visitors on your site, you may want to skip that option, but if you do use it you should ensure that the link opens in a new tab or window so that visitors don't navigate away from your site.

Videos

Another great way to enhance the user experience on your site is to add videos. Not only does this provide useful information and/or entertainment to your visitors, it also keeps them on the site longer, which is another key factor to beating Panda.

To upload a video, simply click the Add Media button we talked about earlier and select the file you want to upload. Once it has loaded you will have the option of entering a title, caption, and descriptions, all of which you should do for SEO purposes. Keep in mind that the video will be inserted as a link that opens the video on another page, not as an actual video on your post.

Thankfully there are plugins that allow you to post actual videos in your posts and pages. One of the most popular is called Secure HTML5 Video Player. This can be found using the WordPress plugin search function or by going to this UR by entering it into your browser. http://wordpress.org/extend/plugins/videojs-html5-video-player-for-wordpress/.

Once the plugin is installed you can use it by inserting some code into your posts. The first step is to upload a video into your WordPress media library like we just discussed. You will also need to upload an image to use as the cover image for the video. Taking and saving a screen cap of the video is a good way to do this, just make sure the dimensions are set to around the same values that you'll be using when you post the video or else the image will be skewed.

Once you have the video and image ready to go, copy their URLs into WordPad or another document, because you will need them later.

Edit Image		
Title	*	Penguins
Alternate Text		
		Alt text for the image, e.g. "The Mona Lisa"
Caption		
Description		
Link URL		http://www.lambertklein.com/blog/wp-content/uploads/2012/09/Penguins.jpg
		(None) (File URL) (Attachment Post URL)
		Enter a link URL or click above for presets.
Alignment		None • Left ○ Center ○ Right

Now that you have everything ready, paste this code into your post where you want the video to go. You can paste it in the Visual or HTML section of the text editor, as either one is fine. The parts that say "video domain name" and "image domain name" are where you enter your video and image information.

[video mp4="video domain name" poster="image domain name" preload="yes" autoplay="no" loop="no" width="640" height="264"]

You may have to alter the width and height to fit the dimensions of your blog. There are also other bits of code and ways of creating this code that can be found in the HTML5 Video Player configuration section, which can be found under the Settings tab in the WordPress main menu.

Embedding YouTube videos in your site is a bit easier. Simply go to YouTube, find the video you want, and click on "Share." A new menu will open. Now click on "Embedded" and you will get an HTML code. Take this code and enter it in the HTML view of the text editor in the post or page where you want the video to appear. You can edit the height and width if you need to as well.

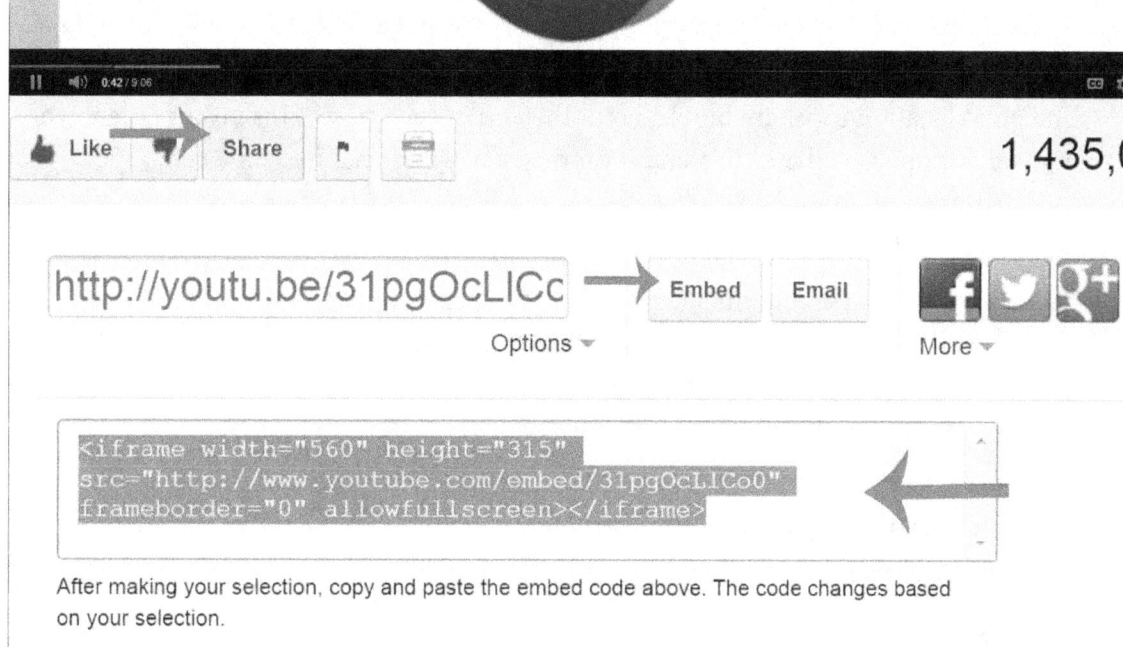

After making your selection, copy and paste the embed code above. The code changes based on your selection.

FAQ and Help Pages

We've already talked about Privacy Policy, Terms of Service, and About pages, but there are other pages you can add to create a more positive user experience. If you find you're getting a lot of questions that cover the same topics, you can create a FAQ page to help explain things to your visitors.

If your site is complex and has a lot of ways for users to interact with it, you may need to create a Help Page. A Help Page will have a list of links to information on a variety of topics that users may have trouble with. This is typically only necessary if your site is highly technical in regards to user interaction.

Social Media Links

Regardless of what kind of site you are creating, you're probably going to want to include social media links. These links allow visitors to share your content with others by clicking Facebook, Google +1, Twitter, and other buttons that you install on your site.

One plugin that we talked about that helps you do this is Slick Social Share Buttons. There are other plugins that provide a similar function, of course, and ultimately it

doesn't really matter which one you use, so long as you get the share buttons on your site in a conspicuous, easy-to-see location.

One great location for share buttons is at the end of each post. This gives readers who enjoyed your post a chance to share it on their favorite social networks.

Opt-in Form

If you are going to be building an email list as a form, or just to keep in touch with your viewers, you need an opt-in form and autoresponder. Popular choices include Aweber, Mail Chimp, and Imnica Mail. Because this is a form of monetization, we'll get into it a bit more later.

http://www.aweber.com/
http://www.mailchimp.com/
http://www.imnicamail.com/

Day 5 Recap

This is what we went over today:

- How to create a post
- How the text editor works
- How to add images and videos to posts/pages
- Proper SEO for posts and pages
- The importance of copywriting for post titles
- The proper way to format your posts for an Internet audience
- What Zemanta does
- How to get visitors to leave comments
- A few key ways to enhance the visitor experience on your site

Today was pretty basic. Content creation isn't hard at all, and there isn't much to adding video and images to your posts either. The most important thing we discussed today was how to properly format your content and how to write compelling titles.

We also briefly touched on the topic of user experience. This is very important, especially when it comes to beating Google's Panda update. I'll get more into that later when I go over how to not only beat Panda, but how to make it work in your favor.

Day 6: Monetization and Traffic

Most of you reading this guide are probably thinking of monetizing your WordPress site somehow, even if you are just creating a blog. While there are many different ways to monetize your website, they are functionally useless if you don't have traffic.

At this point not only should you have a fully functional WordPress site, but you should also have a good idea of how to create compelling, user-friendly content. All that's left now is to monetize your site and drive traffic to it, and you're in business. Today we'll be going over exactly how to do that.

Chapter 22: Monetization

Monetizing your website can be a great way to not only earn passive, or nearly passive, income but to also drastically increase your site's value. You can keep the site forever as a money maker or sell it off for a big pay day. Generally speaking, the more money your site makes, the more you can sell it for.

There are several ways to monetize your site, and the layout, theme, and overall design of your site will be greatly dependent on which methods you are using. Don't forget that you can mix and match monetization methods and aren't obligated to stick with just one.

Google AdSense

AdSense is a program you join that allows you to post AdSense ads on your website. When visitors click these ads, you receive a commission. The commission you receive depends on the ad, but most get you anywhere between $0.10 and $0.50 on average. As you can tell this isn't a lot, so you're going to have to make up for this by getting a ton of people to click those ads.

AdSense sites are primarily content oriented. For example, you could create a site on the different types of cat litter boxes and provide articles and blog posts related to that. AdSense will detect that your site is about litter boxes, if you've done proper SEO like we've talked about, and post ads related to litter boxes and cats in general.

When you create an AdSense site there are several factors you need to take into consideration to be successful. You need to make the site about something that is very specific and preferably something people would be willing to spend money on. Your ad placement also needs to be top-notch, because setting up your ads in the right places will lead to higher conversion rates. There are themes that are specifically designed for this, and we'll discuss those later.

Another thing you have to understand about AdSense sites is the way the content should be written. Because your goal is to get your visitors to click your ads, you don't want your content to be quite as interesting or easy to read as you would on a normal website. While your content should still be useful, don't bother with bolded subheadings, bullet points, or anything else that can possibly distract from the ads. In

fact, longer, blockier paragraphs can actually work to your advantage in this situation so long as you don't cross the line and have massive blocks of text.

Ad Rental

Another method of generating money using ads is offering to rent ad space on your site. If you're getting a lot of traffic, people will come to you and ask to do this most of the time. If not place a banner or page on your site's home page that mentions your ad rental.

When you have an ad rental program you can go about charging your clients in several different ways. You can have a system set up in which they are charged a set price, or you can have potential clients make you an offer. Either way is viable. Typically payment will be set up on a recurring basis. In some cases you may want to offer longer subscriptions at a discounted rate, such as a 1-year subscription at 30% off, so you can get more money up front.

To be successful with this method of monetization, you have to understand the value of your site's traffic. By checking out your analytics you can determine which pages get the most traffic and therefore which pages are worth the most to clients. You should charge more for premium ad space like this while charging less for ad space that isn't as hot. You can also use your analytics data to help advertise your ad rental program by showing potential clients exactly how much traffic they can expect.

Two areas where you should always charge a high amount for ad space are your header/top feature and your sidebar. This is because ads in your header/top feature and in your sidebar will show up on every single page. This makes them extremely valuable.

The best thing about an ad rental program is that it can be combined with practically any other monetization method. Pretty much the only time it's ill-advised is if you are trying to make sure there are no traffic leaks in the event that you're selling affiliate products or your own products. For example, if you're selling an eBook on how to cure gout and a client wants you to put an ad on your site advertising a free report on how to cure gout, that would be an obvious traffic leak and conflict of interest that you would want to avoid.

Affiliate Sites

An affiliate site is one dedicated to selling products as part of an affiliate program. This can take many different forms, such as Amazon reviews sites, single-page sales letter-style websites, and blogs that offer tips and information on things related to the products, then link to the products in a resource box at the end.

While affiliate sites can be very profitable, there are some things to consider. First of all, you need to make sure you're joining a good affiliate program that pays you a reliable and decent commission. Second, you need to make sure that the content on your site is very highly focused and leads visitors to the logical conclusion of buying the products you're promoting. For example, if you have a site that sells throwback football jerseys, you need to make the content on your site about throwback football jerseys, not just football in general.

The last thing to remember about affiliate sites is that your content should focus on a presell, not a hard sell. This is because in most cases you will be linking to a sales page of some sort created by the owner of the products, so leave the selling to them. Your job is to just get your visitors to click through and go to the sales page.

Getting visitors to click your affiliate links requires the use of strong calls to action. You should be using deliberate phrases such as "Click Here for More Info on How to Cure Your Gout Today!" Also be sure to include a healthy dose of hype, big promises, and generally just give them a huge incentive to click your links. You can also use the element of scarcity by mentioning limited time offers and the element of curiosity by saying something like "Click Here to see the Unlikely Cure for Gout that Revolutionized the Medical World!"

Remember, with an affiliate site, the quality of your site is, is only half the battle. If the owner of the affiliate program has a terrible sales page that doesn't convert, it doesn't matter how good your site is. Scout your affiliate program's landing page and sales pages to make sure they're not amateurish garbage before joining an affiliate program.

Selling Your Own Products

Selling your own products is a great business model for a WordPress site. The only catch is that unlike an affiliate site where you simply direct visitors to an affiliate offer,

you actually have to create the products yourself. These products can be eBooks, videos, MP3s, and more.

While you will have to work harder to promote your products, the major advantage here is that each product you create becomes an asset that you own for the rest of your life. This opens up a ton of new possibilities and allows you to use your products in a variety of ways, such as selling them in online bookstores, breaking them up and giving them away as part of a membership site, or giving a mini product away to get people to join a mailing list.

Out of all the ways to monetize your website, this is perhaps the most versatile and can be combined with other monetization methods very easily. The only downside is that it definitely takes more work.

Email Marketing

Regardless of what kind of monetization method you're using on your site, you should also incorporate list building. For example, if you have an AdSense site and you put an email signup form on it, people who click your ad will only be worth between $0.10 and $0.50, while people who sign up to your list can be marketed to over and over again with larger-paying offers.

To build a list you need an autoresponder, which is a piece of software that helps you organize your list, send out timed messages, and create opt-in forms. As mentioned before, popular autoresponders include Aweber, Mail Chimp, and Imnica Mail. Some autoresponders are free while you have to pay for others.

Another important thing to remember is that a list of buyers is worth much more than a list of freebie seekers. While it is acceptable to get people onto a list by offering them a freebie, you want to follow up with a paid offer as soon as possible. Those that accept the paid offer should then be moved onto a separate list, your buyers list. You can then present paid offers to your buyers list more frequently and get a better response.

Also keep in mind that some autoresponders can be configured so that when someone buys a product of yours they are automatically signed up to your list. This is a great way to build a list of buyers right off the bat.

If your site focuses on list building exclusively, you are going to want what is known as a squeeze page. A squeeze page is a website layout that is configured for nothing more

than getting people to sign up to your list. A typical squeeze page consists of an opt-in form and maybe a short blurb as to why someone should sign up. Sometimes a video is used instead of text. In any case, you need to make your offer extremely compelling and straight to the point.

Regardless of how you set up your site, you need to always have your opt-in form above the fold, because many visitors don't bother to scroll down. Your opt-in form should also preferably be in the header/top, or in the sidebar so that it appears on every page. Not every visitor to your site will hit the home page first, after all.

Service Arbitrage

This is an incredibly clever way to monetize your site. This consists of finding a good service online that is sold for relatively cheap, such as website building, content writing, or something of that nature. What you then do is configure your site to center around this service and advertise it. When people place their orders with you, you get the other service to actually do the work for you.

Here is an example of how this works.

Let's say you find a web design service that builds WordPress sites for $40 a site. You can then make your website advertising WordPress site construction for $80. When people place their orders you get the other service to do this and make a $40 profit.

You can even take this one step further by combining multiple services into one. For example, let's say you build a site offering total web development services. You can outsource the site construction, content creation, SEO, and other tasks to individual services that do these things and make a profit off of each transaction.

The main thing to watch out for here is making sure that the services you're getting to do the work for you are quality services that are reliable. For example, while many people on Fiverr do offer quality work, they sometimes disappear without warning. If this happens you need to be able to replace these people as quickly as possible. Also, as a rule it pays to hire each service beforehand in order to get a firsthand look at the kind of work they do, how long it takes them to do it, and their customer service skills.

Testing

There are many ways to monetize your website and there is no "best" way to do it. Additionally many of these methods can be combined with one another. To get the most out of your site it can be a good idea to test different methods and different combinations of methods to see which ones bring in the greatest amount of revenue.

For example, once you have a decent amount of traffic, you can promote affiliate products on your site one week then promote a pure AdSense site the next. Changing the monetization methods on your site does take a bit of work but isn't terribly time consuming. In the end it can be worth it to figure out which methods work the best for your niche and marketing style.

Residual Income

Something you always want to be focusing on with your monetization is residual income. Setting up your site and the monetization method so that it puts money into your bank account with as little effort as possible is key to building your business, because it frees up more of your time so that you can concentrate on expansion.

For example, if you can get your WordPress site to pay a portion of your monthly bills, you can cut back on your work schedule and focus on building more sites or exploring other business opportunities. Once you reach a certain level of residual income you'll even be able to begin pumping that money back into your business and be able to hire virtual assistants to handle most of the day-to-day tasks associated with maintaining and building your websites.

The key to bringing in a substantial residual income is optimization and outsourcing. On every site you build you want to streamline your monetization method so that you're bringing in the maximum amount of money for a minimum amount of time spent working on the site. This is especially important when hiring people to build and maintain your websites, because it will increase their productivity, ensuring that you're getting more for the money you're spending on hiring them. In the end, you want to get things to where you are personally doing as little work in your online business as possible.

Your Site Is an Asset

When you create a website, that website becomes an asset. How much your site is worth depends on two main factors: how much money it earns and how much traffic it gets. Obviously the amount of money it earns is the more important of these two factors and will have the greater impact on how much you can sell your site for.

Another thing to consider is that when you're building multiple sites your revenue tends to fall under the Pareto Principle, which says that 20% of your assets will earn you 80% of your income. This basically means that most of your sites will be underachievers while a select few will be superstars.

To make the most of the Pareto Principle, you should be building up and expanding upon your sites that do well and selling off your sites that underperform. While you may not get much for an underperforming site, you can still make some money by selling it on Flippa, which is preferable to hanging onto the site and paying its yearly domain fees in many cases.

Flippa is the world's most popular place for selling and buying websites. Generally speaking, you can sell a site on Flippa for 6 to 12 times what your site makes in a month. Obviously the longer the site has been around, and the more consistent the income steam has been, the more people will be willing to pay for it. This is a great way to unload unwanted sites or even get a huge payday by selling one of your superstar sites.

Just remember, on Flippa you should be using Escrow for all transactions over $1,000. There are scammers out there who will try to rip you off through PayPal by doing charge backs. Don't let this happen to you, and play it safe with all large transactions.

Chapter 23: Generating Traffic

All the monetization in the world isn't going to do your site any good if you can't drive traffic to it. The simple fact of the matter is that traffic = money. How much money is of course decided by how well optimized your site is and how targeted the traffic you're sending is to your monetization method.

Identifying Your Target Audience

This is something you should do before you attempt to direct any traffic to your site. Having a ton of traffic is practically useless if it's cold and untargeted. You want traffic that is highly targeted and preferably consisting of buyers, if you're selling products or a service.

Identifying your target audience isn't hard and consists of having an in-depth understanding of your niche. For example, if you are in the "cure snoring" niche you should do some research to determine who is most affected by snoring problems. Is it white males aged 20 to 30? Hispanic females aged 35 to 50? These questions and more need to be answered. Dig down deep and get specific data that will help you develop a mental image of the perfect customer for your offers.

Targeted Traffic

Once you understand who your target audience is, you need to figure out where they hang out online and how to get links to your website in front of them. A good example of this is Facebook. The Facebook crowd tends to be of the younger generation, so if the offers you have on your site appeal to this audience you could post ads on Facebook using their ad program. Alternately you could also create a fan page specifically to promote your website. For example, if you're going with the "stop snoring" niche you could make a page centered around that.

The key to getting targeted traffic is to make your traffic generation methods as specific as possible. If the offers on your website relate to the Chicago Bulls, don't target basketball fans in general, target Bulls fans. The principles of attracting targeted traffic should be applied regardless of what traffic generation method you're using. Getting 10 targeted visitors to go to your site is more valuable than getting 50 untargeted visitors.

Google AdWords

AdWords is a system of paid advertising offered by Google that displays your ads on the right side of the page when someone does a Google search. They have some strict regulations, but if you're willing to play by the rules you can generate a lot of targeted traffic very quickly. This can lead to huge payoffs in a relatively short amount of time.

The only downside to AdWords is the fact that it's a PPC (pay-per-click) system that charges you for every person who clicks on your ads. This can add up very quickly, and if your site isn't converting you can expect to lose a lot of money very fast. This makes in-depth testing and understanding of the AdWords system important if you want to be successful.

Facebook and More

AdWords isn't the only PPC system out there. Facebook and other sites have paid advertising programs that allow you to display ads as well. This can be incredibly effective if you have a good understanding of what kind of traffic a website is getting. For example, if your website is selling cat products and you discover another site that is all about cats, posting an ad on that site can be beneficial if it's getting decent traffic.

Many sites out there that get good traffic don't have official ad programs, but you can rent advertising space if you ask them. When negotiating, try to get them to present you with a price first so that you will be in a better position to haggle it down.

The #1 rule of using these methods of traffic generation is testing. If an ad isn't working, pull it, recreate it, and try again. If you just can't generate traffic from a particular site no matter what ad you use, stop advertising on that site, because there is no need to waste your money on it.

Paid Traffic Services

There are many services on the Internet that will send you traffic for a price. These services use a wide variety of different methods to send traffic to your website and most are pretty reliable.

The thing to keep in mind, though, is the fact that not all of these services send targeted traffic. In many cases, services such as these can send you thousands upon

thousands of visitors in a short amount of time, but if the traffic isn't targeted it's not going to be worth your investment.

Do your research and make sure that the company you're going to be doing business with is reputable and does a good job of sending targeted traffic. Ask around and see if you can find people willing to refer or recommend a paid traffic service that they've had good experiences with.

Google Traffic

Traffic from search engines such as Google is known as organic traffic. The key to getting organic traffic is to rank high for your keywords, and that way when someone does a search for those keywords, your site is the first one to pop up in the search results, or is at least on the first page.

To rank high in Google and other search engines, the SEO on your website is very important, as we discussed. However, off-page SEO is going to be even more important.

Off-page SEO consists of backlinks that fall into three major categories: High Authority, Social, and Low Authority, ranked by importance in that order. High Authority links come from sites/web pages with high page authority and high domain authority, which you can check using SEOmoz. Getting links from these sites can be challenging, but you typically only need around five per month to do well.

Social links come from social networking sites such as Facebook, Reddit, and others. These links are very easy to get and you generally only need around 15 per month.

Low Authority links come from article directories, forums, blogs, Web 2.0, and other similar sources. These links are also very easy to get, but for them to count you're going to need around 50 a month.

When it comes to establishing a linking strategy, don't simply have all your links point to the main page of your website. Disperse your links and have them target a variety of pages on your site, with your most popular, high-converting sites taking top priority. It obviously makes sense to post more links to the pages that make you the most money.

All of these links combined will serve to push your website, and its individual pages and posts, up the rankings in Google. It may take a bit of time to see results,

depending on how much competition you have to overcome. Generally speaking, if you see two sites on Google Page 1 for a keyword that have both their domain authority and page authority less than 40, you shouldn't have trouble getting on Page 1 relatively quickly with good SEO.

How targeted search engine traffic is completely depends on your keyword selection. For example, "Buy Samsung Galaxy S2" is extremely targeted (and buyer targeted, which is a plus) while "Samsung Tablets" is significantly less targeted. This isn't to say you can't be successful with fewer targeted keywords, it will just negatively impact your conversion rates, which means you will need more traffic to make a decent amount of money.

Forum Marketing

Forum marketing is, as its name suggests, marketing to forums. The way to do this is to do a few Google searches to find highly targeted forums that have to do with your niche. For example, if your niche is "cat aggression problems" you should look for forums that deal with that or at least have subforums that deal with that topic. Forums that cater to animal or pet lovers in general would do you no good, however, because they would not provide targeted traffic.

One thing you have to remember when doing forum marketing is that most forums do not allow you to blatantly advertise your website and try to sell stuff. Make sure you familiarize yourself with each forum's rules before you begin marketing on them.

Some forums allow you to have a link in your sig to your website, while others allow you to have a link in your profile. When setting these links always make sure you're linking people to your pages/posts that have the highest conversion rates so that you make the most money.

Another rule of thumb when doing forum marketing is to present yourself as an expert in your niche and offer true value to the forum. Try going around and answering people's questions and making useful posts that give tips related to your niche. This will build up your credibility and get more people to click your links and actually buy from you when they get to your site.

Social Networks

One of the great things about social networks such as Facebook, Twitter, and others is that they allow you to both promote your website and create a good number of backlinks at the same time. Every time you create a new post on your website you should also create a post on as many social networking sites as possible. There are services such as OnlyWire (http://onlywire.com/) and plugins that can help make this task a lot simpler.

When creating social network posts, you must make your posts as interesting as possible. Give them good copy written titles, make the descriptions as exciting as possible, and even incorporate images if you feel the need to. Also, don't forget that many of these sites allow you to tag your posts, allowing you to determine what keywords it will come up for in searches on the network.

As with forum marketing, always give top priority to your pages and posts that are converting the best. While spamming is a good way to get banned from a social network, there is nothing wrong with promoting a high-converting page on your site one or two times a week.

Also don't forget that interaction is a huge part of social networks. If someone comments on your post, make sure you respond to them. This will make you look less like a bot and more like a real person. This will build up your credibility and help you to get more clicks in the long run.

Web 2.0

Sites such as Squidoo and HubPages are known as Web 2.0. Sites such as these allow you to create your own pages quickly and easily, and are a great way to reach a larger audience when driving traffic.

The largest benefit of using Web 2.0 is that they already get a lot of love from Google and other search engines. By picking and choosing your keywords wisely, it isn't hard to rank high in the search engine results. Ranking Squidoo posts, HubPages posts, and other Web 2.0 posts, in addition to your own website's pages and posts, can be a great way to really dominate a certain keyword and take over multiple slots on Page 1. This can lead to a sizable increase in traffic.

Also, don't forget that when you create these Web 2.0 pages you need to have very strong calls to action to get visitors to click through to your website, in addition to having a keyword-rich, copy written title. Proper on-page SEO is also a must, and make sure you have at least one call to action above the fold.

The biggest drawback to Web 2.0 is the fact that there are usually ads placed on your page that you have no control over. This can create a traffic leak in many cases. Also the fact that you don't actually have ownership of these Web 2.0 posts and pages that you create prevents them from being true assets.

While Web 2.0 is effective if used correctly, it can be time consuming to create multiple posts using these sites. This is a task that should be outsourced if you can afford it.

Article Marketing

Contrary to many Internet rumors, article marketing isn't dead, it just functions much differently these days. Instead of mass submitting articles to a ton of low-level directories, you should focus on submitting extremely high-quality, highly targeted articles to top-level directories like EzineArticles and others with the intent of getting your articles syndicated.

http://www.ezine.com/

When your article gets syndicated it's published on other websites, allowing you to take advantage of the traffic that the site gets. For example, if you published an article on stopping cat aggression it might get picked up and posted on a site about cats that gets a lot of traffic.

To make the most of this you need to hone your resource box writing skills. Your resource box is a little area at the end of your article that convinces readers to click on links to your website. Making use of copywriting techniques such as scarcity, big promises, curiosity, and very strong calls to action are a must to get a good click-through rate.

While submitting your articles to a lot of different directories isn't as effective as it used to be, it can still help you reach your 50 low authority link quota each month if you're having trouble doing it in other ways. To make this easier on yourself I'd

recommend picking up some software, like <u>ArticleBot</u>, to help with this, or outsource article submission entirely.

http://www.articlebot.org/

Something else that should be said about article marketing is that you don't want your articles on article directories competing with your website's content. To avoid this you should always post content on your site first and make sure it is indexed before posting it to an article directory. Alternately, you can just create fresh content to submit to article directories.

The Traffic Formula

Once you start getting some traffic you can begin to do rough calculations of how much money you're going to be making per month. The formula is as follows:

Search Volume + Conversion Rate + EPA = Income

For example, if you get 100 visitors a day, have a 3% conversion rate, and make $10 per conversion, you'd be making $30 a day. Being able to calculate your income not only gives you an idea of which sites are going to be your superstars, it's also handy for presenting data to potential customers if you decide to sell your site on Flippa.

Chapter 24: Themes & Monetization

While certain themes such as Flexibility and Thesis are good all-around themes, there are actually themes available for specific business models. Here are some popular themes for certain methods of monetization and explanations as to why they work.

AdSense Themes

When creating an AdSense site your primary goal is to get people to click on your ads, of course. One of the key factors to making this happen is ad placement. The simple fact of the matter is that ads placed in certain areas of your site get clicked on more than others. AdSense themes seek to optimize your site by placing ads in these locations to ensure that you're getting as many clicks as possible.

Popular AdSense Themes:

- Heatmap Reloaded
  http://www.top-adsense-themes.com/wordpress-adsense-themes/heatmap-reloaded-adsense-ready-theme/

- Clearness
  http://www.top-adsense-themes.com/Clearness

- Mono Sense
  http://www.top-adsense-themes.com/MonoSense

- Ads Minded
  http://www.sapiensbryan.com/ads-minded-wordpress-theme/index.php/archives/ads-minded-wordpress-theme/

Landing Page Themes

If you're selling your own products you want to make sure you have a good landing page set up that minimizes distractions, focuses attention on the sales copy, and presents a streamlined user experience that guides visitors to the buy button. Good landing page themes are simplistic, straightforward, and designed to support sales copy.

Popular Landing Page Themes:

WP Sales Letter Theme
http://wp-saleslettertheme.com/

Sales Lead
http://thinkdesignblog.com/free-wordpress-theme-saleslead-make-product-sales-pages-fast.htm

Blogging Themes

If you want to make money blogging you need a sleek and modern theme to provide an exceptional user experience to your visitors. This is often referred to as Web 2.0. Because blogs can be monetized in a variety of ways, and often end up incorporating more than one method, you have a lot of options. A good blogging theme presents easy navigation, attractive graphics, and intelligent sidebar setup.

Popular Blogging Themes:

Evolution
http://www.elegantthemes.com/gallery/evolution/

Modernize
http://themeforest.net/item/modernize-flexibility-of-wordpress/1264247

Aware
http://themeforest.net/item/modernize-flexibility-of-wordpress/1264247

Reaction
http://themeforest.net/item/reaction-wp-responsive-rugged-bold/702169

Bloggin Pro
http://www.bloggingpro.com/archives/2007/03/21/blogging-pros-theme-released/

Mimbo
http://www.darrenhoyt.com/2007/08/05/wordpress-magazine-theme-released/

Digital Pop
http://www.writerspace.net/index.php/2007/04/01/digital-pop-wordpress-theme/

Product Review Themes

Selling products from Amazon.com review site, or other online affiliate programs, is always a lot easier when you have a theme designed specifically for that purpose.

These themes make sure that the products take center stage and that ratings, customer reviews, and other important information are easily visible to viewers. In many cases these themes are very image oriented, especially on the main page, allowing visitors to navigate to the products of their choice quickly and easily.

Popular Product Review Themes:

- ProReview Theme
  http://proreviewtheme.com/

- Theme Simple for Amazon Store
  http://wppoint.com/themes/theme-simple-for-amazon-store.html

- WP-Clear
  http://www.solostream.com/wordpress-themes/

- Zenko
  http://www.wpzoom.com/themes/zenko/

- Arras
  http://www.arrastheme.com/

Digital Product/EBook Sales Themes

For sites that specialize in selling digital products, you want a theme that emphasizes the products visually. Relatively large pictures, sidebar images, and a clean design are musts.

Popular Digital Product/EBook Sales Themes:

- eProduct by Templatic
  http://templatic.com/news/eproduct/

- eBook by Templatic
  http://templatic.com/cms-themes/ebook/

- MyProduct theme by ElegantThemes
  http://www.elegantthemes.com/gallery/myproduct/

Directory Website Themes

If your website is a directory, your main emphasis needs to be ease of navigation. Themes that offer muti-variable searches ensure that visitors are able to find what they

need fast and easy. The design should also be clutter free and present information concisely.

Popular Directory Website Themes:

- ⅄ PremiumPress Classified
  http://www.premiumpress.com/classifiedstheme/

- ⅄ eList Elegant Theme
  http://www.elegantthemes.com/blog/theme-releases/new-theme-elist

- ⅄ DirectoryPress
  http://directorypress.net/

Article Directory Themes

The main difference between this type of theme and one for a regular directory is that article directory themes are much more text oriented. This makes a simple design the best because it's easy to drown your visitor in a swamp of text if you're not careful. Themes that allow you to separate many different categories and provide easy navigation are the best.

Popular Article Directory Themes:

- ⅄ Article Directory Theme by Templatic
  http://templatic.com/cms-themes/articledirectory/

- ⅄ Article Directory WordPress Theme by Articlesss
  http://articlesss.com/article-directory-wordpress-theme/

- ⅄ Article Directory WordPress by DailyWP
  http://www.dailywp.com/article-directory-theme/

Magazine/News Themes

These themes provide a healthy balance between text content and image content on the main page. These themes usually separate different posts into blocks and offer thumbnail images to attract attention to each section. In many cases they also have a prominent header on the main page, sometimes in the form of a carousel that rotates different featured posts. A good magazine/news theme presents a balanced view of image and text and makes navigation easy and intuitive.

Popular Magazine/News Themes:

- News Theme by StudioPress
  http://www.studiopress.com/themes/news
- Magazine Theme by StudioPress
  http://www.studiopress.com/themes/magazine
- Bold News by WooThemes
  http://www.woothemes.com/2011/01/boldnews/

Chapter 25: Being an Authority in Your Niche

When you're seeking to monetize a website you want to make sure that you are presenting yourself as an expert in your niche. This is a fundamental aspect of branding, and branding is more often than not what separates the mediocre from the superstars. For example, Nike and McDonald's are considered to be at the top of their industries although (arguably) their products aren't significantly better than their competition.

The reason they're at the top is because they focus on aggressively marketing themselves as the top authorities in their industries. To reach the top you will have to aggressively market yourself as an authority figure in your niche as well. We'll go over some of the factors you need to take into consideration in order to make this happen.

Understanding Your Niche

When you choose a niche, it should either be something you are interested in personally or something you can virtually master in a very short amount of time. To be an authority in your niche you have to be legitimately knowledgeable about it. If you're just faking knowledge and expertise, people will catch on very quickly.

One of the ways to become an authority in a niche that you're new to is to read books by people who are considered experts in the niche. When I say "experts" I mean people who have firsthand experience, if possible. Taking in this firsthand knowledge is the next best thing to having real-life experience with your niche topic.

Remember that speed is the key here. The more complicated your niche, the longer it will take to become an expert. You want something that you can learn the ins and outs of as quickly as possible.

Starting a Blog

If your WordPress site itself isn't going to be a blog, you should consider creating a separate site to function as a blog. It can be another WordPress.org site or simply a WordPress.com or Blogger.com site if you're not actually selling anything on it. Overall I would recommend WordPress.org because you will have more control over the content you post on the site.

The benefit of having a blog is that it helps people get to know you better. It is a well-known fact that people will more readily purchase things from those they know and trust. By giving them an insight into your personal life, people will develop that bond of trust with you, and you can use that to enhance your marketing efforts.

Public Speaking

This is a technique that Timothy Ferriss, author of *The 4-Hour Workweek*, developed that is incredibly effective, if you're willing to come out of your shell a bit. Basically this entails you contacting several nearby universities and offering to give a free 1- to 3-hour seminar about your niche. The more well-known the universities are, the better, and because you're doing it for free, you drastically increase the likelihood of being approved.

Once this is done you now have some notoriety and can use this to enhance your expert status online, but you can also take things one step further. By promoting the fact that you've spoken about your niche at universities, you can convince well-known, big companies such as AT&T, IBM, and others to allow you to give free presentations to them as well. Of course, what companies you contact depends on what your niche is, but the fact that you're offering free presentation and have already done presentations at well-known universities drastically increases your chances of being accepted.

With all these speaking engagements under your belt, you'll have drastically built up your credibility in your niche in a relatively short amount of time. This is one of the fastest techniques for reaching expert status, if you're willing to go through with it.

Join Trade Organizations

If there are trade organizations associated with your niche, you should consider joining a few of them. This will allow you to borrow their authority and make yourself look like more of an expert. In some cases trade organizations will require you to meet certain requirements to be able to join. In other cases you will simply have to pay a membership fee and you'll be accepted.

To find these organization just do a few Google searches and see what turns up. You can also ask others in your niche if they know of any.

Getting the Attention of the Media

Another great way to increase your credibility and establish yourself as an authority in your niche is to get in contact with the media. This can be accomplished in many different ways, but one of the most effective is to create press releases and distribute them via the right channels. Distribution services include PressMethod.com, NewswireToday.com, and many others.

http://www.pressmethod.com/
http://www.newswiretoday.com/index.php
http://socialrealist.com/digital-pr/big-list-of-free-press-release-distribution-sites/

When you write a press release write it with the intent of catching the eye of someone in the media. Make it interesting, and above all else, newsworthy. In most cases if you do get noticed, it will be by someone on a lower-tier media outlet, such as a local radio station, newspaper, or perhaps a local news station. You can then foster connections with these media outlets to work your way up the chain to more prestigious outlets.

In some cases it can be worth it to contact the media directly. This usually works best if you have already done the speaking presentations that we just discussed, because that will give you a boost of credibility. If you're going to do it this way, you have to be prepared to be turned down before you find someone willing to give you the time of day.

NOTE: You can outsource press release writing. Check the Resources section.

Write for a Trade Magazine

If there is a magazine that is closely related to your niche, offer to write an article for them. If they decline you can try offering to interview an expert in that niche instead. The beauty of this is that even if you do just conduct an interview, you will still be listed as a contributor to that magazine and gain credibility.

Make Connections

One of the best ways to ensure that you're viewed as an authority in your niche is to make friends with others that are considered authority figures in your niche. Once again this allows you to borrow the credibility of others and use it for yourself.

The key to doing this successfully is to be able to prove that you have something to bring to the table and show them that you are worth being friends with. If you're a complete newbie in your niche, and have nothing to show for it, most authority figures in your niche probably won't take you seriously. In most cases you should work on getting some experience and credibility under your belt before you try to make these connections. However, there may be situations in which you can convince one of these experts to take you under their wing if you can show that you have potential.

Credibility = Money

In the end, the amount of credibility you have will likely directly impact the amount of money you make. If you become a well-known powerhouse in your niche people will flock to you and practically throw their money into your bank account, as long as you offer them quality products and services. This also makes getting traffic much easier because you will be able to take advantage of word of mouth.

Day 6 Recap

Here is what we went over today.

- The different ways you can monetize your website
- How some monetization methods can be combined
- Why you should always be testing your monetization efforts
- How to find your target audience and why it is important
- Why targeted traffic is important
- Several different methods of driving traffic
- The importance of backlinks
- How to match your theme to your monetization method
- How to become an authority figure in your niche
- Why building your reputation and credibility is important

Some of the things we went over today can be done immediately, such as trying out different themes, while others are going to take time. Building up your credibility, creating backlinks, and finding the best monetization method for your site through

testing aren't things that you can do overnight. These tasks take patience and discipline in order to achieve and see positive results from them.

The real challenge in today's lessons will be not getting discouraged when undertaking the long-term tasks, because it can be easy to get frustrated and give up when you don't see immediate results. What is going to enable you to be successful is your ability to stick with your business model, continue testing, tweaking, and perfecting it, and learning from both your successes and your mistakes.

Remember, there are no failures when it comes to online business, only learning experiences.

Day 7: Analytics

At this point you should not only have a fully functional WordPress site set up with a theme that is conducive to your preferred monetization method, but also an idea of how you are going to drive traffic to your website. Once the traffic starts to flow, it is imperative that you have the capability to analyze that traffic and tweak your website accordingly.

Chapter 26: Installing and Understanding Analytics

Installing Google Analytics

There are a variety of ways to put analytics on your website, but the easiest is going to be to install the Google Analytics. The first step is easy, you head over to www.google.com/analytics and sign up. http://www.google.com/analytics Once you're in your account you'll start by creating a new profile for your website. You do this by clicking on the Admin button then clicking on New Account. You'll then fill out some information, and your new profile will be added.

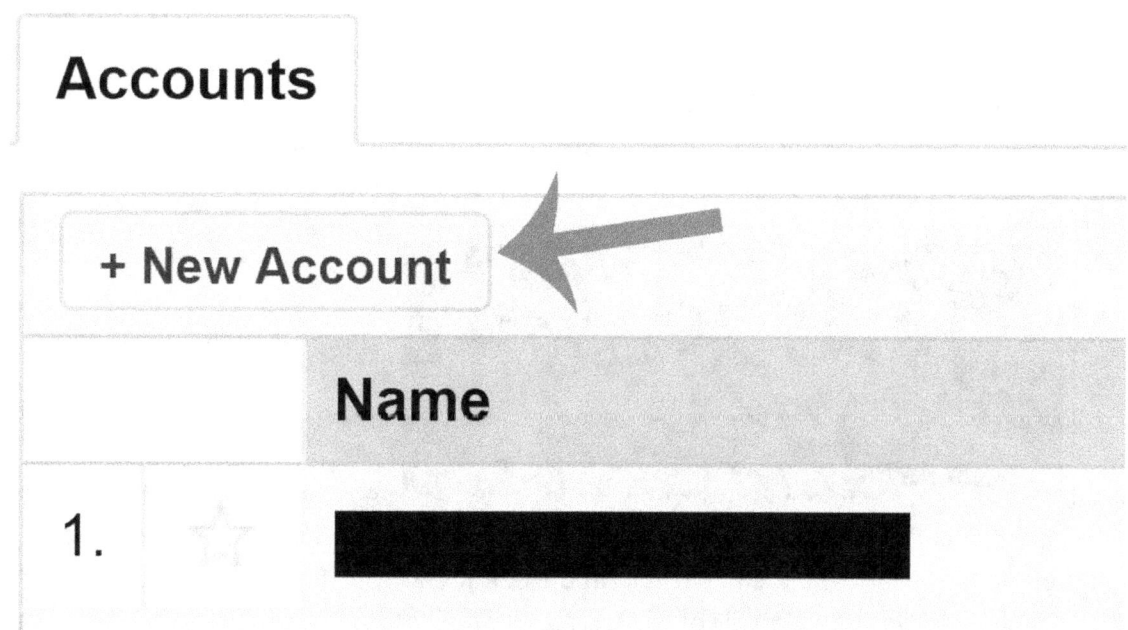

Account Administration

Accounts

+ New Account

Name

1.

Once your account is created click on your username and you will be taken to a screen that shows all of the websites you have added to it. If you want to add another site, click New Property.

Properties	Users	Filters	Data Sources	Account Settings

+ New Property		Show

	Name	↑	Default URL
1.	☆ http://www.1ThinkHealthy.com		http://www.1Think
2.	☆ http://www.coral-cure.com		http://www.coral-c

To get the tracking code you need to click on the website you want to get it for and then click the tab that says "Tracking Code." This will bring up a new page with several things on it. Scroll down and get the code where it says "Paste this code on your site."

Paste this code on your site

Copy the following code, then paste it onto every page you want to track imm
</head> tag. ?

Copy that code and then go into your WordPress account and click on Appearance, then on the "editor" link. Once you're in the editor click on "Footer (footer.php)" which will be on the right side of the screen.

Once you're in this section scroll down in the text box until you see the tag that says
</body> which should be at the very end. Paste in the code just before that tag.

Kindle and PDF Books   7   80   + New

```php
<?php wp_footer(); ?>
<!-- bgwrapper close -->
<?php if (get_option('flex_footer_script')) {
echo stripslashes(get_option
('flex_footer_script')); }?>
</body></html>
```

Once the code is installed you can go back over to Google Analytics to view your stats.
Normally it takes a day or so before the report is generated for your website.

Once you select a website on Google Analytics click on the "Standard Reporting" tab
at the top to get the data from it.

Google Analytics

| http://www.1ThinkHealthy.com - http:... www.1ThinkHealthy.com [DEF... ▾ | Home | Standard Reporting | Cus |

Help   ⊟

Account list › www coral cure com › http://w

221

Chapter 27: Reading Your Stats

When you take a look at your stats page you have to understand how to read your stats and know what they mean. Here is a list of all the stats displayed and what they mean.

Overview

This is a graph tracking visitors to your website. You can select the tabs that say "hourly, week, day, and month" to change how it displays. The graph is an easy way to analyze how much traffic your site is getting overall.

Visits/Unique Visits

This is simply the number of visits your website has gotten, and there can be multiple visits from a single person. Unique visits are visits by different, distinct individuals. The higher this stat is, the better.

Page Views

This stat tracks how many times pages within your site have been viewed in total. The higher this stat is, the better.

Pages/Visit

This is an indicator of how many pages your typical visitor views per visit. The higher this stat is, the better.

Avg. Time on Site

This is a measure of your visitor's time on your site total. The higher this stat is, the better.

Bounce Rate

This is a measure of how many times a visitor lands on one page then clicks off before visiting another page. The lower your bounce rate, the better.

New Visits

This measures the new visitors you get to your site. Obviously the higher this stat is, the better.

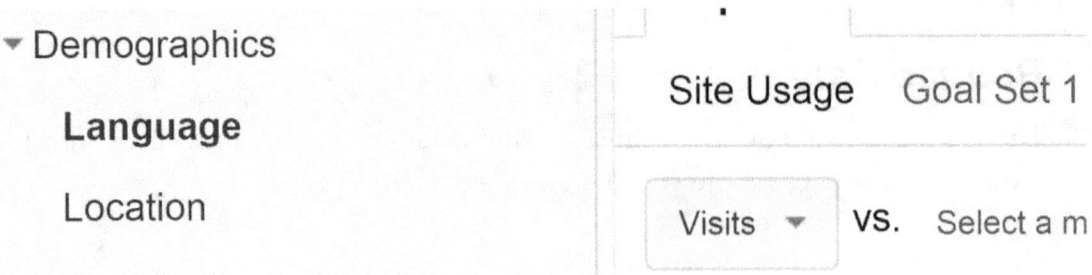

0 people visited this site

Visits: **0**

Unique Visitors: **0**

Pageviews: **0**

Pages / Visit: **0.00**

Demographics

This stat measures where your visitors are coming from and what language they speak. This can be useful if you notice that you have a lot of visitors coming from a particular area and want to focus your marketing efforts on them.

▼ Demographics

Language

Location

Site Usage   Goal Set 1

Visits ▼   VS.   Select a m

Finding New Keywords

Something that upset many website owners late 2011 was the decision of Google to pull the feature from Analytics that monitors what keywords your visitors are using to find your site. This was a great source of new keyword ideas and allowed people to see just what keywords were the most popular for their sites. With this feature now removed, alternate methods have to be used to see which keywords your visitors are using to find your website.

There are several plugins available that are designed to perform this function. Two examples are <u>Whassup Keywords</u> and <u>Hit Sniffer Live Blog Analytics</u>. There are others for you to try out as well, and many are multifunctional.

http://wordpress.org/extend/plugins/wassup-keywords/
http://wordpress.org/extend/plugins/hit-sniffer-blog-stats/

<u>Google Webmaster Tools</u>
<u>http://www.google.com/webmasters/tools</u>
 is another source of this data. This tool allows you to see the top 1000 search keywords that people used to find your site. These stats are only provided for the past 30 days, so you will have to manually record this data if you choose to use this tool to monitor long-term stats.

The reason finding out what keywords are being used to find your site is so important, is because it gives you a valuable insight into which keywords you should target for SEO purposes. You may find popular keywords you've never even thought of before that you can target on your site.

Chapter 28: Beating Panda

Google released their Panda update back in February 2011. This shook things up for a lot of website owners because Panda was designed to rank sites according to new algorithms. These new algorithms are used to ensure that sites providing useful, unique content and a positive user experience are ranked higher than sites that simply follow traditional SEO while offering worthless content. While traditional SEO is still important, there are other factors you must take into consideration now.

There are four main factors you need to concentrate on if you want to not only beat Panda, but use it to your advantage.

Bounce Rate

Panda frowns on a high bounce rate. To overcome this you need to ensure that your bounce rate is **less than 70%**. This means that 3 out of 10 visitors to your site need to visit more than just the page that they land on. There are several ways to encourage this.

The first way is to include a sneeze widget in the sidebar as well as a list of categories and other useful information. You can also include links to related posts in your excerpts on your main page if you have blog posts as your home page. Having these links will get more people to click through to something other than the page they landed on.

Another way to do this is to have a tab or two in the navigation bar that entices people to click on them. This can be a sneeze page such as "Hottest Topics of the Year," a page advertising a super special offer, or something really interesting. The key is to really grab your visitors' attention and get them to click on the navigation tab, then direct them further into the site.

In your posts make sure you have the breadcrumb trail that leads visitors back to the categories section and home page. This way if they land on a post they found in the search engines they can backtrack to these areas. Also make sure that at the bottom of every post you have links to related posts to encourage visitors to click through to those locations as well.

Overall getting a bounce rate of less than 70% isn't hard, but it will take some effort to implement. Just be aware of how important this stat is, and constantly be offering your viewers compelling reasons to explore other areas of your website.

Returning Visitors

This stat should be **kept above 8%**, which again, isn't hard. This is most easily achieved by offering your visitors compelling reasons to visit your site more than once, such as upcoming special offers, new releases, or other interesting events that will happen in the near future.

Another thing you should realize is that if you design a compelling site with unique, interesting information, it will encourage people to come back as well. The truth is, some topics naturally encourage repeat visitors while others don't. For example, if you create a site about the Baltimore Ravens, then Ravens fans will come back again and again as long as you offer them quality information. On the other hand, if you create a site about how to cure snoring and a person is able to purchase the cure in one visit, there is no reason for them to return later.

There are other sites you can create that encourage repeat visitors, such as sites that sell products that need to be replaced often or food items that also need to be bought multiple times. If you can offer your visitors products or a product line that necessitates that they visit multiple times, you should.

A blog can have short blurbs at the end of each blog post that give readers an idea of upcoming posts or special events. Another trick is to break up longer blog posts into multiple parts and have a "click here to read part 2" type link at the end of each post. There are a variety of ways to entice your readers to come back again and again, if you get creative.

Also, having an email list does help to facilitate this as well. You can send out alerts to your list to notify them of special offers on your site and entice many of them to visit repeatedly.

Average Page Views

This is somewhat related to bounce rate. You need to ensure that the average visitor to your site visits **at least two or more pages**. This can be tricky, but if you use the

strategy I talked about earlier of incorporating sneeze page elements as well as captivating reasons to click over to other pages on your site, it isn't that hard.

Another good idea is to have a coupon page or discount page set up in the navigation bar. This will get many visitors to click on it, and once they understand how your discount or coupon system works, they'll then click to another page and use it to make a purchase or at least check out your products/prices.

If your site is a blog, try including teasers at the end of your post that promote other sections of your site. Use the elements of curiosity and big promises to your advantage.

Time on Site

To please Panda you need to ensure that the average visitor spends **at least 1:30** on your website. This may not seem like a lot, but to the practically ADD Internet generation it can be more than you'd think. Fortunately, it isn't that hard to get people to stay on your site longer than a minute and a half if you're offering them compelling content.

The key to this is offering compelling information that keeps the visitor reading. This goes back to providing useful content and a good user experience. Also, if you can continuously prompt your visitors to click links and go deeper into your site, it helps to increase the amount of time they spend on the site. This ties in with both having a low bounce rate and having multiple page views.

Another great way to get people to stay on your site for longer is to include videos in many of your posts. Videos take time to watch and can keep visitors captivated for a decent amount of time. Try including videos as often as possible on your website without overdoing it.

Social Likes

Another factor that is somewhat important to Panda is the amount of social likes you get on your web pages. Social likes are things like Facebook likes, Google +1's and other social points like this. Make sure you're using a plugin to put these buttons on your site or at least have the buttons at the end of every post you make. Optimally you

should have these buttons displayed on every page in the sidebar or header/top feature.

Getting people to click on your social like buttons is best achieved by asking them to click on them. Just politely mention at the end of some of your posts that if the reader enjoyed the post, they should click the like buttons. In some cases you can offer an incentive, such as if a certain post receives a certain amount of likes you will release a free mini product for a limited time to your visitors.

Useful Content and User Experience

As you can tell, Panda is set up to weed out sites that only focus on traditional SEO and don't bother trying to offer a compelling user experience for their visitors. When you're building your site you need to always have your visitors in mind and design things so that they benefit.

Even if your site is an AdSense site, you still need to try and incorporate these factors into your overall design so that the four main statistical requirements are met. This does make it a bit harder to create AdSense sites than it used to be, but ranking high in the search engines will reward you with more traffic, which will in turn help you earn more money.

In the end, there really is no downside to configuring your site so that your visitors get the most enjoyment out of it. They will stay on your site longer, be less likely to "bounce" off of it, and be more likely to hit the various like buttons you have installed. Give your visitors what they want, and they in turn will give you what you want.

Day 7 Recap

What we went over today.

- How to install Google Analytics on your website
- What the different stats on Google Analytics mean
- How to compensate for Google Analytics no longer offering keyword data
- Why it is important to gather data on which keywords visitors are using to find your site

- ∆ The four most important stats for beating Panda and using it to your advantage
- ∆ The importance of social likes
- ∆ The importance of offering useful content and a positive user experience to your visitors

Today was your final day of training. The last step to becoming a true WordPress ninja is being able to read your analytics, understand what they mean, and use that data to optimize your WordPress site on an ongoing basis. These stats will tell you where your strengths and weaknesses lie and what you should be concentrating on to make your website truly excel.

Also of note is that while Panda did have a huge negative impact on many online marketers and bloggers, you should see this as an opportunity. You can now take advantage of a more level playing field and compete more easily against larger websites, as long as you're focusing on offering your visitors useful content and an exceptional user experience.

With the knowledge and tools you now have at your disposal, you can create incredible, and profitable, WordPress websites. All that's left now is for you to take action and make it happen!

Conclusion

This wraps up the *WordPress Domination* guide, and congratulations on making it this far. You now have an excellent set of beginner, intermediate, and advanced WordPress techniques that will allow you to not only build WordPress sites, but also monetize them and drive traffic to them.

The beauty of the WordPress platform is that it's so simple. As you get more experience you should be able to set up complete sites in less than an hour. In fact, some people are capable of doing it in less than half an hour. The point is, you can now create as many sites as you want and begin building a complete online business.

If building multiple sites isn't something that you're interested in, there are other money-making opportunities available to you now, thanks to what you've learned from this guide. Why not take your newfound WordPress mastery and sell a site-building service to others, if building sites for yourself isn't your thing?

As mentioned before, this guide was very specific in some areas while a bit more vague in others, because I can't cover how to set things up for every single hosting company, every single theme, and every single type of site you may want to create. If you ever find yourself stuck, remember that Google and YouTube are your best friends. Also, keep reading for a handy resource section that will be sure to help you with various aspects of WordPress site construction and more.

In the end, WordPress is powerful, but only as powerful as you allow it to be. To truly take advantage of this guide and become a true WordPress ninja, you have to put this knowledge into practice. If you've been following along and doing the lessons as they were taught, good for you! If not, it's never too late to get started and begin mastering the power of WordPress for fun and profit.

Until then, I wish you nothing but success on WordPress and all of your online business ventures!

Your Friend,
Lambert Klein

Resources

Hosting Services

Bluehost
http://www.bluehost.com/

HostGator
http://www.hostgator.com/

iPage
http://www.ipage.com/

Fat Cow
http://www.fatcow.com/

Inmotion Hosting
http://www.inmotionhosting.com/

host monster
http://www.hostmonster.com/

easyCGI
http://www.easycgi.com/

myhosting
http://www.myhosting.com/

Network Solutions
http://www.networksolutions.com/

Autoresponders

Aweber
http://www.aweber.com/

Imnica Mail
http://www.imnicamail.com/

Mail Chimp
http://www.mailchimp.com/

Privacy Policies

freeprivacypolicy.com
http://www.freeprivacypolicy.com/

free generic privacy policy
http://www.inixmedia.com/2010/03/free-privacy-policy-sample-template-for-a-new-website/

FTP

Filezilla   Free
http://filezilla-project.org/

CuteFTP   (This one costs from $25 to $60)
http://www.cuteftp.com/

Press Release Services

List of 50 Free Press Release Services
http://www.avangate.com/company/resources/article/press-release-distribution.htm

Themes

News/Magazine:

News Theme by StudioPress
http://www.studiopress.com/themes/news

Magazine Theme by StudioPress
http://www.studiopress.com/themes/magazine

Bold News by WooThemes
http://www.woothemes.com/2011/01/boldnews/

Article Directory:

Article Directory Theme by Templatic
http://templatic.com/cms-themes/articledirectory/

Article Directory WordPress Theme by Articlesss
http://articlesss.com/article-directory-wordpress-theme/

Article Directory WordPress by DailyWP
http://www.dailywp.com/article-directory-theme/

Directory:

PremiumPress Classified
http://www.premiumpress.com/classifiedstheme/

eList Elegant Theme
http://www.elegantthemes.com/blog/theme-releases/new-theme-elist

DirectoryPress
http://directorypress.net/

EBook/Product:

eProduct by Templatic
http://templatic.com/news/eproduct/

eBook by Templatic
http://templatic.com/cms-themes/ebook/

MyProduct theme by ElegantThemes
http://templatic.com/cms-themes/ebook/

Product Review/Affiliate:

ProReview Theme
http://proreviewtheme.com/

Theme Simple for Amazon Store
http://wppoint.com/themes/theme-simple-for-amazon-store.html

WP-Clear
http://www.solostream.com/wordpress-themes/

Zenko
http://www.wpzoom.com/themes/zenko/

Arras
http://www.arrastheme.com/

Blogging:

Evolution
http://www.elegantthemes.com/gallery/evolution/

Modernize
http://themeforest.net/item/modernize-flexibility-of-wordpress/1264247

Aware
http://themeforest.net/item/

modernize-flexibility-of-wordpress/1264247

Reaction
http://themeforest.net/item/reaction-wp-responsive-rugged-bold/702169

Bloggin Pro
http://www.bloggingpro.com/archives/2007/03/21/blogging-pros-theme-released/

Mimbo
http://www.darrenhoyt.com/2007/08/05/wordpress-magazine-theme-released/

Digital Pop
http://www.writerspace.net/index.php/2007/04/01/digital-pop-wordpress-theme/

Landing Page/Sales Page:

WP Sales Letter Theme
http://wp-saleslettertheme.com/

Sales Lead
http://thinkdesignblog.com/free-wordpress-theme-saleslead-make-product-sales-pages-fast.htm

AdSense:

Heatmap Reloaded
http://www.top-adsense-themes.com/wordpress-adsense-themes/heatmap-reloaded-adsense-ready-theme/

Clearness
http://www.top-adsense-themes.com/Clearness

Mono Sense
http://www.top-adsense-themes.com/MonoSense

Ads Minded
http://www.sapiensbryan.com/ads-minded-wordpress-theme/index.php/archives/ads-minded-wordpress-theme/

Squeeze Page:

Flex Squeeze
http://www.flexsqueeze.com/flexsqueeze/

General:

Flexibility
http://www.flexibilitytheme.com/

Thesis
http://diythemes.com/

Domain Registrars

Go Daddy
http://www.godaddy.com/

Namecheap
http://www.namecheap.com/

Enom.com
http://www.enom.com/

Moniker
http://www.moniker.com/

Reseller Club
http://www.resellerclub.com/products/domain-registration

MelbournIT
http://www.melbourneit.com.au/

Network Solutions
http://www.networksolutions.com/

MyDomain
http://www.mydomain.com/

Plugins

Zemanta
http://www.zemanta.com/

Automatic SEO Links
http://wordpress.org/extend/plugins/automatic-seo-links/

SEO Friendly Images
http://wordpress.org/extend/plugins/seo-image/

SEO Tag Cloud Widget
http://wordpress.org/extend/plugins/seo-tag-cloud/

SEO Title Tag
http://wordpress.org/extend/plugins/seo-title-tag/

Slick Social Share Buttons
http://wordpress.org/extend/plugins/slick-social-share-buttons/

Subscribe to Comments
http://wordpress.org/extend/plugins/subscribe-to-comments/

Personal Favicon
http://wordpress.org/extend/plugins/personal-favicon/

SEO Ranker Report
http://wordpress.org/extend/plugins/seo-rank-reporter/

WP-PageNavi
http://wordpress.org/extend/plugins/wp-pagenavi/

Google Analyticator
http://wordpress.org/extend/plugins/google-analyticator/

Breadcrumb NavXT
http://wordpress.org/extend/plugins/breadcrumb-navxt/

WordPress Related Posts
http://wordpress.org/extend/plugins/wordpress-23-related-posts-plugin/

WP Super Cache
http://wordpress.org/extend/plugins/wp-super-cache/

Google XML Sitemaps
http://wordpress.org/extend/plugins/google-sitemap-generator/

All in One SEO Pack
http://wordpress.org/extend/plugins/all-in-one-seo-pack/

Contact Form 7
http://wordpress.org/extend/plugins/contact-form-7/

Really Simple Captcha
http://wordpress.org/extend/plugins/really-simple-captcha/

Akismet
http://wordpress.org/extend/plugins/akismet/

Hit Sniffer Live Blog Analytics
http://wordpress.org/extend/plugins/hit-sniffer-blog-stats/

Wassup Keywords
http://wordpress.org/extend/plugins/wassup-keywords/

HTML5 Video Player
http://wordpress.org/extend/plugins/secure-html5-video-player/

WP Forum Server
http://wordpress.org/extend/plugins/forum-server/

bbPress
http://bbpress.org/

Simple:Press
http://simple-press.com/

Online Backup for WordPress
http://wordpress.org/extend/plugins/wponlinebackup/

EZPZ One Click Backup
http://wordpress.org/extend/plugins/ezpz-one-click-backup/

WordPress Firewall 2
http://wordpress.org/extend/plugins/wordpress-firewall-2/

cloudsafe365_for_Wordpress
http://www.cloudsafe365.com/how-it-works/

Exclude Pages
http://wordpress.org/extend/plugins/exclude-pages/

PC Hide Pages
http://wordpress.org/extend/plugins/pc-hide-pages/

Tools

Google Webmaster Tools
http://www.google.com/webmasters/tools

Google Analytics
http://www.google.com/analytics

Article Bot
http://www.articlebot.org/

Article Submission Helper
http://www.articlesubmissionhelper.com/

OnlyWire
http://onlywire.com/

Other Social Bookmarking Software
http://www.internetgeeks.org/tech/top-automated-social-bookmarking-software-tools/

SEOmoz
http://www.seomoz.org/seo-toolbar

colorschemedesigner.com
http://www.colorschemedesigner.com/

Article Directorie

s

List of 50 Article Directories
http://www.vretoolbar.com/articles/directories.php

Misc.

Fiverr
http://www.fiverr.com/

Copyblogger
http://www.copyblogger.com/

Tutorial Videos

SQL Database and WP-Config Tutorial
http://www.youtube.com/watch?v=snijbmA0qnY

WordPress Installation on HostGator
http://www.youtube.com/watch?v=3B_k1KqW0Dg

WordPress Installation on Bluehost
http://www.youtube.com/watch?v=uqdWyVpR6HI

Filezilla Tutorial
http://www.youtube.com/watch?v=yr_u2iKfAt0

Registering a Domain Name with Go Daddy
http://www.youtube.com/watch?v=nhtlyNgHPDg

Registering a Domain Name with Name Cheap
http://www.youtube.com/watch?v=JewCEUZrQv8

Installing WordPress

Plugins
http://www.youtube.com/watch?v=BLeAv

BOOK TWO
THE ULTIMATE WORDPRESS THEMES AND PLUGINS GUIDE

60+ Reviews and 190+ total Plugins and Themes!

Introduction

Welcome to the *Ultimate 2013 WordPress Themes and Plugins Guide*! This guide goes over the hottest themes and plugins for 2013. Whether you have a business website, blog, or online store, this guide will come in handy. Choosing the right plugins is incredibly important for your website to reach its full potential. We'll take a look at their pros and cons and show you which ones will enhance your WordPress website, making it easier to use, better looking, and more profitable.

This is an unbiased guide. None of the chosen plugins and themes were selected due to any favoritism on my part, and I'm not being compensated by any software creators to promote them. Each selected plugin and theme was thoroughly researched and deemed to be either one of the best in its particular category or noteworthy for some other reason. I will also go over any negative attributes a plugin or theme might have and recommend alternatives that you may also want to try.

All prices listed in this guide are subject to change. This goes for the star ratings as well. (These aren't my personal rankings; they're taken from the sources where the plugin or theme is available online. All ratings included are on a scale of one to five stars.) This is to give greater insight into the quality of these themes and plugins, since the ratings come from the many people who've downloaded and used the plugins extensively. I do also offer my own opinions, of course.

It should be mentioned that this guide assumes that you already know how to set up WordPress and understand the general idea of what plugins and themes are. If you're completely new to this, go check out my other book, *WordPress Domination*, by typing the following URL into your browser.

`http://www.amazon.com/dp/B007LS0TLE`

It will teach you everything you need to know about web development using WordPress. It is *very* beginner-friendly, but also has neat tips and tricks appropriate for more advanced users as well.

Also, be aware that this guide is intended for use with the WordPress.org website builder. WordPress.com, the free blogging platform, works a bit differently, and the options for it are much more limited.

I'm sure you'll find this guide helpful in getting your site ready for a big year in 2013. Some of the plugins you have come to rely upon might be outdated, or there may be new plugins and themes that do a better job. *The Ultimate 2013 WordPress Themes and Plugins Guide* will uncover all the facts and help make sure you're on the right track to making your website the best it can be.

> Note: The themes and plugins listed in the book may have long URLs to enter. If some of them are too long then there are two other options that you can use.

1. Just search for them on the following sites:

Themes

- ThemeGrade.com
- ThemeForest.net
- NewWPThemes.com
- ElegantThemes.com
- WooThemes.com
- SMThemes.com
- ThemeFuse.com
- TemplateMonster.com
- ThemifyMe.com/themes

Plugins

- CodeCanyon.net
- WordPress.org/extend/plugins
- Yoast.com/WordPress
- StudioPress.com/plugins
- ElegantThemes.com/plugins
2. **Download the PDF version of this book**. This way you can click on the links and will be taken directly to the product of your choice.

This is probably the easiest option. You can download the PDF below.

Just enter the URL below into your browser.

`http://www.lambertklein.com/wppt.pdf`

Before we get started with the meat of the guide, though, let's go over how to install themes and plugins, just to make sure we're all on the same page!

All-Purpose Plugins

The following plugins work well with just about any type of WordPress website. Whether you're building an online store or just want to make a really cool blog, these plugins will help you make your site the best it can be by enhancing various general features. A few of these were spotlighted in my other books, *WordPress Domination* and *WordPress Security* listed below, but we go over a ton more here.

```
http://www.amazon.com/WordPress-Domination-Beginner-
Wordpress-ebook/dp/B007LS0TLE
```

```
http://www.amazon.com/WordPress-Security-Protection-
Crackers-ebook/dp/B007TTSU0W/
```

To visit the download page for each plugin, simply type their URL into your browser. Enjoy!

> **Download the PDF version of this book**. This way you can click on the links and will be taken directly to the product of your choice. **This is probably the easiest option**. You can download the PDF below.
>
> Just enter the URL below into your browser.

```
http://www.lambertklein.com/wppt.pdf
```

W3 Total Cache

Price

Free

Description

W3 Total Cache is a plugin designed to help WordPress sites load faster. It uses a memory-based cache known as memcache. It also does other things, such as offering options for content delivery networks and compressing the file size of your web pages, making them easier to download.

W3 Total Cache

`http://wordpress.org/extend/plugins/w3-total-cache/`

Pros

- One of the fastest caching plugins available
- Compresses your web pages' file sizes for easy download
- Caching options for content delivery networks can help when your web content is posted to social media sites

Cons

- Not all servers are immediately compatible with memcache, which means you may have to go through some additional steps to get it set up
- Advanced options take good knowledge of CSS to use
- Adds a long footnote to your source code that takes some work to remove

Rating

W3 Total Cache is extremely popular and has received a rating of 4.6 out of 5 stars. It has over 2,400 five-star votes.

Conclusion

W3 Total Cache will make your website load super-fast, but it does take some technical know-how to get the most out of it. If you're great with CSS, this could be an amazing plugin for you. If not, you may want something simpler to work with.

Alternate Options

WP-Super Cache

```
http://wordpress.org/extend/plugins/wp-super-cache/
```

— This is a very popular caching plugin that's been around for a while. Not as fast as W3 Total Cache, but still very reliable and easy to use.

Widget Logic

Price

Free

Description

By default, WordPress will normally have your widgets and sidebar options appear on every page. This plugin lets you determine which pages your widgets appear on, giving you greater control over the overall layout of your website.

Widget Logic

`http://wordpress.org/extend/plugins/widget-logic/`

Pros

- Very easy-to-use control field for selecting the pages you want your widgets on

- Has an option for tweaking a widget's HTML

Cons

- The plugin operates through the use of something known as EVAL. Anyone who has the ability to edit widgets on your site can introduce malicious code if they choose.

Rating

Widget Logic currently has a high rating of 4.2 out of 5 stars. It has received over 360 five-star ratings.

Conclusion

Widget Logic lives up to its intent and does a very good job. If you want more control over your widgets, this is a great plugin. The security flaw is a minor issue so long as you're the only one allowed to access your WordPress dashboard.

Alternate Options

<u>Widget Context</u>

```
http://wordpress.org/extend/plugins/widget-context/
```

– While not as popular as Widget Logic, this plugin is actually rated slightly higher, at 4.6 out of 5 stars. Compatibility issues may be an issue with WordPress 3.5 and later.

<u>Sidebar and Widget Manager for WordPress</u>

```
http://codecanyon.net/item/sidebar-widget-manager-
for-wordpress/2287447
```

– This plugin is a bit more advanced than the free ones and has a variety of options, such as the ability to create custom layouts, the ability to drop widgets into page content, variable alignment options, and unlimited custom sidebars. It also requires no coding. It costs $15 for the regular license (for personal websites) and $75 for the extended license (for template creation).

Hint: Go to codecanyon.net and search for this plugin if you rather not type this long URL into your browser. You can do this with other long URLs as well.

WordPress Ajax Contact Form

Price

Regular License - $12

Extended license not currently available.

Description

WordPress Ajax Contact Form is a contact form creation plugin, as its name suggests. Unlike most free variants, this plugin comes with lots of options, including multiple- or single-recipient systems, multiple or single attachments, a script based on open-source framework, a drag-and-drop anti-spam system, reCaptcha integration, and AYAH integration.

WordPress Ajax Contact Form

```
http://codecanyon.net/item/wordpress-ajax-contact-
form-with-attachments/3463740
```

Pros

- Very easy to use
- Easy to customize, since it is based on open-source framework
- Drag-and-drop anti-spam system is very user-friendly
- Extremely flexible overall
- Tons of options and features

Cons

- The many options may seem overwhelming to newbies.

Rating

WordPress Ajax Contact Form currently has a buyer rating of 4 out of 5 stars.

Conclusion

Overall, this is a handy all-in-one contact form creation system. It has practically everything you could ever want wrapped up in one plugin. The only drawback is that if you're new to WordPress or configuring plugins, all those options may seem a bit

overwhelming. Still, for only $12 this is an excellent plugin, though the lack of an extended license may be disappointing if you're a web developer.

Alternate Options

<u>Contact Form 7</u>

`http://wordpress.org/extend/plugins/contact-form-7/`

– Considered one of the top dogs when it comes to contact form creation, Contact Form 7 is very flexible and easy to use. It is currently rated at 4.3 out of 5 stars. The only drawback is that its options are somewhat limited, forcing you to use other plugins such as <u>Flamingo</u>, <u>Really Simple CAPTCHA</u>, and <u>Bogo</u> to get the most out of it. It's still an extremely good contact form creator considering that it's free.

<u>QuForm</u>

`http://codecanyon.net/item/quform-wordpress-form-builder/706149`

– This plugin has gotten a lot of attention lately and currently has a five-star buyer rating. It resembles WordPress Ajax Contact Form in many ways but features an easy-to-use drag-and-drop creation system. It is a bit more expensive at $25 for a regular license (no extended license available, unfortunately), but seems to offer a bit more flexibility than Ajax.

<u>Gravity Forms</u>

`http://www.gravityforms.com/`

– This up-and-coming plugin prides itself on being one of the fastest and easiest to use form plugins available. It also boasts the ability to integrate with several popular web resources, such as PayPal, Aweber, MailChimp, CampaignMonitor, and more. It also has features like a visual form editor, multi-page forms, condition fields and order form capability. On top of all this, Gravity Forms has been pre-optimized to work with several popular theme providers, like Headway Themes, Woo Themes, and Allure Themes.

While slightly lacking the overall capability of QuForm and Ajax, Gravity Forms is still massively popular and currently installed on over half a million WordPress sites.

This is probably due to its compatibility with PayPal and the other themes and properties listed above. It costs $39 for the standard license, which may be worth it if you want something already pre-optimized for a certain theme or to work with Aweber or MailChimp

HTML5 Video Player

Price

Regular License - $20

Extended License not currently available

Description

HTML5 Video Player makes it easy to display videos on your WordPress site without having to rely upon external sources like YouTube. It also allows the creation of a right-side video playlist, or a bottom playlist if you choose. It is the only HTML5 video player currently compatible with Android.

(I want to emphasize that, despite my name, I have no connection to the Lambert Group that created this plugin.)

HTML5 Video Player

`http://codecanyon.net/item/html5-video-player-wordpress-plugin/1613464`

Pros

- Multiple skins to choose from
- Can have a right-side or bottom video play list
- Compatible with both Android and iOS
- Website has a video tutorial to help you get started
- Plays MP4, Ogg video (OGV), and WebM video files
- Multiple adjustable parameters, such as height and width

Cons

- Doesn't support YouTube videos, only HTTP streaming

Rating

HTML5 Video Player currently has a buyer rating of 4 out of 5 stars.

Conclusion

HTML5 Video Player is one of the big boys when it comes to video plugins. Being fully optimized for mobile sets it apart from older models and really gives it an edge. The $20 price is great for what you get, though the lack of an extended license is disappointing.

Alternate Options

Video Player

```
http://codecanyon.net/item/video-player-wordpress-
plugin-youtubeflvh264/719162
```

– This simply named plugin also comes from the Lambert Group. It's a bit scaled down compared to the HTML5 version, but offers a greater range of compatibility, including YouTube, **MP4, M4V, M4A, MOV, MP4v, MP3, and F4V, as well as RTMP compatibility. If you want a player that's more versatile in what type of files it can play, this may be the plugin for you. It is currently rated at 4 out of 5 stars and costs $21.**

VidEmbed

```
http://ithemes.com/purchase/vidembed/
```

– This video player plugin allows you to embed video in a variety of places, even in widgets. Other neat features are the shortcode button for quick and easy embedding, various customizable settings, and a one-year subscription that offers premium support and product updates. It works with multiple file types, including FLV, MP4, and MOV formats, in addition to those hosted on Amazon S3 and YouTube. Even better is the fact that a developer license costs only $20, allowing you to use this plugin on sites built for clients as many times as you wish.

Video Gallery

```
http://codecanyon.net/item/video-gallery-wordpress-
plugin-w-youtube-vimeo-/157782
```

– If you want to put entire video galleries on your WordPress site, this is the plugin for you. Its options may be a bit more limited than other video plugins, but it makes up for it by allowing you to create video galleries that are fully optimized for iOS devices. On top of this, it also has an import/export feature, allowing you to backup your database and keep it safe. The regular license is only $15, and the extended license is $75 — something web developers will love.

All in One Favicon

Price

Free

Description

As you probably know, a favicon is that little symbol that appears on tabs you open in your Internet browser. Having a good favicon is a cool way to make your site stand out to visitors. All in One Favicon allows you to add a favicon of your choice quickly and easily. It supports three file types (ICO, PNG, and GIF) and has been localized for a variety of languages, including Spanish, Dutch, French, German, among others.

All in One Favicon

`http://wordpress.org/extend/plugins/all-in-one-favicon/`

Pros

- Add a favicon to your WordPress site quickly and easily.

Cons

- Has not been updated for WordPress 3.5, although it still functions

Rating

This plugin is rated at 4.7 out of 5 stars.

Conclusion

Nothing fancy here. All in One Favicon does what it claims to do: it adds a favicon to your WordPress site. Though it hasn't been updated for WordPress 3.5, it still works. Also, if you're from a non-English speaking country, you'll appreciate the fact that it has been localized for other languages.

Alternate Options

Personal Favicon

`http://wordpress.org/extend/plugins/personal-favicon/`

– This plugin doesn't differ much from All in One Favicon, and its rating is slightly lower at 4.6 out of 5. It is very basic and easy to use, getting the job done with no fuss.

Calendarize It

Price

Regular License – $25

Extended License – $125

Description

Calendarize It is a calendar program designed to be very flexible and work with a variety of different types of WordPress websites. It has plenty of options, such as support for custom fields for events, support for reoccurring events, an easy point-and-click interface, and support for shortcodes. Perhaps the best element is the fact that you can take advantage of the "try before you buy" feature by visiting their web page.

Calendarize It

```
http://codecanyon.net/item/calendarize-it-for-
wordpress/2568439
```

Pros

- Designed with a very broad target audience in mind
- Very versatile
- A point-and-click system that's easy to use
- Multiple event scheduling options
- Sidebar mini widget calendar option is very convenient

Cons

- Not designed for the needs of any specific industry
- Huge number of options can be overwhelming

Rating

Calendarize It currently has a buyer rating of 4 out of 5 stars.

Conclusion

Calendarize It is one of the most versatile WordPress calendars available. If you need to keep track of events and dates on your WordPress site, you can't really go wrong with this plugin and its massive amount of options. The only noteworthy drawback is that if you need a calendar for a specific industry, there may be something more specialized for you out there.

Alternate Options

WordPress Pro Event Calendar

```
http://codecanyon.net/item/wordpress-pro-event-
calendar/2485867
```

– This sleek and easy-to-use calendar has several notable features: Google Maps support, cross browser support, and a responsive draggable/touchable interface. The regular license is a great deal at $15, while the extended license is $75.

WordPress Events Calendar

```
http://codecanyon.net/item/wordpress-events-
calendar/910386
```

– This calendar's a bit more scaled down than the others, but is a steal at only $10 for the regular license and $50 for the extended. If you just need a good, basic calendar, this is a great choice.

Calendar

```
http://wordpress.org/extend/plugins/calendar/
```

– This free calendar is extremely popular and has had nearly 350,000 downloads. It features a variety of handy options, such as mouse-over functionality, various sidebar/widget options, and full internationalization for a broad appeal worldwide.

FontPress

Price

Regular License – $15

Extended License - $75

Description

One of the main limitations of the WordPress website building format is that it doesn't allow you to change fonts. This plugin takes care of that problem and provides you with the ability to add and use unlimited fonts of your choice. It comes with more than thirty fonts already installed and allows you to edit the color, size, and line height of your text.

FontPress

```
http://codecanyon.net/item/fontpress-font-manager-
plugin/1746759
```

Pros

- 30+ fonts to use from the start
- Can upload unlimited custom fonts
- Can edit font attributes, such as color, shadow, size, and more
- Typography shortcode makes it easy to use; no CSS required
- Website offers video tutorials

Cons

- Nothing notable

Rating

FontPress currently has a buyer rating of 5 out of 5 stars.

Conclusion

There really isn't anything not to love about FontPress. It solves all the font issues of WordPress quickly and easily. It even has tutorials on how to use it, making it extremely newbie friendly.

Alternate Options

Use Any Font

`http://wordpress.org/extend/plugins/use-any-font/`

- This free font plugin has several attractive features. It supports compatibility with all the major browsers and operating systems, including mobile ones like Android and iOS. It also has an easy-to-use setup with no CSS needed. Since it stores the fonts on your server, it doesn't impact load times for visitors. There aren't a lot of good free font plugins out there, but this one is a gem.

After the Deadline

Price

Free

Description

WordPress's default spellchecker isn't the greatest. To pick up the slack, After the Deadline is a great choice. It features a contextual spell checker, advanced style checking, and intelligent grammar checking. In addition to all this, it is available on multiple platforms, allowing you to install it in Chrome, Firefox, and more in addition to WordPress. Best of all: it's free!

After the Deadline

`http://www.afterthedeadline.com/`

Pros

- Accurate spelling and grammar checker that utilizes artificial intelligence
- Contextual spelling check is a must for professional writers
- Available on several platforms
- Tutorials on the website make it very newbie-friendly
- Really good value for a free plugin

Cons

- Developer licensing may be a bit restrictive.

Rating

This plugin is rated at 4.6 out of 5 stars.

Conclusion

This free plugin may not have tons of options or features but it really doesn't need them. It's good at what it does and makes writing directly in the WordPress dashboard much easier. The website tutorials will get you up and running with this incredible plugin fast.

Alternate Options

Pro Writing Aid

`http://wordpress.org/extend/plugins/prowritingaid/`

– This free plugin not only looks for spelling and grammar errors, it also checks for overused words, clichés, and redundancies. It is rated 5 out of 5 stars, but only has one rating at this time and hasn't been optimized for WordPress 3.5 yet.

Google XML Sitemaps

Price

Free

Description

Probably the most popular XML sitemap generator at over 9 million downloads, this old favorite gets the job done quickly and easily. It generates a sitemap that helps the crawlers from Google, Bing, Yahoo!, and others to index your website and pages more easily, which is essential when it comes to getting highly ranked in search engines.

Google XML Sitemaps

```
http://wordpress.org/extend/plugins/google-sitemap-
generator/
```

Pros

- Easy to install and use
- Still considered the best XML sitemap plugin by many
- Works without hassle

Cons

- Nothing significant

Rating

4.6 out of 5 stars, with nearly 3,000 five-star ratings.

Conclusion

After all these years, Google XML Sitemaps is still king of the hill. You really can't go wrong with this one.

Alternate Options

<u>XML Sitemap</u>

```
http://wordpress.org/extend/plugins/xml-sitemap-xml-
sitemapcouk/
```

– This free plugin also provides an XML sitemap for the search engines. It is rated 5 out of 5 stars, but only has one rating at this time. It also provides a shortcode for use on HTML sites if you want. It has not yet been optimized for WordPress 3.5 as of this writing.

P3 (Plugin Performance Profiler)

Price

Free

Description

This is a lesser-known plugin that's nevertheless very useful, especially if you're installing lots of plugins on your WordPress site. P3 checks your plugins and looks for performance issues. If a plugin is slowing down your website, P3 will find it and let you know.

P3 Plugin Performance Profiler

`http://wordpress.org/extend/plugins/p3-profiler/`

Pros

- Helps to optimize your website's load time
- Easy to use

Cons

- Only works with certain browsers (Chrome, Firefox, Safari, Opera, IE9)

Rating

This plugin has a rating of 4.6 out of 5 stars.

Conclusion

This is a very handy plugin to have, especially when you're installing a lot of plugins and don't know if they are slowing down your website or not. Those who don't use mainstream browsers might view the limited variety of support available as a drawback.

Alternate Options Nothing notable

Plugins for Search Engine Optimization (SEO)

Search engine optimization is all about satisfying the search engines, particularly Google, so that you can get your website and its pages ranked highly. A higher ranking means more exposure. To help with this, there are plenty of plugins that enhance the various SEO-related factors of your WordPress site.

WP-PageNavi

Price

Free

Description

Internal linking structure and navigation are a big part of SEO these days, so it pays to make sure you can get things set up the way you want. WP-PageNavi makes it easy to structure your internal navigation and linking. It comes with several options, though many people simply install it and let it do its thing.

WP-PageNavi

```
http://wordpress.org/extend/plugins/wp-pagenavi/
```

Pros

- Very easy to use
- Multiple options to give you complete control over your navigation structure
- Great for SEO

Cons

- Your web host needs to have PHP5 for this to work

Rating

WP-PageNavi has a four-star rating and has been downloaded over 3 million times. It's very popular.

Conclusion

Still considered one of the best navigation plugins around, WP-PageNavi is loved for its simple yet effective design.

Alternate Options

Zamango Page Navigation

```
http://wordpress.org/extend/plugins/zamango-page-
navigation/
```

– This free plugin features a variety of advanced page navigation options and customizability using CSS and HTML. Has a rating of 4.4 out of 5 stars.

GD Pages Navigator

```
http://wordpress.org/extend/plugins/gd-pages-
navigator/
```

– This plugin allows you to edit the hierarchy of the page display as well as a dynamic list of pages, depending on which page is currently displayed. It is also notable that it is configured for both Serbian and English. This plugin is free.

Simple Selection Navigation Widget

```
http://wordpress.org/extend/plugins/simple-section-
navigation/
```

– Another free plugin, this one is rated 4.9 out of 5 stars. Simple Selection Navigation Widget focuses on implementing navigation via widgets, as its name implies. If this is how you want to do navigation, this is a good choice; it has plenty of options to work with.

Breadcrumb NavXT

```
http://wordpress.org/extend/plugins/breadcrumb-navxt/
```

– This popular free plugin is designed to allow easy page navigation by adding "breadcrumb" trails to posts and pages, linking visitors back to parent categories or pages. These links are great for SEO as well. The plugin comes with over 10 languages installed and is very popular among bloggers and Internet marketers.

Google Analytics for WordPress

Price

Free

Description

Keeping track of your WordPress site's stats is very important, and Google Analytics is one of the best tools out there. This plugin allows you to track tons of metadata about your site, like outbound links and download tracking. It also uses an asynchronous Google Analytics tracking code for exceptionally accurate results.

Google Analytics for WordPress

```
http://wordpress.org/extend/plugins/google-analytics-
for-wordpress/
```

Pros

- Very easy to use
- Tons of options
- Allows you to connect your Google AdSense and Google Analytics accounts
- Installation instructions are available on the website
- Allows tracking of custom variables

Cons

- Nothing notable

Rating

This plugin has a rating of 4.3 out of 5, with close to 4 million downloads.

Conclusion

Google Analytics for WordPress is still considered by many to be the standard for using Google Analytics on WordPress. It can track just about any stat you need, making it easy to see where your site is succeeding and where it needs work. This is a critical part of SEO.

Alternate Options

Google Analytics Dashboard

```
http://wordpress.org/extend/plugins/google-analytics-
dashboard/
```

– This free plugin allows you to display Google Analytics data in your dashboard. It also lets you embed the data onto your site if you want. The major drawback is that you'll need to get a Google Analytics code and then use another plugin, such as Google Analytics for WordPress, to make it work.

Google Analyticator

```
http://wordpress.org/extend/plugins/google-
analyticator/
```

– This one allows you to display your Google Analytics results right there in your dashboard. However, there have been reports of bugs and compatibility issues. Despite this, this free plugin is quite popular and has been downloaded over 2 million times.

WordPress SEO by Yoast

Price

Free

Description

There are a variety of plugins designed to ensure that all SEO criteria on your website are met. This particular plugin is designed by WordPress SEO consultant/designer Joost de Valk (whose first name is pronounced "Yoast"). WordPress SEO by Yoast really goes the extra mile in providing you with a huge arrangement of options, including search engine result previews, in-depth page analysis, automatic WordPress optimization, XML sitemaps, metadata insertion, social integration, breadcrumb integration, and much more. This plugin just about does it all.

WordPress SEO by Yoast

`http://wordpress.org/extend/plugins/wordpress-seo/`

Pros

- Handles just about every SEO factor you could think of
- Massive amount of options and settings
- Designed by a WordPress SEO consultant
- Very easy to use
- Newbie-friendly despite its complexity

Cons

- Nothing notable

Rating

The plugin has a rating of 4.7 out of 5 stars and has been downloaded over 3 million times.

Conclusion

This may just be the SEO plugin that takes the crown from the longtime favorite, All in One SEO Pack. It does practically everything you could ever want an SEO plugin to

do in a way that's easy to understand and use. Just about any WordPress site could benefit from this plugin.

Alternate Options

All in One SEO Pack

`http://wordpress.org/extend/plugins/all-in-one-seo-pack/`

– Probably the most popular free SEO plugin ever with over 13 million downloads. It's simple, effective, and still considered the SEO plugin standard by some. It does have a 3.8-star rating, though, as some people have had minor problems with it.

Headspace2 SEO

`http://wordpress.org/extend/plugins/headspace2/`

– This is another free SEO plugin. This one lets you easily fine-tune the SEO on your WordPress site. Additionally, it allows you to add Google Analytics, Statcounter, Microsoft Live verification, Yahoo! Site Explorer, and many other neat options.

SEO Rank Reporter

`http://wordpress.org/extend/plugins/seo-rank-reporter/`

– This free SEO plugin works a little differently than the others. What it does is track various keywords that you're targeting on your site and report how you rank for them. (This is *much* easier than checking manually.) Since many SEO plugins lack this functionality, it makes a great companion for them.

SEO Smart Links

Price

Original Version – Free

Personal Version - $79

Professional Version - $149

Business Version - $299

Description

SEO Smart Links makes it easy to interlink your web content using your selected keywords. It also allows you to set a "no-follow" attribute to certain links and open them in a new window or tab. Interlinking like this is great for SEO and the no-follow option is great for linking to affiliate offers.

SEO Smart Links

`http://wordpress.org/extend/plugins/seo-automatic-links/`

Pros

- Makes interlinking much less tedious
- Can give a good SEO boost
- Great for affiliate sites that need no-follow links
- Free updates

Cons

- Premium versions are very expensive for what they do
- Bug fixes are almost exclusively limited to the paid versions

Rating

The free version is rated at 3.9 out of 5 stars and has been downloaded over 600,000 times. The paid versions have been downloaded over 300,000 times.

Conclusion

SEO Smart Links is very good at taking the hassle out of internally linking keywords in your web pages. However, the main drawback is that the premium versions get preferential treatment but may not be worth the price.

Alternate Options

SEO Smart Links+

`http://wordpress.org/extend/plugins/seo-smart-links/`

- Functions exactly the same as SEO Smart Links. It may be the better choice if you find that SEO Smart Links has bugs or compatibility issues. This plugin is free and rated at 4 out of 5 stars.

Automatic SEO Links

`http://wordpress.org/extend/plugins/automatic-seo-links/`

– This free plugin is very broad in scope. It will take words and link them to whatever you want; however, it will do this every single time the selected word appears on your site. This is only useful in certain scenarios, as you can imagine.

Vulcan Links to Keywords

`http://wordpress.org/extend/plugins/link-to-words-in-posts/`

– This plugin is like the one above, only it links all the selected keywords in a single post, giving you a bit more control over what you're doing. On the other hand, this also means you'll have to do this for every post or page on your site.

Outbound Link Manager

`http://wordpress.org/extend/plugins/outbound-link-manager/`

– Want to just regulate your outbound links? This free plugin can help. It allows you to regulate no-follow attributes, update tag and anchor text, and remove links

altogether if you need to. Best of all, it allows you to do this in bulk across the entire site if you want.

SEO Friendly Images

Price

Free

Description

When it comes to on-page SEO, many people forget how important it is to make sure the images are optimized. This plugin makes optimizing your images very easy by allowing you to add alt and title attributes to them. This gives them a good SEO boost to help you rank higher.

SEO Friendly Images

`http://wordpress.org/extend/plugins/seo-image/`

Pros

- Very easy to use
- Can add alt/title tags automatically or according to the options you select
- Makes images useful for SEO purposes

Cons

- Nothing notable

Rating

SEO Friendly Images has a rating of 4 out of 5 stars and has been downloaded over 800,000 times.

Conclusion

It is important to make your images work toward your overall SEO goals, and this plugin gets the job done. With no notable flaws or complaints from users, this may be the best plugin of its kind available.

Alternate Options

<u>SEO Image Renamer</u>

```
http://wordpress.org/extend/plugins/seo-image-
renamer/
```

– A free plugin designed to rename images after they've been uploaded to the WordPress media gallery. Has a three-star rating; people seem to either love this plugin or hate it.

<u>WP Image SEO</u>

```
http://wordpress.org/extend/plugins/wp-image-seo/
```

– Another free plugin that changes your images' title and alt tags to give you an SEO boost. However, this plugin is rated at one star, and people have had trouble getting it to work.

WordPress Flash Tag Cloud

Price

Free

Description

When it comes to SEO, some people say that installing a tag cloud is a big help. Others say it doesn't matter. And still others say it can hurt your ranking. If you do want to install a tag cloud, this plugin lets you do it with style, utilizing fancy Flash animation.

WordPress Flash Cloud

```
http://wordpress.org/extend/plugins/wp-
flashflyingtags/
```

Pros

- Looks cool
- Functions as a tag cloud should

Cons

- Can be distracting

Rating

WordPress Flash Tag Cloud has a rating of 4.2 out of 5 stars.

Conclusion

If you want a tag cloud on your site and you want it to look cool, this is the plugin for you. However, a tag cloud serves no purpose to the visitor whatsoever; it's really only for the search crawlers. There is no practical reason to draw attention to your tag cloud.

Alternate Options

<u>SEO Tag Cloud Widget</u>

`http://wordpress.org/extend/plugins/seo-tag-cloud/`

– This is another free plugin that puts a tag cloud on your site. This one isn't as flashy as the one above, so it may be better for those of you who don't want your tag cloud to stick out. It also has an optimized HTML markup.

<u>Fast Category Cloud</u>

`http://wordpress.org/extend/plugins/fast-category-cloud-wordpress-plugin/`

– This is another cloud generator, only this one is for categories, not tags. It gives you several display options, such as color fading, shown post counts, limited categories, and more. It also has a cache option to ensure that it doesn't affect the load time of your site.

SEO Title Tag

Price

Free

Description

Title tags are probably the most important on-page SEO factor. The problem is that post titles should be short and catchy, making it hard to incorporate the proper keyword phrases. SEO Title Tag allows you to override the title tags for your posts, pages, categories, and pretty much any title tag on your entire site, and replace them with SEO-optimized tags while keeping your original titles. In other words, it lets you please both the search engines and your visitors, having the best of both worlds.

SEO Title Tag

`http://wordpress.org/extend/plugins/seo-title-tag/`

Pros

- Excellent for on-page SEO
- Very quick and easy to use
- Can edit titles on a very large scale

Cons

- Hasn't been updated since 2009
- May suffer from compatibility issues in the future if it isn't updated

Rating

3.8 out of 5 stars, with over 300,000 downloads

Conclusion

This is a great plugin that provides a much needed function: optimizing your title tags. Not only that, it also allows you to do so in a very convenient and hassle-free manner. The only drawback is that the creator seems to have abandoned the plugin, making it susceptible to issues of compatibility as new WordPress versions are released. This

great plugin may eventually become unusable, which is a shame, since there aren't many options available for this sort of thing.

Alternate Options

Category SEO Meta Tags

```
http://wordpress.org/extend/plugins/category-seo-
meta-tags/
```

– This is a much narrower plugin that allows you to edit your category tags to make them more SEO-friendly. It is good at what it does, but it doesn't really do much overall.

AutoSEO

http://wordpress.org/extend/plugins/auto-seo/

– This free plugin allows you to edit your title tags manually across your site all in one go, much like SEO Title Tag. It is also highly customizable and claims to be extremely fast. So far, though, only just over 6,000 people have downloaded it, so it is relatively untested as far as plugins go.

Social Share Plugins

Something that is steadily becoming more important for SEO these days is the presence of social indicators, such as "likes" on Facebook and "+1's" on Google+. Because of this, it is a great idea to have social share buttons on your site, which you can do using plugins.

Digg Digg

Price

Free

Description

Digg Digg is a plugin that ads a social share bar to your WordPress site. The cool thing about it is that it can be set to display on every page, and can even be made to scroll with the screen so it is always visible. It features buttons for many popular social media sites, like Facebook, Twitter, Reddit, StumbleUpon, and many more.

Digg Digg

`http://wordpress.org/extend/plugins/digg-digg/`

Pros

- Has plenty of social media buttons to choose from
- Highly visible, which attracts more clicks
- Very customizable, allowing you to set it up how you want

Cons

- Some people claim that it slows down their websites' load times

Rating

This plugin has a rating of 3.5 out of 5 stars, with over 500,000 downloads.

Conclusion

Digg Digg makes it very easy to get the social signals you need for SEO purposes in a way that doesn't force you to manually put social buttons all over your site. Though a few people have said it slows down their website, most have had no problem with it, and the developer has endeavored to make it so that the plugin doesn't affect load times. If there is a problem, they're working on it.

Alternate Options

AA's Dig Dig Alternative

`http://wordpress.org/extend/plugins/aas-digg-digg-alternative/`

– This plugin is a direct competitor to Digg Digg, as the name suggests. It has much of the same functionality, only it claims to also have faster load times, cleaner code, less code overall, and be easy to customize. It has a rating of 4.8 out of 5 stars but only around 3,600 downloads.

Social Box

`http://codecanyon.net/item/socialbox-social-wordpress-widget/627127`

– This plugin comes in the form of a widget that you can place in your sidebar. Instead of focusing on "likes" and "+1's," it encourages people to actively subscribe to your social media accounts, such as following you on Twitter or subscribing to you on YouTube. It also shows your current subscriber count as well. This doesn't give you immediate SEO juice, but it could be useful in the long run if you're trying to get more followers/subscribers. Social Box costs $6 for the regular license and $30 for the extended license.

Slick Social Share Buttons

`http://wordpress.org/extend/plugins/slick-social-share-buttons/`

– This free plugin is very similar to Dig Dig. It does, however, have the additional option to open and close the social box as well as an "auto-close" feature that some visitors to your site may like if they find a floating social bar obnoxious. Slick Social Share Buttons has a rating of 4.4 out of 5 stars and is a favorite of many bloggers.

Social Media Tabs

```
http://wordpress.org/extend/plugins/social-media-
tabs/
```

– This plugin allows you to create widgets with social media tabs as well as snippets from your various social media feeds, like tweets and Facebook posts. Social Media Tabs is a free plugin and rated at 4.6 out of 5 stars.

Social Network Tabs

```
http://codecanyon.net/item/social-network-tabs-for-
wordpress/1982987
```

– It functions much like Social Media Tabs, in that it can display feeds in addition to social buttons, but it has many more options. With over 17 social networks to choose from and over 70 feed options, this is an exceptional social tab plugin. Additionally, the tab box can be displayed on any edge of your browser, or you can place slide-out tabs in your actual content, giving you plenty of ways to work with this plugin. Social Network Tabs is a great deal, at only $12 for a regular license.

WordPress Social Share Buttons

```
http://codecanyon.net/item/wordpress-social-share-
buttons/2927356
```

– A simple, straightforward social share plugin. This one allows you to place social share buttons in multiple locations across your site, using a stylish floating panel. It also has anti-spam capabilities and has been optimized to keep it from overlapping your content on mobile devices. WordPress Social Share Buttons costs $8 for a regular license.

FB Page Integrator

Price

Regular License - $8

Extended License - $40

Description

If you like building Facebook pages to work closely with your main website, this plugin can be a big help. It allows you to edit Facebook fan pages using WordPress, which can save a lot of time.

FB Page Integrator

```
http://codecanyon.net/item/fb-page-integrator-
wordpress-plugin/308746
```

Pros

- Can help you save time if you're using a Facebook page in conjunction with your main website
- Once set up, it's easy to use

Cons

- Must be frequently updated to keep up with Facebook's changes
- Setup can be complicated, since the instructions are vague.

Rating

This plugin currently has a buyer rating of 4 out of 5 stars.

Conclusion

FB Page Integrator is great at what it does: allowing you to work on your Facebook fan page from your website's interface. The only issue is that the instructions to get it set up are extremely vague, which may cause some to get lost. Also, since this plugin works closely with Facebook, it tends to need to be updated whenever Facebook is updated. Fortunately, so far the developer has been really good about putting out updates.

Alternate Options

<u>Facebook Walleria</u>

`http://codecanyon.net/item/facebook-walleria-`
`wordpress-plugin/634775`

– Functions much like FB Page Integrator but also allows you to embed lots of Facebook content directly into your site. This includes albums, photos, feeds, comments, videos, and more. Even better is the fact that it allows you to update all of this, and even interact with your fans directly, from your website. While this plugin may be slightly better than FB Page Integrator, it also costs more: $14 for the regular license and $70 for the extended.

<u>Facebook Fan Page</u>

`http://wordpress.org/extend/plugins/facebook-fan-`
`page/`

– This free plugin doesn't function like FB Page Integrator, but it does allow you to install a Facebook fan page widget on your site. It includes wall posts and user comments from your fan page, as well as the ability for people to "like" your content. It also displays photos of featured fans.

<u>Facebook AWD All in One</u>

`http://wordpress.org/extend/plugins/facebook-awd/`

– This plugin is a greatly scaled down version of Facebook Walleria and FB Page Integrator that's available for free. It still has many useful options, such as content publishing from your website, "like" buttons, an activity box, and more. It's rated at 4.3 out of 5 stars and has been downloaded over 100,000 times.

WordPress Like Locker

Price

Regular License - $7

Extended License not available

Description

This plugin is somewhat controversial, as it "locks" selected content on your website and forces the viewer to "like" it (using Facebook) to unlock it. This can be a double-edged sword; you could get a lot of likes this way if you have compelling content, or it could have people click away from your site and increase your bounce rate, which is bad for SEO. If you're going to use this plugin, it is recommended that you offer a good amount of compelling content and only lock selected parts after you've got your visitors hooked.

WordPress Like Locker

`http://codecanyon.net/item/wordpress-like-locker-like-to-read-plugin/166051`

Pros

- Very easy to install and use
- Can get you lots of likes

Cons

- Effectiveness of the plugin is contingent on how you use it
- Can work against you if used improperly

Rating

This plugin has a buyer rating of 4 out of 5 stars.

Conclusion

This plugin could be extremely effective if you take the time to use it correctly. For example, you could write a compelling blog post and promise something interesting in the final paragraph, which you lock using the plugin. Or, if you're running a website that's more of a store, you could use it to lock discount codes or coupons.

However, many people may be wary of liking something they haven't seen yet, and may click away from your site if you don't give them a good reason to click the like button. Use with discretion.

Alternate Options

Facebook Like Content Locker

```
http://wordpress.org/extend/plugins/facebook-like-
content-locker/
```

– This free plugin is essentially a simpler version of WordPress Like Locker. Rather than allowing you to select what you want to lock, it locks your entire blog. As you can imagine, the effectiveness is greatly diminished. That's probably why this plugin has only a 1.3 star rating, out of 5.

Social Locker for WordPress

```
http://codecanyon.net/item/social-locker-for-
wordpress/3667715
```

– Functions basically the same as Facebook Like Locker, allowing you to lock parts of your content and forcing visitors to use social buttons to unlock it. The difference is that this one allows visitors to unlock the content using Facebook, Twitter, or Google+. It also comes with built-in analytics tools and is highly customizable. Social Locker for WordPress costs $21 for the regular license and $105 for the developer license, so it's a little on the expensive side.

Social Video Locker –

```
http://codecanyon.net/item/social-video-locker-for-
wordpress/2861710
```

This plugin allows you to lock videos and force visitors to share them on Facebook, Google+, Twitter, or LinkedIn before watching. It works with both YouTube and Vimeo videos and comes with a variety of options, such as the ability to allow visitors to unlock all videos on your site by unlocking one, or the ability to put a timer on videos, forcing visitors to have to press social buttons multiple times to view the entire

thing. Social Video Locker costs $20 for a standard license and has a 5 out of 5 star rating.

<u>Security Plugins</u>

Now we're going to go over plugins that help make your WordPress sites more secure. Preventing things like hackers, viruses, and spam is very important. Some of you may recognize a few of these from my other book, <u>WordPress Security</u>, which you should check out for more information on how you can keep your site safe from a variety of threats.

Security Ninja

Price

Regular License – $10

Extended License - $50

Description

Security Ninja is the #1 top-selling security plugin on CodeCanyon for a reason. It performs over 31 security tests, including brute force tests, one of the most common hacking techniques. It also checks your site for other threats including malicious code, exploits, and more.

Security Ninja

`http://codecanyon.net/item/security-ninja/577696`

Pros

- Very comprehensive all-in-one security plugin
- Easy to use and understand, even for newbies
- Their website allows you to log in and test the plugin

Cons

- Designed to work with other plugins, such as Core Scanner, Scheduled Scanner, and Login Ninja, which must be purchased separately

Rating

Five stars out of five, with ratings from over 200 buyers. This is a very popular plugin.

Conclusion

Security Ninja is a great plugin for any website, taking care of multiple security tasks in an easy-to-understand manner. The only drawback is that the add-ons to enhance its use must be purchased individually. Whether or not they're worth it is up to you.

Alternate Options

<u>**Bulletproof Security**</u>

```
http://wordpress.org/extend/plugins/bulletproof-
security/
```

– This free plugin packs in a lot of functionality to protect your site against attacks. It includes protection against XXS, RFI, Base64, Code Injections, and much more. It also protects your vital .htaccess files. While this plugin is fast and easy to use, it can be a bit harder to understand due to the hacker jargon used. Even so, it is very popular, with a 4.7 out of 5 star rating and over 450,000 downloads.

<u>**Ultimate Security Checker**</u>

```
http://wordpress.org/extend/plugins/ultimate-
security-checker/
```

– This is a free plugin that scans your WordPress site and gives it a security rating based on various parameters. The only drawback is that it doesn't actually fix vulnerabilities detected in your system. Still, it's very newbie-friendly and can give you an idea of how secure your site is.

<u>**Exploit Scanner**</u>

```
http://wordpress.org/extend/plugins/exploit-scanner/
```

Works much like Ultimate Security Checker and also scans plugins for malicious code as well. However, it also doesn't actually fix any detected exploits. This plugin is free and has been downloaded over 400,000 times.

<u>**WordPress Sentinel**</u>

```
http://wordpress.org/extend/plugins/wordpress-
sentinel/
```

– A free plugin that watches over your files, particularly your admin files, and notifies you of any changes. This is a great defense against hackers who may attempt to insert malicious code into themes, plugins, or other files.

<u>**WP Email Guard**</u>

`http://wordpress.org/extend/plugins/wp-email-guard/`

– Having your site crawled by spammers is bad news, especially if they get a hold of your email address. This free plugin safeguards any mention of your email address on your site from being scraped and spammed. Extremely useful, but hasn't been updated since 2009.

Email Obfuscate Shortcode

`http://wordpress.org/extend/plugins/email-obfuscate-shortcode/`

– Provides shortcode to keep your email address from being scraped by spammers. This free plugin has been updated for WordPress 3.5.

Wordfence

Price

Free

Description

This security plugin has some unique features, so it deserves an extended review. What sets Wordfence apart from the pack is the fact that not only does it detect threats, but it can also repair any of your core, theme, and plugin files that may be infected or corrupted. This is the only WordPress security plugin capable of this at this time.

Wordfence

`http://wordpress.org/extend/plugins/wordfence/`

Pros

- Can scan multiple sites from one control panel a real time saver if you have more than one site
- Continuously scans for a huge number of threats, including backdoors, malware, and phishing
- Protects your login from brute-force hackers
- Gives you a real-time view of all traffic on your site.

Cons

- The ability to block countries and do scheduled scans is only available in the paid version.
- Not quite as newbie-friendly due to the huge amount of options and hacker jargon

Rating

Wordfence has a very high rating of 4.8 out of 5 stars and has been downloaded over 200,000 times.

Conclusion

Wordfence may seem a bit complicated at first, but the fact that it can actively fix certain security problems makes it a great plugin, especially since it is free. Also, the fact that it can scan multiple sites from one control panel is a huge plus for anyone with more than one site.

Alternate Options

WordPress File Monitor

```
http://wordpress.org/extend/plugins/wordpress-file-monitor/
```

 – Actively monitors your WordPress files and emails you when changes are made. This plugin is free, but hasn't been updated since 2010. If it isn't updated again, it may become obsolete.

WP Security Scan

```
http://wordpress.org/extend/plugins/wp-security-scan/
```

– This is a free plugin that also scans your WordPress site for vulnerabilities and exploits. While it won't fix them, it will suggest actions you can take to correct the problems. Key areas that it helps with include passwords, file permissions, database security, and WordPress admin protection. WP Security Scan is very popular, with over one million downloads, but has a fairly average rating of 3.4 out of 5 stars.

Admin SSL

```
http://wordpress.org/extend/plugins/admin-ssl-secure-admin/
```

– This plugin uses private SSL to help secure your WordPress admin area and keep it safe from hackers. This can be a bit on the technical side, but it does have installation instructions and a FAQ. Admin SSL is free but hasn't been updated since 2009. It may become obsolete soon.

Theme Authenticity Checker (TAC)

`http://wordpress.org/extend/plugins/tac/`

– This is a free plugin that searches the source code of themes you download for malicious code. This is a great choice if you often download new themes to try out.

Antivirus

`http://wordpress.org/extend/plugins/antivirus/`

– This clearly named plugin does what you'd expect: it scans your WordPress site daily for viruses and malicious injections. If something suspicious is found, you're notified in your admin area and by email. It supports multiple languages.

AskApache Password Protect

Price

Free

Description

Password hacking is one of the oldest tricks in the book for hackers, and the "brute force" method can be devastating to unprotected WordPress sites. AskApache protects your login using HTTP Basic Authentication or the more secure HTTP Digest Authentication. It also has anti-spam capabilities and can protect against other common exploits.

AskApache Password Protect

`http://wordpress.org/extend/plugins/askapache-password-protect/`

Pros

- Great for password protection
- Various extra options and capabilities

Cons

- Hasn't been updated since 2010
- If your web host isn't Apache, it won't protect your .htaccess files

Conclusion

AskApache is great for password protection, which is important since that is what many hackers will target first. The main drawback is the lack of recent support and the fact that your .htaccess files won't be protected unless your site is hosted with Apache. Still, .htaccess protection isn't the main purpose of this plugin anyway, and there are other plugins that can take care of that.

Alternate Options

<u>Login Security Solution</u>

`http://wordpress.org/extend/plugins/login-security-solution/`

– This is a free plugin that has a variety of handy features. In addition to protecting against brute force password hacking, it also tracks usernames, IP addresses, and passwords. It also checks login failures for these factors, slowing down response times when multiple attempts are made, which frustrates would-be hackers.

<u>One-Time Password</u>

`http://wordpress.org/extend/plugins/one-time-password/`

– This plugin is designed to give your login info an extra layer of protection in environments like shared Internet connections at cafés and other public places. It allows you to log in using passwords that only work once. This way, if your password is stolen by a keylogger or other underhanded method, it won't work again. It may seem slightly inconvenient to do it this way, but if you're constantly using a shared connection, it could prevent you from having your password stolen and your account compromised.

SI CAPTCHA Anti-Spam

Price

Free

Description

Protecting a WordPress site against spam is very important if you allow visitors to comment. Bots will spam you relentlessly if you don't take measures to stop them. This plugin not only protects your comments from spam, but also guards your registration, lost password, and login systems for extra security. It allows trackbacks and pingbacks, and also supports 18 different languages.

SI CAPTCHA Anti-Spam

```
http://wordpress.org/extend/plugins/si-captcha-for-
wordpress/
```

Pros

- Provides good anti-spam protection using CAPTCHA
- Protects more than just your comments section
- Great for deterring bots
- Supports multiple languages

Cons

- Several people report spam getting through to their site anyway

Rating

This plugin is rated at 3.8 out of 5 stars, with nearly 1.5 million downloads.

Conclusion

This plugin is great for protecting your comments against spam, along with other critical areas that bots will try to get into, such as the registration screen. Despite its popularity, some have claimed that spam still gets through sometimes, though they are in the minority.

Alternate Options

<u>Akismet</u> –

`http://wordpress.org/extend/plugins/akismet/`

By far the most popular anti-spam plugin for WordPress, though that may have to do with the fact that it comes preloaded on every WordPress installation. Akismet's biggest drawbacks are that it only works for comments and that you have to sign up to their site to get an API key to make it work; it no longer works automatically. Even worse is the fact that if you make any money from your website, Akismet requires you to pay a subscription fee. Still, many people consider it to be the anti-spam standard.

<u>Antispam Bee</u>

`http://wordpress.org/extend/plugins/antispam-bee/`

– This free plugin is considered by many to be the best alternative to Akismet and actually has more functionality and options. The biggest drawback here is that it is in German, which may alienate people who don't speak that language. However, you can enter the following URL into your browser to get a full review of the plugin in English, with a listing of all of its features to help you decide if Antispam Bee is for you.

`http://www.mydigitallife.info/antispam-bee-review-best-free-akismet-alternative-for-wordpress/`

WP-DBManager

Price

Free

Description

No security system is 100% guaranteed to defend against any and all hacking attempts. This makes it very important to back up your data, so if you do get hacked, you won't lose everything. WP-DBManager does this and much more, giving you plenty of database management options to work with, including optimization, repair, back up, restore, delete files, drop/empty tables, and run selected queries.

WP-DBManager

```
http://wordpress.org/extend/plugins/wp-dbmanager/
```

Pros

- Very comprehensive database management plugin
- Supports automatic scheduling for various tasks

Cons

- Some options may be hard for newbies to understand

Rating

WP-DBManager has a rating of 3.9 out of 5 stars and has been downloaded over 750,000 times.

Conclusion

One of the best free database management plugins around. It backs up your data to keep it safe, and performs a number of other handy tasks. However, some of the more advanced options may be a bit technically complex for those not experienced with database management.

Alternate Options

WP-DB-Backup

`http://wordpress.org/extend/plugins/wp-db-backup/`

– A very simple and straightforward free plugin that allows you to back up your data. Extremely popular, with over 1.5 million downloads, but hasn't been updated since 2010. Due to this, it may become obsolete in the future.

Simple Backup

`http://codecanyon.net/item/simple-backup/104945`

– This is another very straightforward plugin. This one can also be scheduled to perform backups automatically using cron, though that may be a bit complicated for those not technically inclined. The regular license costs $8, while the extended one costs $40.

VaultPress

`http://vaultpress.com/`

– This is *not* a plugin, but it may just be the most comprehensive and complete security system for WordPress available. VaultPress is a subscription-based service, starting at $5 a month per site, that performs a variety of security functions like real-time database backup, automatic site restoration, daily security scans, and review/repair of security threats, just to name a few.

Themes for Stores and Affiliate Sites

When choosing a theme for a store or affiliate site, what you need can vary depending on the type of store or site you're building. For example, an Amazon affiliate store would be set up differently than a store that sells health supplements and related products. Sites like these need to have a strong visual element, especially on the main page. Here are a few themes that are great for stores and affiliate sites.

Affiliate Theme 2.0

Price

Standard Package – $77

Premium Package – $97

Deluxe Package – $147

Description

Affiliate Theme 2.0 is a simple WordPress theme designed specifically for affiliate sites. The main page is very clean, featuring a strong visual element and limited navigation options that help push potential customers where you want them to go. Sidebar and widget options are restricted to internal pages and posts, allowing easy navigation for viewers once they've clicked on a product or offer.

The main benefit is probably the selection of various skins for the site, allowing you to customize it to fit what you're selling. Some examples of included skins are Amazon, travel, dating, and web hosting.

The Standard Package is $77 and comes with five skins, six unique template pages, and tutorials/support. It also has 10 pre-made niche header graphics included as a bonus. Best of all, it can be used on an unlimited number of sites with no developer's license needed.

The Premium Package costs a bit more, but comes with 50 niche headers. The Deluxe Package is the same as the Premium Package, but comes with installation, which is honestly kind of unnecessary; installing a theme is easy.

Afilliate Theme 2.0

`http://www.affiliatetheme.net/`

Pros

- Very sharp, clean look
- Very good use of images on the main page
- Includes several skins to use
- Setup wizard makes getting started easy

- The Marketplace allows for the purchase of additional skins/services
- The Marketplace also allows you to sell skins and services
- Support and tutorials are included at no extra charge

Cons

- May be a bit too simplistic for some people
- Deluxe Package doesn't really justify its price

Conclusion

Overall, Affiliate Theme 2.0 is a very solid affiliate theme that allows you to customize it with various skins while still maintaining the simple and sharp look of the site. It's easy to use, and support and tutorials are readily available if you need them. On top of this, the Marketplace has plenty of stuff for you to buy and sell, making this a very good deal for $77. Web developers will love the fact that they don't have to pay extra for a developer's license.

InReview

Price

$39.

As of this writing, this price not only gets you this theme, but the other 80 themes from Elegant as well, which is an incredible bargain.

Description

Making a review website to sell products used to be a lot of work. Most people would take a standard blog template and add in the graphics, pictures, and other necessary bells and whistles manually. InReview, made by prominent theme designers Elegant Themes, makes creating a review website much easier.

The site has the standard navigation options at the top, beneath the header, and then allows a space for a message of your choice. This is a great place to advertise a sale, discount, or other special promotion because it will get a lot of attention there. Below that, you'll find a featured item area that can be configured to rotate among several products; once again, this makes for a great opportunity to showcase special offers and hot deals.

Just below all this comes the real meat of the theme: tons of product placements. On the left/center, you can have pictures showcasing several products with short snippets from the reviews as well as their star ratings. In the right-hand sidebar, you can have smaller product pictures with ratings as well, grouped using widgets like "Top Editor-Rated Products," "Top User-Rated Products," and others. Other widgets displaying recent comments/posts are also available.

InReview

`http://www.elegantthemes.com/gallery/inreview/`

Pros

- Constantly being updated by Elegant Themes for best performance
- Compatible with all major browsers
- Convenient star rating system for both you and your users to use
- Designed for easy affiliate integration

- Complete localization for easy translation for foreign customers
- Comes in five unique colors
- Exceptional support in case you need help
- Plenty of theme options, shortcodes, page templates, and more
- Eighty themes for the price of one

Cons

- Main page can become cluttered if you don't know what you're doing
- Intelligent use of images and image placement will be needed to use this theme effectively

Conclusion

InReview is an amazing template for review-style stores and sites, taking a lot of the work out of the process. The star system allows you to rate products across various categories as well as give them an overall rating. It also allows users to give ratings in the comments section, encouraging user participation. Additionally, it allows for easy creation of "buy it now" buttons that can be given a call-to-action of your choice.

The amount of options you get is very impressive, and the main page does a great job of showcasing your products and their ratings, which is a surefire way to get people clicking on them. The only real issue is that the main page can become cluttered and messy if you don't know what you're doing. Overall, though, InReview can save you a lot of time and effort when setting up a review site.

Also, eighty themes for the price of one is one of the best deals I've ever seen. However, I have no way of knowing how long this offer will last.

ProReview Theme

Price:

Single Site License - $37

Multi-Site License - $69

Developer License - $119

Description

ProReview claims to be the best review theme online, and it could be right about that. Optimized for two of the most popular affiliate programs around, Amazon and ClickBank, this theme has a lot to offer. The easy-to-use options panel offers a great deal of control and the ability to customize the theme to your liking.

ProReview features a rather standard header and top navigation area and has a prominent slider that can feature multiple products. The slider also has a little bar on the right, showcasing three additional products of your choice. This is a great way to show off your best-sellers and really maximize your profits. Below this, you can add a little "welcome to the site" blurb if you want before you get into the product listings.

The product listings are done very well; they're located on the left/center with large pictures, a star rating, and a review snippet. Additionally, it has a "Visit Site Now" button that takes visitors directly to the offer using your affiliate link. Since the ultimate purpose of a review site is to get people to the main website to buy the offer, this is a huge plus for this theme. You can also insert banner advertisements between the review listings on the main page if you feel the need, though this could be a distraction.

The right sidebar has plenty of options, too. You can insert widgets displaying top-rated products, social media widgets to help spread the word about your site, and even a product-review video if you want. You also have the option for traditional blog-style posts on the main page but, once again, that could end up being a distraction for potential customers.

The product review pages themselves look great, featuring attractive images, star ratings, and a "Visit Site Now" button right up at the top; a very smart move. Comments also allow visitors to add their own star ratings.

ProReview Theme

`http://proreviewtheme.com/`

Pros

- Fits a lot of information on the main page without seeming cluttered
- Star-rating system is convenient to use
- Sidebar has lots of great options
- Easy to place banner ads if you want to
- Works great with video
- Easy navigation

Cons

- The overall design is set up like a traditional blog, which some may consider old-fashioned
- Adding too many features like banner ads and blog posts could distract customers from the products

Conclusion

ProReview is a very solid review theme, especially as it was developed specifically for the Amazon and ClickBank affiliate programs. However, it would also be a good theme for practically any review site you could imagine. It has plenty of options to really make your site unique while still looking sleek and attractive.

The main benefit to this theme is how it manages to pack in a ton of useful info about various products on the main page without overwhelming a potential customer. The inclusion of ads and blog posts could work against you, though, if you decide to use them.

Magazine Basic

Price

Free

Description

This WordPress theme is, as its name says, very basic. However, it is also very customizable and offers a lot of different layout options, including the placement of your sidebars, the width/height of the theme, and color options. Getting this theme to look good for an affiliate/review site will take some work, but it is so versatile that it can accommodate practically any site you could ever want to make.

For example, you can place your main content in the middle and have two sidebars, or just have a single sidebar and let your content take up a larger area. You can also add sliders, special headers and footers, and much more. There is really a lot you can do with this theme.

Magazine Basic

`http://themes.bavotasan.com/2008/magazine-basic/`

Pros

- Versatile
- Simple and attractive
- Easy to use
- Plenty of places for ad placement
- Free

Cons

- Will take some work to get set up
- You'll need to have at least some knowledge of web development to make your site look attractive
- Design is very simple looking

Conclusion

Magazine Basic is an excellent all-purpose theme that can be used for just about anything, including affiliate/review sites. The base design has very few distractions for potential customers, but looks somewhat dated. The theme is so versatile that you're going to have to do some work to get it to look how you want, and it will take some web design know-how to do that. If you're familiar with web design and want a free theme that you can do all kinds of things with, this is a good choice.

Zenshop

Price

Free

Description

Zenshop is a theme specifically designed to work with the e-commerce plugin Cart66, which I'll go over later. The theme looks very sleek and professional, considering it is free, and has a lot of potential for various types of affiliate/review sites as well as other forms of e-commerce.

It doesn't have much of a header, sacrificing that space in order to fit more important things "above the fold," like the large, bold product slider and the product listings below it. Those product listings are displayed on the main page in a grid-like fashion with big, prominent images. There are no star ratings or review snippets, only a link for more information and the price.

The product review pages also have massive images up top and a simple yet stylish look. The sidebar contains various widgets, such as a shopping cart recap, categories, ads, etc. There are a lot of options to work with here.

Zenshop

`http://www.fabthemes.com/zenshop/`

Pros

- Visually impressive
- Simple layout won't overwhelm potential customers
- Plenty of sidebar options
- Very visually oriented
- Add-to-cart button
- Plenty of footer options

Cons

- No fancy features, like a star-rating system

- Simple layout can look plain and unexciting

Rating

Zenshop has a rating of 4.35 on FabThemes.

Conclusion

In the end, Zenshop is a visually striking theme that gets the job done. The use of large images is definitely an eye-catcher, but there are no bells and whistles to really take the theme to the next level. The simplistic look has both positive and negative qualities, but still manages to be attractive. Overall, this theme is great if you're looking for something free; just don't expect a lot of neat features and options to play around with.

Plugins for Stores and Affiliate Sites

There are many great plugins for stores and affiliate sites. Some transform your theme into a virtual storefront, while others add much-needed functionality like a shopping cart.

MaxBlogPress Affiliate Ninja

Price

Single-Site License - $37

Developer License - $97

Description

This plugin functions as a link tracker, allowing you to obtain accurate stats so that you can better optimize your affiliate site. However, it does much more than that. MaxBlogPress Affiliate Ninja also allows you to create redirect links, cloak your links, manage links by groups, create no-follow links, turn your keywords into links, and more. When it comes to configuring your affiliate links, this plugin does it all.

MaxBlogPress Affiliate Ninja

`http://mbpninjaaffiliate.com/ninja-trial-2.php`

Pros

- Lots of options
- Easy-to-use dashboard with stat tracking
- Helps to prevent affiliate theft
- A big time-saver
- A big help when it comes to split testing anchor text
- Smart caching system keeps your site running smoothly

Cons

- It is completely oriented around affiliate links and offers no other features.

Rating

None available

Conclusion

If you want more control over your affiliate links, this plugin has what you need. Used correctly, it can help you improve conversion rates and the amount of money you

make by allowing you to optimize your links based on accurate data. It has a lot of features, but they all have to do with links and nothing else.

Alternate Options

<u>Pretty Link Lite</u>

`http://wordpress.org/extend/plugins/pretty-link/`

– This free plugin offers quite a bit of functionality. Its main purpose is to shorten links, much like tinyurl.com, only it uses your own domain to do it. It also offers link tracking both on your site and anywhere you use the link-shortening function. Pretty Link Lite is currently rated at 4.1 out of 5 stars and has been downloaded close to 600,000 times.

<u>Amazon Affiliate Link Localizer</u>

`http://wordpress.org/extend/plugins/amazon-affiliate-link-localizer/`

– This free plugin is a major time-saver for anyone with an Amazon store. It automatically changes any link to Amazon into your affiliate link so you don't have to do it manually over and over again. It also directs customers to the Amazon store appropriate for their region; for instance, if you get a customer from the UK, it will direct them to the UK Amazon site. This is a great way to keep from losing international sales.

<u>Amazon Link</u>

`http://wordpress.org/extend/plugins/amazon-link/`

– Very similar to Amazon Affiliate Link Localizer, this plugin has a few extra features, including a search tool, affiliate tracking IDs, and a caching system to keep your site running smoothly. It's also free and has a rating of 3.7 out of 5 stars.

Affiliate Links Manager

`http://wordpress.org/extend/plugins/affiliate-links-manager/`

– This free plugin includes a few essential functions: affiliate link tracking via Google Analytics, link redirects, and server load reduction.

Affiliate Link Cloaker

`http://wordpress.org/extend/plugins/alc/`

– Very simple free plugin that cloaks links. It can also be configured to work manually or automatically. Good for preventing affiliate theft.

attentionGrabber

Price

Regular License - $12

No Extended License Available

Description

This plugin displays an eye-catching notification bar on your website. This is very simple, but useful; it's great for promoting sales, discounts, and other special offers. It has plenty of customization options, animation affects, a click counter, and modules for Facebook likes, Twitter, and Google+. It can also incorporate RSS, ATOM, and Twitter feeds as well.

AttentionGrabber

```
http://codecanyon.net/item/attentiongrabber-
wordpress-notification-bar/242027
```

Pros

- Great way to draw attention to special sales and hot products
- Plenty of ways to customize it so it fits with your theme
- Has many handy features
- Can help increase sales, newsletter signups, and Facebook likes

Cons

- The notification bar looks kind of basic when it could have been more eye-catching.

Rating

This plugin has a 5 out of 5 star rating from over 200 buyers.

Conclusion

Drawing your customers' attention to special deals and other important information is easy with this plugin. It's very simple to use, but has enough options to allow you to customize it to your liking. Extra features like incorporating Facebook likes and Twitter feeds are a really nice touch.

Alternate Choices

EZ Notification Bar

```
http://codecanyon.net/item/ez-notification-
bar/2478002
```

– This plugin is like a scaled-down version of attentionGrabber. It is fully customizable and actually a bit more impressive graphically. It is also cheaper at only $5 and fulfills its primary function very well.

WordPress Notification Bar

```
http://wordpress.org/extend/plugins/wordpress-
notification-bar/
```

– Very simple notification bar with customizable color and multi-site functionality. Has a rating of 4.9 out of 5 stars. Free.

Duplicator

Price

Free

Description

This plugin allows you to quickly and easily duplicate WordPress sites. If you're creating multiple niche sites that follow the same template and layout, this plugin can save you a lot of time. It also functions as a backup utility.

Duplicator

`http://wordpress.org/extend/plugins/duplicator/`

Pros

- Makes it very easy to clone sites
- Huge time-saver
- Can be used to back up sites in case you get hacked
- Works in only three steps

Cons

- Takes a bit of technical know-how to use

Rating

4.8 out of 5 stars.

Conclusion

This plugin is handy when you want to make multiple sites fast, which is a common strategy among those involved in e-commerce. The only downside is that a certain level of technical knowledge is needed to use it.

Alternate Choices

<u>NS Cloner</u>

```
http://wordpress.org/extend/plugins/ns-cloner-site-
copier/
```

– This website cloner is meant to work with WordPress Multisite, not single installations. Easy to use and free. It has a rating of 5 out of 5 stars, but only two ratings so far.

<u>XCloner</u>

```
http://wordpress.org/extend/plugins/xcloner-backup-
and-restore/
```

– This is an up-and-coming free plugin that allows you to back up your files and database. Still takes some technical know-how to use. It has a score of 4.4 out of 5 stars and has been downloaded close to 150,000 times.

ReviewAZON Pro 2.0

Price

$79

Description

One of the most well-known Amazon store plugins, ReviewAZON 2.0 has a ton of functionality and features. It transforms an ordinary site into an Amazon store quickly and easily. It gives you the ability to use the star rating system, insert affiliate links, insert buy buttons that look just like the ones on Amazon.com, and much more. One of its best features is the fact that it can take info straight from Amazon such as product rating, list price, sale price, customer reviews, and more. And this is just the tip of the iceberg.

ReviewAZON Pro 2.0

`http://reviewazon.com/`

Pros

- Many, many features. Everything you'd need to turn your site into an Amazon store.
- Very easy to use
- Takes out much of the hassle of setting up your own store
- Can turn just about any theme template into a functioning Amazon store
- Includes lifetime updates and access to the members-only support forums.

Cons

- The amount of options available may be overwhelming at first

Rating

None available

Conclusion

The price of $79 isn't exactly cheap, but you do get a ton of value for your money with ReviewAZON 2.0. It has everything you could ever need to turn your site into a fully functional Amazon store. It's also very easy to use, though it can be easy to get overwhelmed by the sheer amount of things you can do with this plugin. This may be the ultimate Amazon store plugin.

Alternate Options

WP Zon Builder

```
http://www.wpzonbuilder.com/
```

– This is another Amazon store builder with plenty of options. This one features multi-national functionality to help cater to an international audience. This plugin seems geared toward sites that feature more product graphics on the home page. It comes with an unlimited site license for $99.

phpZon Pro

```
http://www.phpbay.com/phpzon-pro-wordpress-
plugin.html
```

– This $79 plugin comes with a lot, including the ability to list a product by ASIN, display product description snippets, display product features, and SEO URL features. The end result looks really good and is great for sites that need to list large numbers of products.

Amazon Reloaded

```
http://wordpress.org/extend/plugins/amazon-reloaded-
for-wordpress/
```

– A free plugin that makes it easy to get both image and text links from Amazon for use in your store. It can be configured to put your affiliate tag in these links automatically, saving you a lot of time. While it may not have the functionality of the paid plugins, it does its job well.

Affiliate Easel for Amazon

`http://wordpress.org/extend/plugins/affiliate-easel-for-amazon/`

– This free plugin has a variety of functions, allowing you to quickly and easily get the info you need from Amazon to post on your site. It also supports easy insertion of your affiliate ID. However, at this time it only supports compatibility with the US Amazon store. It has a rating of 2.1 out of 5 stars.

WordPress eStore Plugin

Price

$49.95

Description

WordPress eStore Plugin has a massive number of features for turning your site into a fully functional e-store. It has an integrated shopping cart, affiliate software integration, Amazon S3 integration, product display templates, secure download manager, the ability to create membership sites, and much more. It also comes with a standard multi-site license, which is always great. Included as part of the deal are a bunch of other plugins: Extra eStore Shortcodes, eStore Bulk Item Purchase, and eStore Post Payment Actions, among others.

WordPress eStore Plugin

```
http://www.tipsandtricks-hq.com/wordpress-estore-
plugin-complete-solution-to-sell-digital-products-
from-your-wordpress-blog-securely-1059
```

Pros

- You get a lot for what you pay
- Can be used to create any kind of store and sell any kind of product
- Comes with a multi-site license
- Has squeeze page capabilities for list/newsletter subscription
- Product display template looks very sharp

Cons

- Has so many features that it may take some time to set everything up
- Jack-of-all-trades, master of none

Rating

None available

Conclusion

If you want an all-purpose e-store builder, this is a great plugin. You can use it to build Amazon stores, ClickBank stores, bookstores, wholesale stores, etc. The only issue here is that it isn't optimized for any one type of store. If you're building an Amazon store or ClickBank store in particular, there may be better plugins for your specific needs. However, at only $49.95, this is still an excellent value and may prove more useful if you want to build many different types of stores, since it comes with a multi-site license.

Alternate Options

<u>Cart66</u>
`https://cart66.com/`

– This popular plugin is great for selling both physical and digital products. It features both Amazon S3 and PayPal integration, making it a great choice for anyone who sells their own products, like e-books, mp3s, or anything else you create on your own. Additionally, it is pre-optimized to work with certain themes, such as ZenShop. It even calculates rates for UPS, USPS, FedEx, and Canadian and Australian shipping. If you want to set up an e-commerce site that isn't an affiliate site, this is a great plugin. Just be aware that the free standard version has fewer features than the pro version, which starts at $89.

<u>Shopp</u>
`https://shopplugin.net/`

– One of the most flexible and versatile e-commerce plugins available. It offers integration with PayPal, Google Wallet, and 2Checkout.com. It also has many add-on integrators, like real-time shipping rates, order fulfillment services, cloud storage, and more. A single site license is $55; a developer license is $299.

<u>Quick Shop</u>
`http://wordpress.org/extend/plugins/quick-shop/`

– This is a free plugin that adds a variety of essential options for e-commerce sites, such as a shopping cart, a checkout page, and multiple product display options. Lacks

many of the features of paid plugins, but has the bare minimum needed for a store. Has a rating of 3.7 out of 5 stars and has been downloaded almost 100,000 times.

<u>**PG Simple Affiliate Shop**</u>

`http://wordpress.org/extend/plugins/pg-simple-affiliate-shop/`

– Allows many handy options, like the ability to attach testimonials, product descriptions, and images. You can customize banners and buy-now buttons, too. This is a free plugin with a 5 out of 5 star rating but only 3 ratings so far.

Responsive Pricing Table – Pure CSS

Price

Regular License - $4

Extended License - $20

Description

Sometimes, certain items or services for sale need special price tables to show different variations and pricing options. This plugin uses CSS and HTML to take care of that, so you don't have to bother uploading images. The interface makes this plugin very easy to use without you having to do actual CSS and HTML coding; it does it for you! It is very flexible and allows you to create a wide variety of pricing tables to fit your needs. It also comes with "yes" and "no" icons to help you differentiate product versions and features.

Responsive Pricing Table – Pure CSS

```
http://codecanyon.net/item/-responsive-pricing-table-
pure-css/3162267
```

Pros

- Easy to use
- Very flexible and customizable
- "Yes" and "no" icons are very convenient
- Pricing tables look sleek and professional
- Animated and non-animated tables available
- 252 total pricing tables

Cons

- This relatively new plugin has only 15 purchases so far, so it hasn't gotten a lot of feedback yet

Rating

None available

Conclusion

Responsive Pricing Table – Pure CSS makes it easy to add pricing tables to your e-commerce website. This is particularly great for sites that sell software and services. It has a ton of options and is very flexible, letting you create a table perfect for your site. However, it is very new and hasn't gotten a lot of feedback yet, making its true performance somewhat unknown. Still, it doesn't cost much.

Alternate Choices

<u>uPricing</u> –

```
http://codecanyon.net/item/upricing-pricing-table-
for-wordpress/145538
```

This is another price table creator for WordPress. While it lacks some of the functionality of Pure CSS, it does have all of the core components, such as multiple templates, customizable fonts/colors, and a live preview feature. It costs $15 for the standard license and $75 for the extended, and has a four-star rating with over 900 purchases.

<u>Price Table</u> –

```
http://wordpress.org/extend/plugins/pricetable/
```

Just like the name of this free plugin, Price Table is basic but functional. It uses CSS3 to allow you to create drag and drop price tables quickly and easily. Nothing fancy here but it gets the job done.

Pricing Table –

`http://wordpress.org/extend/plugins/pricing-table/`

This is another free pricing table plugin with basic functionality. It looks a bit better than Price Table and features slightly more options, such as the ability to highlight a featured column as the best value in the package.

Multipurpose Bookshelf Slider

Price

Regular License - $12

Extended License - $60

Description

The name says it all: this plugin allows you to display product images in an attractive, "bookshelf" style. As you might imagine, this is an excellent plugin for selling e-books and physical books. It also works really well for selling DVDs, CDs, mp3s, comics, or any other product that relies on having a strong, clear visual image. It is meant to display images in gallery style and has been optimized to work with the WooCommerce plugin. It can also display videos as well, making it great for product video reviews.

Multipurpose Bookshelf Slider

```
http://codecanyon.net/item/multipurpose-bookshelf-
slider-wordpress-plugin/2228996
```

Pros

- Great for displaying product images in a professional, visually powerful manner
- Easy to use and configure
- Cross-browser compatibility
- Widget and shortcode full setup

Cons

- May not work as well with products like jewelry, pet supplies, etc.
- Virtually useless for selling services

Rating

This plugin has a buyer rating of 5 out of 5 stars.

Conclusion

This plugin can add a distinctive, professional visual element to your e-commerce site. It is easy to use and very functional, but may not be much use for certain types of e-commerce sites. If you're selling books, though, this one is a real winner.

Alternate Options

Image Gallery Reloaded

```
http://wordpress.org/extend/plugins/image-gallery-
reloaded/
```

– Creates a great, yet somewhat generic image gallery for your site. It can be useful for certain categories, or on the home page if your theme lacks an inbuilt gallery. It's fully customizable and features a slide-show function. This plugin is free and has a rating of 3.9 out of 5 stars.

iFrame Images Gallery

```
http://wordpress.org/extend/plugins/wp-iframe-images-
gallery/
```

– Free plugin that creates a very simplistic image gallery scroll bar. Must be scrolled manually using a slider. Nothing fancy, but may be useful in certain situations.

Pinterest Plugin

```
http://wordpress.org/extend/plugins/pinterest-plugin/
```

– Pinterest is a very popular new social media site that revolves around creating image galleries. This plugin puts the "Pin It" button on selected images on your site, allowing viewers to quickly and easily pin them to their Pinterest galleries, using the alt-code of the image as the default title. This can lead to a lot of great traffic from Pinterest to your website. This plugin is free and is rated at 3.4 out of 5 stars.

CBPress

Price

Free

Description

This plugin allows you to turn your site into a ClickBank store and sell their products as an affiliate. It can import a full marketplace of products and categories, as well as allowing you to fully edit the product information to your liking. You can import from ClickBank category lists, or create your own product lists if you want. In addition to this, you can also add affiliate products from other sources than ClickBank.

CBPress

`http://wordpress.org/extend/plugins/cbpress/`

Pros

- Put ClickBank products on your site quickly and easily
- Allows for plenty of customization
- Allows the promotion of non-ClickBank products as well
- License allows you to use it on multiple sites

Cons

- There have been issues with updates and support
- A few people have reported compatibility issues with WordPress 3.5

Rating

This plugin has a rating of 3.4 out of 5 stars

Conclusion

Overall, this is a good plugin for creating a ClickBank-based affiliate store. It doesn't have quite the number of options or capabilities that Amazon plugins have for Amazon stores, but keep in mind that this plugin is free. Some people have raised concerns about the amount of support that this plugin gets from its developer.

Alternate Choices

CB Storefront

`http://wordpress.org/extend/plugins/cb-storefront/`

– Similar to CBPress, this free plugin allows you to create a ClickBank storefront by presenting ClickBank products using their feed and your affiliate ID. It uses shortcode to insert the product galleries on your website pages, so there is some manual work involved. However, these listings are also self-updating, so once you have it set up, you're good to go.

ClickBank Sale Notification

`http://wordpress.org/extend/plugins/clickbank-sale-`
`notification/`

– Enjoy the feeling of knowing you just made a sale from your store? This plugin sends you an email notification every time you make a sale. It also notifies you of re-bills, refunds, chargebacks, and cancel re-bills. It may be best to create a specific email account just to use with this plugin; you don't want your main email account being flooded if you make a ton of sales. This plugin is free.

Themes for Blogs

Blogging is still probably the number-one way WordPress is used. If you've switched over to WordPress.org from WordPress.com or another free provider, you'll be happy to know that you have a lot of options when it comes to getting a great theme for your blog.

Sahifa

Price

Regular License - $45

Extended License - $2250 (no, that's not a typo!)

Description

Sahifa is an extremely good-looking theme built to accommodate a magazine, news, or blog style. It was designed with mobile capability in mind and features HTML5 functionality. The homepage builder is drag-and–drop, making it very easy to use, even for newbies. It has a ton of options and features, including 30 custom widgets, 70+ shortcodes, 8 page templates, 500+ Google web fonts, unlimited sidebars and unlimited colors. It even has a rating system built in that can use stars, percentages, and more. Other features include an integrated favicon uploader, a logo uploader, custom gravitar uploader, and full screen background options.

As for how it looks, Sahifa is very crisp and professional. The homepage is very image-oriented, making it great for blogs that use a lot of images for their posts. The theme has a large featured image at the top that can function as a slider; below that, you can have a recent posts section, a blog roll, banner ads, and more.

The default main page has a sidebar, allowing you to display such information as social buttons, Facebook widgets, Flickr Widgets, popular posts, etc. All of this is fully customizable (and image heavy, of course), making it look great.

Sahifa

`http://themeforest.net/item/sahifa-responsive-wordpress-newsmagazineblog/2819356`

Pros

- Massive amount of features and options
- Great for a variety of blog types, especially image-oriented ones like news sites
- Highly customizable for a unique look
- Very crisp, clean, and professional-looking

- Easy to use
- Useful features, like the rating system, that you wouldn't expect a blog theme to have

Cons

- The amount of options may be overkill for a simple blog
- Easy to get overwhelmed with the sheer amount of things you can do with this WordPress theme
- Extended license is insanely expensive

Rating

Sahifa has a buyer rating of 5 out of 5 stars from over 200 buyers. It has been purchased close to 2,000 times, making it a very popular paid theme.

Conclusion

I don't think I've ever come across another WordPress theme with the amount of options and features that Sahifa has. There are literally tons of things you can do with it, making it a great choice for practically any blog, and even for review style e-commerce sites, thanks to the ratings system. On top of that, it looks incredible and can give any blog an aura of professionalism. You get a huge amount of value for $45. At the same time, this may be overkill for those who want just a simple blog.

The Style

Price

$39. Currently there is a special offer where if you buy this theme, you get all of Elegant Themes' other themes free. Eighty themes for the price of one is an exceptional deal.

Description

This is another great theme from Elegant Themes. *The Style* is a heavily image-based theme that is very simple but visually striking at the same time. The homepage consists of a very large header and a navigation bar; the rest is taken up almost completely by pictures, with short snippets of the blog post underneath them. Mousing over an image provides a larger excerpt and prompts the reader to click to read more. Each image also has the category prominently displayed on it for easy navigation.

This bold visual style is perfect for news and political blogs. In fact, any blog that is very picture oriented, such as travel blogs or personal blogs, can really benefit from this avant-garde theme style.

While there is no sidebar on the main page, there is a customizable footer where you can place info that would normally belong in the sidebar. Also, there is a sidebar within the actual blog posts. You can add various widgets, such as social buttons, recent posts, popular posts, and much more.

The Style

`http://www.elegantthemes.com/gallery/thestyle/`

Pros

- Very bold and striking visual design looks amazing
- Very easy to use and set up
- Cross-browser compatibility
- Perpetual updates
- Complete localization
- Comes in five unique colors

- Excellent support

Cons

- Homepage may be considered somewhat simplistic by some
- Doesn't have a huge amount of features and options compared to some other themes
- If you don't add a lot of images, it isn't going to look good

Conclusion

The Style manages to be both simple yet extremely bold in design. It is a definite eye-catcher that will "wow" your readers. The heavy visual design is great for holding the attention of the modern Internet generation as well. The only downside is that you're pretty much forced to use lots and lots of images — one per blog post at the bare minimum. Also, while this theme looks amazing, it isn't exactly loaded down with options and features like some other themes are. Then again, its strength lies in its simplicity. The eighty-for-one sale by Elegant Themes going on as of this writing is also an incredible offer.

Headlines

Price

Standard Package – $70

Developer Package – $150

Description

Headlines is a great looking blog theme from popular theme creator WooThemes. It features customizable header and navigation options, allowing you to alter the theme template to your liking. The homepage consists of blog post snippets with large, visually striking visuals on the left/center and a right-hand sidebar. This allows the theme to have an old-school design while incorporating a fresh modern look. You can also place a featured blog post if you want.

The sidebar widgets are very easy to customize and the unique ones included with the theme are great. One standout is the all-in-one widget that incorporates popular, latest, comments, and tags into a single tabbed widget. The blog post pages themselves look great and, once again, stick to a strong visual style while retaining a traditional blog feel.

HeadLines

`http://www.woothemes.com/products/headlines/`

Pros

- Successfully blends a classic and modern blog look
- A control panel that's very easy to use
- Integrated favicon and header upload
- Dynamic images options
- Various layout and navigation options
- Designed to work with Google Analytics

Cons

- May not be fancy enough for some people

- A little expensive for what you get
- Doesn't excel in any particular area

Conclusion

Headlines looks great while keeping things simple and stylish. Sticking to a classic blog format and not getting too fancy is this theme's greatest strength and its greatest weakness. It doesn't have a lot of bells and whistles compared to some blog themes, but it is still very solid and looks and functions great. The price may be a bit much for some people, though, considering the lack of features.

Rapido

Price

Limited Options - Free

Standard License - $29.95

Developer License - $49.95

Description

Rapido is a great looking theme by New WordPress Themes, known for their good work. This theme is similar to Headlines, but opts for a sleeker, more modern look. The most striking thing about Rapido is its large image slider on the homepage. It is a real eye-catcher and makes the homepage look really great while drawing attention to your featured blog posts. The header and top navigation are fairly standard, allowing you to have two navigation bars if you want. It also makes it easy to insert banner ads, social buttons, and more.

Below all of this is the blog posts section, featuring large images, post snippets, and a "read more" button. Impressively, each entry manages to fit in additional information, like date, category and comment links, without the entry seeming cluttered.

The sidebar can be configured to display even more blog entries, in a similar yet scaled down fashion. This is a great opportunity to show off some of your most popular posts. Best of all, this doesn't clutter up the homepage and actually enhances the look. You can add plenty of widgets to the sidebar of your choices as well, including Facebook widgets, tag clouds, and ads. There is also a comprehensive footer area where you can add any additional information and widgets that you want, or even more ads if you need them. This is a great blogging theme to use if you want to incorporate AdSense or other types of banner advertising.

Rapido

`http://newwpthemes.com/rapido-free-wordpress-theme/`

Pros

- Looks extremely sharp, stylish, and modern
- Very easy-to-use control panel

- Get a lot for what you pay
- Very good support system on the forums
- Compatible with all major browsers
- Easy gravitar upload for comments
- SEO optimized
- Very reasonably priced developer license

Cons

- Free version doesn't allow editing of your footer or access to the support forums
- Some people have had trouble getting the big image slider on the main page to work

Conclusion

New WordPress Themes is a great publisher and this is one of their best creations to date. Rapido is a very sharp looking theme that's great for blogging. The control panel makes it very easy for newbies to customize and use as well. One of its best features is how easy it is to insert ads, making this an excellent theme for AdSense and other ad-based sites. This theme has virtually no shortcomings if you buy the standard version. The only mishap is the fact that some people have had problems getting the slider to work. There are threads on the support forums that help with this, though.

Plugins for Blogs

When it comes to hosting a successful blog, two of the most important factors are encouraging user participation and gaining exposure. The good news is that there are plenty of plugins that can help you spread your content around the Web as well as get your readers involved.

Thank Me <u>Later</u>

Price

Free

Description

This plugin allows you to automatically send an email to anyone who comments on your blog. This is a great way to help people feel more involved and appreciated, encouraging further participation. Also, if you're running an e-commerce site, you can use this email to notify people of a sale, hot deal, or encourage them to sign up for your newsletter if you have one. There really is a lot you can do with this if you get creative.

<u>Thank Me Later</u>

`http://wordpress.org/extend/plugins/thank-me-later/`

Pros

- Allows customization of multiple emails to make them more personal
- Schedules when emails are sent
- Opens the door for tons of marketing possibilities
- Makes visitors feel appreciated

Cons

- Lacks any advanced features

Rating

Thank Me Later has a rating of 4.8 out of 5 stars.

Conclusion

This very simple plugin can have a big impact on your blog if you use it correctly. By making your visitors feel appreciated when they comment, you encourage them to further participate. And the more people who participate on your blog, the more word of it will spread and the more traffic you'll get. This plugin is also a great one for e-

commerce, as it allows you to "get your foot in the door" in a somewhat subtle way for all kinds of marketing strategies.

Alternate Options

Subscribe to Comments

`http://wordpress.org/extend/plugins/subscribe-to-comments/`

– This free plugin allows visitors to subscribe to be notified of further updates in the comments section of your blog. This is very handy for getting repeat visitors to your site, which is great for SEO and encouraging participation.

Usernoise Pro Advanced Modal Feedback and Debug

`http://codecanyon.net/item/usernoise-pro-advanced-modal-feedback-debug/1420436`

– This plugin adds a unique feedback window to your blog, allowing you to more easily gather user feedback from your visitors. It is compatible with iPad and Android tablets and 99.5% of themes. This is a great way to get feedback for your blog and let your visitors recognize that you value their opinion. It costs $10 for the regular license and $50 for the extended license, and it has a five-star buyer rating.

WordPress Related Posts

Price

Free

Description

This plugin has been a huge favorite for a long time now and for good reason. When your visitors finish reading a blog post, it is important to direct them to other pages in your blog and not just leave them hanging. This plugin adds a list of related posts and thumbnails to the end of every post, ensuring that readers have somewhere to go next. It's also highly customizable and records click-through statistics as well.

WordPress Related Posts

```
http://wordpress.org/extend/plugins/wordpress-23-
related-posts-plugin/
```

Pros

- Performs an essential function
- Customizable
- Keeps track of CTR stats
- Very easy to use
- Mobile-ready

Cons

- May need to disable this on certain posts if you want to direct visitors to a specific location

Rating

WordPress Related Posts is rated 4 out of 5 stars and has been downloaded close to 600,000 times.

Conclusion

This is a great plugin to help keep visitors within your site for that extra bit of SEO juice. It is also customizable and can feature a thumbnail image to get a higher CTR.

The stat tracking is great too, letting you know which links are the most effective. There really is nothing bad to say about this plugin.

Alternate Options

RelatedPosts

`http://wordpress.org/extend/plugins/related-posts/`

– This free plugin also shows related posts but does so using a sidebar widget. If you'd rather keep your related post links out of the main blog post area and in the sidebar, this may be a good choice for you. It is rated at 3.7 out of 5 stars.

Efficient Related Posts

`http://wordpress.org/extend/plugins/efficient-related-posts/`

– This is a free plugin that provides related posts, but with a twist. Instead of choosing which posts to display when a viewer clicks on the blog post, it does it only when the post is created or updated. The reason for this is that eventually other related-post plugins can slow down your site if you have hundreds of posts being accessed by tons of people each hour. If you have a very popular blog with tons of content, this is a good choice for you. It does require PHP5 to run, however.

Tweet Old Post

Price

Free

Description

This plugin is designed to allow you to get the maximum amount of value from your blog posts by tweeting them on a timed schedule. This can keep older posts relevant and have them keep bringing in traffic long after they've been published.

Tweet Old Post

`http://wordpress.org/extend/plugins/tweet-old-post/screenshots/`

Pros

- Get more traffic by tweeting old posts
- Set-it-and-forget-it design
- Easy-to-use control panel

Cons

- Tweeting old posts too often could annoy your followers

Rating

This plugin has a rating of 3.8 out of 5 stars.

Conclusion

This is a great plugin when used wisely. However, if you overdo it and constantly tweet old posts, you'll be seen as a spammer. This should be used with discretion to get traffic to older posts that need some love.

Alternate Options

<u>Tweet Posts</u>

`http://wordpress.org/extend/plugins/tweet-posts/`

– The name says it all; when you make a blog post, it sends out a tweet to notify your followers. It also adds the appropriate metatags to activate Twitter Cards and looks at the post formatting to decide what the message should look like.

<u>Tweetily</u>

`http://wordpress.org/extend/plugins/tweetily-tweet-wordpress-posts-automatically/`

– Functions much the same as Tweet Old Post, but in a somewhat more random fashion. However, it also gives you more options to work with, such as the ability to set hashtags and set links back to your site. It is currently rated at 4.6 out of 5 stars.

<u>Social Discussions</u>

`http://wordpress.org/extend/plugins/social-discussions/`

– Not only does this free plugin allow you to enable social sharing to over 30 networks, it also allows you to automatically publish your blog posts to over 25 networks. Great for getting maximum exposure. It is currently rated at 3.9 out of 5 stars.

Media Grid

Price

Regular License - $16

Extended License - $80

Description

If you run a blog based on a service you provide, it pays to have a portfolio to showcase your samples. Media Grid makes it easy to create an attractive portfolio using vivid visual representations of your work. It features one-click setup and eight predefined styles. Additionally, it has full media support for video and audio, and has Pinterest, Twitter, and Facebook sharing as well. Best of all, it is optimized for mobile, allowing you to take your full portfolio with you anywhere you go, including job interviews.

Media Grid

```
http://codecanyon.net/item/media-grid-wordpress-
responsive-portfolio/2218545
```

Pros

- Create attractive visually represented portfolios
- Mobile optimization is a huge plus
- Very easy to use and newbie-friendly
- Inclusion of video and audio is also handy
- Can put together images of various dimensions, creating a very striking look

Cons

- Social media sharing is only optimized for Twitter, Facebook, and Pinterest

Rating

This plugin has a four-star buyer rating and more than 2000 downloads.

Conclusion

If you need a visually represented portfolio on your website, this is one of the best plugins you'll find. Image creation and arrangement is easy and looks great. The fact that it is mobile optimized lets you show anyone your portfolio no matter where you are; no more missed opportunities. The only drawback is that it is only optimized to share with Facebook, Twitter, and Pinterest at this time. It could benefit from share options with LinkedIn, Google+, and others. Overall, though, this is an excellent portfolio plugin.

Alternate Options

Showcase

`http://showcase.dev7studios.com/`

– This gallery plugin offers slightly less functionality than Media Grid, but it does have an easy-to-use drag-and-drop interface. The regular license is $14 and the extended is $70, making it just slightly cheaper than Media Grid.

Fanciest Author Box

Price

Regular License - $10

Extended License - $50

Description

If you want a great looking author box at the end of every blog post, then Fanciest Author Box is a great choice. In addition to adding a professional-looking author box, it also features social media share tabs on the box, reminding readers to share your post to their favorite social media sites. Even better is the fact that if you don't want your author box at the end of your posts, you can use a widget instead of the shortcode to place it in the sidebar instead.

Fanciest Author Box

`http://codecanyon.net/item/fanciest-author-box/2504522`

Pros

- Very easy way to incorporate your author box into your blog
- Integrated social media tabs are a useful addition
- All major social media networks available for use
- Highly customizable
- Thumbnail image easy to integrate
- Can set your own color scheme
- Can be translated into other languages

Cons

- Nothing notable

Rating

This plugin has a five-star buyer rating.

Conclusion

Fanciest Author Box gets the job done, letting you add your author box either at the end of posts, the beginnings of posts, or in the sidebar. It's very easy to use, highly customizable, and the social media tabs are an excellent addition. There's nothing bad to say about this one.

Alternate Options

DT Author Box

```
http://wordpress.org/extend/plugins/dt-author-box/
```

– A free plugin similar to Fanciest Author Box, but geared to work for multiple authors on the same blog. It allows the standard text snippet and thumbnail images, and also has a link to the author's website and/or Twitter account. It comes in several different languages.

Fancier Author Box

```
http://wordpress.org/extend/plugins/fancier-author-
box/
```

– Made by the same developer as Fanciest Author Box, this is a free, slightly scaled-down version. There are no widget options or social media tab options. Still, it is an adequate author box generator.

WordPress Post Planner

Price

Regular License - $16

Extended License - $80

Description

If you run a multi-author blog, it can be hard at times to keep everything organized, especially if you're working on a strict schedule. WordPress Post Planner makes it easy to keep all authors on the same page, thanks to its various features. You can assign planners, due dates, custom statuses and more to each author. It also allows you to assemble checklists to make sure all necessary tasks are completed. It offers email integration as well, making communication easy. Aside from all the editorial benefits, WordPress Post Planner also allows you to easily insert references, images, and files into your blog posts. It's multi-site compatible, making it a valuable asset if you're trying to run multiple blogs.

WordPress Post Planner

`http://codecanyon.net/item/wordpress-post-planner/2496996`

Pros

- Offers a variety of useful editorial and managerial tools
- Helps to keep multiple authors organized and on task
- Multi-site compatibility is a huge plus
- Content editing software is a great feature
- Makes life as an editor/manager much easier

Cons

- Isn't going to magically make you a good editor/manager if you don't already possess those skills
- There is a certain learning curve involved in using this plugin

Rating

This plugin has a five-star buyer rating

Conclusion

If you're an editor or manager struggling to keep everything together on a multi-author WordPress site, this plugin is a godsend. It will work wonders in keeping everyone organized and working as a team while helping to eliminate miscommunications and misunderstandings. The main drawback here is that this is only a tool; you're going to have to be the one with the managerial skills to use it. Also, while this plugin isn't overly complex, it will take some time to learn how to use it to its greatest effect.

Alternate Options

Co-Authors Plus

`http://wordpress.org/extend/plugins/co-authors-plus/`

– This free plugin allows you to assign multiple bylines to your blog posts if you have multiple authors. Not comparable to WordPress Post Planner but could come in handy in some situations.

Themes for Squeeze Pages

Squeeze pages are designed for one purpose: to capture leads. This usually takes the form of trying to get people to sign up to an email newsletter or sign up for a CPA offer. In any event, these are themes that have been designed for this very purpose.

OptimizePress

Price

$97

Description

OptimizePress is a theme built for multiple types of Internet marketing: sales pages, sales letters, landing pages, launch pages, one time offers and, of course, squeeze pages. The real benefit here lies in this theme's simplicity. It focuses on its task of getting people to fill out your signup form and that's it.

To facilitate this goal, the squeeze-page mode of this theme is extremely simple. It consists of a headline, video, and signup form, all above the fold. This is fully customizable, though, so if you want to swap the video out for something else, you can.

OptimizePress

`http://www.optimizepress.com/`

Pros

- Extremely simple and focused
- Like having several themes in one
- Many Internet marketers swear by this theme
- Split testing is very easy, due to the simple design
- Easy to set up and use overall

Cons

- Price may be a turn off to some

Conclusion

OptimizePress has a reputation of being a juggernaut in the world of Internet marketing; it's incredibly popular. Its simple design never deviates from its purpose. If you make a squeeze page, it works to get people to sign up with you. If you make a sales letter, it works to make sales for you. It never does anything to distract the visitor from doing what you want him or her to do; that's the power of this theme. The price

is a bit steep, but you are essentially getting several themes in one, which does help to justify it a bit.

Profits Theme

Price

$97

Description

Profits Theme is similar to OptimizePress in that it is essentially several themes in one. It, too, can be used for sales letters, launch pages, etc., in addition to squeeze pages, but ultimately it is a bit more versatile and less simplistic. You can even turn it into a blog if you want.

When using this theme for a squeeze page, you have lots of options. You can set it up essentially any way you want. If you know what you're doing, this is great. If you aren't that familiar with squeeze pages, this may not be so great unless you find a tutorial online to help you out. The amount of freedom and options available may be intimidating for inexperienced users.

Profits Theme has a ton of options, features, and bells and whistles. The sheer amount of stuff you have to work with is comparable to Sahifa. You can create "buy now" buttons, Johnson boxes, testimonial boxes, guarantee seals, free trial buttons, and more — much, much, much more. This is literally just the tip of the iceberg.

You can use video, text, and columns in your squeeze pages. You can have pop-ups on your pages that prompt people to sign up for your newsletter. You can have one-time offer pages for visitors to land on after they sign up. You can have different sign up forms on different pages. All this can be done through a simple, easy to use, drag-and-drop interface that thankfully makes the complexity of this theme a little easier to bear. In fact, one testimonial states it's so easy, "a 12-year-old could do it."

Profits Theme

`http://profitstheme.com/`

Pros

- You get a lot of options and features for your money. **A lot**.
- Can create sites in many different Internet marketing styles
- Not restrictive at all; you have total freedom

- Plenty of graphics and other resources to use as well
- Looks very professional and sharp

Cons

- Can easily lead to information overload
- If you're not a web designer, you're probably going to need tutorials
- There is a learning curve involved here

Conclusion

Profits Theme's greatest strength is also its greatest weakness: you have a massive number of options and can do pretty much whatever you want. This is almost like a complete web-design kit rather than a theme, because you have so much to work with. Some marketers rate this theme as being slightly superior to OptimizePress, and you certainly get more than your money's worth here. The question is whether you are skilled enough to use it properly. If you get this theme and don't know anything about web design, you might be better off hiring someone who does to create a squeeze-page masterpiece with it.

Squeeze Theme

Price

$147

Description

Squeeze Theme is built primarily for squeeze pages and is meant to work with Squeeze Plugin, which we'll get to later. This theme is relatively simple and allows you to control various options from the control panel, including the header, appearance, display settings, footer settings, squeeze-form settings, and more.

The main page of the theme is similar to OptimizePress in simplicity, but has a few more things going on, namely a navigational bar and some things in the footer. This is all up to you; you can make it as complex or as simple as you like. You can also place the opt-in form any place you like as well, giving you plenty of options.

In addition to this, Squeeze Theme also can be converted into a sales page or a blog. There are support forums that can help with this and other questions if you get lost. The color picker makes it easy to create a nicely color-coordinated site, as well.

One of the best options that this theme offers may be its stat-tracking feature. Combined with the ability to design unlimited variants of your squeeze page in the main panel, this allows you to split test to your heart's desire and with minimum effort. This can really ramp up your opt-in rate if you stick with it.

Squeeze Theme

`http://www.squeezetheme.com/`

Pros

- Simple enough for newbies, but complex enough for web designers that want to do more with it
- Optimized for squeeze pages
- Stat tracking and unlimited variant creation makes split testing very easy
- Color picker helps to make sure the site is attractive
- Great looking overall theme design

- Support forums will help you if you get lost or stuck

Cons

- The price is a bit higher than what you'd expect
- Using this theme for anything other than squeeze pages will take a bit of a learning curve
- Some knowledge of how a squeeze page should be set up will be required

Conclusion

Squeeze Theme is a happy middle between the ultra-simplicity of OptimizePress and the hyper-complexity of Profits Theme. It gives you the freedom to do what you want, but is also simple enough that building a squeeze page shouldn't be that hard, even for beginners. The only real drawback here is the price, which is honestly a bit steep for what you get.

FlexSqueeze

Price

$127

Description

From the makers of the popular Flexibility theme comes FlexSqueeze, a theme dedicated to being a squeeze page hybrid. The reason I say "hybrid" is because, while you can make just a single-page squeeze page if you want, this theme makes it easy to work an opt-in box into a highly visible location on a blog, e-commerce store, or sales page. You have a lot of options, and this may be Profit Theme's equal in versatility, if not in sheer volume of features and options.

What sets this theme apart are the huge sub-header and footer areas that were also present in Flexibility. These areas are great for putting in whatever you want: ads, widgets, blog rolls, et cetera. But the sub-header is a particularly great place to put your opt-in box; use a video or something to give people a compelling reason to sign up before diving into the rest of your site's content.

There are quite a number of special features included with this theme. You get 10 widget locations, tons of templates to make things easy on you, unlimited colors to choose from, built in ad placement, the ability to export your settings to duplicate your sites quickly and easily, one-click color schemes, designs and layouts, and more. It also comes with full customer support in case you need help.

FlexSqueeze may just be the most well-rounded squeeze page theme available.

FlexSqueeze

`http://www.flexsqueeze.com/flexsqueeze/`

Pros

- Templates make squeeze page creation easy
- Plenty of freedom to create what you want
- Can be used to create more than just squeeze pages
- Can make really nice looking squeeze page hybrids

- Over 300 total theme options
- Comes with over 75 custom favicons, or you can upload your own
- Integrated breadcrumb navigation that's very nice
- AdSense-optimized
- Great customer support

Cons

- There will be a learning curve for newbies
- Will take some work to create a site that doesn't look simplistic

Conclusion

FlexSqueeze is very well rounded, offering plenty of options for veteran web designers to play with and easy-to-use templates for newbies. Creating a blog/squeeze-page hybrid or e-commerce/squeeze-page hybrid has never been easier. On top of that, FlexSqueeze looks great… but only if you take the time to make it look great. The templates are nice, but a bit simple looking; it's going to take some extra effort to bring out FlexSqueeze's true potential. When all is said and done, though, this squeeze-page theme is a solid choice for both newbies and veterans alike and should get more credit than it does.

Plugins for Squeeze Pages

When it comes to plugins for squeeze pages, there are several options to help you capture leads. Many revolve around getting the visitor's attention and making sure that they understand why they should sign up using your opt-in form.

PopUp Domination

Price

$77

Description

Everyone hates pop-ups, but they are one of the best ways to increase your subscriber count and capture leads. PopUp Domination is a pop-up device that looks great while displaying crucial information, like an eye-catching headline, bullet points that explain why the reader should sign up, and even a product image. PopUp Domination claims that it can't be blocked by ad-block software, and that over 15,000 of their customers experience a 500% increase in signups practically overnight.

PopUp Domination

`http://www.popupdomination.com/live/`

Pros

- Looks very professional
- Easy opt-in box integration
- Large "X" that allows readers to easily click it away if they want, so fewer people will get upset and leave your site
- Can't be blocked by ad blockers
- Lets you use copywriting elements like headlines, bullet points, etc.
- Configured with analytics to allow easy split testing for conversion optimization
- Specific page targeting
- Many customization options

Cons

- People who hate pop-ups are still going to hate this
- Somewhat expensive

Rating

None available

Conclusion

PopUp Domination looks great and allows you to create really effective lead-capturing ads. The inclusion of elements such as bullet points, headlines, and product images was a great move and can really help increase conversions. Overall, the pop-ups look great, too — very professional — and the rather large "X" in the corner is convenient for viewers who want to get rid of it right away. This is a very solid popup plugin that does everything right.

Alternate Options

Ninja Popups

```
http://codecanyon.net/item/ninja-popups-for-
wordpress/3476479
```

– A cheaper alternative to PopUp Domination with even greater functionality, this $16 plugin can pretty much do it all. Key features include the ability to put social "like" buttons in your pop-up and the fact that the plugin is already optimized for integration with several of the most popular autoresponder services, like Aweber and MailChimp. It even allows you to lock pages of your website until readers either click a "like" button or sign up using your opt-in form.

WordPress PopUp

```
http://wordpress.org/extend/plugins/wordpress-popup/
```

– This free pop-up plugin doesn't have autoresponder integration, but it can still come in handy. It can be set on a timer to pop up after visitors have been on a page for a certain amount of time. It has an option that allows visitors to click it away so that it never displays again, and another option to select which visitors see it. It's currently rated at 4.1 out of 5 stars.

Optin Revolution

```
http://wordpress.org/extend/plugins/optin-revolution/
```

– One of the few free popup plugins that's comparable to PopUp Domination and Ninja Popups. This one has a lot of functionality and options, as well as the all-important ability to integrate your opt-in box directly into the pop-up. There are

video training tutorials on the site as well, making it very newbie-friendly. This plugin has a rating of 4.9 out of 5 stars.

<u>**WPSubscribers**</u>

`http://www.wpsubscribers.com/`

– This plugin offers plenty of options and features, but the one that stands out the most is the fact that you can place your pop-ups on any page or post you want, allowing you to get more targeted and increase your signup rate. It has tracking analytics, can auto-fill your visitor's name and email into the opt-in form, and allows visitors to subscribe while commenting. This plugin costs $47 for the triple license and $97 for an unlimited license that allows you to use it on an unlimited number of sites and gives you top customer support priority.

MyMail

Price

Regular License - $25

Extended License not available

Description

MyMail is a newsletter management system. It gives you a wide variety of handy options so that you can have better control over email list campaigns from your WordPress dashboard. Its tracking options will help you to optimize your campaign, and you can use the scheduling feature to set up emails to go out when you want them to. You can also send out specific emails to specific people on your list. Another great feature is that you can actually create your newsletter right in your WordPress dashboard. There is also an option that checks your emails to make sure nothing will get it sent to the recipient's spam folder.

MyMail

```
http://codecanyon.net/item/mymail-email-newsletter-
plugin-for-wordpress/3078294
```

Pros

- Lots of customization options
- Feature that checks for things that will put your email in spam folders is invaluable
- Being able to manage your campaign from your WordPress dashboard is very convenient
- Has double opt-in support
- Has multi-language support

Cons

- May take a bit of a learning curve to figure out how to use all of the options

Rating

This plugin has a 5 out of 5 buyer rating.

Conclusion

Managing email newsletters from your autoresponder account can be annoying, especially since some of them can be hard to learn. This plugin not only simplifies a lot of that, it also adds a lot of functionality that most autoresponder services lack. The ability to pre-check your emails for spam factors is great, and the tracking options are also a must-have. This is a very good all-around newsletter management plugin.

Alternate Options

WordPress Email Newsletter Plugin

`http://codecanyon.net/item/wordpress-email-newsletter-plugin/149180`

– This is another plugin that has a ton of options and functionality for creating and managing a newsletter from your WordPress dashboard. It has scheduling, templates, and bounce tracking, just to name a few features. It costs $25 for the standard license and $125 for the extended. It also has a buyer rating of 4 out of 5 stars.

Email Newsletter

`http://wordpress.org/extend/plugins/email-newsletter/`

– This plugin allows you to send emails to registered members of your site, essentially allowing you to have a newsletter without the need for an autoresponder. It is kind of basic in comparison to some of the others, but it is free.

Newsletter

`http://wordpress.org/extend/plugins/newsletter/`

– Another basic WordPress-based email newsletter system. This one allows unlimited emails and unlimited subscribers and offers configurable themes to work with. It is rated at 4 out of 5 stars and has been downloaded over 200,000 times.

Squeeze Plugin

Price

$97 for unlimited use

Description

This plugin is meant for use with the FlexSqueeze theme, but in truth it can turn any WordPress theme into a squeeze page. The drag-and-drop interface lets you build a squeeze page in minutes, inserting video and autoresponder codes with a click of your mouse. The overall appearance of the squeeze page looks very simple, but it gets the job done.

Squeeze Plugin

`http://www.squeezetheme.com/`

Pros

- Very easy to use and newbie-friendly
- Simple design is free of distractions for visitors
- Video integration is very easy to use
- Can be used to turn any page on your site into a squeeze page

Cons

- Somewhat expensive
- Some people may not like the simple design

Rating

None available

Conclusion

Squeeze Plugin is a great squeeze-page creation plugin. It covers all the basics and is extremely newbie-friendly. The main drawback is that you're paying close to $100 and don't exactly get a huge amount of bells and whistles in return. Still, the plugin does what it is designed to do, and does it very well.

Alternate Options

<u>WordPress Squeeze Page Plugin</u>

`http://www.wpsqueezepage.com/`

– This plugin allows you to build just about any kind of squeeze page you could imagine. It has tons of options, including the ability to integrate Google Content Experiments for easy split testing and optimization. It also comes with special members-only support area access. This plugin costs $47.

<u>WordPress Landing Pages</u>

`http://wordpress.org/extend/plugins/landing-pages/`

– This free plugin allows you to create a variety of landing pages for your WordPress site. It offers stat tracking for easy split testing, templates, and the ability to easily clone landing pages. It has a rating of 4.7 out of 5 stars, but only three ratings.

<u>Simple Newsletter Signup</u>

`http://wordpress.org/extend/plugins/simple-newsletter-signup/`

– This free plugin lets you insert opt-in forms quickly and easily. It's optimized to work with third-party autoresponders, such as MailChimp, Constant Contact, and others. It is a relatively new plugin with no ratings yet, though it has close to 1,000 downloads.

Themes for AdSense

AdSense is a classic way to make money using WordPress. AdSense ads can be inserted into just about any type of site, and you make money when people click on them. However, some themes have been created specifically with AdSense revenue in mind.

HeatMap

Price

$67 for lifetime membership

Description

Developers and analysts often use what are known as "heat maps" to map out the spots on a web page where an ad will get the most clicks and make the most money. The HeatMap theme is built around that principle, setting things up and guiding you so that you place your ads in the statistically most successful positions. It also has a variety of other useful features, such as ad rotation, authority skins to make your site look great, social media button integration, site cloning, and internal SEO features, just to name a few.

How the overall look and design of the site turns out is up to you. You have a huge amount of freedom to make your site how you want. HeatMap also caters to affiliate sites, squeeze pages, sales letters, and more if you want to create those types of websites as well.

HeatMap

`http://heatmaptheme.com/`

Pros

- Very targeted ad positioning that's great for newbies
- Loaded with features and options
- Can create and optimize many different sites for ads
- SEO and social integration is a huge plus
- Logo and favicon uploaders
- Page templates are a time-saver

Cons

- The number of options and amount of freedom can be intimidating for newbies

Conclusion

HeatMap has been a favorite among AdSense marketers for some time now, and for good reason. It takes you by the hand and shows you exactly where you should be placing your ads, leading to higher click-through rates. The only issue is that the huge number of options and the ability to customize your site any way you want may leave some people feeling lost.

Adsense Pro Ultimate

Price

Regular License - $69

Developer License - $149

Description

This theme focuses on being as simple as possible, allowing users to create sites that don't distract from the ads for a higher CTR. This also has the side effect of producing very fast-loading sites, since they aren't bogged down by extra bells and whistles. Other features include AdSense integration, favicon integration, analytics/stat management, and tracking code integration.

Adsense Pro Ultimate

`http://ctr-themes.com/themes/adsense-pro-ultimate/`

Pros

- Simple design for fast loading and maximum CTR
- Analytics and stat tracking helps you optimize your ads and ad placement
- Very versatile overall

Cons

- Simplistic look may be considered dated by some
- Optimal ad placement will take some know-how to implement

Conclusion

Adsense Pro Ultimate is a great theme for a pure AdSense site. It covers all the basics very well and has some great features like stat tracking and code integration. The main issue here is that it really isn't suitable for anything other than a pure AdSense site that uses a blog format. Then again, if your goal is to make money with AdSense, you probably don't need anything more fancy, anyway.

MaxSense

Price

$69 for lifetime membership

Description

MaxSense is an AdSense theme designed to focus around a blogging platform. Since you will need compelling content to draw people to your site, this is a reasonable approach. The placement of ads can be edited to your liking, allowing you to place ads in sidebars. It also comes with integrated analytics and stat management as well.

The sleek and modern look of the theme gives it a slight edge over themes like Adsense Pro Ultimate in the overall appearance department. The use of thumbnails really enhances the main page and keeps visitors from bouncing.

MaxSense

`http://www.adsensepress.com/maxsense-wordpress-theme`

Pros

- Looks sharp and modern
- Great for blogs that want to incorporate AdSense
- Analytics and stat tracking are plusses
- Compatible with all major browsers
- Footer area is fully customizable

Cons

- Ad placement seems somewhat limited
- Seems more like a blog theme than an AdSense theme

Conclusion

While this theme does look great, I can't help but feel that it leans more toward being a blog theme with AdSense thrown in as an afterthought. This is mainly due to the

limited way in which ad placement is implemented. It has some nice features, though, and is easy to set up. If you run a blog and want to put ads on it, this isn't a bad choice.

CTR Theme

Price

$67. However, you can get it for free when subscribing to one of CTR Theme's hosted plans, which start at $4.99 a month.

Description

Despite its simplicity, CTR Theme manages to look very professional and attractive, albeit in a basic kind of way. Its ad placement strategy is based on the placement recommendations from Google AdSense, so it comes from a reliable source. It also has an ad placement randomizer that helps to prevent readers from automatically filtering out the ads in their mind. Other features include super-fast load times, social media integration, and multiple sub-themes.

CTR Theme comes with several layout options. Some feature images, others have a prominent header, and there's still another that's just text. In each case, the ads are placed in very prominent locations as dictated by Google. At the same time, the ads don't come across as being obnoxious, which is great. To the untrained eye, some of these layout options don't even look like pure AdSense sites.

CTR Theme

`http://www.ctrtheme.com/`

Pros

- Simple yet attractive
- Multiple layout options
- AdSense integration based on Google's recommendations
- Powerful core features
- Easy to use
- Comes with a bonus: AdSense Link-Building Secrets guide

Cons

- This is a pure AdSense theme, so it may not be good for affiliate sites, dedicated blogs, etc.

Conclusion

CTR Theme is a very focused, attractive AdSense theme. It aims for one thing, getting people to click on ads, and it does it well. It has plenty of features and options, including several layouts, so you can set the site up the way you want within certain parameters. Because of its simplicity, it is very newbie-friendly and easy to use. However, due to its ultra-focused nature, it probably isn't what you want if you're trying to put ads on a popular blog or your affiliate site. If you're trying to concentrate on AdSense revenue, though, this is one of the best choices available. Also, an unlimited site license is included with your purchase so you can create an army of AdSense sites using this theme if you want.

Plugins for AdSense

There are a variety of plugins that make using AdSense a bit easier. Some of these are redundant with certain AdSense theme functions, while others work to complement AdSense themes.

Click Missile

Price

$47, but reduced to $27 as part of a special offer

Description

Click Missile was created by the developers of HeatMap. It shows you exactly where the hottest spots on your site are for ad placement, similar to the way that HeatMap functions. The benefit here is that this plugin can be used for any site, making it great for hybrid sites. For example, if you wanted to put AdSense on your affiliate site, this would show you where to place your ads for maximum CTR.

Click Missile

http://heatmaptheme.com/click-missile-ads-placement-plugin-for-wordpress/

Pros

- Shows you where to place your ads. Great for AdSense newbies
- Works with any site
- Optimized for mobile devices
- Allows you to place ads for certain categories and tags

Cons

- AdSense veterans who already know where to put their ads may not find this as useful

Rating

None available

Conclusion

Click Missile is great for anyone just getting started with AdSense and ad revenue generation as a whole. It shows you exactly where you should be placing your ads for the highest click-through rate and allows you to place ads by category or for posts with certain tags. Being mobile optimized is also a huge plus. The only problem is that

veterans of AdSense and other programs might not find it all that useful if they already know where to put ads.

Google AdSense Plugin

```
http://wordpress.org/extend/plugins/adsense-plugin/
```

–This is a free plugin with basic functionality. It allows you to place ads on your site quickly and easily, and has some customization options as well. Also features multi-language capabilities.

All in One AdSense and YPN Pro

```
http://wordpress.org/extend/plugins/all-in-one-
adsense-and-ypn-pro/
```

– This is a free plugin that allows you to place not only AdSense ads on your site, but ads from the Yahoo! Partner Network as well. Comes with options that grant you a lot of control over where your ads are placed on your site and an ad randomizer to prevent readers from developing "ad blindness."

Easy AdSense

```
http://wordpress.org/extend/plugins/easy-adsense-
lite/
```

– Here is another free plugin. This one has the benefit of enforcing Google's "only three ad blocks per page" rule to keep you out of trouble. It also displays ad blocks based on post length, keeping your layout looking nice and clutter-free. It has a rating of 3.2 out of 5 stars.

WP Auto Post ADS

```
http://wordpress.org/extend/plugins/wp-ads-auto-post/
```

– A very basic free plugin that allows you to add AdSense to your site automatically. Features iFrame, HTML, and JavaScript support. This plugin is rated 5 out of 5 stars by three voters total.

Google Adsense Report Pro

Price

Free

Description

If you don't have a fancy ad plugin or theme that tracks your stats automatically, this plugin can be a great help. Google Adsense Report Pro allows you to track various ad data in your dashboard and even provides graphics and dollar currency support. It is also available in Spanish.

Google Adsense Report Pro

```
http://wordpress.org/extend/plugins/google-adsense-
report-pro/
```

Pros

- Helps you optimize your CTR by tracking your stats
- Very simple and easy to use
- Makes a great addition to any theme or AdSense insertion plugin that doesn't feature tracking

Cons

- It's nothing but a tracking plugin

Rating

Has a five-star rating, but only one person has rated it so far. Has over 2,000 downloads.

Conclusion

A very handy free plugin if you need stat tracking and analytics. The data is easy to read and understand. The only drawback is that it doesn't do anything else. Then again, it wasn't designed to.

Alternate Options

Ad Logger

```
http://wordpress.org/extend/plugins/ad-logger/
```

– This free plugin collects data not just on AdSense clicks, but on Amazon, Facebook, and Twitter as well. It also has a bombing prevention function that stops bots or malicious people from clicking your ads repeatedly, which can get you in trouble with Google. The general concept is solid, but the implementation of this plugin may be a bit too advanced for some, since it saves the data to your MySQL database. It has a rating of 2.6 out of 5 stars.

Google AdSense and Google Analytics Remover

`http://wordpress.org/extend/plugins/google-adsense-and-google-analytics-remover/`

– Your AdSense data can become skewed when you log in to your WordPress account to work on it. This free plugin blocks out ads and removes data collection when you're logged into your WordPress account to keep your data as accurate as possible.

Better AdSense Targeting

Price

Free

Description

One of the main keys to success with AdSense is being able to target your ads to your website's demographic and content. This plugin works to improve your targeting and ensure that your ads match your content by allowing you to select which areas of your site are used to select ads from the network.

Better AdSense Targeting

`http://wordpress.org/extend/plugins/better-adsense-targeting/`

Pros

- Increases ad targeting, which increases CTR
- Great for sites that have content that is unrelated to the main theme
- Easy to use

Cons

- No real special features or options

Rating

Better AdSense Targeting is rated 4.7 out of 5 stars.

Conclusion

This is a very handy plugin for sites that have a lot of varied content, such as personal blogs or travel blogs. Better AdSense Targeting makes sure that the ads displayed are ones that are relevant to the reader's interests, helping to increase CTR. It doesn't do anything fancy, but then again, it really doesn't need to.

Komoona's Google AdSense Companion

Price

Free

Description

This is another plugin that allows you to place AdSense ads on your WordPress site, but this one works a little differently. In addition to basic AdSense functionality, it also allows you to set a minimum price for ads. If the AdSense ads that are to be displayed have a lower payout than the set price, Komoona will replace them with alternate, higher value ads. In addition to this, it can also be configured to allow independent advertisers to create and upload ads automatically. This plugin is available in over 20 languages.

Komoona's Google AdSense Companion

```
http://wordpress.org/extend/plugins/komoona-ads-
google-adsense-companion/
```

Pros

- Has basic AdSense insertion functionality
- Allows you to regulate the value of your ads to some degree
- Simplifies working with independent advertisers on your site
- Relatively easy to use and has detailed instructions on how to set it up

Cons

- Some may view this as unnecessary

Rating

This plugin has a rating of 3.7 out of 5 stars

Conclusion

Komoona is an interesting plugin that provides a unique function. It could increase your overall revenue stream, but some may feel that it is unnecessary. It is free, though, so it wouldn't hurt to give it a try if you're interested.

Plugins for Forums, Chat Rooms, and Membership Sites

I won't be going over any themes for these types of sites because really just about any theme could be used. It is the plugins that you use that will give the functionality you need for these types of options on your WordPress site.

Simple:Press

Price

Free for the core plugin.

Support plugins require a membership: $39 for a two-month plan or $99 for a twelve-month plan

Description

The Simple:Press plugin adds a forum to any WordPress site with its own forum template/theme. It has sub-forum support and a variety of handy features, such as forum ranks/badges for members, automatic thumbnail and pop-up enlargement, user-defined signatures, smileys and custom smiley upload, and much more. In short, it has pretty much everything you could ever want in a forum, including security, SEO, and language features.

The overall look of the forum is simple and clean, but it's also highly customizable. You can choose the colors, set thumbnail graphics for each sub-forum, and create your forum in any way you choose. It's nothing fancy, visually speaking, but it doesn't really need to be.

This plugin is designed to work with a ton of support plugins for additional functionality. Examples include private messaging, post previews, polls, an admin bar, CAPTCHA, font resizing, and post rating. (And that's just the tip of the iceberg.) Furthermore, these plugins are all made by the same developer, so you won't' have to worry about compatibility issues. However, it must be mentioned that access to the support plugins requires a membership fee. ($39 for 2 months; $99 for 12 months)

Simple Press

`http://simple-press.com/`

Pros

- Very well rounded forum plugin
- Tons of options and features

- You can select which features you want using the additional plugin system
- Forum looks clean and simple
- Core plugin is free

Cons

- Forum setup may be considered basic looking by some
- Must pay a membership fee for support plugins

Rating

None available

Conclusion

This is an excellent forum plugin that has all the functionality you could ever want in a forum. The design looks very clean and is easy to use, not cluttered and clunky like some forum designs. The only thing holding this product back is the fact that you have to pay a membership fee for support plugins that have important functions. While you do get access to all the support plugins for a very reasonable price, the reoccurring fee will turn some people off.

Alternate Options

<u>Forums</u>

`http://wordpress.org/extend/plugins/zingiri-forum/`

– This free plugin is an easy way to add the very popular myBB forum software to WordPress. While the forums look very modern and eye-catching, and the plugin does have good functionality, some have reported encountering bugs. Still, this is good forum software for free, especially if you're a fan of myBB. It has a rating of 2.7 out of 5 stars.

<u>Mingle Forum</u>

`http://wordpress.org/extend/plugins/mingle-forum/`

– This is a unique forum plugin for WordPress that has more features than you'd expect from a free product. You can choose from several skins, all of which look really

good. Other notable features are the use of BB code, hot/very-hot topic icons, user signatures, SEO friendly URLs, and quick reply, just to name a few. This plugin has a rating of 3.9 out of 5 stars and there is plenty of support for it on its main site, including support forums.

Vanilla Forums

`http://vanillaforums.org/`

– This is a professional-level forum plugin that is actually more than just a plugin. To get this to work, you're going to have to go through some technical stuff, especially if you're planning on installing this on your own host. If you are technically skilled enough to do this, you'll be rewarded with a *very* high-end forum with excellent functionality and options. This plugin has both free and paid versions.

Premise

Price

$165

Description

Premise is a plugin designed for membership sites that offers plenty of features to help facilitate long-term profitability. It allows you to create a variety of landing pages, using video content and more. It also has templates for each page type, along with more than 1,100 custom graphics. It comes with an e-book, "The Premise Copywriting Approach," and even has copywriting tips inside WordPress to help you better convince people to sign up with you.

On top of all that, it allows you to accept recurring payments and drip-feed content on a precise schedule. It's got built-in checkout pages and the ability to set up password-protected content libraries, too. You'll also be happy to know that it works with any WordPress theme or framework. Furthermore, it also allows easy split testing and optimization.

Premise

`http://getpremise.com/`

Pros

- Many helpful features
- Geared towards making you as successful as possible
- Easy to use
- Works with any theme or framework
- Integrated checkout page and payment-processing with PayPal and Authorize.net
- Can create private forum areas

Cons

- Takes some web design skill to fully implement all of its features

Rating

None available

Conclusion

Premise is a very robust membership site plugin that does practically everything you could possibly want it to do. The integrated checkout and payment processing is amazing and the copywriting tips and e-book will work wonders for you if you don't know anything about writing copy. The developers of this plugin have gone out of their way to try and make you successful. The only drawback is that it will take some web design knowledge to implement all of the features on your site; this isn't the kind of plugin that you just install and you're good to go.

Alternate Options

Membership Lite/Membership Pro

`http://wordpress.org/extend/plugins/membership/`

– This plugin adds a lot of membership functionality to your WordPress site by providing subscribers access to content based on their membership level. The Pro version ($19 or $39.50, depending on what you get) allows unlimited membership levels and subscription levels, while the free Lite version is limited to two. A very solid membership plugin. The Lite version is rated 3.9 out of 5 stars.

Magic Members

`http://www.magicmembers.com/`

– This is a very comprehensive membership plugin with plenty of features, such as sales reports, multi-lingual integration, Simple:Press forum integration, controlled content management, payment integrating, S3 Amazon support, and much, much more. It also has excellent support, including tutorials, training, updates, and customer service. A single license costs $97; you can get a three-user license for $197 and unlimited for $297. This is an extremely powerful membership plugin.

SabaiDiscuss

Price

$20

Description

This plugin adds a question-and-answer area, sort of like Yahoo! Answers, to your WordPress site. The layout is very clean and organized, as the minimalist style works well with just about any theme. Other features include a voting system, easy moderation, an abuse reporting function, profile pages, a reputation system for members, and an easy cloning system.

SabaiDiscuss

`http://sabaidiscuss.com/`

Pros

- Simple and easy to use for administrators and users
- Question-and-answer style is very popular
- Many options and features
- Looks great with any theme

Cons

- More simplistic than a true forum

Rating

None available

Conclusion

SabaiDiscuss is a great plugin if you want to add a Q&A section to your site in the vein of Yahoo! Answers. It allows users to interact with one another in a simple yet fun way while sharing useful information. This is, of course, much less functional than a true forum but its charm is in its simplicity.

Alternate Options

<u>Question and Answer Forum</u>

`http://wordpress.org/extend/plugins/question-and-answer-forum/`

– A free plugin that also functions with a sort of question-and-answer format. This one is very basic, but does allow user profile pages and customization by theme. It also comes with a neat widget that will show the last five questions. It has a rating of 3.8 out of 5 stars.

<u>SD Questions and Answers</u>

`http://wordpress.org/extend/plugins/sd-questions-and-answers/`

– This free plugin has basic Q&A functionality, but the catch is that only the admin can create questions for the guests to answer. In that regard, it functions more like a feedback or polling option than a true discussion forum. Still, it can be a great way to encourage interaction on your site without letting the guests get out of control.

<u>WP Feedback and Survey Manager</u>

`http://wordpress.org/extend/plugins/wp-feedback-survey-manager/`

– This is a free plugin that allows you to collect feedback and survey data from your site. It is similar to SD Questions and Answers, but in this case it's more for data collection than encouraging interaction. The data gathered is displayed in a variety of charts and graphs. This plugin has a rating of 4.8 out of 5 stars.

Chat and Chat Pro

Price

Free/$19

Description

Chat and Chat Pro are plugins designed to create direct live chat on your WordPress site. With the chat box enabled, you can easily communicate directly with your members and they can communicate with each other. This has great application for both social and commercial interests. The free variant offers just a basic chat box, while the Pro version offers many advanced features, such as the ability for any Facebook/Twitter user to join the conversation, selecting which roles are mods, changing colors, enabling emoticons, disabling avatars, and archiving chats.

Chat and Chat Pro

`http://premium.wpmudev.org/project/wordpress-chat-plugin/`

Pros

- Free version gets the job done and the Pro version has a lot of handy features
- Good for both commercial and social sites
- Very easy to use

Cons

- Free version is obviously designed to make you want to purchase the Pro version

Rating

Free version is rated at 4.4 out of 5 stars

Conclusion

Chat and Chat Pro are both great chat plugins. While the free variant is a bit basic, the Pro version has plenty of great options and functionality. While the free version is

intended to get you to buy the Pro version, it isn't a bad deal at all at $19 if you want a chat program on your site with more advanced functions.

Alternate Options

Quick Chat

`http://wordpress.org/extend/plugins/quick-chat/`

– This is a very comprehensive free plugin that features a decent number of features like multi-lingual capabilities, the ability to block certain words, and the ability of an admin to ban users from chat. It is rated 4.5 out of 5 stars and has been downloaded over 100,000 times.

Banckle Live Chat

`http://wordpress.org/extend/plugins/banckle-live-chat-for-wordpress/`

– This is a free live chat plugin that gives you plenty of administrative control. You can define filter rules, create notifications, and even create surveys for post-chat sessions. It is also fully customizable.

HTML5 Online Chat Widget, aka RumbleTalk

`http://wordpress.org/extend/plugins/rumbletalk-chat-a-chat-with-themes/`

– This free plugin features Facebook and Twitter integration and has a strong focus on being mobile-friendly. It also has a theme library, an option to ban trolls, a private chat feature, and supports 29 languages. It's rated at 4.1 out of 5 stars.

Final Word

As you can see, there are plenty of plugins and themes for WordPress, and this is just a small fraction of what is available. There are literally thousands and thousands to choose from, making it easy to find something for your unique needs.

I did my best to present some of the most popular plugins as well as some alternate options that you may not have heard of before. If you're looking for something specific and didn't see it listed here, try searching through the various sites listed in the resources section.

Ultimately, this goes to show just how versatile and easy WordPress is to use as a website-building platform. There really are options for everyone and every type of site imaginable. Finding the perfect plugins and themes to build your site the way you want has never been easier.

If you want more information on how to build WordPress websites and keep them safe from hackers, check out my other books, _WordPress Domination_ and _WordPress Security_. They complement this book perfectly and will help you use WordPress to its fullest potential.

Thanks for reading. I'm always glad to have the opportunity to share information regarding this incredibly customizable and easy-to-use website-building platform. Whether you're building a site for fun or for profit, I wish you the best of luck!

Your Friend,

Lambert Klein

www.LambertKlein.com

Resources

Didn't find what you were looking for in the guide? Try these sources; you'll find access to thousands of great plugins and themes for your WordPress site. Enjoy!

Themes

- ThemeGrade.com
- ThemeForest.net
- NewWPThemes.com
- ElegantThemes.com
- WooThemes.com
- SMThemes.com
- ThemeFuse.com
- TemplateMonster.com
- ThemifyMe.com/themes

Plugins

- CodeCanyon.net
- WordPress.org/extend/plugins
- Yoast.com/WordPress
- StudioPress.com/plugins
- ElegantThemes.com/plugins

If you have found this book useful then please leave an unbiased review on Amazon at:

`http://www.amazon.com/dp/B00B35YH4G`

WordPress Top Plugins and Themes Review Book

Thanks!

BOOK THREE
WordPress Security: Protection from Hackers

Introduction

Hello, everyone, and welcome to *WordPress Security*, the guide that'll teach you how to lock your WordPress site up so tight that even the most "1337" hackers won't be able to get into it. Not only will this perfect defense ensure your privacy and safety, it will give you peace of mind as well.

You may remember the brief security chapter I had in my previous guide, *WordPress Domination: Beginner to Ninja in 7 Days*.

`http://www.amazon.com/dp/B007LS0TLE`

This guide expands on that in a major way to show you a combination of beginner, intermediate, and advanced anti-hacking techniques, as well as a few other neat WordPress security tricks to keep your website protected.

The WordPress platform has become immensely popular for those who build websites online. This is due to an easy-to-use interface that requires no knowledge of complex coding, such as HTML or CSS, to use. WordPress also comes with some pretty heavy-duty security systems already in place. This is great for those who are new to website security and anti-hacking systems.

The problem lies in the fact that even the best security systems are vulnerable to crafty hackers who use the latest hacking and cracking techniques to get into your data. While the motivations of hackers and crackers can vary, 99% of the time, their intentions aren't good. Their intrusions can lead to serious consequences, like lost data, damaged coding and, in a worst-case scenario, identity theft.

The good news is that you can significantly beef up your WordPress site's inherent security with relative ease. You don't need to be a coding wizard to lock down your site and keep unwanted guests from accessing sensitive info or going on a code-destroying rampage within your system.

Most of the techniques I'm going to share are incredibly simple and can be done in a matter of minutes. Others may be a bit more advanced, but I'm going to walk you through the process and make sure that you have a good understanding of how to implement these security procedures so you can protect your site.

Now that you understand what this guide entails, let's get started and turn your WordPress site into an impenetrable Internet fortress!

<u>Chapter 1: Hackers and Crackers: The Critical Difference</u>

Every once in a while, you'll hear a news report about a hacker breaking into a system in a large company or causing some sort of trouble. Many people aren't aware, however, that the media incorrectly uses the term "hacker" when describing the situation.

Hackers are shown in television and movies as a sort of super-intelligent criminal. Sometimes they are fighting against a corrupt government or otherwise using their abilities for good. Other times, they are malicious and are terrorizing people with their skills. There are all sorts of fantasy hacker scenarios in entertainment, but when's the last time you saw a movie on someone labeled as a heroic or criminal *cracker*?

Reporters usually mix up the word "hacker" with the correct term, "cracker." Unless you enjoy computers or work closely with them, you probably don't know the difference.

In this guide, we will be using the term "hacker" to refer to someone that's breaking through your WordPress website's security. However, it is important that you understand the difference between the two phrases.

First, let's define what they mean. We'll start with the more popular expression, "hacker."

Hackers

A hacker is a person who is familiar with the internal systems of a computer or network. Hackers are enthusiastic about computers and enjoy exploring and learning about how they work. They are often computer programmers or designers.

The media often portrays the word in a criminal sense, and this is often where the non-technical crowd gets confused. When you hear on the news about a hacker attacking a bank, what they're actually referring to is a cracker.

It's important to realize that there is nothing illegal about being a hacker. The word doesn't imply that anything illicit is taking place. It is no more illegal to hack a system you own than it is for you to look under the hood of your car.

However, when someone else comes along and starts looking under your car's hood without your permission, then that is where the line gets crossed. There may also be laws regarding what kind of modifications you can make to your own car, such as installing tinted windows.

Hackers occasionally get in trouble by going too far. Once a hacker starts performing illegal actions through hacking, they can be correctly classified as a cracker.

Crackers

Crackers are also computer and network enthusiasts. The difference is that crackers use their knowledge of computer systems to break into secured systems that they have no authority over. Such actions include (but are not limited to) breaking into systems they do not have permission to access, stealing information, and corrupting data.

Even the legitimate use of the term "cracker" doesn't necessarily mean that something illegal is happening, though. Most crackers do their work illegally, but not all. Some companies hire crackers to intentionally break into their systems. This may sound crazy, but the goal is to expose weak spots that a real cracker could exploit so that they can be patched up.

Here, the cracker is legally doing an act that would normally be illegal. This is similar to how police may hire minors to attempt to buy alcohol at a bar, in an effort to test if the bar is following the law about checking the IDs of patrons.

If you really want to get your vocabulary correct, you'll have to throw some adjectives on there. Criminal crackers or malicious crackers are a few you could use.

You can think of crackers as being a type of hacker. Additionally, you could say crackers are hackers, but hackers aren't crackers. It's like saying all German Shepherds are dogs, but not all dogs are German Shepherds.

Why the Confusion?

Not a lot of people run around calling any dog they see a German Shepard. After all, a Golden Retriever and a Dalmatian are different breeds and wouldn't be classified as a German Shepard. So why have the words "cracker" and "hacker" become mixed up?

It may be in part that they sound so similar. They rhyme, and cracker has only one more letter than hacker. Additionally, their definitions are very similar.

Some hackers take offense to the use of the term. With the way the word is portrayed in movies and in the news, it leads people to believe that all hackers are crackers, and that being a hacker automatically means you commit crimes.

Remember, it isn't incorrect to refer to a cracker as a hacker, just as it wouldn't be wrong to call a German Shepard a dog. But when someone who isn't familiar with technological terms only hears the word "hacker" to describe these people, they have no reason not to believe that's the correct word.

With how the word "hacker" is used in the media, and has been for years, it can be acceptably used to refer to a cracker. Also, from this point forward, this guide refers to anyone attempting to break into your WordPress system as a hacker. However, it is important to know the difference between the two. This way, you can clarify if need be, and not make assumptions about people based on simply if you know they're a "hacker."

What Do Hackers Want?

What does a hacker stand to gain by breaking into your website? Some see it as a way to make a monetary gain. For example, a hacker who tries to steal credit card numbers from a bank may be trying to steal someone's bank account or identity. An identity can be sold and resold to a variety of buyers who would use it for illegal business practices.

Sometimes the hacker isn't after your money, however. Maybe you just happened to upset the wrong person, who then decides to have a vendetta against your website or blog. They may try to hack your site and take your server offline, disrupting business. They could also edit your website and put damaging information on your pages that would drive away readers or customers.

Perhaps a hacker stumbles onto your website. Suppose you've made a statement on your site that contradicts a strong belief the hacker holds. Instead of deciding to go on their merry way and agreeing to disagree, they may take this as a reason to attack you.

Also, there are hackers out there that simply love the idea of doing something naughty. These hackers tend to be in the younger generations, so they're looking to entertain themselves and prove how "cool" they are to their friends and strangers. They may not mean any serious harm to you, but the damage they can cause should still be taken seriously.

Hackers may look at your security system as a personal challenge, as if you're daring them to attack. Their pride compels them to try and take control of your system. There's no greater satisfaction for them than when they succeed—the more difficult the lock, the more interested they will be.

Whatever the case, it's important to keep your security tightly locked and updated. You never want to put your WordPress site at risk of being hacked. Following basic security precautions, keeping your system up-to-date, and having good security systems are vital to securing your website.

Chapter 2: Basic Steps to Stop a Hacker

Now that you have an idea of what the difference between a hacker and cracker is, and why they may try to get into your site, we can concentrate on preventing a security breach. Most of these techniques are very basic and easy to implement; others are a bit more advanced, though not hard. First, let's start by examining what you can do to prevent offline or in-network threats to your website.

Offline and In-Network Threat Prevention

Believe it or not, many people have their WordPress site's security compromised not by an online hacker, but rather by someone offline or within their network, such as a LAN or cloud-computing group. In fact, people tend to overlook this aspect of website security so often that this is one of the easiest ways for hackers to get into your system. All the online security in the world won't matter if your website isn't protected from real-life threats.

Shared Computers

This is one of the most common ways to have your website broken into. Many people share computers, either at work, at home, or in public places such as libraries and net cafes. When you access your website's admin area on a shared computer, you are putting yourself at risk. Due to this, it is advised that you don't access your admin area on *any* shared computers.

However, realistically there may be times when you have to do this. If you only have one computer in your home, then this may be unavoidable. But there are ways to compensate for this security risk.

The first and most basic rule is to not click the "Remember Me" box on the login screen. This will ensure that you, or a potential threat, will have to type in the login info manually each time.

When you're done working on your site on a shared computer, *always* log out. If you want to be extra safe, you can go into the computer's history and delete the cookies as well.

Never access your website's admin area on shared computers in libraries, hotels, net cafés or similar places. You have no idea how secure these computers are. A crafty hacker could have installed a key-logger program or some other exploit that can record your login information and get into your account. For this same reason, you should also avoid accessing your admin area from a friend's smart phone or tablet device.

File Transfer Protocol

FTP is one of the easiest ways to upload files to your WordPress site, but if you aren't careful, it could present a security risk. When you use FTP, not only are you gaining access to your WordPress site, but also every single file that is on your hosting server. If you have multiple sites, a hacker would only have to get into your FTP account to access them all. This could be disastrous.

Reducing the risk of an FTP-based intrusion is much the same as preventing other offline and in-network threats: limiting access. When you use your FTP client, make sure you create a password-protected profile for each website, as well as the root domain if it will let you. Different FTP programs will have different security measures, but most should have this basic function.

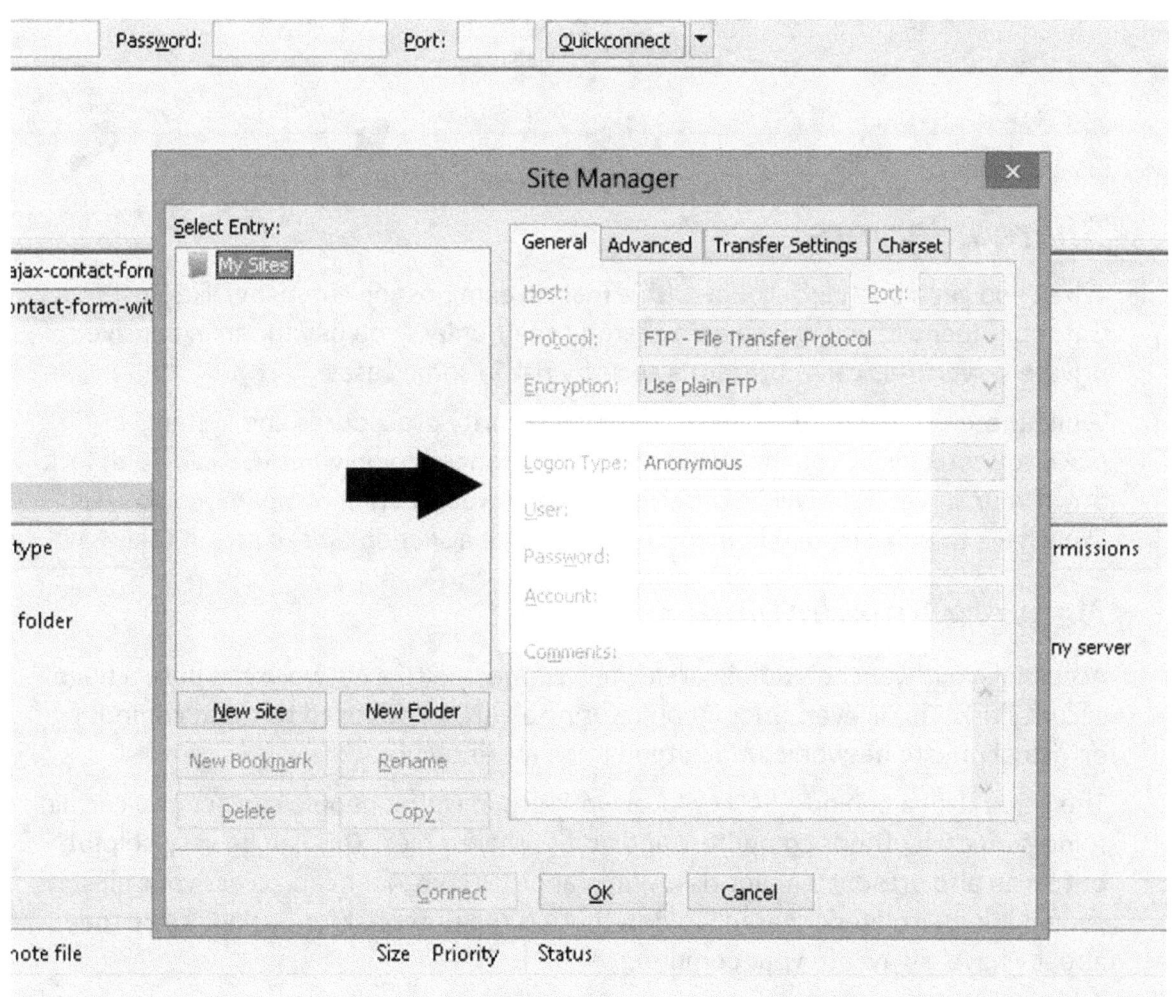

Also, while the quick-link can be a handy way to quickly access your files using an FTP program, you're going to want to avoid using this, especially on a shared computer. If for some reason you do use this function, make sure you delete the history once you're done transferring files.

Shared Servers

When you get a hosting account with a mainstream hosting company, like Host Gator or Bluehost, you will be on a shared server unless you pay for an expensive private server. This can represent a security risk in some cases.

While these companies do have exceptional security procedures and systems in place to protect you, you may want to get additional info on what you can do to lock down your server. This will be different for each web-hosting company, so you will likely have to email or call them if they don't have a section on security in their FAQ.

Network Vulnerabilities

Accessing your website's admin area while connected to a network can pose a huge security risk. This is even truer if you're using a LAN, as opposed to cloud computing or virtual private networks, which tend to be more secure.

The general idea behind a LAN or local work-group is that people can get into certain folders on each other's computers and access shared files. This can be very helpful, but it can also present a major risk. When another computer can access your files, even if it is an isolated "shared" folder, there is the potential for hacking since they already have a way into your computer.

Even worse, if one computer on the network gets hacked, the hacker could potentially access all the computers on the network, including yours. This can pave the way for viruses, Trojans, root-kits, key-loggers and other nasty surprises. If you're accessing your admin area or using FTP to access your web server, this could spell disaster.

The most obvious way to prevent this from happening is simply to not access your admin area while on a LAN. If you have no choice but to do so, make sure you speak with your network administrator and ensure that proper security protocols are in

place for every single computer on the network. Remember, a chain is only as strong as its weakest link.

Generally speaking, cloud-computing networks and VPNs have top-notch security systems in place to prevent intrusion. Security protocols include Internet Protocol Security, Transport Layer Security, Datagram Transport Layer Security, Secure Shell (a great alternative to FTP), and more.

Username Issues

If your user name is obvious, it makes it much easier for a real-life threat to get into your admin account. Whatever you do, do not use "admin" as your username for your admin account. Once someone knows your username, it isn't hard for them to use brute force tactics to hack your password.

If you have named your admin username "admin," I would recommend making another admin account and deleting that one.

To create a new admin account, simply click the tab on the left-hand menu in the WordPress admin area that says "Users," then click where it says "Add New." Give the new account administrative privileges, log out, log into that new account, and then delete your old admin account.

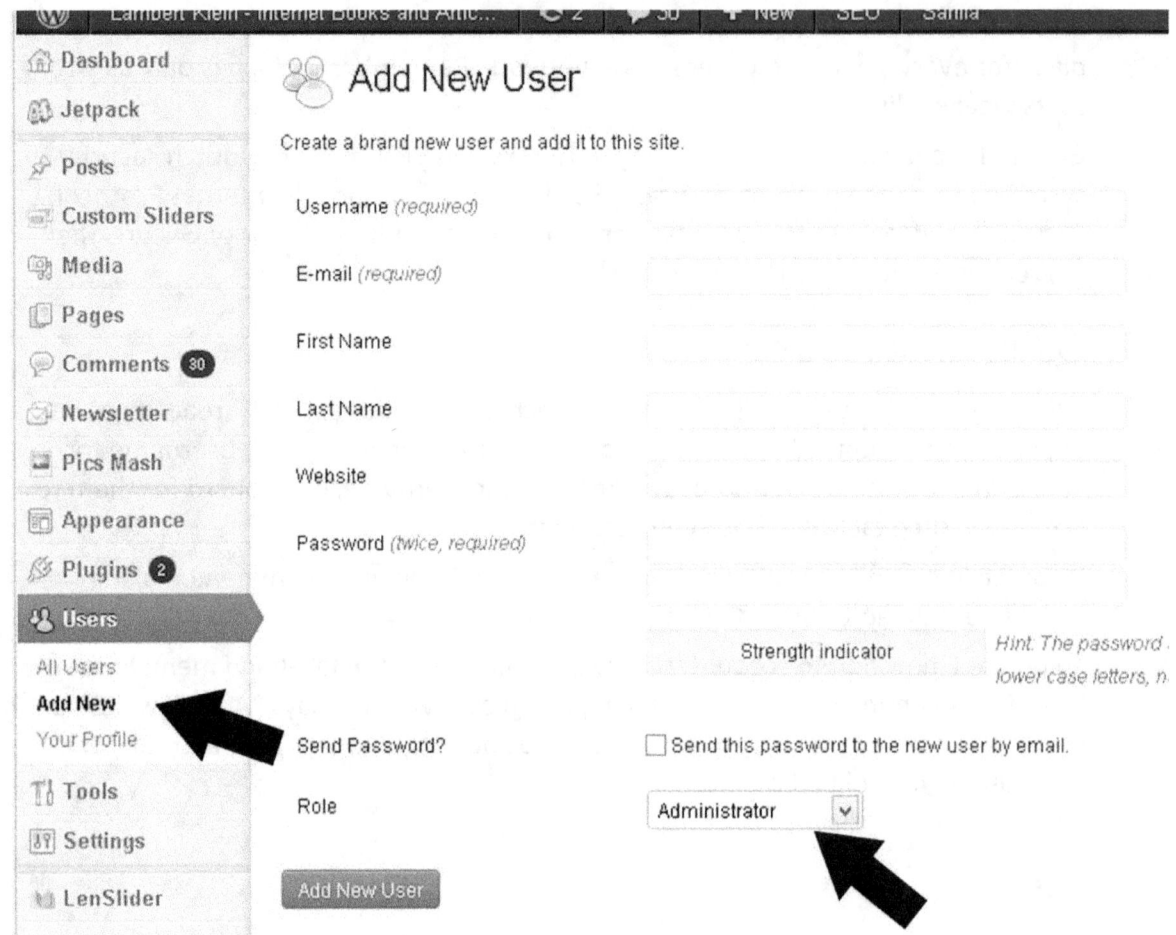

Online Threats

While offline threats are probably the greatest threat to your WordPress security, online threats can be just as dangerous if you're unprepared. Online attacks can come in many different forms, from corrupt plugins that rewrite your files to SQL injection attacks to brute force password hacking. Fortunately, for every hacking technique, there are countermeasures to prevent it.

File Permissions

Certain files in your WordPress folders are "write–accessible." This means that anyone who can access them can rewrite them; no special permissions are needed.

While this is necessary in many cases to allow your WordPress site to function (some plugins rewrite files), there are certain files that need to have this disabled for security purposes.

Take a look at this list of files that should not be writable:

- The root directory (except .htaccess, if you want WordPress to automatically configure rewrite rules for you)
- /wp-admin/
- /wp-includes/
- /wp-content/plugins/

Keep in mind that /wp-content/ itself should be writable. Making it unwritable could cause problems.

To change a file from writable to unwritable, it is easiest to use a FTP program such as Filezilla, although you can do this via your cPanel as well. To do this in Filezilla, all you have to do is right-click the file you want to alter and select "File Attributes." A new window will pop up that will allow you to change the permissions. Unclick the boxes that say "Write" for both Group and Public. This will ensure that only those with admin access can rewrite these files. Go through and do this for all the files listed above and any others you don't want to be writable.

Plugin Threats

Plugins are a handy way to change the functionality of your WordPress site and make it easier to use. While 99.9% of plugins are safe to use, there are some out there that have been designed by hackers to exploit your system. As previously mentioned, some plugins actively rewrite some of your WordPress files to function, and this can lead to a security breach. Though the risk of being hacked by a bogus plugin is very small, you can decrease your chances even further by following a few simple steps.

The first and most obvious way to prevent a bad plugin from allowing a hacker access to your system is to only download plugins from trusted sources. When you find a plugin, either through using the WordPress plugin search or a search engine like Google, you want to make sure that it comes from a reputable source.

Look for signs that the plugin is the real deal. Does the plugin have a lot of good ratings? Does it have a website explaining how it works? A hacker's plugin will often times have no effort put into the webpage where you download it, and it won't have any ratings since it is just a cheap attempt to hack people's WordPress accounts. If you are unsure about a plugin that you want, do a Google search to see if other people are talking about it or have discovered that it is a hacker plugin.

Scanning plugins for viruses and Trojans is another way to ensure that your system isn't exploited. To do this, don't download a plugin directly from the WordPress search, but instead go to the download page and download it onto your hard drive. You can then use your anti-virus/anti-malware software to scan the file and confirm that it doesn't contain any nasty surprises. It is recommended that you do this for themes as well, since they too can contain malicious code.

Keep in mind that just because a plugin is free from viruses and malware doesn't mean that it can't exploit your system. A hacker plugin may be built to exploit your system without the use of viruses, Trojans or stuff like that. This is why it is important to make sure you're only downloading plugins that are trustworthy.

Another bit of advice is to always make sure that your plugins are kept up-to-date. An out-of-date plugin can pose a security risk because, as hackers improve their hacking techniques, WordPress, plugins and other security systems have to evolve as well. If you have any inactive plugins on your WordPress site, delete them to ensure that they aren't used as an exploitation method.

Computer Vulnerability

We'll get into this a bit later when we discuss how to protect your computer from viruses, malware and more, but I just need to explain why this is important. When your WordPress site is attacked, the hacker doesn't necessarily have to target the site itself or even your web hosting server. If your computer has no virus protection or firewall, the hacker can get in that way as well.

If your computer becomes compromised by a hacker, this then opens the door for him or her to get into everything, including your WordPress site and web hosting. One of the most important rules of protecting your WordPress site is to ensure that your computer's security is top-notch. Lock your computer down with the latest virus protection, firewall and other security features to make sure that it isn't compromised by a hacker.

Router Security

Another major threat to your WordPress security, and your computer's security as a whole, is your router. This is especially true if you're using a wireless connection, as it is very easy for external sources to "piggyback" onto your network.

Piggybacking causes several problems aside from being a major security hazard. If you pay for your Internet connection per Gigabyte, the intruder will increase your monthly bill. Having an intruder on your network will also decrease your connection speed as well.

One of the main ways hackers exploit a wireless connection is via packet sniffing. This technique scans the data passing through your wireless network for cookies, passwords, usernames, HTTP requests and much more. Any sensitive data could potentially be intercepted and exploited.

The first thing you're going to want to do to prevent this from happening is to change your router's username and password. Hackers are crafty individuals and can get lists of default usernames and passwords for virtually any router in existence. Leaving your username and password as default is like leaving the key to your house sitting on your doormat.

Username and Password

In most cases, you can access your router's setup screen by typing "192.168.1.1" into your browser. (The IP address could be different, such as 192.168.3.1. Check your router's documentation.) You will then be prompted to enter your username and password. If you are unsure of what they are, try checking the manual your router came with. If for some reason you can't get this to work, then do a Google search for more info or contact the manufacturer. In any case, make sure you get that username and password changed as soon as possible.

SETUP   **ADVANCED**   **TOOLS**   **STATUS**

ADMINISTRATOR SETTINGS

The 'admin' and 'user' accounts can access the management interface. The admin has read/wri
access and can change passwords, while the user has read-only access.

By default there is no password configured. It is highly recommended that you create a
password to keep your router secure.

Save Settings   Don't Save Settings

ADMIN PASSWORD

Please enter the same password into both boxes, for confirmation.

Password :

Verify Password :

SSID

Another thing you're going to want to do while you're in your router's admin area is
change the SSID name, which is basically the name of your network. In most cases,
this will simply be listed as "default" or as the name of the manufacturer of your
router. Changing this won't necessarily give you additional protection against
hackers but it will ensure that no one accesses your network by accident.

SETUP	ADVANCED	TOOLS	S

WIRELESS

Wireless Network Settings

Use this section to configure the wireless settings for your D-Link Router. Please not changes made on this section may also need to be duplicated on your Wireless Clier

Save Settings   Don't Save Settings

WIRELESS NETWORK SETTINGS

Enable Wireless : ☑

Wireless Network Name : thinkhealthy   (Also called the SSID)

Enable Auto Channel Scan : ☑

Wireless Channel : 2.437 GHz - CH 6 ⌄

802.11 Mode : Mixed 802.11ng, 802.11g and 802.11b ⌄

Transmission Rate : Best (automatic) ⌄   (Mbit/s)

Channel Width : Auto 20/40 MHz ⌄

Visibility Status : ⦿ Visible ◯ Invisible

WIRELESS SECURITY MODE

To protect your privacy you can configure wireless security features. This device supp wireless security modes, including WEP, WPA-Personal, and WPA-Enterprise. WEP is wireless encryption standard. WPA provides a higher level of security. WPA-Personal require an authentication server. The WPA-Enterprise option requires an external RAD

Security Mode : None ⌄

For example, if you and a neighbor both have Linksys routers and your signals are overlapping, there is the possibility that they could get on your network by accident or vice versa. This could slow down your connection and increase your monthly bill, as described earlier.

WEP/WPA2 Encryption

You'll want to make sure you enable encryption while in your router's admin page, as well. This will make it much harder for others to encroach onto your network. To do this, set the network to use either WEP or WPA2 encryption methods. If your router is older than 2006, use WEP. If it was made in 2006 or later, use WPA2, which is more secure but incompatible with older routers. In most cases, you will also be prompted to enter a password. Make it something hard to guess, such as a random string of numbers, symbols and letters.

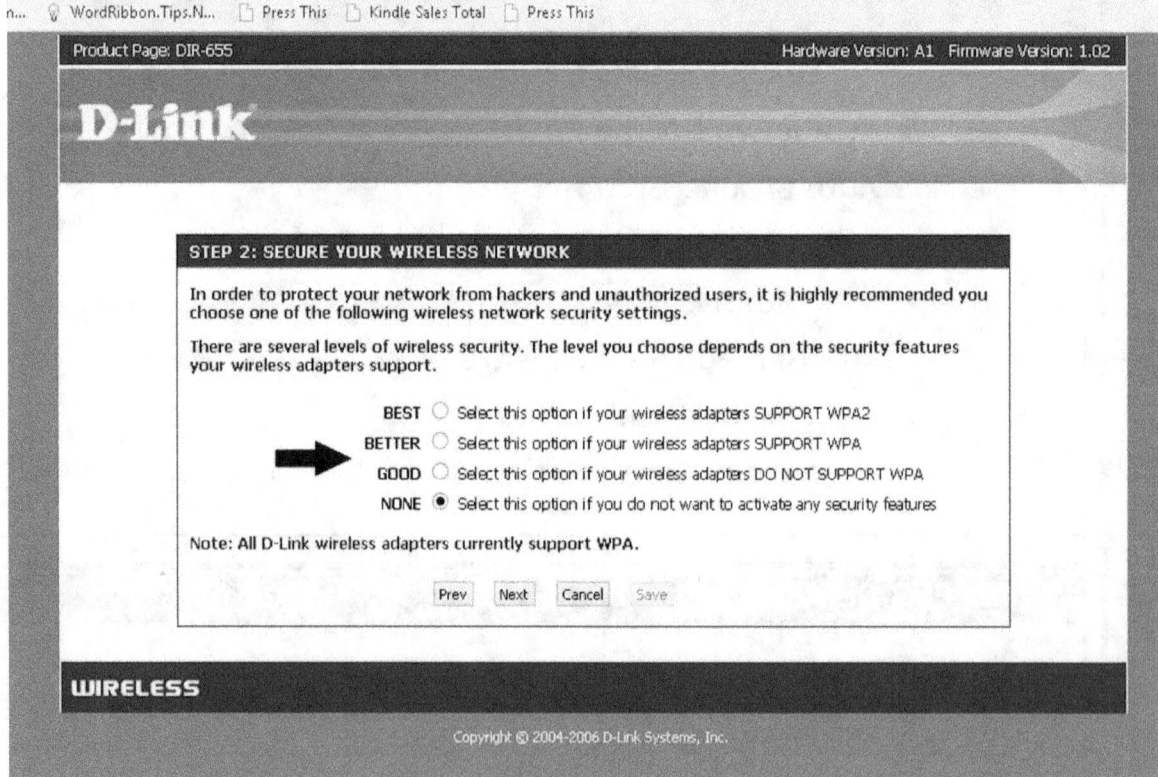

MAC Address Filtering

Each wireless device, from laptops to smart phones, has what is known as a MAC address, which is like an IP address for wireless use. To ensure that unauthorized devices don't access your router, you can make it so that only pre-approved devices are allowed to connect to it. This is because MAC addresses are hard-coded into your networking equipment, so that one address only lets one single device connect to the network.

The first step to pulling this off is to decide which devices you want to allow connecting to your wireless network. Once that's done, you need to get the MAC addresses of all these devices. To find this on a computer, you'd typically open up the command prompt and type in "ipconfig/all." This will show the MAC address beside where it says "Physical Address."

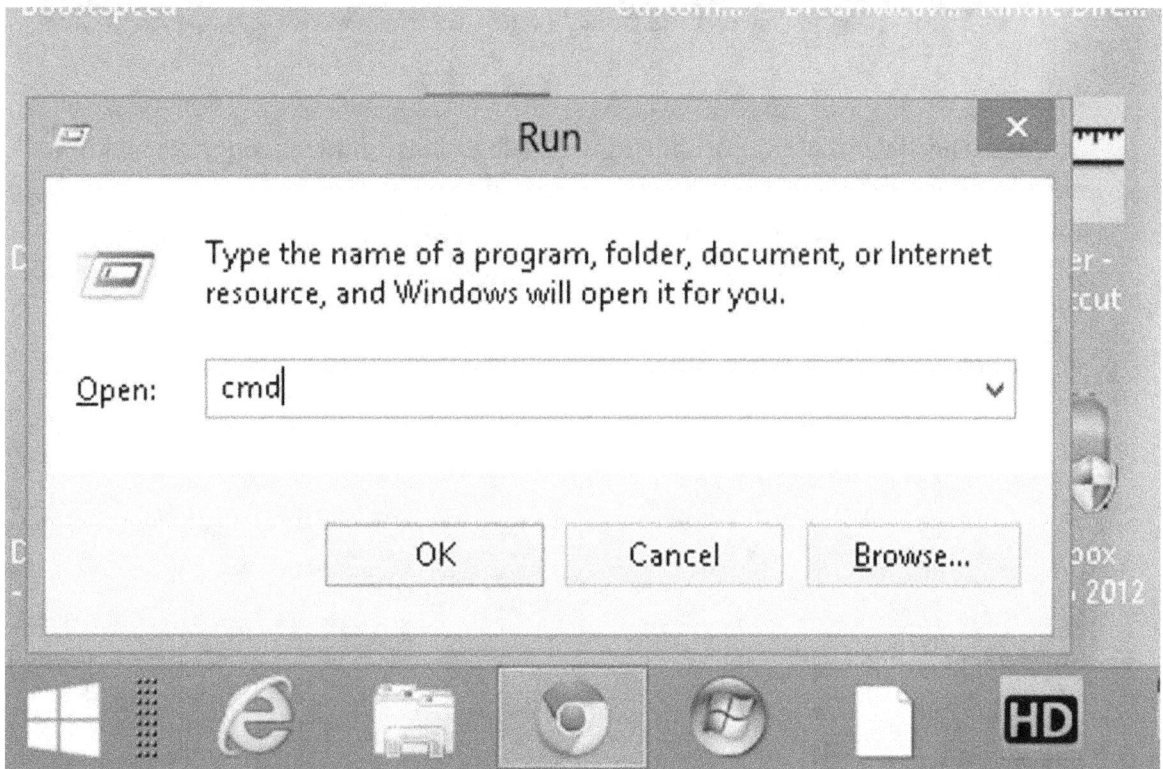

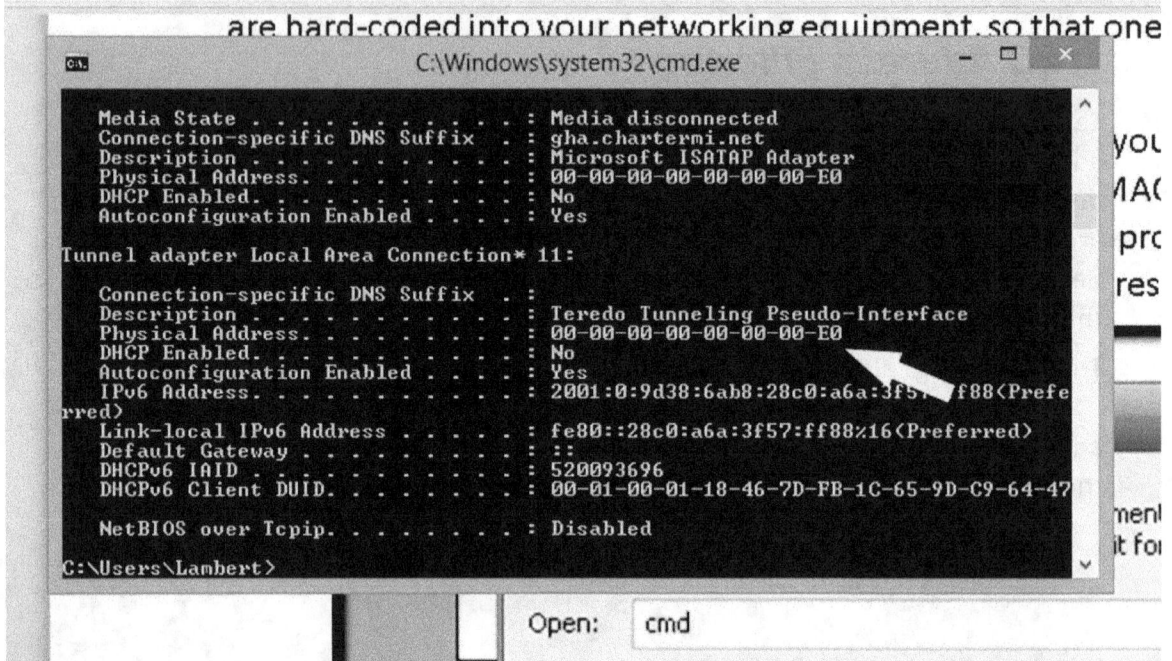

For smart phones and other portable devices like tablets, this can generally be found under "network settings," though this can vary for each device.

Once you have the entire list of MAC addresses you need, you can then add them to the filtering section in your router's administrative area.

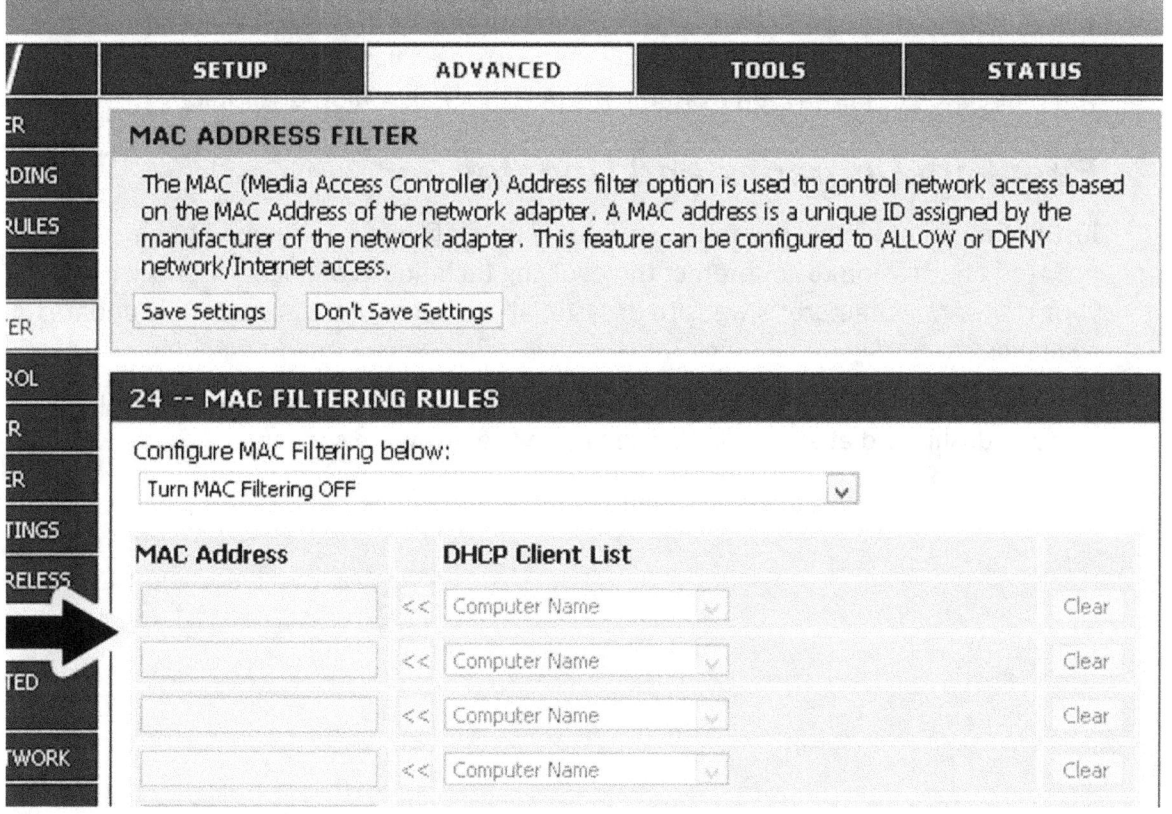

Reducing the Signal Range

Most routers typically have a pretty large wireless range. This can work to your disadvantage, especially if you live in an apartment complex. Fortunately, it is easy to deal with this by changing the mode of your router from 802.11n or 802.11b to 802.11g. You can also use a different wireless channel.

Other, simpler methods include wrapping tinfoil around your router's antenna, placing the router in a box or even hiding it under the bed. Keep in mind that these methods can sometimes cause signal interference.

Another method is to use anti-WiFi paint.

```
http://news.bbc.co.uk/2/hi/8279549.stm
```

Yes, such a thing actually exists. This special paint is designed to absorb radio signals and would easily confine your router's signal to a single room if the walls were covered with it. This could be especially useful in an apartment complex... though you'd need to get permission from the property manager first, of course.

Firmware Upgrades and Updates

Just like most other security software, your router's firmware will need to be updated on occasion to counteract the evolving techniques of hackers. Check in at your router manufacturer's website occasionally to see if there are any new updates available.

To check which version of firmware your router is currently running, access your router's dashboard at 192.168.1.1, then go to the firmware section.

D-Link

DIR-655	SETUP	ADVANCED	TOOLS	STATUS

ADMIN

TIME

SYSLOG

EMAIL SETTINGS

SYSTEM

FIRMWARE

DYNAMIC DNS

SYSTEM CHECK

SCHEDULES

FIRMWARE

The Firmware Upgrade section can be used to update to the latest firmware code to improve functionality and performance.

If you would like to be notified when new firmware is released, place a checkmark in the box next to Email Notification of Newer Firmware Version.

Save Settings   Don't Save Settings

FIRMWARE INFORMATION

Current Firmware Version : 1.02

Current Firmware Date : 2006/10/13

Latest Firmware Version : 1.02

Click here to access firmware online.

FIRMWARE UPGRADE

Note: Some firmware upgrades reset the configuration options to the factory defaults. Before performing an upgrade, be sure to save the current configuration from the Tools -> Admin screen.

To upgrade the firmware, your PC must have a wired connection to the router. Enter the name of the firmware upgrade file, and click on the Upload button.

Upload :   Choose File   No file chosen

Upload

FIRMWARE UPGRADE NOTIFICATION OPTIONS

Automatically Check Online
for Latest Firmware Version :   ☑

Email Notification of Newer
Firmware Version :   ☐

Other Prevention Tactics

Now that you understand some of the basics when it comes to protecting your WordPress site and your computer from both offline and online threats, let's get into some of the other ways you can protect yourself from hackers. Some of these techniques are a bit on the technical side, but ultimately pretty easy to pull off.

Update WordPress and Plugins

As mentioned a few times, hackers are constantly evolving their techniques to crack into WordPress. To counter this, WordPress continuously improves their software, as well. This makes it very important to update WordPress as soon as possible when a new version comes out.

Also, make sure that you're updating your plugins when they need to be updated. Frequent updating combined with deleting unused plugins will help to ensure that they are not exploited and used by a hacker to gain access to your site.

Backing Up Your Websites and Databases

We're going to get into how to create and backup SQL databases a bit farther down the road, but for now I just want to get across the importance of doing it. This is actually more of a "damage control" technique than an anti-hacking technique.

In a worst-case scenario, if you get hacked, the hacker may decide to completely wipe your data when they're done doing whatever it is they broke into your WordPress site to do. This can destroy months or even years of hard work. This is why your website needs to be backed up.

Backing up your website is pretty simple and typically consists of either using a plugin to do it, manually backing up the SQL database you created, or both. I'll go into this in more detail later. I recommend having multiple databases for multiple sites, so that if a hacker gets into one website, they can't also get into every site on your server.

Your web hosting should back up your data as well if they're doing their job. Before you purchase web hosting, make sure you verify that they do this for you. Most companies, like Host Gator and Bluehost, do this automatically at regular intervals.

.htaccess Lock-Down

Your .htaccess file is one of your most important files when it comes to WordPress security. By default, it is at risk of being exploited by cunning hackers, but a few simple changes will make it much more secure and prevent people from using it to invade your WordPress site.

The first thing you should do is make a copy of your .htaccess file. When editing files, you can sometimes screw things up and render your entire website inoperable. This will ensure that if something goes wrong, you can re-upload the original file and start over.

To find the .htaccessfile for the root domain, you're going to go from the root folder down to the public_html folder and look in there. The file will be below any add-on domains you may have and folders like wp_admin.

public_ftp
public_html
? ruby

Filename	Filesize	Filetype	Last modified
Templates		File folder	1/14/2013 1:51:...
webassist		File folder	1/14/2013 1:51:...
wp-admin		File folder	1/14/2013 1:51:...
wp-content		File folder	2/7/2013 9:58:5...
wp-includes		File folder	1/14/2013 1:51:...
.htaccess	7,340	HTACCESS...	2/7/2013 10:18:...
00EA2163BDDC(...	40,088	JPEG image	2/29/2012 1:13:...
400.shtml	130	SHTML File	7/7/2005 5:11:2...
401.shtml	162	SHTML File	6/25/2003 11:1...

To access the .htaccess file for add-on domains, you have to click the folder for that add-on domain that's in your public_html file under the root folder.

Keep in mind that the contents of your .htaccess file may differ a bit between your root domain and your add-on domains. Also, sometimes your .htaccess file will be hidden, and you'll have to select "Show Hidden Files." In Filezilla, this is done by clicking on "Server" then "Force showing hidden files."

Editing your .htaccess file can have a variety of results, some of which can be unpredictable, depending on which folder you place it in. Some web hosting companies may not provide you with .htaccess files, so you may have to create them yourself, which is relatively simple.

To create a .htaccess file, simply open a text editor like Notepad and paste in the following:

```
# BEGIN WordPress
<ifmodule mod_rewrite.c>
RewriteEngine On
RewriteBase /
RewriteCond %{REQUEST_FILENAME} !-f
RewriteCond %{REQUEST_FILENAME} !-d
RewriteRule . /index.php [L]
</ifmodule>
# END WordPress
```

Save the file as ".htaccess" and upload it into the folder of your choice. This will typically be the public_html folder, but it can go in other folders, too, such as the main folder for each add-on domain.

Protecting Your wp-admin Folder

The next thing you want to do is limit which IP addresses can access the admin area of your WordPress site. This will ensure that even if they crack your username and password, a hacker can't get into your admin area. Keep in mind that a side effect of this will be that you will also be unable to access your admin area from any computer that is not listed in the file.

To do this, go into your .htaccess file by right-clicking on it and selecting "view/edit." Then, add the following code:

```
AuthUserFile /dev/null

AuthGroupFile /dev/null

AuthName "Access Control"

AuthType Basic
```

```
order deny,allow
deny from all
#IP address to Whitelist
allow from 123.456.789.012
```

(Swap out the IP address 123.456.789.012 with your own IP address.)

You can add other IP addresses as well if you have multiple devices you want to grant access to, or if you have other trusted individuals who need to access your site from their computers.

An alternate, simpler code you can use is:

```
# deny access to wp admin
order deny,allow
allow from xx.xx.xx.xx #
deny from all
```

Replace the "xx"s with your static IP.

This technique is only viable if you use a static IP address. A dynamic address, which changes constantly, won't work here because this limits access to your admin folder to specific IP addresses.

Protection .hta Files

You can also strengthen your .htaccess file by adding the following code to your domain's root .htaccess file:

```
# STRONG HTACCESS PROTECTION</code>
<Files ~ "^.*\.([Hh][Tt][Aa])">
order allow,deny
deny from all
satisfy all
</Files>
```

What this does is prevent any external access to files that have .hta, drastically decreasing the chances of an external source hacking these files.

While you're doing this, you also need to limit your .htaccess file's write access. In your FTP client, you can simply enter the numeric value 644. This will give the following permissions:

Owner: Read, Write

Group: Read

Public: Read

Protect Your wp-config.php File

You can also secure your wp-config.php file by adding this code at the very bottom of your htaccess file:

```
<Files wp-config.php>
```

```
Order Deny,Allow

Deny from All

</Files>
```

Ideally, you should do both, as this will also help to limit unauthorized access to your wp_config.php file.

Another method of protecting this file is through adding custom security keys. When you get into your wp-config file, you'll find a section that looks like this:

```
define('AUTH_KEY', 'put your unique phrase here');

define('SECURE_AUTH_KEY', 'put your unique phrase here');

define('LOGGED_IN_KEY', 'put your unique phrase here');

define('NONCE_KEY', 'put your unique phrase here');
```

What you want to do is go to **https://api.wordpress.org/secret-key/1.1/** and get your own secret security keys. You'll then use them to replace the bottom four "define" rules, so that they look something like this:

```
define('AUTH_KEY','1j+_ .[6c1=13n rhZBhjXd0o|miL<baCpYhqZrl}o2a|irZy-
]Wy8PYW+a]zE]5');

define('SECURE_AUTH_KEY','s8p1+WgH0{Ph/)Vr;pFggsp{xoh8Cy>>#/+]EJ|P|yQ
fS* /SJO7XuK#G3&f1rnZ');

define('LOGGED_IN_KEY','h$eIl%#nZ|.}z-U)Z:O$u,y c[N;7^j-
x,)Zs*wUHheGO-(KKpONVC664X$uO$Mt');

define('NONCE_KEY','d=>/Uh@%RnZ|*<bGq[2<_R@spP*oE[7oE?<#%xyoowmU0XzxK
DjhyLXLcifX32k');
```

Encryption of user data will make your login passwords a lot stronger than they were previously.

Prevent Directory Browsing

Another security system you want to implement is adding a bit of code to your .htaccess file that prevents directory browsing. If a hacker is able to browse your website's directory, they can potentially find exploits that they can use to get into your system. Here is the code:

```
# disable directory browsing
Options All -Indexes
```

Put that into your .htaccess file in the root directory of your website.

Protecting Your wp-content File

Your wp-content folder is very important and can contain a lot of sensitive data. To ensure that this data isn't compromised, locate the .htaccess file in your wp-content folder (not the root .htaccess file) and add this code:

```
Order deny,allow
Deny from all
<Files ~ ".(xml|css|jpe?g|png|gif|js)$">
Allow from all
</Files>
```

As you can see, it is somewhat similar to the code that protects your wp_config.php file. If there isn't a .htaccess file in your wp-content folder, simply create one with the above code and any other security code you want in it.

Preventing Script Injections

Script injection is a sneaky way hackers can get into your files using an SQL exploit. The good news is that there is a very easy way to prevent this. Just paste the following code into your .htaccess file in your root folder.

```
# protect from sql injection
Options +FollowSymLinks
RewriteEngine On
RewriteCond %{QUERY_STRING} (\<|%3C).*script.*(\>|%3E) [NC,OR]
RewriteCond %{QUERY_STRING} GLOBALS(=|\[|\%[0-9A-Z]{0,2}) [OR]
RewriteCond %{QUERY_STRING} _REQUEST(=|\[|\%[0-9A-Z]{0,2})
RewriteRule ^(.*)$ index.php [F,L]
```

Another way to help prevent script injections is to change the prefix of your tables. By default, the prefix is "wp_"... and every hacker knows that. The prefix can be easily changed by using the WP Security Scan plugin. Browse to this URL **http://wordpress.org/extend/plugins/wp-security-scan/** to visit the download page for more info.

Keep Search Engines from Indexing Your Admin Area

Google and other search engines have very efficient crawlers that go through your site and index its pages. Unfortunately, they can also end up indexing your admin area if you're not careful.

To prevent this, you're going to want to create a robots.txt file to place in your root directory. The file should contain the following code:

```
Disallow: /wp-*
```

Browse to http://www.robotstxt.org/robotstxt.html for more detailed information on how to create and configure a robots.txt file and where it goes.

Delete Inactive User Accounts

This should go without saying. If you have user accounts on your WordPress site that no one uses, they should be deleted. Accounts created by users other than you can have weak username and password security that can be potentially exploited and used by hackers to gain entry into your site.

Using HTTPS

While most sites use HTTP, sites that need extra security, such as payment processors like PayPal, use HTTPS. This is an improved version of HTTP that you can use on your site for additional security.

By using HTTPS, your username and password will be encrypted, ensuring that they are lot harder to decode if they happen to be intercepted by a hacker.

There are two basic ways to enable HTTPS on your site. The first is the manual way, which is done by adding the following code to your wp-config.php file:

```
define('FORCE_SSL_LOGIN', true);
```

The other method is by using the plugin Admin-SSL, which you can get by *Browsing to* http://www.kerrins.co.uk/blog/admin-ssl/ . It's free, so I encourage you to donate to the creator if you choose to use it.

Security Plugins

I've already mentioned a couple of plugins you can use to beef up your security. Here I'll go down a complete list of all the best security plugins you can use on your WordPress site. Remember to always keep your plugins up-to-date!

Browse to the following URLs for links to the download pages for these plugins.

WP Security Scan

`http://wordpress.org/extend/plugins/wp-security-scan/`

Scans your WordPress installation for security vulnerabilities, exploits, and anything else you should know about. It also suggests corrective measures you can use to beef up your security.

Admin-SSL

`http://wordpress.org/extend/plugins/admin-ssl-secure-admin/`

Uses private SSL protocols so secure your login page, admin area, and more. This allows you to use HTTPS for maximum encryption of sensitive data.

WordPress FireWall2

`http://wordpress.org/extend/plugins/wordpress-firewall-2/`

Protect your WordPress site with a powerful firewall. This plugin is an updated version of the popular WordPress FireWall.

Bulletproof Security

`http://wordpress.org/extend/plugins/bulletproof-security/`

This is a high-end security plugin for WordPress that protects against XSS, CSRF, SQL Injection and much more. This is a great alternative to manually configuring your .htaccess files if you struggle with that.

WP-DB-Backup

`http://wordpress.org/extend/plugins/wp-db-backup/`

If a hacker attacks, you'll find how essential it is to have a backup of your data. This plugin also allows you to back up other tables within the same database.

Antispam Bee

`http://wordpress.org/extend/plugins/antispam-bee/`

A cutting-edge anti-spam plugin. This program eliminates incoming spam by analyzing it thoroughly, including the ping. This plugin is also anonymous and registration-free.

SI CAPTCHA Anti-Spam

`http://wordpress.org/extend/plugins/si-captcha-for-wordpress/`

Fight off spambots with this handy plugin, which adds a captcha form to your comments section, login page and more. Works incredibly well with Akismet, another popular anti-spam plugin.

Blackhole

`http://perishablepress.com/blackhole-bad-bots/`

Having a robots.txt file in your root directory sometimes isn't quite good enough. Blackhole traps any bots that make it past your robots.txt file. This sophisticated software also does a WHOIS lookup on the bad bots and records their activity, so that all future bots of the same origin are permanently denied access to your files.

AskApache Password Protect

`http://wordpress.org/extend/plugins/askapache-password-protect/`

This plugin is designed to add multiple layers of security to your website. By using additional password protection, you can build a virtual "wall" of defense around your website.

TAC (Theme Authenticy Checker)

`http://wordpress.org/extend/plugins/tac/`

Did you know that viruses, exploit kits and more can be sneaked in with themes as well as plugins? This plugin checks the source files of all your installed themes for malicious code and other bad stuff.

Antivirus

`http://wordpress.org/extend/plugins/antivirus/`

This plugin constantly checks for dangerous viruses, malware and exploits designed specifically to target WordPress. It also comes with multilingual support.

WP Email Guard

`http://wordpress.org/extend/plugins/wp-email-guard/`

Worried about your email address being scraped off of your website by bots? This plugin converts all of your emails within the body of your posts to Javacode, making it readable only by real humans and not malicious bots.

WordPress File Monitor

`http://wordpress.org/extend/plugins/wordpress-file-monitor/`

Manually monitoring your WordPress files for any signs of hacking is a chore. This plugin will monitor your WordPress files for any additions, changes or deletions. When a change is detected, you can have the plugin email you.

Ultimate Security Checker

`http://wordpress.org/extend/plugins/ultimate-security-checker/`

This plugin scans your WordPress installation for literally hundreds of known security threats, and then gives you a security rating based on how well protected you are.

Outsourcing WordPress Security

A lot of this security stuff for WordPress is somewhat technical. The good news is that these tasks can be outsourced; there are several different ways to go about this.

The first way is to hire a professional computer security firm to take care of this for you. These firms typically range in price from moderate to expensive. This is a case of "you get what you pay for," though, and your site will be ultra-secure if you choose this route. The only problem is that it may not be economically feasible for you unless you run your own business.

Another way to do this is to hire a freelancer from a site like Freelancer.com. These freelancers typically charge less, but are still adequately knowledgeable about WordPress security and can lock up your site pretty tightly. If you feel the need, you can pay your freelancer to do monthly or weekly security checks on your site. In fact, in most cases, the only things you'll be missing out on by hiring a freelancer rather than a security firm are advanced software solutions for security issues and 24/7 systems monitoring.

Chapter 3: Computer Virus Protection

There are all sorts of programs out on the Web that can get into your computer and mess you up. Viruses, spyware, adware, Trojans and worms are a few types, and they can be difficult to remove without the right tools. The best option is to install the proper protection software and keep your system safe from the beginning.

When protecting your WordPress site, it's very important to keep your entire computer or network secure. An infected file on your computer could corrupt your website's data; a key-logger hiding in your system could give your passwords away to a hacker.

The more you understand about virus protection, the better equipped you will be for defending yourself and your data.

Keep your System Updated

Windows operating systems have automatic update features that allow you to download the latest security patches for your OS. These come straight from Microsoft and should be installed as soon as possible.

Microsoft has gotten pretty good at keeping their systems secure and Apple computers are inherently much harder to hack or infect with malicious programs. Because of this, many malicious programmers choose to get through to your data by exploiting weaknesses in the browsers you use. This means it is important to keep your browser up-to-date as well.

Many browsers tell you right away when there is a new version out. Some will even update automatically.

Holes in a browser aren't the only way to get into your system. Popular plugins like Adobe Flash Player are constantly under attack from new viruses, which can also leave you exposed. Update your plugins regularly. As with browsers and system updates, these will usually notify you when there's a new version released.

Windows OS also has programs such as Windows Defender that act as basic anti-virus tools. Windows Defender can be helpful, but it shouldn't be the only program you rely on. Windows Defender isn't updated nearly as often as a commercial security program would be because it isn't intended to be your main defense. Find

quality anti-virus and anti-malware programs, or you could find yourself dealing with difficult system-damaging traps.

What to Buy

How do you know which virus protection you should buy? There are many different programs you can buy, so you need to know what you want in software security.

Your first task is to find a product with all the features you need. Here is what you're looking for when shopping:

- Real-time Scanner: This feature actively scans all data that comes through your network. It can find and quarantine viruses and malware before they hide or install themselves in your system.

- Heuristic Scanner: This process helps catch viruses and other programs that might not be in the software's virus database yet. It uses what it knows about other malicious programs to find new threats and contain them before damage can spread.

- POP3 Email and Webmail Scanner: It should be able to detect malicious programs in attachments both on POP3 email programs and web-based mail systems like Hotmail or Gmail.

- Instant Message Protection: Sometimes, worms and other programs will try to get into your system through instant message clients via infected computers on your contact list. A decent security software package will be able to block this.

- Scheduled Scans: Set your protection software to run an automated scan on specified days or times. It's important to run full scans frequently in case something has managed to sneak past the real-time scanner.

- Script Blocking: Scripts may be used to execute harmful programs on your computer through the browser. Your software should be able to identify harmful scripts and stop them.

⅄ Automatic Updates: Thousands of new viruses are written every day. Keeping your software up-to-date is a high priority, and automatic updates make that easy.

The next thing to keep in mind is the cost. Some protection programs are subscription based, while others have a one-time fee for security. There are even some free options available online. While you shouldn't put your security at risk to save some money, there are quality programs available that are either cheap or free.

Additionally, some programs have basic packages but offer better protection for a higher cost. Make sure that the price you choose gives you all the features you need. You don't want to buy software thinking you're getting the whole package when you actually only got half.

Configure your Protection

Once you've selected your protection and installed it, you'll want to configure it. You may be tempted to just let it do what it wants, but you'll quickly find that anti-virus software needs to be customized. If you don't tell it what to do, you could end up not activating the features you need, or even have safe software blocked.

Read the Manual

Many people neglect the manual when they first open a new product. They go by an "I can figure it out myself" mentality that can lead them to problems. Now, you don't have to sit down and read the instructions front to back, but when you come up to something you're having trouble with, it should be the first place you look.

If you bought your program in a box, it should come with a paper manual that can answer some basic questions you may have. Some even come with a digital manual located on a disk in the box. If the manual doesn't help you ,or you downloaded your software online, go to the company's website. They will most likely have an FAQ, knowledge base, or support system that can help. Online directions and support are likely to be the most up-to-date instructions you'll find.

Basic Configuration

Start with the automatic scanner. You want to be sure this is set to run at a time when your computer will be on, but you won't be working. For example, if your scanner is set to run at midnight, but you turn your computer off at 11:00 PM every night, this may prevent your anti-virus from finding an infection. Also, you don't want to run the scanner while you're working, as that can slow your computer's performance greatly.

The automatic updater needs to be set to check for updates every day, which is the default setting for most programs. Some programs will allow you to check for updates several times a day. You want to have the latest updates for your systems, and new updates could be published at any time. The more often you update, the safer you will be, but once a day is usually fine.

You also need to become familiar with your whitelist, which is composed of software you want your security systems to leave alone. Security programs can sometimes interfere with or block software you use regularly by mistaking it for a threat. If this happens, you'll need to know how to tell the program that this software is safe. Also, you will want to make sure that all the features you need are enabled. Some may be disabled by default.

Chapter 4: Backing Up your Website's Data

Imagine that one day, you go to your website and find the entire thing has been ransacked by a hacker. Your database has been destroyed and there's nothing left of your hard work. Now imagine that you hadn't taken the time to back up your disks and there's no way to get your data back.

What if your hard drive malfunctioned because your system overheated? Or maybe you were in the middle of moving and someone dropped your computer down a flight of stairs. What would you do?

Life happens. These scenarios are entirely possible, which is exactly why you need to take the extra steps to back up and secure your data. The first step to do so is to decide on a method. How are you going to do it?

Remember, your web host will have backups of your data on their servers, but for extra security, you may want to create your own. If something were to happen to their building, such as a fire or a flood, you could lose your server and your backups. Also, if they go out of business and you haven't made your own copies, you could lose all of your data without warning.

One method you could use would be to upload your files to cloud storage, which is an increasingly popular option right now. For a more down-to-earth choice, there's also RAID configuration through multiple hard drives, as well as NAS systems. If you have a large budget and need the extra safety, you could decide to combine some of these methods.

Let's take a look at these storage methods.

Cloud Storage

Cloud storage is incredibly popular. It's easy to use and gives you access to your files anywhere with an Internet connection. If you have a lot of files you need stored, it can save you a lot of money.

Storing your backup "in the cloud" basically means uploading your data to a remote server. That server is regularly backed up so the company won't lose your data in the event of a malfunction.

Cloud services usually charge a monthly or yearly subscription fee. Some offer discounts for larger purchases. Some services put a limit on how much storage

you can have, but there are unlimited options available that you should look for. You'll want to shop around and see what the best deals are.

Cloud storage is great because you don't have to deal with maintenance and upkeep for the storage servers. You never have to worry about upgrading your storage hardware, either.

If you work across multiple computers, you can set up your cloud storage to automatically sync to your computers. That way, you can have access to everything you need, no matter what computer you are using.

You should keep security in mind, and cloud storage does offer encryption to help keep your information safe. However, the more remote servers there are that hold your data, the more you risk having your data compromised. A disgruntled or unethical employee could turn your data out to someone else.

Remember, storing data on a cloud server means that you're sharing your data with at least one other person. The fewer people you have handling your data, the more secure it will be. If you have confidential documents, you may want to consider storing the data yourself, or make sure you find a storage solution that doesn't compromise your privacy or that of your clients/users/etc.

Cloud storage companies are also not immune to damage, just like the rest of the world. If a fire were to destroy the building and equipment that stored your data, your backups would be gone. In addition, if the company were to go bankrupt, you could lose your data without any warning.

Extra Hard Drives

If you want more options, you can also buy an extra hard drive for your system. Running your own hard drives can give you extra security and control over your data. You can also set up your hard drives so that your entire network has access to them.

Your hard drive will likely come with software to help automate your backups. This software can update your backup as soon as the original file is saved. You don't have to worry about whether or not you uploaded the latest changes to your backup.

Of course, adding your own hard drives isn't without its own fair share of problems. If there is a technical issue, it's your responsibility to get it fixed. This

could mean spending time finding the solution yourself, or hiring someone to do it.

Another problem with maintaining your own backups is that it can be costly. Hard drives themselves can cost hundreds of dollars. You will also need to upgrade them every few years or so, as they become old and slow. You will have to pay for the extra electricity to run these servers, as well.

If you only plan to run one or two extra drives, or you don't need a lot of space, then the costs may not be so bad. In fact, it may even turn out to be cheaper than renting space on a cloud server for years. However, if you have a lot of valuable data you need to back up, then the price tag will increase quite a bit.

Picking a Hard Disk

When choosing a brand of hard drives, you'll want to keep some things in mind:

How much storage do you need? You don't want to buy more than you'll need. You may think that you'll fill it eventually, but keep in mind that technology ages very quickly and you may need to upgrade sooner than you expect. Any disk space not used by the time you upgrade was wasted money.

Do I want an internal or external drive? Internal drives don't require any extra desk space; all you need is the right cords and connectors inside your machine. External hard drives give you portability and are easy to install, but require more physical space.

How do I install this? If you aren't familiar with installing new hardware into your computer, you'll need to find some instructions to help you out. If you aren't comfortable taking your computer apart yourself, you can take your system into a shop and have a technician do it. However, they may charge you quite a bit for a relatively easy procedure.

What is the failure rate for this drive? You don't want to buy a drive that isn't going to last. For example, if you decide you want to buy a

solid-state drive, it would be helpful to know that these have a higher failure rate than hard disks.

Set Up a RAID

A more advanced option is to set up your own system and store your data across multiple disks. You can link multiple hard drives together on your system to create a RAID (Redundant Array of Independent Disks). A RAID uses special software to spread your data across multiple drives. If a drive fails, then the other drives would be able to restore the lost data.

The cost of a RAID depends on how many hard disks you include and what size storage they are. However, the benefits may be worth the cost. When you're in control of your storage, there are automatically fewer people who have access to your data. Remember, the fewer people involved, the more secure it is.

Network Attached Storage Devices

What if you had personal cloud storage—a device that you could set up for your own private network that was wireless and could connect all your devices? If this sounds good to you, then maybe a network attached storage (NAS) device is what you're looking for.

An NAS device uses RAID technology to keep your data safe. You connect it to your own network and assign it an IP address of its own. Then, you can connect to the device easily. You can also set up user profiles with password protection and even data encryption to help stay secure.

Creating SQL Databases

In addition to backing up your WordPress site itself, you are also going to want to back up your SQL database. This has the additional benefit of allowing you to restore lost data in the event of a hack. You may remember this from my previous guide, WordPress Domination.

You can find it at: `http://www.amazon.com/dp/B007LS0TLE`

Creating an SQL database is pretty easy, but the steps you take may differ depending on who your web hosting company is. In WordPress Domination, I

went over how to do this with Host Gator. This time, I'm going to show you how to do it with Bluehost, since they are a popular web hosting company, too.

Start off by selecting "My SQL Database" on your cPanel. It will have a little dolphin picture on the icon.

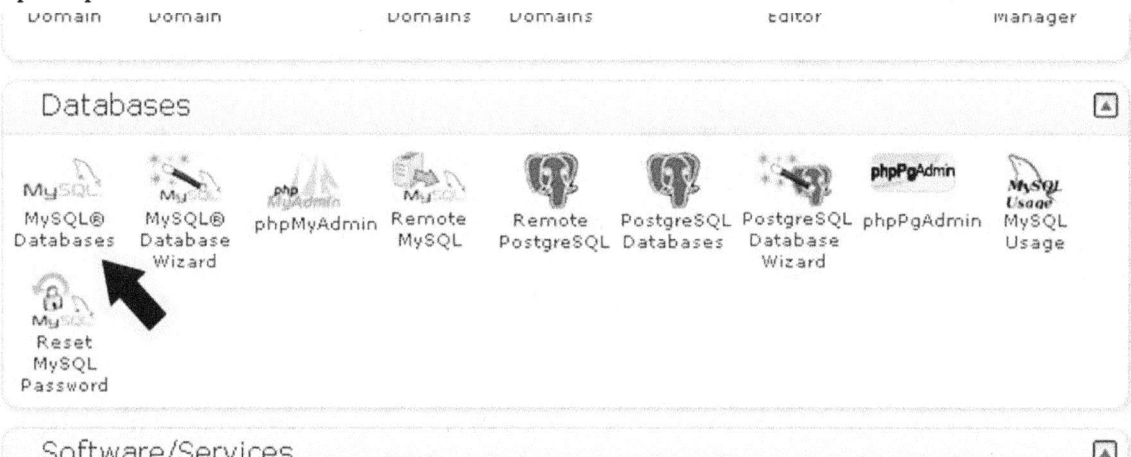

On the next screen, enter the name of your new database. It can be whatever you want, but there will be a character limit. Also, your cPanel username will be added to the front of this database name automatically upon creation. Once you're done, click "Create Database."

Create New Database

New Database:

Create Database

Once it is on there, click the "Go Back" button on the next screen to return to the previous screen. Now, we need to create an SQL user, so scroll down to the part

that says "Add New User." Enter any username you want, but be aware that this too will have your cPanel username added to the front of it.

Next, you need to create your password. Refer to the passwords chapter later in this guide for more details on how to create ultra-secure passwords.

When you're done, click "Create User."

MySQL Users

Add New User

Username: ▮▮▮▮▮▮_ [   ]

Password: [   ]

Password (Again): [   ]

Strength (why?): [Very Weak (0/100)   ]   [Password Generator]

[Create User]

The last thing you're going to do is link the username you just created with the database you just created. Scroll down to where it says "Add User to Database." Now, select the user and database and hit "Add."

Add User To Database

On the next page, select "All permission," then click the "Make Changes" button.

☐ **ALL PRIVILEGES**	
☐ ALTER	☐ ALTER ROUTINE
☐ CREATE	☐ CREATE ROUTINE
☐ CREATE TEMPORARY TABLES	☐ CREATE VIEW
☐ DELETE	☐ DROP
☐ EXECUTE	☐ INDEX
☐ INSERT	☐ LOCK TABLES
☐ REFERENCES	☐ SELECT
☐ SHOW VIEW	☐ TRIGGER
☐ UPDATE	

Make Changes

See how easy that was?

Browse here **http://www.youtube.com/watch?v=mtQqg_I_oZ0** for a video tutorial so you can watch how this is done on Bluehost. If you have a different hosting company, the steps you follow will probably be similar.

Browse to https://my.bluehost.com/cgi/help/5 **for a link on how to back up an SQL database on Bluehost and** https://my.bluehost.com/cgi/help/4 **for how to restore an SQL database on Bluehost. Also, you can go to**

`http://support.hostgator.com/articles/cpanel/how-to-backuprestore-your-mysql-database` **for info on how to back up and restore an SQL database using Host Gator.**

Optimally, you should create an SQL database for every WordPress installation on your server. This will ensure that if a hacker gets into one site, they won't have immediate access to your other sites.

Chapter 5: You've Been Hacked! Damage Control 101

Sometimes, no matter how much security you put on your WordPress site, a hacker gets in. Though these situations are rare, they do happen, and you should be prepared to deal with this in order to minimize the damage.

Finding the Source of the Hack

The very first thing to do if you have been hacked is to find out how the intruder got into your site. They could have gotten in from an infection in your computer itself, so that is one of the best places to start. Run a scan of your entire computer to see if you find any Trojans, root-kits, viruses or any other malicious software that could have been responsible for the hack.

If you find that your computer has been hacked, it is suggested that you look up info online as to how to handle the situation. Browse here `http://www.switched.com/2011/02/23/what-to-do-if-your-pc-gets-hacked/` for some info to get you started.

If the hack came from an infected plugin, SQL injection or another attack that went after your WordPress site directly, you'll need to check with your hosting provider. They can confirm whether or not it was an actual hack and tell you what you should do.

Changing Your Passwords

Once you've determined the source of the hack, you should immediately change your passwords. This includes those for your website, your FTP, your SQL databases and your cPanel. If you really want to play it safe, you can change your password for every place online where you need one.

If your computer itself was hacked, it is recommended that you change the passwords on all your user accounts. In some cases, you may even want to delete your user account and create a new one. Keep in mind that this should be done *after* you have confirmed that your computer, server, website and everything else are no longer compromised and are fully protected from repeated hacking attempts.

Also, be sure to check your WordPress user's area. Make sure the hacker didn't create a new user, especially one with admin privileges.

Upgrade to the Latest WordPress Version

If you haven't already done so, upgrade WordPress to the most recent version. This will ensure that, if the hacker took advantage of an outdated WordPress version, they won't be able to attack your system the same way again.

Another thing you're going to want to do is change the secret keys for your WordPress site. These are the randomized keys that you get and insert into the .htaccess file that we talked about earlier.

Check Your Files

If the hack was directly against your WordPress site, you want to make sure you scan all of your files to ensure that there are no malicious programs hiding within them. Also scan your plugins, themes and other possible sources of entry.

Keep in mind that sometimes even the best virus and malware scanners can miss bits of malicious code that have been inserted into your files. This is especially true for your .htaccess file.

Check the .htaccess File

Make sure that your .htaccess file hasn't been compromised. Since this file is so important to security, you need to make sure that it hasn't been altered with malicious code. Make certain you scroll through the entire code; hackers like to hide their code in hard-to-notice locations.

To easily locate malicious code, compare your .htaccess file against a clean .htaccess file. (You can do this for any other files you check manually, too.)

A default .htaccess file will look like:

```
# BEGIN WordPress
<ifmodule mod_rewrite.c>
RewriteEngine On
RewriteBase /
RewriteCond %{REQUEST_FILENAME} !-f
RewriteCond %{REQUEST_FILENAME} !-d
RewriteRule . /index.php [L]
</ifmodule>
# END WordPress
```

or, in some cases, simply like this if it is a placeholder devoid of any real code:

```
# BEGIN WordPress

# END WordPress
```

Keep an eye out for strange code that you didn't add.

Also, keep in mind that a hacker may decide to change the access permissions on your .htaccess file or other important files on your server. Change them back to their original settings as soon as possible if they have been altered.

Malicious Code to Look Out For

Here are some bits of code that could signify a hacker:

```
eval ()

base64_decode ()

POST: Array
(
[cookie] => wordpressuser_c73ce9557defbe87cea780be67f9ae1f=xyz%27;
wordpresspass_c73ce9557defbe87cea780be67f9ae1f=132;
)

<?xml version="1.0"?>

<methodCall>

<methodName>test.method

</methodName>

<params>

<param>

<value><name>`,'')); echo

`_____BEGIN_____';

passthru('id');

echo

`_____FIM_____';

exit;/*</name></value>

</param>

</params>
```

```
</methodCall>
```

Malicious code like this could be in *any* .php file on your WordPress site. Since malicious code can be so hard to find, a complete deletion/uninstall of your site may be necessary.

Sometimes, malicious code will be sneaked in as an image and added to the activated plugins list. To see if this has happened, go into PHPMyAdmin, locate your site's options table, and then find the active_plugins record. Look for code that looks like this:

```
../uploads/2008/05/04/jhjyahjhnjnva.jpg
```

If you find this code, delete it. Note that there may be multiple instances of this code. If you are having a hard time tracking them all down, just delete your active_plugins record and reinstall all plugins.

Delete Everything (optional)

If the attack was directly against your website and not an intrusion into your computer, you may want to consider deleting your site in its entirety, since malicious code can be hard to find. This is why it is important to back up your files so that you can upload a clean copy of the site that is free of malicious code in this situation.

If you decide to do this, make sure that your backup files haven't been compromised as well. If the hacker got into your hosting server, there is a chance that he or she could have done something to your backup files too.

In some cases, you may even want to go so far as to completely remove the installation of WordPress from your server and do a fresh install. This will ensure that no malicious code remains in your files, as they will all have been completely deleted, even the folders themselves.

Back to Normal

If you do get hacked, use it as a learning experience. Figure out how the hacker got into your site and install security measures to make sure that it doesn't happen again. There is a chance that the hacker may try again, so it is very important that you defend against future attacks, especially those that use the original method to get into your system.

Chapter 6: DDoS and What to Do if You're Attacked

DDoS stands for Distributed Denial of Service. DDoS attacks are carried out by hackers using compromised computer systems that all target the same system. They flood the selected server with requests and force the system to go offline. Due to how easy it is to carry out a DDoS attack, they are fairly common.

You can think of your website as a room. Only so many people can stand inside this room at once, but that's okay, because you normally don't reach maximum capacity, anyway. However, if someone were to come by and fill your room with boxes, no one would be able to get inside.

This is similar to what a DDoS does. All of the controlled computers contact the website at the same time. The server responds to their requests, using up all of the system's resources. Because of this, legitimate users won't be able to access your website. It is difficult to track these attacks down, because the computers used for the crime could be in different locations all around the world.

If you think you might be targeted by a DDoS attack, try to confirm it. If you host your website on your own server, is your Internet connection slower than usual? The massive amounts of requests you'll be getting will slow your entire connection. If your website is remotely hosted, then does your site time out when you try to connect?

I'm Under Attack! What do I Do?

You need to be aware of your options when you create a defense plan. Ideally, you'll have a plan prepared before you get attacked, but sometimes things just don't work out that way. Unfortunately, just as extra security can cost a bit of money, so should you be prepared to spend a bit more to get your site back up.

Call in Some Help

If you're being DDoS attacked, you want to contact your ISP (if you host yourself) or your web host. You also want to call your security network. It could be that they already know; they're likely to have already noticed the spike in traffic.

Your web host will want to deal with this problem as quickly as you do, since the high requests can slow down multiple servers in their network. It's a good idea

to contact them instead of just letting them handle the situation on their own, because their method of dealing with it may not be the one you want. For example, if you are being DDoS attacked, your web host may redirect your traffic to null. This basically means that all incoming traffic will be sent to a non-existent server, meaning no one will be able to connect to your website.

Ask your host if they offer alternate solutions. Some hosts will offer mitigation services for DDoS attacks, like firewalls and proxies. Firewalls, switches, proxies and scripts can help sort out fake requests and let the good ones through. These may be costly, however, and not all hosts will offer them.

Your network security will work with you and try to help you through your problem. (After all, that's why you pay them, right?) Your web host, on the other hand, may have specific policies regarding what to do in this situation. They are not guaranteed to act in your favor, and it's a good idea to read the policies on their site to see how they might react.

If the attacks are small, you may have the option to upgrade to a better hosting plan that would allow you to take the brunt of the attack and still let legitimate users through. This may be a good answer if you find you are consistently attacked; however, if you choose to take this course of action, your attacker may decide to step up their methods as well. Talk to your provider about your options.

If you run your own server, try installing firewalls. Configure these firewalls along with your switches, routers, etc. to sort out the spam and let the real people through to your website.

File a Police Report

DDoS attacks are illegal, and you should report the crime to your local authorities. This won't help you get your server back online, and you will probably never know if your report helps lead to any arrests. But giving the information to the police can help lead to solutions in the long run. If you call, be sure to dial their non-emergency number; don't tie up 911 or your local emergency number. Expect them to ask a lot of questions, because odds are they don't have a DDoS specialist on staff.

However, you may want to check your local disclosure laws before you report the attack. Once you tell the police, they may have the ability to tell whomever

they want, and this could give your website negative attention. In rare instances, they may even confiscate your computer for investigation into the attacks.

Wait it out

Sometimes the simplest solutions are the best. (Well, maybe "best" isn't the right word.) If you've stepped up your security and upgraded your servers, and the attacks continue to take down your site, there isn't a whole lot you can do.

DDoS attacks are difficult to track down and stop, but they can't last forever. The longer a DDoS attack continues, the more the hacker risks being caught. It's also likely the hacker will get bored or lose interest. Sooner or later, they will stop.

There is no guarantee that, once the attack has stopped, that they won't try again. The more spam you can filter out through your firewalls and other security systems, the better. But if your methods aren't working, your only choice may be to wait

Chapter 7: Password Tricks

Having a strong password is one of the most fundamental ways to stop hacking attempts. The "brute force" method of hacking is when a hacker uses a program to try thousands, if not millions, of password combinations to get into your account. The secret key method discussed earlier, as well as other strategies and tricks, can help reduce the chance of a hacker getting into your website this way.

Creating a Strong Password

The first step to password protection is to create a very strong password. Passwords that use all numbers, all letters, or a simple combination of the two aren't as strong as you'd think. To get around this problem, here are some basic tips for creating a strong password.

- Make sure it is more than eight characters long.
- If you can, include numbers, symbols, and a combination of uppercase and lowercase letters
- Avoid guessable passwords, such as dictionary words, names of family or loved ones and birth dates.

Another thing you want to do is visit a site that will gauge the strength of your password. You can use a pretty good one by using this website `http://www.passwordmeter.com/`.

These passwords can be very hard to remember, so it is recommended that you either physically write down your passwords and store them in a very secure location or take the time to thoroughly memorize them. Memorization can be helped by saying the password out loud on a regular basis or by associating mental images with the password using mnemonic memory techniques.

You can also go to `http://www.wikihow.com/Create-a-Password-You-Can-Remember` for some tips on how to create an easy to remember password, but be aware that some of the tips in this resource do not focus on creating a strong security password.

Change your Password Regularly

Another thing you should be doing is changing your WordPress passwords regularly. You can do this once a month, or even once a week if you want to be

really secure. This will ensure that hackers don't have an easy time accessing your site.

Also, make sure that, in the event that you need to allow a web designer, security systems expert or anyone else to modify your site, that you delete their user accounts when they're done. If they will be working with you on an ongoing basis, ensure that you also change their password regularly as well.

The Static/Variable Method

Since changing your password regularly can strain your brain in a major way when it comes to recall, you can use this little trick. Have one half of your password be very hard to guess and always remain the same. The second half will be an easy-to-remember phrase or word that you can swap out at regular intervals with other easy-to-remember word combinations.

Here are a few examples:

- G8)?gR02ndogfood
- uq!8P29L*beartrap
- aR'_e+89K^gonefishing

Concentrate on memorizing the hard part. You'll only need to do that once, and then swap out the easy-to-remember part as needed.

Alternate Key Strokes

Another clever way to create a password is simply to change the position of your hands on the keyboard. While this doesn't make use of special symbols, it can be handy in cases where you aren't allowed to create a password using those symbols.

For example, if you move your fingers one key to the right from the default position, "dogfood" becomes "fphgppf." Used creatively, you can easily remember your password using this technique while throwing off hackers who look for common words at the same time.

Password Protected Pages

Also, remember that you can also password-protect specific pages on your website. If you are doing this, you need to ensure that there is no intrusion into these areas. To help facilitate this, use a different password than the one you use to log into your admin account. This can confuse hackers and make it hard for them to access multiple private areas.

Another great thing about this is the fact that multiple password layers buy you time in the event of a hack — the extra time may be enough to take care of the hacker problem before they get into all of your data.

The #1 Rule

The most important thing to remember about your WordPress passwords is to make sure that they are not the same as any other passwords you use online. Your admin area, cPanel, webpages and anything else passworded should each have its own unique password. If you use the same password for everything, a hacker's job is much easier and they can get into all of your data in one fell swoop.

Conclusion

Keeping your WordPress site secure does take some time and effort. There are a variety of threats out there that you'll need to prepare for. Learning what steps you can take is just the first part; now you'll need to put them into action.

The Internet is always changing and hackers will keep trying to come up with new ways to get into your system. You'll need to stay on your toes and keep one step ahead of them. There are plenty of tools and tricks you can use that will keep you in the game.

There are all sorts of plugins and software programs that you can use to keep unwanted intruders at bay. Avoid simple mistakes that leave you exposed, such as password sharing and using public computers. Stay updated on all of your programs and plugins. Also, keep your files backed up, so if the worst happens, you still have all of your data saved. Having strong passwords can keep hackers from ever getting in.

Getting hacked isn't the end of the world. It can be quite the thorn in your side, but you always have options available to you. Your security network and web host can help you regain control of your site, while security software can help you clean up your system and prevent future attacks.

Losing control of your website can be unsettling, and it may take some time to clean up, but there's no such thing as an adversity that you can't learn from. Hackers are out to ruin the Internet for the rest of us, either for their own enjoyment or for some sort of gain. However, there are tons of ways to protect yourself and keep using the largest network in the world.

Your Friend,

Lambert

Resources

Anti-virus for Windows

avast! Antivirus

```
http://www.avast.co
m/
```

AVG Internet Security

```
http://www.avg.com/
```

Avira Antivirus
Premium

```
http://www.avira.co
m/en/for-home-
avira-antivirus-
premium-v1
```

McAfee AntiVirus Plus

```
http://home.mcafee.
com/store/antivirus
-plus
```

Norton AntiVirus

```
http://us.norton.co
m/antivirus/
```

ZoneAlarm Antivirus +
Firewall

```
http://www.zonealar
m.com/security/en-
us/zonealarm-
antivirus-
software.htm
```

Anti-virus for Mac

Avira Free Mac Security

```
http://www.avira.co
m/en/download-
start/product/avira
-free-mac-security
```

McAfee VirusScan for
Mac

```
http://www.mcafee.c
om/us/products/viru
sscan-for-mac.aspx
```

Norton Antivirus for Mac

```
http://us.norton.co
m/macintosh-
antivirus/
```

Misc. Free Protection

Comodo Firewall for
Windows

```
http://personalfire
wall.comodo.com/
```

ZoneAlarm Free Firewall
by Checkpoint

```
http://www.zonealar
m.com/security/en/t
rialpay-za-
signup.htm
```

Misc. Paid Protection

Comodo Antivirus and
Firewall

```
http://personalfire
wall.comodo.com/
```

Sandboxie

```
http://sandboxie.co
m/
```

ZoneAlarm PRO Firewall
```
http://www.zonealar
m.com/security/en-
us/zonealarm-pro-
firewall-anti-
spyware.htm
```

**Cloud Storage
Companies**

JustCloud

```
http://www.justclou
d.com/
```

SkyDrive

```
http://windows.micr
osoft.com/en-
US/skydrive/home
```

ZipCloud

```
http://www.zipcloud
.com/
```

Livedrive

```
http://www.livedriv
e.com/
```

SOS Online Backup

```
http://www.sosonlin
ebackup.com/
```

SugarSync

```
https://www.sugarsy
nc.com/
```

Mozy

```
http://mozy.com/
```

Amazon S3

```
http://aws.amazon.c
om/s3/
```

DropBox

```
https://www.dropbox
.com/
```

External Hard Drives

Seagate FreeAgent
GoFlex Drives

```
http://www.seagate.
com/www/en-
us/products/externa
l/external-hard-
drive/
```

Seagate Expansion Hard Drives

http://www.seagate.
com/www/en-
us/products/externa
l/expansion/

Western Digital External Desktop Hard Drives

http://www.wdc.com/
en/products/externa
l/desktop/

LaCie Desktop Hard Drives

http://www.lacie.co
m/products/range.ht
m?id=10033

SQL Tutorial

Bluehost: MySQL Database Creation

https://my.bluehost
.com/cgi/help/6

Host Gator: How do I create a MySQL database, a user, and then delete if needed?

http://support.host
gator.com/articles/
cpanel/how-do-i-
create-a-mysql-
database-a-user-
and-then-delete-if-
needed

Security Plugins

Login and Admin

Semisecure Login Reimagined

http://wordpress.or
g/extend/plugins/se

misecure-login-
reimagined/

Login LockDown

http://wordpress.or
g/extend/plugins/lo
gin-lockdown/

Chap Secure Login

http://wordpress.or
g/extend/plugins/ch
ap-secure-login/

Admin SSL
http://wordpress.or
g/extend/plugins/ad
min-ssl-secure-
admin/

Backup

WP-DB-Backup

http://wordpress.or
g/extend/plugins/wp
-db-backup/

Remote Database Backup

http://wordpress.or
g/extend/plugins/re
mote-database-
backup/

WP-DBManager

http://wordpress.or
g/extend/plugins/wp
-dbmanager/

BackUpWordPress

http://wordpress.or
g/extend/plugins/ba
ckupwordpress/

myEASYbackup

http://myeasywp.com
/plugins/myeasyback
up/

Spam Block

Antispam Bee

http://wordpress.or
g/extend/plugins/an
tispam-bee/

NoSpamNX

http://wordpress.or
g/extend/plugins/no
spamnx/

Aksimet

http://akismet.com/

Defensio Anti-Spam

http://wordpress.or
g/extend/plugins/de
fensio-anti-spam/

SI CAPTCHA Anti-Spam

http://wordpress.or
g/extend/plugins/si
-captcha-for-
wordpress/

WP-reCAPTCHA

http://wordpress.or
g/extend/plugins/wp
-recaptcha/

Blackhole

http://perishablepr
ess.com/blackhole-
bad-bots/

Security

Secure WordPress

http://wordpress.or
g/extend/plugins/se
cure-wordpress/

WP Security Scan

http://wordpress.or
g/extend/plugins/wp
-security-scan/

AskApache Password Protect

http://wordpress.org/extend/plugins/askapache-password-protect/

TAC (Theme Authenticity Checker)

http://wordpress.org/extend/plugins/tac/

HTTP Authentication

http://wordpress.org/extend/plugins/http-authentication/

AntiVirus

http://wordpress.org/extend/plugins/antivirus/

Replace WP-Version

http://wordpress.org/extend/plugins/replace-wp-version/

WP Email Guard

http://wordpress.org/extend/plugins/wp-email-guard/

WordPress File Monitor

http://wordpress.org/extend/plugins/wordpress-file-monitor/

wp-dephorm

http://wordpress.org/extend/plugins/wp-dephorm/

WordPress Firewall

http://wordpress.org/extend/plugins/wordpress-firewall/

Secure Contact

http://wordpress.org/extend/plugins/secure-contact-form/

Fast Secure Contact Form

http://wordpress.org/extend/plugins/si-contact-form/

Content Security Policy

http://wordpress.org/extend/plugins/content-security-policy/

FTP Programs

Cyberduck

http://cyberduck.ch/

FileZilla

http://filezilla-project.org/

JSCAPE

http://www.jscape.com/

WinSCP

http://winscp.net/eng/index.php

RAID Setup Tutorial

Windows

How to set up a RAID array on your motherboard

http://www.youtube.com/watch?v=rgo0OPSw9_E

RAID 0 & RAID 1 Setup Guide (NCIX Tech Tips #77)

http://www.youtube.com/watch?v=RYBtmVMtH1g

RAID 5 & RAID 10 Tutorial & Explanation (NCIX Tech Tips #79)

http://www.youtube.com/watch?v=TuwjadbtUCY

Mac

How to set up RAID on a Mac 2012

http://www.youtube.com/watch?v=NbG1G3sNqwk

Mac Pro RAID installation

http://www.youtube.com/watch?v=U41beKVajao

External Hard Drive Setup

How to Set Up and Connect an External Hard Drive to your Mac

http://www.youtube.com/watch?v=ocKvU9yzPAc

Western Digital 750GB External Hard Drive

http://www.youtube.com/watch?v=-xok11PpjAE

Network Attached Storage Devices

A short cartoon explaining what a NAS can do for your home network

http://www.youtube.com/watch?v=-1L_2G6rLIO

Western Digital Network Products

http://www.wdc.com/en/products/network/

Buffalo Tech - NAS Product Selector

http://www.buffalotech.com/products/network-storage/product-selector/

Security Firms

eSoft

http://www.esoft.com/network-security-solutions/web-security-solution/

Miles Consulting

http://www.milesconsultingcorp.com/IT-Outsourcing.aspx

SecureWorks

http://www.secureworks.com/

Trustwave

https://www.trustwave.com/encryption/

Places to Hire Freelance Security Help

Freelanced Social Network

http://www.freelanced.com/jobs/network-security/us

Freelancer

http://www.freelancer.com/jobs/Computer-Security/

Guru

http://www.guru.com/

Secret Key Generator

Secret Key Generator

https://api.wordpress.org/secret-key/1.1/salt/

About the Author

Lambert Klein is that inspirational older brother you wish you had—that guy who knows all the ways to be successful at online marketing and is willing to share his secrets with you.

After leaving his job in construction, Lambert was determined to learn about Internet marketing. He successfully reinvented himself as an authentic and dedicated writer focusing on Internet solutions and Internet marketing. He started out writing for other people, and soon realized that he could work on his own projects exclusively and produce a generous income.

His uncompromising passion to write quality content has driven his four websites to wild success. He found that the people around him were constantly coming to him for advice on Internet marketing. That was the moment he knew that he would begin writing books about Internet solutions.

Lambert has authored several PDF reports and e-books, as well as a variety of Kindle books, covering such subjects as blogging, search engine optimization, weight loss, and natural anti-aging. He's most proud of the response to his most popular book on Amazon Kindle, entitled *WordPress Power Guide*.

Lambert calls Marion Township home, where he lives on seven acres of beautiful Michigan countryside. There, you will find him hiking with his wife Lynn or strumming on his guitar. On the weekends, he enjoys heading to the ballpark to take in a Detroit Tigers baseball game, playing with his cat Mitts, or enjoying a double scoop of chocolate ice cream.

It's said that you should find someone whom you want to be like and copy them. Lambert Klein is that guy. He knows Internet marketing, he's making money, and he's willing to share his knowledge with you.

Contact Information: http://www.lambertklein.com/

Lambert Klein

Top 10 Ways to Make Money with WordPress

This is probably what a lot of you are here for, my special report on the *very best* ways to make money with WordPress. I touched on monetization a little in WordPress Domination but I want to get more in-depth and share with you some really high-octane money making methods.

Whether you're into WordPress for blogging, charity, or to actually sell stuff, more money in the bank is always a good thing!

Let's get started!

Method 1: Ads

Okay, I'm sure you already know about AdSense since I've already gone over that a bit. It is probably the easiest way to incorporate ads on your site thanks to the various plugins associated with it. However, there are other ways to put ads on your site, some of which will pay you much more than AdSense!

Media Buys

First let's talk about media buys. The concept is simple: someone wants to advertise something so they pay someone else to display

their ads. This most commonly refers to TV and radio commercials but it can also apply to WordPress sites as well.

Let's say you have a website that blogs about car repair and gets a good number of visitors a month. You could use this to your advantage by approaching various car repair businesses and propositioning them. Tell them that you're getting a ton of traffic and ask if they would be interested in placing an ad on your site.

When you do this, make sure you explain the benefits. You want the businesses you approach to understand very clearly what's in it for them. Increased traffic, making more sales, getting new clients, etc. that's the sort of thing you want to tell them about.

Also remember that media buys work both ways. If you're selling stuff on your site and need more traffic, look for sites in your niche that get lots of traffic and see if they'll let you place an ad on their site.

Here is a big tip when doing this: always try to get the other person to make the first monetary offer. This will greatly strengthen your position when haggling whether you're selling ad space or buying it.

Ultimately this method can make you more money than AdSense if you're targeting big spenders and making it worth their while. Also, the income tends to be more consistent than AdSense as well since you'll likely be offering monthly plans to people.

Ad Networks

<u>AdSense</u> - It's easy and it works. However, there are other ad networks out there. Let's go over a few.

<u>Bidvertiser</u> – This ad network functions like a combination of AdSense and Adwords. It allows you place ads on your site and make money when they get clicks. It also allows you to post ads to put on other people's sites if you want, similar to Adwords.

<u>Chitika</u> – Similar to Bidvertiser in the fact that it offers both ad publishing and ad advertising. Chitika also has options for search targeted ads and mobile ads.

<u>Clicksor</u> – Also offers options for both publishers and advertisers. It's been around since 2004 and has an interesting traffic reseller program as well.

<u>Amazon Associates</u> – You don't have to create an entire store to make money from Amazon. They have plenty of text and image ads you can put on your site. Keep in mind that it may not be available in your state or area of the world though.

<u>Kontera</u> – This ad network places a strong focus on branding and reaching people who fall into certain demographics. Their site is honestly a little hard to understand though.

Overall ad revenue is probably one of the most powerful, and most popular, methods of residual income for WordPress users. No

matter what kind of site you have you can benefit from ad placement!

Method 2: Donations

Believe it or not, you can make decent money with donations. The catch is you have to make people want to donate. Just putting a donate button on your site and hoping for the best isn't going to work.

So how do you get people to donate their hard earned money to you? Simple. Offer compelling content. So long as you're giving people great content on a regular basis for free, there will always be a percentage who will gladly "tip" you.

Just try not to make this seem like "ebegging" as some people like to call it these days. Explain why you are collecting donations and present it in a way that doesn't seem greedy or like begging.

Something like "If you like my content then feel free to leave a tip here" tends to work well. Saying "I need $300 to pay my rent, donate here" on the other hand isn't going to work.

Also keep in mind that this method relies heavily on building a positive relationship with the visitors to your site. The more they like you, the more they're going to tip you. So make sure you're interacting with them on a regular basis. Social media like Twitter, Facebook, and more are great for building this kind of relationship.

To accept donations you're going to have to create a donate button. This is usually done through a payment processor like PayPal. It is extremely easy to set up and your payment processor should have instructions on how to do it.

Method 3: Membership Sites

One great way to make money off of a WordPress site is by turning it into a membership site. Now keep in mind that the entire site doesn't have to be membership based, you can section off certain parts of it that are "members only" like special forums or premium content. Multi-layered membership sites like this that offer a good combination of free and paid content do really well.

The key to making this work is to offer very compelling content. If you can hook your visitors with your free content, there is no doubt that you can get a percentage of them to pay for more exclusive content. So don't' be afraid to toss out a few freebies to see who will bite and go for the paid stuff.

Other ways membership can work is to have a free newsletter but also have a super special paid newsletter. You just have to make sure that the paid newsletter has tons of value for your subscribers. You can accomplish this by linking them to various coupons and special offers related to your niche or by giving them awesome free content of your own like eBooks, videos, and stuff like that.

Another popular way to sell a membership option is to offer one-on-one consulting if your site is one that would be good for

something like that, like a business motivational site or a dog training site. How much you charge for this service is up to you but you can have an option where members get a certain amount of your time per month.

Also be aware that you can have multi-leveled memberships. Maybe the Bronze membership people get access to special blog posts and articles, Silver gets access to the private forums, and Gold members get to speak with you directly for a half an hour a month. How you do this is up to you but this is a great way to target people of all income levels.

Remember how I said ads were the most powerful method of residual income for WordPress sites? Scratch that. If done right membership sites have the potential to earn you a full-time income on auto-pilot if you're outsourcing most of it.

Method 4: Creating a Store

If you want to make you're entire site an online store you probably already get this. However, even if you're running a blog just to post your thoughts on stuff or maybe you're just running a charity website, there is always room for a store. Let me give you an example.

Let's say you have a blog about videogames. You just love videogames and like blogging about them and don't really care about promoting products or anything. Why not tack on a store to your site for visitors who have money to spend?

This sort of thing isn't hard. Thanks to Amazon, you can find just about any product you want to sell. And if you don't like Amazon or maybe they don't offer their affiliate program where you live, there are TONS of affiliate programs online that you can use to "stock" your store.

Even in cases where you may not be able to think of a related product, like if your site is about internet memes, there are sites that allow you to create custom t-shirts, mugs, and other merchandise on demand. Put the meme on a shirt (as long as it isn't copyrighted) and start making money!

Regardless of what kind of store you make, make sure you're directing people to it. This is especially important on the home page. A "hot deals" widget in the sidebar is always great since it will show up on every page on your site.

For those of you who want your entire site to be a store, there are tons of themes and plugins that will work wonders for you as we went over in the themes and plugins part of the book. Just make sure you familiarize yourself with how Internet marketing works for ecommerce, it will make a big difference, trust me.

Method 5: Affiliate Offers

Okay, maybe promoting affiliate offers appeals to you but you don't want to actually have a store on your site. This could be due to the fact that you're only promoting a very small number of offers which

would make a store section impractical, or for other reasons. Regardless, it is very easy to incorporate affiliate offers into your site.

One of the best ways to do this is to simply have a very short blurb at the end of your various blog posts and articles directing readers to a related product. For example, let's say you just wrote a blog post about home first-aid. At the end of the post tell readers that they can get a hot deal on a first-aid kit if they click your link, and then link them to an offer for a first-aid kit.

Once again, a "hot deals" sidebar widget is a good idea as well.

Just make sure that the products you're promoting are a part of some sort of affiliate program so you can get compensated. This goes without saying I suppose.

Also be aware that various affiliate programs have resources to help you sell their stuff such as banner ads, graphics and much more. Take advantage of these resources to really boost your sales!

In any event, the key to making this work is to not be too overbearing in your attempts to sell. Remember, leave the selling to the sales page that you're going to link to. Your material should just warm the potential customers up a bit and get them interested.

Method 6: Website Creation

This has probably got you scratching your head but hear me out. Thanks to this guide you now know how to make WordPress sites. With a little practice you can have a site up and running in probably 15 minutes or so. Would you trade 15 minutes of your time for several hundred dollars?

Small businesses around the world are in desperate need of people who can build sites for them and are willing to pay literally hundreds of dollars (sometimes thousands) to get it done. Yes, building WordPress sites may not seem like that lucrative of a job but trust me; there are people with more money than time on their hands who are willing to pay big bucks to have you do this.

To be successful with this you're going to have to really be on top of your game when it comes to marketing your services. That's beyond the scope of this guide but to make things easy on you I'm going to link you to a few places where you can get started selling your services. Keep in mind that these places aren't where you're going to find the big money clients (you'll probably have to contact them directly) but it is a great way to build up your portfolio while making some money doing it.

*Warriors for Hire
*Digital Point Services
*BlackHat World
*Elance
*Guru

<u>*Odesk</u>

Another thing to keep in mind is that you can increase the value of your work by combining your website creation service with graphics design, SEO, and other web design related services. If you don't want to do this yourself, find other freelancers who will and mark up their prices so that you make a profit when creating sites for your clients.

Also be aware that you can purchase premium themes with developer licenses that allow you to use them for a business such as this. This can make things much easier on you when mass producing websites. Check back in the themes and plugins section for examples.

Oh yeah, one last thing. Don't forget to offer your clients support and maintenance services for residual income. For example, you could sell a website for $200 then offer support and maintenance for $50 a month. Just be sure to price to your market; some clients will be willing to pay thousands for a site and hundreds a month for maintenance. Use your brain and come up with a price that works for both you and the client.

Method 7: Joint Ventures

Joint Ventures can be thought of as affiliate programs without an official affiliate program. In short, you'll be approaching business owners (sometimes they'll approach you) and tell them you'd be

512 ULTIMATE 2013 WORDPRESS THEMES AND PLUGINS GUIDE

interested in promoting their products or services for a commission.

For example, let's say you have a blog that's dedicated to showing off your dogs and just talking about dogs in general. You could then approach Joe's Online Obedience Classes and tell him you'll put ads on your site, or write blog posts promoting his business in exchange for a commission when people hire him through your links.

In some cases you can even charge for leads, not just sales. This is usually more appropriate if the leads you send tend to convert very well and if you're sending a high volume of leads. Ultimately it is the other business's job to turn leads into sales so you could say that just delivering the leads is all you should be responsible for.

Another great way to do a JV is to do a joint mailing with someone. For example, if you have a decent sized subscriber list to a newsletter, you can make a deal with other people in your niche and do a cross promotion. This is where they promote your site to their list and you promote them to yours. This can lead to more traffic for both of you that can be monetized in various ways.

Ultimately the moral of the story here is that you should be forming positive relationships with others in your niche, especially the "big dogs" if you can. Getting a popular figure on your side and either paying you for traffic or promoting your site can lead to big money very quickly.

Method 8: Website Flipping

Website flipping can be very lucrative if done right. It isn't as easy as it was a few years ago but if you know what you're doing you can still make very easy money doing this. Let's go over a few of the most important aspects of modern day website flipping.

First off, there are two ways to do this. Either make a site from scratch and sell it or buy a site then resell it for a profit. In either event there are certain factors that will drastically increase your site's value and help you sell it.

Sales

A website that is proven to make money is worth money. Period. If you have a site that made $100 in a month you can flip that for 6 to 12 months worth of profit; $600 to $1,000. The key to make this work is consistency. A site that made $100 a month 5 months in a row is much more likely to sell for a high price than one that only did it in its first month.

On top of that, many website selling places won't let you sell sites that aren't old enough. For example, a site may require your domain associated with the site to have been registered for at least 2 or 3 months before you sell it.

This is to prevent fraudsters who build sites and make sales through black hat methods (such as getting a friend to do it, or doing it through an alternate account of some sort) to pad their

stats. They then sell the worthless site for big money, ripping off their client.

However, if you know how to make legitimate sales and have the patience to do so for several months, site flipping can be a gold mine.

Traffic

In the world of Internet marketing people love to say that traffic = money. Because of this, sites that have lots of traffic always sell for more. Keep in mind that traffic is no substitute for sales, since sales prove that the traffic actually converts. However, traffic is still a major selling point.

What you can do is build a site, or buy one for cheap, drive a ton of traffic to it, and then resell it under the premise that the buyer can monetize that traffic for big bucks. Like I just said, this obviously isn't as attractive selling point as a site that is already making sales but it can work.

Appearance

Another, quicker way to make sales doing this is to purchase sites that are poorly designed but have potential and fix them up, then resell them. This is very similar to how many people do real-estate flipping in real life. Buying a site, installing a premium theme on it to make it look great, then reselling it is very quick and easy to do. Just don't expect to make massive profits doing it this way if you don't have traffic and sales to boost its value as well.

Domain Name

Domain flipping is an industry in and of itself. However, it also applies to website flipping since most sites are going to have a domain associated with them. In some cases, the domain may even be worth more than the site itself. Take a moment to study up on what makes a domain valuable and how domain flipping works. It will be a big help when it comes to site flipping.

For example, let's say you're building a site just for the purpose of selling it. The domain name is very important here. The domain "bestdogtraining.com" will sell for a lot more than "aw3somedawgtraning4U.info" just because the domain name is so much better.

Here are a few general rules for domain names:

*The shorter the better

*Avoid using hyphens

*Don't use numbers unless it makes sense

*.coms are almost always worth the most

*Make it memorable

*Don't use weird spellings

*Make sure it is SEO optimized for your main keyword for your site

*The domain name you want is probably already taken so use adjectives like "best," "now," "today," etc. to get what you want. For example "bestdenverplumber" or "hotvideogamereviews"

For site flipping purposes it generally is a bad idea to try and get a domain name that is focused on branding. For example, don't get something like "xingu.com" and make a site about web development intending for that to be the name of the company. For one thing your client may already have their own business name and second of all, branding is their job, not yours.

Where to Sell

There are many places where you can sell complete sites, such as certain sections on forums like the <u>Warrior Forum</u>, <u>Digital Point</u> and more. However the most popular site flipping website is <u>Flippa.com</u>. I'd recommend checking it out if you're interested in site flipping.

Method 9: Sponsored Posts and Reviews

If you like blogging and/or writing reviews, why not get paid to do so? This is very similar to the JV stuff I just talked about but works a little differently. The general idea behind this is that you'll write blog posts and reviews that someone pays you to do.

An example of how this works is someone approaching you and offering to pay you to review their new dog collar on your dog blog. Of course in most cases they're not going to come to you, you're going to have to go to them.

Once again, seek out similar sites and businesses in your niche and see if you can find people who would be willing to pay you blog about their products and services. The more traffic you have coming in to your site the better of course, that will be a major selling point when you proposition them. If you have other stuff for sale on your site and you have an audience of proven buyers, that's even better.

One thing to keep in mind here is that your credibility with your audience will be an issue. You should always say that a sponsored post is a sponsored post, don't try and deceive your readers. Also realize that a small percentage of your readers are going to call you a sellout no matter what. That's just part of the deal.

Staying honest about sponsored posts and keeping them in their own section on your site can go a long way towards minimizing the negative reaction from some of your readers though. Keep that in mind.

Method 10: Creating WordPress Themes and Plugins

Even if you're not a professional coder or developer, you can still do this believe it or not. As you probably guessed from the plugins and themes section in this book, developing software for WordPress is a big money industry. Here is how you can get a piece of it.

First off, if you're not interested in learning how to do this yourself, hire a developer. In most cases WordPress developers are reasonably priced and aren't going to charge you an arm and a leg for their services. Creating WordPress software is surprisingly simple if you know how, this isn't brain surgery.

Once you have a developer you have to tell him or her what to create. Put your thinking cap on and decide what kind of WordPress software would sell the best. When doing this it is always a good idea to look at both what is already selling and search for any gaps in the market that you could exploit by creating a brand-new product.

When your developer gets done making your awesome new software you then have to decide where to sell it. You could sell it from you own website, from a software site like CodeCanyon.net, or from sites like Clickbank.com. Even eBay is an option if there is a market for your software there.

Conclusion

Ultimately there is no single *best* method when it comes to making money with WordPress. It all depends on your particular skill set and how much effort you're willing to put forth. Maybe you're an awesome developer who can create hot WordPress themes and plugins. Maybe you're a pro blogger who can talk your readers into buying products and using your donate button. Or maybe you're good with web design and can place ads on your site that get massive click through rates.

In the end I wish you the best of luck. You really can make money with WordPress, very easily in fact, if you're willing to give it a shot.

Patience and discipline are very important, so stick with it and never give up. You'll soon find yourself making the money you deserve with WordPress!